MW00806103

Giving Voice to my Music

Choral Composers in Conversation
with David Wordsworth

Preface by Sir Andrew Davis

Foreword by David Hill

Edited by Leslie East

KAHN & AVERILL • LONDON

Published by Kahn & Averill
2-10 Plantation Road
Amersham, Buckinghamshire, HP6 6HJ
United Kingdom

www.kahnandaverill.co.uk

A CIP record of this book is available from the British Library

Book design by Økvik Design

Printed in Great Britain by Halstan UK, Amersham
www.halstan.co.uk

ISBN 978-0-9957574-5-5

Cover Photograph: The London Youth Chamber Choir (with kind permission)
www.londonyouthchoirs.com/chamber-choir

Founded 24 January 1813
Under the immediate patronage of
Her Majesty the Queen

Registered Charity No 213693

www.philharmonicsociety.uk

February 2021

Giving Voice to My Music

Whatever besets our nation, we come out singing. Even as the pandemic stopped so much music in its tracks, people found ways to keep singing together, with a profusion of online choirs, and countless instances of people singing on their doorsteps and in their streets. The 2017 Big Choral Census found that over 2 million people nationally get together regularly to sing: in choral societies, chamber choirs, rock and gospel choirs, church choirs, and more. At Wigmore Hall, we've seen in our 'Singing with Friends' programme the tremendous benefit that singing brings to those living with dementia, their families and carers, and there are many further examples nationwide of singing in groups enriching our collective wellbeing. As such a singing nation, it's fitting that one of the world's greatest choral works – Beethoven's Ninth Symphony – was commissioned here in the UK, by the Royal Philharmonic Society. We are tremendously grateful that proceeds from this book will come to the RPS, to help us continue our longstanding tradition of supporting composers and commissioning such works, and playing our part in ensuring the nation's bright choral heritage gets the recognition it deserves.

John Gilhooly

John Gilhooly OBE
Chairman, Royal Philharmonic Society and Director, Wigmore Hall

48 Great Marlborough Street, London W1F 7BB, United Kingdom   admin@philharmonicsociety.uk   +44 (0)20 7287 0019

Contents

THE COMPOSERS

THE APPENDICES

Preface

BY SIR ANDREW DAVIS

David Wordsworth, who I met through an enormous mutual admiration for Michael Tippett, has complied a marvellous diversity of characters and talents, many of whom I have worked with, to form a truly intriguing book that will appeal to all who love to sing and listen to our great heritage of choral music, which is so alive and flourishing right now despite our dire circumstances. The personalities and their answers are constantly fascinating and I can't wait to read the whole thing from end to end!

Andrew Davis

March 2021

Foreword

BY DAVID HILL

We are still amidst the pandemic which continues to ravage the world, and yet creativity has been one of the opportunities, as opposed to threats, of the past year. Were anyone to choose the twenty-four composers to be featured in a book which discusses their backgrounds and lives in choral music, then David has come up with what many would regard as the premier division and devoted a huge amount of his time in writing this book.

The format of asking each of them the same question and then hearing their responses shows the diversity of musical upbringing, teaching and other influences – all combining to create their individual voices. We are truly blessed to know that composition, in all its forms, is a central aspect of music-making and that the choral scene, in particular, is enjoying the fruits of incredible talent. The '24' featured in this book are themselves inspirations for so many aspiring composers around the world. Reading their stories reminds us that, no matter what their background, colour or religion is, composing – like so many of the arts – is a process everyone can enjoy.

During my career, I have had the privilege to have worked alongside many of the featured composers and I can honestly say that has been the most important aspect of my musical life. I am constantly in awe of how they approach the process and the results they produce. David has encapsulated their illuminating conversations in such a way as to engage the reader about each of the interviewees. To each of them, there is a debt of gratitude for opening up their thoughts and experiences: I know it will be a book I will pick up time and time again.

David Hill MBE
Musical Director, The Bach Choir
Principal Conductor, Yale Schola Cantorum
Rutland, January 2021

Introduction

BY DAVID WORDSWORTH

This book came about primarily as a result of the strange times that we all have found ourselves living in from March 2020, and that many, at the time of writing, still are living in to a lesser or greater extent. Amongst all the chaos and personal tragedy associated with the Covid-19 pandemic, a very particular sort of havoc was forced upon the choral world. Looking back, little in history has stopped the live rehearsal and performance of music in quite the same way – be it war, revolution, poverty, political repression, somehow music has gone on, but not in the last year. People have not just been missing their choirs, be they professional singers, amateur choral societies, chamber choirs or church choirs; for many there has been a feeling of what can only be described as bereavement. As more than one of the composers in this book has said, there is nothing quite like singing in a choir, be it a religious, spiritual, or social experience – it adds a special ingredient to life that one cannot get anywhere else.

Along with most choral conductors I had been wondering what to do, how to keep my choirs entertained and fulfilled and to keep their interest alive. Having found that a little virtual rehearsing went a very long way, I decided to offer talks about various standard repertoire pieces, the Fauré and Mozart Requiems for instance. I then became concerned that people would, in time, have had more than enough of my voice and so had the idea of interviewing some of the composers that the choirs had been associated with and broadcasting this over Zoom during our regular rehearsal time. Cecilia McDowall very kindly agreed to be the first interviewee. The Addison Singers have had a particularly long working relationship with Cecilia; we have sung a good deal of her music, she has written pieces for us and, living close by as she does, has never been anything but supportive to the choir(s), attending rehearsals and concerts whenever she could.

The interview went well, and it suddenly occurred to me that although there had been several books of interviews with composers of what one might call 'concert music', there had never, at least as far as I could tell, been a book of this kind devoted to choral music. Thankfully, Leslie East, Chair of the Association of British Choral Directors and Editorial Consultant to Kahn & Averill thought this was a good idea too and I am grateful to him for the encouragement to pursue this idea, particularly at a time when it was possible to guarantee catching the composers at home and willing to talk, either via Zoom (in the vast majority of cases), by email or phone.

My aim was to try and talk to a broad range of composers, but inevitably, there will be some people who will be annoyed that I have left a particular composer out, or even annoyed that I have left a particular composer in. A couple of composers declined to take part, but in these situations, to paraphrase Abraham Lincoln, one cannot hope to begin to please all of the people all of the time. I wanted to get a perspective from other parts of the world too, hence the inclusion of composers from the US, the Baltic States, Poland and Finland, as well as including just a few of the extraordinary collection of composers actively involved in choral music here in the UK. Some are known almost exclusively for their choral music (some like that more than others as you will read), for some it is an important part of their wider activity as a composer; some hardly need an introduction at all, some should be better known; all have something interesting to say about their music, their influences, attitudes to choirs, singers and conductors and life as a composer in the early twenty-first century.

David Wordsworth

London, March 2021

www.davidwordsworth.co.uk

Editor's note

Representing conversations on the page is not straightforward. On one hand, one wants the discussions to make sense and easy to read. On the other, the flow of the conversation, the interaction between interviewer and interviewee, needs to be captured. Transcribing recorded conversations is not easy and the outcome may often seem rambling. But the interviews represented here always had their own coherence and logic. The editor's task therefore is to try to capture the flow while, through appropriate punctuation, making the coherence and logic even clearer.

So, sometimes questions are not questions but statements that lead logically to the interviewee's next thought. Sometimes a thought is interrupted, as in any normal conversation, as part of the to-and-fro of exchanging ideas. The ellipses (…) indicate where conversation is continuous or ironically leaves a thought hanging in the air. In contrast, sometimes a question demands or generates greater thought. Where this was significant it was important to indicate this thus: '[Long pause]'. Some statements conveyed special emphases and exclamation marks are used to capture these.

Titles of works are indicated in italics while individual movements and text titles are rendered in inverted commas. Technical terms are also italicised.

Inevitably, because these are conversations, names, terms and titles are often spoken of without explanation. Where an explanation of a name, term, or title could be helpful to the reader it has been marked with an asterisk (*). This indicates its inclusion in the Reference section. Many names appear in more than one interview.

Leslie East OBE

The Composers

Judith Bingham

BORN 1952

DW: *Can you tell me about your first musical memories? Was there much music in the home when you were growing up?*

JB: My father loved classical music – he played the piano and taught me the rudiments early on. It was essentially a working-class family with aspirations, and he was quite a snob. He sneered a bit at my mother's tastes which inclined more to songs from the shows. My elder brother liked Buddy Holly*, Roy Orbison*, rock-and roll. My father belonged to the World Record Club, so he bought me those pieces that he considered children's pieces – *Swan Lake*, *The Sorcerer's Apprentice** – but he played all the classics, not really going any further than Sibelius*, although I remember him dipping his toe in Tippett*, so to speak. My mother had a good voice and everyone noticed that I could sing well, from 18 months according to her. I was often asked to sing solos at school, which I hated, being very shy. My earliest memories are of piano pieces by Grieg*, who I still love – my father would have the radio on over breakfast and say 'who is this piece by?', which trained me to listen in a very analytical way quite early on.

DW: *I don't think there was much encouragement about the prospect of you being a professional musician. You were singing in amateur choirs and played the oboe at school.*

JB: It was inconceivable at school and at home that a girl could become a composer, although I always knew I would be. I didn't have any confidence as far as doing that professionally until I was at the Academy [RAM*]. I played the oboe badly at school and didn't enjoy it, but I was always singing and in choirs. I started voice training when I was 16 with a well-known bass in Sheffield called John Dethick. He was really good and taught me how to breathe properly and gradually strengthen my voice. It started to seem possible that I might be a singer – my mother was just about OK with this, but really thought I should be a nurse or a teacher. My father was rather withdrawn and didn't express an opinion as such. When I was 16 I joined the Sheffield Philharmonic Chorus, which was wonderful. They sang with the Hallé and all the star conductors – Barbirolli* of course – I sang in his last *Messiah* – also Giulini*, Rudolf Schwarz*, Charles Groves*, Maxim Shostakovich*...

DW: *The urge to write music was always there.*

JB: Yes, I think I was about three when I started to make things up on the piano. Until I was a teenager I had no idea that women composers existed. My composition was rather secret, a way of dealing with a dysfunctional family. I did show some pieces to my teachers at school – I wrote a big Masque for a school competition. It was the only entry but it didn't win as it had dissonances in it, which were not allowed! There was a feeling of being slapped down and they probably felt it was for my own good.

DW: *You obviously remember those early pieces – I think you developed a love of Berlioz* in particular.*

JB: I don't think I wrote anything down until I was about 11. The piano pieces, many of which I still have, are tonal, sometimes modal, not strikingly original; on the other hand if I had shown them to anyone they might have been surprised that I was doing that on my own. There was the Masque I mentioned, an opera about Caligula, pieces with unusual instrumental line-ups. My teens coincided with a golden age of pop music – the Beatles*, the Stones*, the Who*. There was huge disapproval at home, shock even, because I liked such bad music! I never went to pop concerts but I did join the Beatles fan club! Berlioz became my great mentor and friend, probably as a result of doing his Requiem with the Hallé, though I already knew *Symphonie Fantastique* of course. The Sheffield Chorus also took part in a concert version of *Les Troyens*. I loved all things French and in Berlioz I found someone who I thought understood me. I read his Memoirs, his *Treatise on Instrumentation*, and studied his scores, learning so much before I got to the Academy.

DW: *You went to the Royal Academy of Music to study singing and composition, but found it singularly unhelpful.*

JB: I thought it would be like the Moscow Conservatoire – full of brilliant people – but that wasn't the case at all. I was shocked that no one in my digs had ever heard any Mahler* and had no real curiosity outside their subject. The other problem was that I had never had a composition lesson and had never had anyone pass any comment about what I was doing. The only other woman composer there was Odaline de la Martinez*, who moved in a very different circle. I realise now that I was excluded from a lot of groups because I was a woman, but also I didn't fit into any of the new music trends – the Manchester School*, and the Electroacoustic set, led by Paul Patterson*. Everything about me jarred with new music of the time. I discovered early music, French Baroque in particular, and was trying to integrate these mad French ornaments into my music, and worse still, I used tonal chords... It was very fascistic then, new music – Boulez* and Stockhausen* set the tone. I wrote to Boulez and said that I thought that pop music and film music, both very tonal of course, would have a real influence in the future. He didn't reply of course. I see now that I was very much part of that group of composers like Tavener* who were trying to shift music away from the post-war scene, the cloud of the Holocaust. Now I feel that Boulez and Stockhausen were part of a group of composers at the end of a movement, not the Messiahs as they themselves thought.

DW: *Your official teachers at the academy included Malcolm MacDonald*, Eric Fenby* – remembered as amanuensis to Delius of course – and Alan Bush*, but wasn't it Hans Keller*, a musicologist, that first took you seriously as a composer?*

JB: The Academy is a very different place now to how it was then. A lot of the teachers were quite old, past retirement age, and very locked in their ways. Malcolm was a nice man, he mainly wrote for brass and military bands. Eric Fenby would just put a red pencil through anything I took to him – he was irascible and rather bitter. Alan Bush – I wanted to study orchestration with him, but instead he made me do two years of Palestrina species counterpoint, no doubt because he felt I lacked discipline, although again I felt as though I was being slapped down and told to mind my place! I was demoralised and unhappy when I left the Academy. I went home to Norfolk for a year to live with my parents and worked in Debenhams in Kings Lynn. A friend suggested I send some scores to Hans Keller, who at the time was Chief Assistant, New Music, at BBC Radio 3. He wrote an encouraging letter back and offered to teach me, telling me 'you won't like it'. I was so naive and had no idea he was a famous teacher and writer and he never mentioned it. I could still cry, thinking about it now, as it was only years later that he told me he knew I didn't have any money to pay for lessons but that he wanted to encourage me. I never got to thank him properly and never knew he had Motor Neurone Disease until he had died. I felt huge shame about this because Hans was so selfless, and he saw something in me even though I was so young and bolshie!

DW: *Can you say what it was that he taught you?*

JB: Hans called what he did 'anti-teaching'. He never suggested anything was wrong, he asked me how I felt the piece, and when I expressed doubts, we'd talk them through. He really knew my pieces before I saw him, took me very seriously and helped me to take myself seriously too. Some of the things he said I didn't understand for a long time – 'why do you think the first idea is the spontaneous one?'. It was very psychological teaching, not surprising from someone who came from Vienna.

DW: *For a while you were combining the life of a professional composer with that of a professional singer – quite a rare thing I would imagine, at least since the Renaissance.*

JB: It was very rare when I was young and people often commented on it. Now, with the resurgence of interest in choirs, there are several well-known singer/composers around, who also conduct – Owain Park* and Hilary Campbell* for instance.

DW: *You sang in the BBC Singers for over a decade – I would imagine that singing in a virtuoso choir like that was probably the best education any composer who wanted to write choral music could wish for.*

JB: I'm tempted to say yes to this! In the '80s and '90s the Singers worked with Boulez, Berio*, Xenakis*, Birtwistle*, Ligeti*, Lutosławski*, Tippett*, Reich*, Tavener, Penderecki*, Stockhausen, Arvo Pärt*, just everyone, and thousands I've forgotten. Virtually no women – the very occasional piece by Elizabeth Maconchy*, Nicola Le Fanu*, Judith Weir* and me of course. I've written 14 commissions for the BBC Singers over the years – the Singers and BBC Symphony Chorus have gone right through my professional life in a major way. I think every composer should be in a choir, even a bad one! It is a fantastic education, just learning by osmosis how to write for and balance voices, but also the psychology of a choir. So much rehearsal time can be saved by understanding how individuals and sections react to the notation of the music.

DW: *How did you find your own voice? You have said that you felt as though you didn't particularly fit in anywhere.*

JB: My catalogue of juvenilia and early pieces finishes in 1974 and contains over 70 pieces, so I was writing a lot. I think my harmonic language was recognisable fairly early – the mix of French music, '60s TV music, maybe a little Elgar* and Vaughan Williams*. People talk about Messiaen* too, and I get that, but I hadn't really heard any until the '80s, apart from *O sacrum convivium* perhaps. David Hill* says that my style in the '90s was English with a French accent, which is OK but it ignores the jazz influence. I hardly wrote any choral music to begin with. Most of what I wrote before joining the Singers was instrumental/chamber music, some solo vocal music too. A breakthrough piece was *Hymn before Sunrise in the Vale of Chamouni*, with words by Coleridge* and Shelley*. I think I always was a square peg in a round hole. When I was younger people said my music was refreshingly more traditional and easier than the norm – right of centre – though they often sneered when they said that. Now people tell me my music is hard and dark. I've always just tried to be myself. As I've got older Russian music and literature has been a great influence. For some reason Russian composers do the most brilliant endings, the hardest thing when composing. I always tell students to start thinking about the ending when you start a piece!

DW: *Two of your most notable early successes were big orchestral pieces* – Chartres *and* The Temple of Karnak. *Do you regard these pieces as in some way your real opus 1?*

JB: Sorry to disappoint you, but I have never felt 'this is me'. The mythology that surrounds composers, that there needs to be a eureka moment, really it isn't true. Everything is striving, and disappointment continues throughout your life. One moment you think you are a genius and the next a fraud. *Chartres* was an important piece for me because it came at the end of a difficult chapter in my life and the start of a new chapter. When I was young I was thinking of myself as Berlioz and that, like him, I would be famous for writing operas and orchestral music. I've written a lot of orchestral music but most of the pieces have fallen on deaf ears, which is painful, given the amount of work they take. Maybe it is latent sexism, preferring women to stick to smaller forms and leave the big stuff to men.

DW: *Am I wrong to suggest that you imagine choral music orchestrally too? I'm thinking of some of the vocal effects you use – vocal trills, singing 'mm', 'ah' or 'non' or a combination of them; there is a wonderful effect in the Christmas cycle* A Cold Spell *marked 'shivery', where the choir are instructed to sing rapid single notes to 'v v v v'.*

JB: My first concern is 'The Idea' – there is a point when I click with that idea – a text, a story, a dramatic idea. The idea has to be brief and it's important to me that the commissioner is satisfied and surprised. I remember performing a great piece by Edward Cowie* with the [BBC] Singers, *Hest Bank*, in which he creates the sound of birds on the west coast of the UK. It was the first time I have heard voices used instrumentally and I'm sure it influenced me. The humming thing has become a bit of a signature, but I like adding it to a texture as it brings out the overtones, and adds a magical gloss to the sound. It also keeps singers in touch with the notes and can be very helpful in cueing the next entry. But it still has to be a legitimate part of the piece, you have to think about that and not use it wantonly. A background tapestry of sound can also create a mystical sense of otherness, or apprehension, in sacred music.

DW: *You find inspiration from a wide subject matter – most directly Shakespeare for* A Shakespeare Requiem, *a football match in the trenches between English and German soldiers (*A Christmas Truce*), but also aspects of nature, landscape, visual art, films, literature... Can you say what the balance is between inspiration and technique?*

JB: The last part of the question doesn't mean much to me – everything has to be balanced. The music has to be as strong as the idea. I've had criticism in the past that the idea is more interesting than the music, but I know that's because the critic has only heard the music once. I do like to collage ideas together and like to set things other than poetry or prose – newspaper articles (in *A Christmas Truce*), knitting patterns – anything that fits the idea.

DW: *I wanted to ask you about your wonderfully poetic titles – it is quite rare for anything to be given just an abstract title...* Unpredictable but Providential *is a great title,* My Heart Strangely Warmed, Salt in the Blood *– titles that heighten the curiosity in some way.*

JB: Titles are VERY important. The best ones always come before I start writing the music – I hate struggling for a title. They are usually part of a text. I've written five settings of the Missa Brevis* – another one soon – but nowadays quite a lot of people, including publishers, are out of touch with the church world, and don't understand what something like Coll Reg* means. Also, church music gets performed a lot in a concert now, and I think a subtitle is more helpful and memorable. My second Missa Brevis, *The Road to Emmaus*, was when I first thought of developing the Mass like a drama that only came to a climax in the voluntary. I wrote a prelude, a Preamble, a bit like an overture, that presented the themes. The whole thing was inspired by Caravaggio's 'Supper at Emmaus'*. A communion motet depicted the moment when Christ breaks bread and is recognised. Baroque gestures, the melodrama of them, have been a big influence in my later music. I don't think I could ever call something by an abstract title.

DW: *And sometimes your starting point is a work by another composer – for example Wesley* *in* The Darkness is no Darkness; *Parry* *in* Distant Thunder; *Stanford* *in* The Drowned Lovers *and Tallis* *in* The Spirit of Truth *– these are re-workings or fantasies on well-known pieces, designed to be sung alongside their original inspirations. Can you say a little about how these pieces came about?*

JB: I must have sung Wesley's *Thou wilt keep Him in perfect peace* in church over Christmas. I was playing it through and noticed how odd some of the harmonies are, and oddly spaced too. I wondered what would happen if you took out the odder chords and made a new piece using those harmonies – *The Darkness is no Darkness* is the result. The words are taken from the same Psalm as the Wesley but reworked to sound more like a love song, so that the two halves of the piece are about secular and sacred love. My piece should never be sung without the Wesley, it says so at the front of the score, but this still happens. It pains me to think of it because it doesn't have a proper ending. The other re-workings are done on the same principle; they only use harmonies from the 'parent piece'. I was trying to choose a piece from each century of British music, but obviously that didn't work out.

DW: *Can you say a little about texts? Is finding the right text an involved process? You must do a lot of reading.*

JB: I do read a lot, especially books about art and history. Also, the natural world – well, I'm a magpie, I'm interested in so many different things. I come back to a subject I like. At the moment I'm reading about the human biome – I imagine many people are reading about viruses and bacteria now! I read a lot about Christianity from all different points of view. I rarely want to set a famous text such as 'There is no rose'. When I did the *Corpus Christi Carol* it took a long time to chase the famous settings out of my mind. I have worked with living poets several times, which is challenging, because I am a control freak with my ideas, but it is good for me. The worse thing is being given a text to set – I was asked to set 'O Clap your hands' once and did a terrible setting of it, because I disagreed with it and could not make it happy! It's so aggressive to me, almost offensive!

DW: *Could you say how a piece starts once you have the text?*

JB: The period before you start the composition is incredibly important. Some composers do a lot of formal planning and stick to that plan. I like a visual backdrop to my desk that has images to keep me in the zone. At a certain moment I feel like I'm ready to start improvising and in the next day or so the piece will start. I always feel that I'm never going to write again and so it is always a relief to get going. I use an old Yamaha synthesiser, which has the advantage that I can record and multi-track onto it. I start with pen and paper, but once I've done a chunk I start putting it on the computer. This is a good stage for 'tarting it up' as Richard Rodney Bennett* used to say. It's important for me that every part, whatever the genre, has equal weight, the parts all have integrity and there are no fillers. I don't compose for long. If I do I tend to go wrong and force the process which is never good.

DW: *You have had long and close associations with a number of choirs, the BBC Singers of course – you were their Composer in Association for a while – but also, choirs in the US such as VocalEssence and the St Louis Chamber Chorus. Does it help to have the sound of the choir you are writing for in your head? As a singer you must be aware of how different choirs sound in different countries.*

JB: Yes, I take all commissions very seriously and try to write for the forces I'm given. Choirs do sound very different from country to country, but it is up to the conductor to adjust these things. It pays dividends to ask lots of questions I have found – how many people, any good solo voices, male or female altos, ranges – VERY important – ability – conductors will generally tell you that their choir is better than it is! Where will they sing? Acoustic? – those sorts of things. Professionals will generally be of a standard, but amateurs have a huge range of ability. I do prefer a lighter sound, as a lot of vibrato will obscure the harmony.

DW: *I read somewhere that you objected, quite rightly, to being called a 'choral composer' – you have written a lot of choral music of course, but lots of chamber music and orchestral works, made important contributions to the repertoire of wind and brass bands etc. Do you feel that you have to some extent been pigeon-holed?*

JB: There used to be a lot of snobbery about choral music, but this isn't really the case now. There are so many good choirs now –Tenebrae for instance, Stile Antico, Voces8 –

very youthful groups, and one shouldn't under-estimate the effect of having women in collegiate choirs and girls in cathedrals, this has fed into the high standards of many smaller choirs. I think I was pigeon-holed in a sexist way, but musicians often only know you for what you have written for their instrument or voice.

DW: Do you see yourself to be part of an English choral tradition in any way? Is there anything in your music that sounds particularly British or English?

JB: I remember when I wrote my first Mass for Westminster Cathedral, going past the building on the number 22 bus and suddenly thinking I was now part of that tradition. I am a patriotic person, especially proud to be English. Although we have been vilified for shameful moments in our history, we have a culture that is a staggering achievement – no need for me to list the painters, composers, novelists and poets. Englishness in my music is to do with the weather, the sea, the kind of English mysticism you find in Samuel Palmer* or Vaughan Williams. Writing an anthem for the re-interment of Richard III was such a privilege, and that day in Leicester Cathedral was one of the best days of my life.

DW: I think I'm right in saying that you earn your living exclusively from composing. With this in mind, you must be pretty disciplined when it comes to working hours and deadlines.

JB: Yes, I diarise everything carefully, and am quite good at working to a deadline. There is an element of trade when writing to commission, and if you want to make a living from it you have to be disciplined. Doing a good job so that people get a piece that fits the brief, but also surprises them, means that they will have a good attitude to commissioning again – you don't ruin things for the next composer.

DW: Are you ever surprised when you hear a piece for the first time?

JB: No, and I don't think you should be.

DW: Do performers ever find things in your music that you didn't know were there?

JB: I think that's called interpretation!

DW: Do you ever revise? Have you ever experienced composer's block?

JB: There generally isn't enough time to revise so I try to get the piece right the first time. It's very hard to get back into a piece again. I did have composer's block once in the early '80s, though it was more that I couldn't finish pieces and what I was writing was terribly turgid. I started having therapy, and my therapist suggested drawing what I was trying to say instead of composing, and it was incredibly effective. But my problems then were in any case to do with family, so not just about composing.

DW: *Are you self-critical? Does the act of composition get easier as you get older and more experienced?*

JB: Yes, terribly self-critical. There is always a voice saying 'give it up – you're never going to get it'. Composition never becomes any easier and I always get that imposter syndrome.

DW: *Do you think about an audience when you are writing?*

JB: It's easy to start worrying about the audience – I find that's a common thing amongst young composers – they worry people will be bored. As one hopes there will be many audiences it is probably best to block those thoughts out. However, I love it when someone comes up to me after a performance, and I've noticed that older women often do that – I think it is terrific that they feel they have a voice in their culture and aren't invisible.

DW: *Do you enjoy rehearsal and premieres?*

JB: Premieres are stressful, regardless of if the performance is good or not. I feel very exposed – it's worse of course if there are lots of wrong notes. I've had performances where afterwards I felt as though I had been mugged! The trouble is that people are always trying their best and nobody actively tries to sabotage a performance, so you must always thank people as it might have been a stressful experience for them too. Mind you, I once went to hear a choir who were nowhere near ready to perform the piece. A tenor came up to me afterwards – he was elated. 'That was wonderful', he said, 'it's the first time we've got through the piece without stopping'! So for them it was a big success. But a lot of premieres are wonderful, and very emotional. I do enjoy rehearsals, and love to see other musicians.

DW: *I'm not sure you have held any official or regular teaching positions, but you have certainly done a good deal of teaching and running workshops for young composers. To begin with, can composition really be taught and secondly, as someone who was a professional singer, what do you find are the main problems for young composers when writing choral music, or perhaps it isn't just young composers?*

JB: If a composer isn't a singer, I think the main problem is understanding tessitura. You can make such a difference to the way a chord sounds by understanding where the notes sit in the voice. Writing on a keyboard with your two thumbs in the middle often produces a muddy sound in the alto and tenor parts. Composing can be taught, and there are always people that are not full-time composers that want to learn – teachers, arrangers, organists etc. The real McCoy, people like me, with a vocation, have generally already started writing before they get to college level. Some will want to stay in education, making a living to fund their writing. Someone like me will be ploughing their own furrow and not really surface for a few years. High-art composers usually have a very particular mix of characteristics to their personality. It's a rare thing, obviously.

DW: *Do you have any particular advice for a young composer?*

JB: Peter Maxwell Davies* said, 'my advice is, don't listen to anything I say'. I do think it would be great if every composer had performing experience because it gives you realistic and humane goals – to stand in front of several thousand people at a late night Prom and sing a top C on the word 'scream' with a diminuendo on it – every composer should have to do that. But then the composer also has to sit in the audience and hear bad performances – that is a lesson in itself. The thing that sorts out the sheep from the goats is risk taking. British composers have a particular affliction, worrying that they are giving away too much about themselves, worrying about boring people, worrying about what their 'particular set' will think about them. You have to take the risk to be truthful – being truthful is THE RISK, it's hard to do, but it transforms the music. Being truthful also means acknowledging who you are. You have to develop your ideas – read, read, read and think. If you are setting a religious text, spend some time really engaging with it. It has nothing to do with being a Christian; find something real and truthful to tell about the text you are setting. There is nothing worse than cynical settings of Christian texts, and there is a lot of that around. I think my main advice though is to guard your integrity, because you can't get it back once it is gone. It can be tempting to do things for money or because it seemed like a laugh at the time, but stuff comes back to bite you. Take yourself seriously.

DW: *Is there anything in particular that you are longing to write?*

JB: No, I mean, I'm happy to write what fate throws at me.

DW: *Elgar quotes Ruskin at the end of* The Dream of Gerontius* – 'This is the best of me…'. Can you say which piece or group of pieces of yours might fall into that category?*

JB: No. Other people will say, 'I think this is your best piece', when it is the only piece they have studied or learned, and they have only heard one or two in total. Some of the choices have been just bizarre. I would certainly choose another piece of Elgar if I were him – the text of *Gerontius* makes me cringe, it is embarrassing in places and brings out the worst kind of choral singing. (Sorry!) Also, it is a very male thing to try and single one piece out – your favourite symphony, that kind of thing. I think in a more linear way.

DW: *We are recording this interview at a very worrying and difficult time – how have you been dealing with lockdown?*

JB: I have chronic asthma and last February I was in my own self-imposed lockdown as it was so cold, so I just slid into the lockdown that was ordered by the government. I like living on my own and have had work to keep me going. I feel very lucky compared to most of the performers I know. My main anxiety has been about catching the virus. Being ill all the time has slowed me down, but I am never short of things to do.

DW: *What would you say are your five favourite choral works?*

JUDITH'S FIVE FAVOURITE CHORAL WORKS

Handel *Dixit Dominus*

Ligeti *Magyar Etudok*

Mahler *Symphony No.8*

Poulenc *Figure humaine*

Rachmaninov *All-Night Vigil*

Bob Chilcott

BORN 1955

DW: *Can you tell me about your background? Did you come from a musical family?*

BC: Not at all. I was about five when I started to learn the piano with a local teacher, who was also organist at the church where I was a member of the choir. The assistant organist at that time was Andrew Davis, later Sir Andrew, the conductor. It was a good choir, boys and men, a lot of music going on. I did quite well early on and started to give recitals when I was about seven or eight, but my father died when I was 12 and we just didn't have the money to take the lessons much further. I was playing the viola too and, as there were not many viola players around, we decided I should go on with those lessons instead. I missed out on about three years of piano lessons at a crucial time and although I got to be a reasonable pianist, I think I would have been much better if circumstances had been different. It was actually the vicar at the church that suggested I should go for a chorister trial and as a result I got into the Choir of King's College, Cambridge* and went there at eight years old.

DW: *This would be in 1963, when Sir David Willcocks* was Director of Music.*

BC: Yes, just after the time he had started to put together *Carols for Choirs 1**, and they were making a series of recordings of the music of Tallis* for Argo, including *Spem in Alium**...

DW: *Music that at that time was not so well known…*

BC: Yes, that's right, it was an incredible experience. I remember that this was also the time that the Cambridge Press published the Cambridge Hymnal. A fellow chorister was Simon Grant who many years later was singing with the BBC Singers when I was conducting them. We were rehearsing that lovely carol by Elizabeth Poston, *Jesus Christ the Apple Tree*, and Simon reminded me that we had sung in the first performance. The now famous Willcocks arrangement of *Tomorrow shall be my dancing day* was in the same book – I can still see David coming to our choir practice with it written out on those old xerox sheets that went a horrible brown colour after about two minutes. We did the first stereo recording that King's ever did, for EMI – it was called *Sing Praises* and we started touring too – we went to Germany in 1965. This was only twenty years after the war of course and I think some of the parents were still a little nervous about that trip, but we stayed with families and had a wonderful time. We sang Bach and Brahms - for me that was very significant, especially Brahms, who is so important to me now – there was something in the air, it was just rather special.

DW: *Willcocks was quite tough on you all I think.*

BC: He was very demanding and treated us like professionals – it didn't matter how young we were. He could be very fierce but we all loved him all the same. There was such a lot going on. Willcocks was growing the choir and developing an international reputation. The concerts with Benjamin Britten*were a big highlight, singing the *War Requiem** and the *Spring Symphony* with him conducting. He was so charismatic and brilliant and we were all completely star-struck! I remember being at the Festival Hall in London and getting to that last chorus in the *Spring Symphony*. The boys sing 'Sumer is Icumen in' and I was completely overwhelmed; I could hardly sing myself. I thought, I don't know what this is, but I've got to do it!

DW: *Then came the famous recording of the Fauré* Requiem.*

BC: That was a little later, just before my voice broke. We recorded it for television to begin with and had a female soprano for the 'Pie Jesu'. Hermann Prey sang the baritone solo. He was very grand, very good-looking and swept in wearing a long cloak I remember. He sang beautifully but somehow, just slightly under the note, so Willcocks stood in front of him pointing upwards! When it came to the LP, the producer, Christopher Bishop, said that it had to be a boy singing the 'Pie Jesu' and I was lucky, I got it!

DW: *Were you writing anything at this time?*

BC: That came later when I was at secondary school. I would have been about 14. My friend David Angus, who later worked as a repetiteur and conductor with some of the great opera companies, played the piano very well and composed, and I just thought I'd like to do that. Oddly enough I remember watching a Hollywood film about Chopin*, very much heart on sleeve stuff, and straight after that I wrote some Chopinesque piano pieces. I'm sure they were probably dire! I wrote an Oboe Concerto and a Cello Concerto, all carefully written out – even then I was concerned with how the music looked. I wrote a lot of music. That's all I was really interested in.

DW: *All hidden away now...*

BC: They certainly are! I borrowed from everything I heard.

DW: *So what did these pieces sound like?*

BC: The big influence was Vaughan Williams*. I loved twentieth-century English music, Finzi and Delius, but I also enjoyed pop music, so that was in there somewhere.

I did play in a band which was no doubt pretty awful. I remember a significant moment in my teens was when I heard Stockhausen's *Gesang der Jünglinge** – it just staggered me. I had never heard anything like that before. Then I had a friend who was keen on music and we used to go to concerts all the time. I remember lots of Messiaen* – the *Vingt Regards sur l'Enfant-Jésus** was my 'go to' piece, all very adolescent but hugely important.

DW: *And then back to King's College - as a student and a tenor? This was around the time that Willcocks left?*

BC: Yes, he was there for a term and in January 1974 Philip Ledger came, another incredible musician. I had a friend, Julian Pike, who was and is a good composer, he was mad on Bruckner, so we used to sit and listen to the Mahler and Bruckner symphonies, again going into all this adolescent ecstasy. I sort of gave up composing myself. There were some pretty remarkable contemporaries including Judith Weir* and Robert Saxton*. Robert was a bit older and kept going off to London to hear his pieces being performed and everyone was saying how brilliant Judith was, blazing a trail. This was also the time that John Rutter* was writing his early carols, conducting the choir at Clare College. The kind of musical language that he used, and I felt close to, was so far away from the language that everyone thought was the one that all composers should be using. I went down to the Royal College of Music [RCM*]to study composition and just felt out of it, but I was also studying singing and this rather took over my life. I sang with the John Alldis Choir – lots of premieres of seriously demanding music, Xenakis*, Nono*, Finnissy*, Berio* – it was terribly exciting.

DW: *But exciting as it was, you were conscious that it was not the sort of music you wanted to write.*

BC: No, I just felt it wasn't for me. I was singing in a vocal group we had started in Cambridge and I did some arranging for that. We did a concert in London and luckily the brilliant arranger Neil Richardson came. He was doing a lot of work for the BBC, programmes like Friday Night is Music Night on BBC Radio 2. He asked me to do some continuity arrangements and that sort of thing. I loved doing it.

DW: *You must have been learning on the job here – you really have to know what you are doing in that kind of situation.*

BC: Absolutely. I learnt quickly because you had to! Everything was hand-written of course. You would get arrangements by Gordon Langford, Peter Knight, Richard Rodney Bennett*, and you would be asked to re-score them for different ensembles, literally over-night. It really put one on the spot. You certainly learnt how to orchestrate and learnt what worked and what didn't. I met Ron Goodwin too – a fine composer and a really nice guy. I asked him if I could orchestrate for him but he did everything himself. He was quite brilliant, would write 15 minutes of music a week and orchestrate everything himself – incredible really. This led to some television work, I even remember doing 'Comedy Tonight' for Frankie Howerd*!

DW: *So you were doing all that and were a 'jobbing singer' too?*

BC: I was singing with the BBC Singers, various other choirs, all kinds of things, and then in 1985 I was asked to arrange something for the King's Singers for an album they were doing. Grayston (Bill) Ives had to back out of the group, I subbed for him, then Bill decided to leave shortly afterwards, and I got the job.

DW: *The King's Singers are a world-renowned group now, but at that time, it is hard to over-estimate how huge they were – concert tours, albums, Saturday night peak TV – almost pop stars?*

BC: Yes, when I started with the group it was beginning to happen in North America too. Whenever we did a concert with an orchestra, I used to do an arrangement, you know –in places like Toronto, Pittsburgh, Minnesota – and I would sit there thinking 'how lucky am I'? Then we did a Christmas album and I did a lot of arrangements for that which became quite successful.

DW: *The King's Singers have always sung a huge variety of music – madrigals and Bach*, Simon & Garfunkel and the Beatles*, and then a lot of new pieces, Penderecki* and Ligeti* for instance...*

BC: We had some fantastic commissions and we always worked with the composers of course which was fascinating - Takemitsu and Maxwell Davies* wrote for us, John McCabe* wrote us a fantastic piece, William Mathias* too. The most thrilling for me, because I got to know him quite well, was György Ligeti. We worked with him over a period of eight years on his *Nonsense Madri-*  *gals* which were incredibly hard, even harder as he kept revising them as we went along! He knew that I listened to a lot of music and we used to talk about that a lot – what I had listened to or what I should listen to. I showed Ligeti a few early pieces of mine and he was encouraging. He said very sweetly, in heavily accented English, 'Very simple music but very good music'.

DW: *All that arranging I suppose kept your creative interest on the boil a little?*

BC: Yes, it did help a lot. Then I had a break, thanks not for the last time to John Rutter. He had a longstanding arrangement with Hinshaw Music in the USA and it was through him that the King's Singers had a series of arrangements published under their own name, including some that I had done. John was incredibly supportive.

DW: *You left the King's Singers in 1997 and decided that you would take the jump and be a full-time composer?*

BC: Yes, I became associated with OUP [Oxford University Press] in 1995, again thanks to John who had sent some of my music on, including some pieces I wrote called *The Modern Man I Sing*. I wrote these for the Toronto Children's Choir and the tenor Ben Heppner, who was a Patron of the choir. One of those pieces was *Mid-Winter* and became my first OUP publication. I just thought that I was 42 and needed to give it a go whilst I still had the energy. I certainly never intended to do any conducting, it just wasn't of interest to me, but then fate took over and I got asked to direct the choir at the RCM, so again, I 'learnt on the job'. I didn't have a clue! But I worked hard at it and then realised how important that sort of contact with singers was for me.

DW: *Do you think at that time, this would be the late '90s, that there was less pressure on you to write in a way that was expected of you? That someone who wanted to write diatonic music could do so without being shouted down?*

BC: Yes, definitely. I remember going to see a couple of publishers in the US, and they said, 'This is great, write us something, as long as it sounds like John Rutter...'. That was always the line – he had a massive presence there and still does. It was at the same time that composers like Górecki* and Tavener* were bringing about a change of attitude with their music. Tavener's *Song for Athene* was sung at Princess Diana's funeral and became incredibly popular. Then, the aftermath of the release of all the East European countries from Soviet control brought us music by Pärt*, Tormis* (whom I met – the King's Singers' commissioned him). They had musical languages that people really responded to and became popular with both choirs and audiences.

DW: *It was still true that choral music, certainly music for children that you were writing a lot of, was looked down upon.*

BC: Yes, choral music in general but writing music for children did put you at the bottom of the pile! I remember going to the ADCA* convention in San Diego in 1997, and I met conductors of children's choirs who were fighting to be noticed. Since then the whole upper-voice arena has blossomed. I think now the phrase 'children's choir' is a bit of a misnomer really.

DW: *Is there a piece that you think you can say 'that's me', a sort of opus 1, or maybe you were not so concerned about finding a voice, you just wrote what you wrote.*

BC: I think I just did what I did and didn't really think about my own voice as such, but there is a piece, fairly early on, *The Making of the Drum*. I wrote it for a choir in Oxford. A few years later I did it with the BBC Singers and I felt that it represented a kind of fusion of the energy I had in the King's Singers and identified it as the sort of sound-world I wanted to pursue for a while. Maybe *Canticles of Light* a little later too – quite an important piece for me I think.

DW: *A big part of the process for you is finding texts I think?*

BC: I spend a lot of time looking around for texts, especially when writing pieces for children. I realised I had come from the English music tradition and that I knew all those liturgical texts back to front. If someone had said to me, would you write a Mag & Nunc* at that time, I don't think I would have known what to do. I felt rather straight-jacketed and would go into a default sound-world without having much to say. Finding texts to set for children was kind of liberating – something that wasn't sacred, but had energy and a real message. It gave me the chance to express what I wanted rather than what I felt people wanted from me. Even now I feel when I'm asked to write an anthem I find it rather hard. I really felt that I didn't have a voice for that kind of thing until the *Requiem* came along. After that I was much more confident and had a bigger canvas to work with. Another important thing has been collaborating with poets and asking them to write texts for me. I've been working with Charles Bennett for some years. He has written some wonderful texts for me and then more recently I've been working with a young poet called Delphine Chalmers. The idea of writing words for a composer to set is a whole different kind of thing. Charles and Delphine would be the first to admit that I think.

DW: *You find that many of your musical ideas come directly from reading the text.*

BC: Yes, I think so. This has helped me to define my role as a composer, in particular trying to communicate with the people I'm writing for, especially writing for children or amateurs. I want to communicate something of the world I find myself living in.

DW: *Having said what you have said about the English choral tradition, do you still feel very much part of that?*

BC: I do, but I think luckily, when one looks at the musical landscape now, it has blossomed into something that is very wide and more inclusive. At one time it would have been characterised just by music for the church but I think this is less so now. It is defined by community and by all the work being done re the positioning of singing here, so that there are so many composers that have something different to say.

DW: *You mention the Requiem which I think might have been a bit of a turning point. You were writing lots of shorter pieces but, since the Requiem, there have been regular works on a larger scale – Salisbury Vespers, St John Passion, Christmas Oratorio...*

BC: It was certainly a turning point. In a funny way I feel more at ease with a big canvas - it enables me to build a bigger picture of what it is I want to say. I loved writing the John Passion – it tells a story and I felt I had something to say in my own way, the same with the Christmas Oratorio.

DW: *You have of course built up a sound technique over the years but does the act of writing music get easier the more experience you have?*

BC: I still find it difficult and probably always will. It's trying to find ways of re-evaluating one's own language and developing it. I am pretty keen on the technical side – if you give someone a well-crafted piece they will enjoy it. I think for a long time about detail, just looking to find ways of making it better. I would be disappointed if someone told me a piece was badly written. I look at things I wrote 15 years ago and am not sure I could do them now – I had a different sort of energy, I was in a different place then.

DW: *With that in mind you wouldn't go back and revise?*

BC: No, not really. Although recently I took another look at a piece I wrote for the Houston Chamber Choir in 2003, *Circlesong*, that sets indigenous American texts. I thought it was quite a good piece – quite bold texts. I had to revise it a little as it was originally for two choirs and I changed some of the language to try and make the text more gender neutral and universal, more fitting for these different times. But when I heard it I was surprised – it was actually rather good! I wasn't ashamed of the piece.

DW: *What do you think the balance is between inspiration and technique? Do you believe in inspiration?*

BC: I do believe in inspiration. Occasionally you can hear a couple of notes or even one note in your head and it can suggest a whole world. I remember hearing the writer Ian McEwan speak once and he said that he can be inspired by just one word and then it grows organically – I think it is like that sometimes. On other occasions, I can spend days and weeks on thinking about how to make things work, how to structure something.

DW: *And this is where your practical experience as a singer and conductor comes in?*

BC: Yes, I think of the people that have got to be able to sing the piece. As you well know, with professional choirs you might if you are lucky have one rehearsal and with amateur choirs more often than not, one rehearsal with orchestra, and what you want is someone to say 'we can do that piece because we can do a good job in the time we have and with what we have available'. Let's do a piece that will sing itself – I like writing that sort of piece. It doesn't mean to say that a piece is easy to bring off well, but just something that is practical and will work in all these circumstances.

DW: *Are you quite disciplined in your writing, do you work regular hours every day?*

BC: Yes, I try to. I start about 9.30am and go through to 6.00pm – unless I need a gin!

DW: *What do you do when you get stuck? Do you go away and come back later?*

BC: I tend to stick at it and just look at the blank paper. It has so much to do with your energy levels. I know a lot of composers who work late into the night and I just can't. I find regular hours during the day help focus the mind.

DW: *You still write by hand I think.*

BC: I like the physical contact with the pencil and paper – I couldn't imagine not doing that. If I was twenty-five or something I would probably have a Great Wall of machinery but not now. In any case, I don't like looking at a screen for hours on end.

DW: *I've seen you conduct Birtwistle* with the BBC Singers, children's choirs, amateur choral societies, all kinds of things. Talking as a conductor, do you have a different approach and when you are conducting your pieces do you need to stand aside from it a little?*

BC: It's a good question – the biggest problem I find when conducting my music is getting the tempo right – I find that really hard. I've found doing the OUP choral samplers so helpful – lots of different short pieces, different styles and I just have to sit there with my metronome! With my own pieces I'm often wrong and have to think very carefully, stand back from it and think. I have enjoyed conducting other people's music very much too. It is fascinating to see how other composers do things and deal with the problems that I have.

DW: *So when you go to performances of your music as a listener do you sit on your hands?*

BC: No, I'm quite relaxed. I'm just thrilled they are doing the piece. I like to support them.

DW: *When you are writing a big piece does listening to music put you off? Maybe it is a different part of the mind?*

BC: No, I listen to lots of music all the time – I'm able to detach myself a little. I listen to a great deal of early music and I find that invigorating, a lot of Lieder too – it just puts me in a better place.

DW: *Composing is a solitary thing and you like the balance of that with conducting, bringing you into contact with singers and players.*

BC: Yes, that's why I write – to hear it and perform it. You know, you want it to be functional and rewarding for people. It is a spiritual thing for me to be part of the whole process of why you are doing a piece and bringing the music to life.

DW: *Are you ever surprised when you hear a piece for the first time?*

BC: Not really, I've got a good inner ear and know how it is going to sound.

DW: *In that case are you surprised with what others find in the music?*

BC: Yes, sometimes. They sometimes find something or emphasise something that takes me by surprise. Nicholas Cleobury did that with the premiere of the *Requiem* with the Oxford Bach Choir. He did a great job and I was a little surprised, but in a good way.

DW: *You spend 99% of the time writing for the voice – do you ever feel you would like to write something else, an orchestral piece, chamber music?*

BC: Not really. I need words! I have a solo song-cycle coming up and so I'll have to think very differently about that, still words of course, but in a very different way. It's a bit like saying as a conductor, would you like to conduct a Bach Passion? No thank you, I'd rather hear someone else do it. I'm not sure I have anything to say. The same thing with instrumental music. I'm happy doing what I do.

DW: *Is there anything you are longing to write?*

BC: Not at the moment. I'm writing a big piece for the RSCM* next year, and I wanted to write something that responded not just to the bad side of the situation we are in at the moment but something that looks forward. That was just an idea that came to me. I wrote a children's opera recently with Charles Bennett and I really enjoyed that, so maybe another one of those, a stage piece for kids.

DW: *You must get far more commissions than you can possibly take. How do you decide which commissions to take?*

BC: All the big pieces recently have been my idea and my publisher and I have gone out and found people that would be interested in taking them on. You reach people in a different way. That I've rather enjoyed.

DW: *Elgar quotes Ruskin at the end of* The Dream of Gerontius* – 'This is the best of me…'. Can you say which piece or group of pieces of yours might fall into that category?*

BC: There are a couple of hymns in my *St John Passion* that I'm rather proud of. I think I hit on something that surprised even myself. With that piece I did make a big journey. I feel good about it, so perhaps that is some of the best of my work. There again some of my simplest pieces for children too, for what they are, they function in a real way and I'm happy with those.

DW: *What about teaching composition – can it be taught?*

BC: That's difficult. I once asked John McCabe for some composition lessons, Robert Saxton too, and they both said the same thing: only if I gave them some ideas! I like teaching but the conducting I rather think of as teaching really, certainly in the area that I occupy, just encouraging people to think of something differently – 'would this make you do something better' – I think that is what I can do best.

DW: *What advice would you give to young composers?*

BC: The best advice is to get a routine going – it is a long way from A to B. It's like practising the piano, you only get better by doing it long hours and being disciplined.

DW: *We are recording this interview at a very difficult time – how are you dealing with lockdown?*

BC: From a composing point of view the last few months have been very productive and of course I haven't had any trips to make, so the concentration level has been high. Then, I was driving back from taking my daughter to school not long ago and was listening to John Rutter's magnificent orchestration of the Howell's *Coll Reg** and I sat in the car with tears streaming down my face. There was one part of me that I was thankful to be part of this tradition but also incredible sadness about all we have to lose and I think about that a lot. It doesn't matter if you are at the top of the tree or at the bottom, if there is no performing there is no money for performers, but more than that, we are completely crippled. It is just horrific – we just sit here and wait!

DW: *What would you say are your five favourite choral works?*

BOB'S FIVE FAVOURITE CHORAL WORKS

Bach *Singet dem Herrn*

Brahms *Fest und Gedenksprüche* Op.109

Akira Miyoshi *Ikiru*

Sheppard *Media Vita*

Vaughan Williams *Five Mystical Songs*

Jonathan Dove

BORN 1959

DW: *Can you tell me about your earliest musical experiences? Were your parents interested in music?*

JD: I come from a family of architects. Both my parents, my sister, her husband and my brother are all architects – architects as far as the eyes can see. My mother played the piano beautifully and, particularly when we were younger, I would hear her playing as I was drifting off to sleep. She would play pieces like *Clair de Lune**, Handel's *Largo*, a bit of *Oklahoma**, and I would go down to the piano next morning and try to play them myself. That was the beginning of music making for me. My mother was a churchgoer, a Catholic, my father less so until recently – he would come to church on special occasions. Interestingly, they had both designed the choir loft at the local church that we used to attend, Our Lady of the Star of the Sea in Greenwich. When I was nine I started singing in the choir, a very humble choir, nothing elaborate, just hymns really. I was probably 12 when I started to play the organ, playing for a few services and weddings, and remember being very impressed with the power of the organ as a child. I was no virtuoso but I took my Grade 8 and could get through the Widor *Toccata*. It was more of an effort to play Bach* Preludes and Fugues, especially the pedal parts – you can't really sight-read those. What I could do was to make music up on the spot, so rather than practise for months I could make something festive and colourful up for people to leave the church. So you could say that I became a composer out of laziness!

DW: *But this is really something an organist needs to be able to do...*

JD: Well, yes, I could improvise if the bride was late and make sure I got back to F major for the entry of the bride.

DW: *I read somewhere that you liked to improvise music to books that you were reading.*

JD: I remember doing that with *The Hobbit**, but I'm not sure about anything else. I was always interested in the story-telling possibilities of music. I don't recall what this music sounded like but on some days it could be quite angry and dissonant and on other days something pleasantly tuneful. I couldn't really find a way to write down the music I wanted to hear until much, much later; I was nearly thirty actually. What I improvised probably sounded like whatever I was listening to at the time.

DW: *Do you remember what that might have been? Were you interested in pop music of the time?*

JD: Not really. My brother certainly listened to a lot of pop music. On the whole this sort of music has tended to appeal to me when it is twenty or thirty years out of date. It just didn't excite me at the time. The choir at school were not bad; we had an ambitious Head of Music who wanted to put on proper concerts – Lessons and Carols at Christmas; we did the Vaughan Williams* *Mystical Songs*, the Vivaldi* *Gloria* and the Fauré* Requiem. An even more formative experience was singing with hundreds of other kids, when a large number of choirs joined together for special concerts. That was my first experience of the sound of a massed choir and I think my interest and indeed obsession with community music making comes from that, trying to recapture that experience. In my teens I went to the ILEA [The Inner London Education Authority] Centre for Young Musicians in Pimlico on Saturdays, an amazing education and completely free of charge of course. I was in a choir at the CYM run by a very enterprising man called Iain Humphries, and I remember singing *Rejoice in the Lamb* and *St Nicholas* – so there was quite a bit of Britten* early on. I took up the viola and played in the London Schools Symphony Orchestra and I remember the thrill of playing Elgar*, Sibelius*, John Ireland's* *A London Overture*, pieces by Malcolm Arnold*. Then, through university, I was still playing the viola, especially the piano, accompanying singers, but I didn't really get involved in the choral or chapel side of things particularly. I'm not sure I even went to the services – up too late the night before! Theatre music from the shows has been an important part of my life. In my twenties, I remember playing in the pit for a production of *On Your Toes*. I got the sack as my concentration became less the more performances we did, so there was quite a range of music going on.

DW: *I know you were interested in theatre from an early age too, clearly important to you later as an opera composer. Is it true to suggest that some of your choral works are like little dramas too, certainly pieces like* The Passing of the Year *and* There was a Child, *also shorter pieces such as* The Three Kings *and* Seek Him that Maketh the Seven Stars? *This is all part of your wish to tell stories, even in a short anthem.*

JD: Yes, I think that is what I try to do, be a storyteller. Even in an anthem there is certain drama or narrative. That's certainly what I have felt.

DW: *Then you went to Cambridge?*

JD: Yes, it was a general music degree at Cambridge and I studied composition with Robin Holloway* in my last year. I know Robin didn't suit everyone but we always got on very well. I remember the most important composition lesson I ever had – for my first lesson I took along a twenty-page serial organ solo and on page two Robin said in that endlessly imitated way of his, 'I'm bored already' – I could feel my lower lip trembling a bit, but as I crashed through the other 18 pages I realised he was right and if

I wasn't writing the kind of music I wanted to hear, why wasn't I, and when was I going to? There was no particular stylistic requirement from Robin, but what he was great at was trying to work out what you were trying to say and encouraging you. Most of the time I didn't finish pieces and we would end up playing Mahler* symphonies on two pianos! Robin was really very helpful, but it was many years after that that I really got going compositionally.

DW: *It took you a while to find your own voice I think.*

JD: To be honest, I'm not sure I had a real idea of what I wanted to write and I had a problem with getting past about bar four in any idiom. I suppose that I felt that I should be writing difficult, dissonant or unpredictable music of one sort or another and to write things like octaves and triads was unforgivable. In my last year at university I discovered the American minimalists, Steve Reich* in particular, and that was a revelation. He was writing music that was diatonic, using the chords I loved in middle-period Stravinsky* and giving them a strong pulse. Most of the new music I was hearing at that time seemed to have no pulse – it was angular. Reich somehow felt new and it took a while for me to absorb all that. After university, I was playing the piano for a living, but I wrote a few things that were somewhat Reichian!

DW: *Can you say when your first acknowledged pieces started to appear? Is there an opus 1?*

JD: I wrote a group of pieces around 1988/89 thanks to the choral conductor Simon Halsey*, to whom I owe a good deal throughout my career. He took on the Salisbury Festival and I wrote a solo organ piece for Thomas Trotter*, a choral piece for Simon's father Louis Halsey* and his choir, and a piece of music theatre, *Music for Drowning* for two dancers and two singers, in which I also played the piano, sang and acted – quite an off-the-wall piece in some ways. I had been working for a year as Assistant Chorus Master at Glyndebourne and was then offered the post of Chorus Master, but I realised that this was the time for me to move on.

DW: *You would have probably gone on to be a conductor…*

JD: Yes, that is almost certainly what would have happened. I enjoyed being Chorus Master very much but I felt that composing was what I really wanted to do. My first officially-published work was *Figures in a Garden*, a wind serenade for the Mozart bi-centenary in 1991, commissioned by Glyndebourne. I extensively revised the organ solo, *Niagra*, and that was published much later. The Salisbury choral piece I haven't published – it was a little experimental – but the Christmas carol *Welcome all Wonders* became my earliest published choral piece. When I did come back to music for the church, after being away from that world for a while, it rather surprised me that the texts still appealed and touched me enough to want to find music for them. Even though I would not consider myself a churchgoer, there is something about the theological imagery and the rituals of worship that still inspires me to write music. I'm not steeped in the Anglican choral tradition at all. I didn't grow up singing it or hearing it. I still don't know many pieces by Herbert Howells* for instance and I have to say that kind of music doesn't grab me particularly.

DW: *All the work you did as a repetiteur* and chorus master must have been a wonderful learning experience compositionally, showing you how to write for the voice sympathetically.*

JD: It was very unconscious really; it isn't a clinical study as such – one falls in love with certain sounds and starts to think how one can make this line or this chord sound better. I had no particular training to be a chorus master – I was asked by the conductor Ivor Bolton* to prepare a group of amateur singers to make up the chorus in *Così fan tutte** at the Britten Pears School in Aldeburgh. It all felt rather improvised. I must have picked up things from other conductors, but I found my way through.

DW: *You mentioned earlier your interest in working with amateur singers and players. Your music is sung by great choirs of course, but when you are writing are you aware of the fact that further down the line your pieces will be sung by groups that are not King's College, Cambridge*, or Tenebrae, or whoever?*

JD: I think a formative experience was when I was asked to write an anthem for the Annual Service for the Friends of the Royal Academy of Arts in 1995.

DW: *That would be* See him that Maketh the Seven Stars?

JD: That's right. I was told that the choir would turn up half an hour before so the choral parts had to be more or less sight-readable, but that the organ part could be as hard as I liked, as the organist would have the music in advance. As a result that has in a way set the pattern for a lot of what I've done since. I think there was some sort of instinct about what would be possible for singers. The music I write is not theoretical or of cerebral construction. I'm singing through the choirs – it all begins with me singing and playing something and I generally think that if I can sing or play it then others can too. There is an impulse to perform that is the basis of the music. I've been around a lot of amazing singers of course, but I've had about three singing lessons in my life and I don't think that is a disadvantage really. The range I have is I think close to what most people might have. I've had the odd complaint that my tenor parts are too high – but you can't please all of the people all of the time!

DW: *Choral music starts with text of course, so presumably musical ideas grow out of that. Do you start with trying to create an atmosphere? Going back to* Seek Him that Maketh the Seven Stars, *that glittering accompaniment and the feeling of awe and wonder in the text comes through in the music so beautifully...*

JD: In that case certainly it was about finding an atmosphere. It was a long hunt for the right words, I remember that and that is often the case. When someone commissions a piece, I'm often grateful that they have a text in mind.

DW: *Really – you don't think that restricts you in any way?*

JE: No, a lot of the hard work is already done when I get the text. The words usually tell me how they want to be sung and I just write it down. They might tell someone else a different story perhaps but there it is. If you are looking for words, I'm looking for something that engages or moves me. There is a feeling for the kind of sound that might come out of the words but on the other hand, the kind of sound one can have in mind can also inform the search. In the case of the text for *Seek Him that Maketh the Seven Stars*,  the night sky was a very enticing idea and everything followed on from that, whereas in the *Missa Brevis*, because I was asked to write in Latin, there was a sort of liberation. I did write a Mass in English as a teenager which I would dread to hear now, but there are certain constraints somehow for an Englishman setting English – it is impossible for an Englishman to 'forget' how English sounds: it is of course part of our DNA. My music tends to be an amplification of the qualities that are already there. With Latin you have more freedom and that offered the rhythmic playfulness of the 'Gloria' in the *Missa Brevis** for example.

DW: *I was going to ask you about the liturgical pieces. In the case of the Te Deum and the Missa Brevis, does the baggage associated with texts concern you? Having already said that you didn't have much to do with the Anglican choral tradition, this was probably not the case. That wonderful 'Gloria' in the Missa Brevis really does blow the dust off a few hundred years of, shall we say, less invigorating settings.*

JD: I think being almost innocent of what has been done in the past does free one up a little. I just sit and consider that if these are the words that are being used at this particular point, what is it that I want to hear? That can also mean perhaps re-inventing the wheel. Matthew Owens* asked me to write a Service for Wells Cathedral and I was imagining the scene in the Magnificat, Mary getting this news; thinking operatically it is a woman's scene, so that meant that upper voices had to be prominent. I do realise this is not such an original idea, but as I don't know the repertoire so well, it still feels fresh for me.

DW: *The other thing that strikes me about your music is its positivity – clearly there are dark moments, in your song-cycle* Damascus *for instance, or in* For an Unknown Soldier *where you set war poetry, but so much of it seems to be uplifting and optimistic.*

JD: It isn't something I consciously set out to do, but I think when my musical voice settled, I would have been around 30, and I remember one particular opera commission that came my way. At that moment I thought the thing I could do was magic and comedy – that just seemed to fit the sort of music I wanted to make. The more 'difficult' side of modern music was born out of a very disturbed part of human history, but I was born in a safer time, so that level of cosmic anxiety was not my level of experience. I had a very safe and loving upbringing, music and theatre were valued and there was plenty to feel happy about. I suppose, going back to Steve Reich, those chords and that pulsing energy I found was my kind of music. I think, later in life, I have looked for darker subject matter, certainly in the two works you mentioned. Also, I've just finished a piece setting an anthology of texts about exile, for baritone, cello and orchestra, so that is a painful subject. The piece I wrote before that, *The Tin Soldier*, starts with toys coming to life, so there is a magical, playful aspect, although the ending is rather less happy when he goes up in flames with the ballerina! Maybe I have a celebratory side in my nature. I discovered that I could write operas that make people laugh!

DW: *But that is a very difficult thing to do. Two of your most successful operas –* Flight *and* The Adventures of Pinocchio *– have a lot of bright, cheerful music...*

JD: It is just congenial to me. I know many would say that the best way of killing a joke is to set it to music, but it is just my musical idiom. I've found that operatic ensembles for instance work better when you are working diatonically or at least modally, which is what I do, and if you haven't got pulse, then comic timing is going to be tough!

DW: *Have you ever been beaten by a text?*

JD: When I was writing *For an Unknown Soldier*, I was setting poems by poets that fought in the First World War – some died and some survived. I originally intended to find diary entries and letters, as I was anxious to do something as different as I could from the *War Requiem**, so I thought I couldn't set any Wilfred Owen*. Then I felt that the letters and diaries didn't gain anything by being sung and that the poems were essentially letters home from the trenches too. I did feel I could tell a story and if I told the story of one soldier, from the patriotic and jingoistic beginning to the moment of despair and death, that would work. The piece was co-commissioned by Portsmouth Grammar School and the London Mozart Players; there was a strong connection for some reason with the poet Edward Thomas*, so they asked me if I could include something by him. I read quite a lot and, wonderful poetry though it was, I couldn't find any music that would add to the experience of the poetry. There is something in his mode of utterance, the time it takes to sing a phrase, the meaning of the words would be lost; it would just defeat comprehension. Then the tenor James Gilchrist* asked me to write a song that set an English contemporary of Heine*, as set by Schumann*, so I looked at Wordsworth* and Coleridge* – big, expansive poems, so far from the rather short, terse texts of Heine in *Dichterliebe*. James was keen on Byron*, but I just thought, 'you can't sing this stuff', more a question of tempo – the poems seem to demand being read at 'speaking speed', so, holding that up with music, allowing the melody to come out, the poem just loses out. I've sometimes thought that I do better with poems that have rhyme and metre, although having said that I set beautiful prose in *In Damascus* and I sometimes set that very happily. I don't think there is any rule about this; every composer feels different about it. That beautiful piece by Samuel Barber*, *Knoxville: Summer of 1915*, sets prose by James Agee*, but sounds incredibly poetic.

DW: *I wanted to ask you about another popular piece,* The Three Kings, *that you wrote for the King's College* Service of Nine Lessons and Carols, for the Millennium – what kind of restrictions are imposed on you for such a piece? Do they just say, 'please write us a carol'?*

JD: The text has to be approved. I was very lucky that a senior cleric at King's provided me with quite a collection of texts and two jumped out at me. One was 'Run Shepherds Run', by William Drummond*, which I subsequently set for the Spitalfields Festival when I was Artistic Director – it just didn't seem like the right thing for this event. Then I came across the Dorothy L. Sayers* poem, which actually moved me to tears, because it was so surprising...

DW: *Yes, in my ignorance, I knew Sayers as the creator of the fictional detective Lord Peter Wimsey, but didn't realise she was a poet too...*

JD: Exactly and it is such a surprise – you would think that the old king would be the one with the myrrh and the idea that it is the young king that has this and the old king's hands are full of gold, that seems to say so much more, not just about the treasure, but about whole-life experience and it opened up so many possibilities – that reversal of expectation excited me.

DW: *There again, the piece is like a mini-drama, each of the kings has a particular musical character...*

JD: Yes, with a feeling of folklore and ancient tradition...

DW: *When writing for an occasion like that is there ever a feeling of terror – that the first performance would have an audience of millions?*

JD: I don't remember feeling that particularly. Our school choir used to mount a Service of Nine Lessons and Carols: I even sang <u>that</u> solo at the beginning of *Once in Royal David's City*; we had the books of *Carols for Choirs* * so it felt as if I belonged there in some way. I haven't really thought about that before. I had plugged into that part of the English choral tradition and it was probably very important. What you are hoping for from a carol is something catchy, that people will remember, and not such an abstract idea.

DW: *A piece of yours I particularly like is* The Passing of the Year *– it just seems such a perfect combination of words and music. The bell-ringing in the last setting – Tennyson's 'Ring Wild Bells'* * – is just so energising and it seems to me as if the music has always been there...*

JD: I've played the piano part for that piece quite a few times now, with Voces8...

DW: *That is a very hard piano part...*

JD: It is sort of sobering. When I wrote the piece I could play every note – of course when I'm writing I'm playing the same bar over and over again, so that makes it possible. Now having to play the whole piece I do have to practise quite a lot each time. I was thrilled when a bell-ringer came up to me a while ago and thanked me for that last movement, telling me how well I had musically described the unpredictability of the ringing. I've often enjoyed bellringing but wondered what would happen if one of the ringers had been for a drink beforehand – in my setting of *Ring Wild Bells* it is never a metronomic sequence. Perhaps some bells have a longer distance to travel – it makes it all the more human somehow. I was simply asked for a piece by the London Symphony Chorus with piano and I started to look for poems that would make sense delivered by a large body of people, because some poems it seems to me just don't. Some poems, if you want to hear them sung at all, need to be sung by only one person as opposed to a choir. With the Tennyson* 'In Memoriam' it is a very particular and universal response to a tragedy, but there is something in the rhetoric of the last lines, 'Ring in a thousand years of peace...' - it does feel as if he is speaking of so many people and there is something about choirs singing on behalf of the community. As I wrote the piece it suddenly dawned on me that the poems that I chose reflected different moments of the year – I came across 'Answer July' by Emily Dickinson*, and thought what a great rhythm; I wanted to set 'Farewell, earth's bliss' (Thomas Nashe*) because of the line, 'Brightness falls from the air...' which I think is one of the most extraordinary lines in poetry and it made sense as an autumnal piece, so there was quickly a feeling of a journey through the piece.

DW: *Are you a disciplined composer? Do you work regular hours?*

JD: It isn't exactly 9 to 5 but it is pretty regular. There may be stretches when I'm just looking for texts, spending hours in bookshops or the library or engrossed in my own anthologies. I may have to read lots of books. For example with *For an Unknown Soldier* it took weeks to find the right words. As I say, once the words are there half of the work is done. I'm nowhere near manuscript paper at this time. Then it's a process of sketching, finding the right key, instruments, rhythm and throwing a lot away; actually, the melody comes last most of the time.

DW: *Does writing music get easier with experience? Are you self-critical?*

JD: It gets easier and harder! The danger is that you have already written quite a lot of music and there is the chance of accidentally writing the same piece again. Having said that, certain pieces yield quite a lot of discoveries and suggest something else to investigate in another piece. I suppose that experience means that you are able to come up with something plausible, but it is perhaps harder to find something really authentic. This is a very strange experience; I don't think I have talked about this in an interview before and this is something that I think has only happened recently with choral music. Three or four times I've finished a piece and thought it was fine and then at the very last minute, I write a new piece. I wrote a set of Hebrew psalms for David Hill and the London Bach Choir...

DW: Psalms for Leo?

JD: Yes, that's right, and in the first of those pieces I came up with something plausible, but I was getting a bit depressed whilst working on it. I'd finished the piece and orchestrated it too. I kept waking up thinking that the tempo wasn't right and it hadn't got the earthy feel I wanted. Then I started to think that there wasn't anything in this piece that William Walton* couldn't have written, so that isn't good. I think two or three days before David was going to come over and hear the piece, I suddenly had a completely different idea, which had the earthy rhythm I wanted, and wrote something else, which I thought was much too difficult, and then a third version that finally felt great and was achievable by the choir. It happened with a shorter piece too, *Te Lucis Aeternam*, that I wrote for Wells Cathedral. Again, I'd written and finished it – then I woke up at four o'clock one morning and had second thoughts and came up with a simpler idea at the last minute. I don't think it is specific to age or experience as I don't have this problem with orchestral or instrumental music.

DW: *Do you think about the audience when you are writing?*

JD: I think about myself being in the audience and if I can satisfy myself then it might satisfy other members of this imaginary audience. I don't know how one could write theoretically for an audience, because you never know what is going on in people's heads. Perhaps it does get harder and harder to please oneself.

DW: *Are you ever surprised when you hear a piece for the first time?*

JD: It always sounds better, more vivid and technicolour. The voices in my head are not as loud and bright. Like many composers nowadays, I work with a computer that can give a reasonably close idea of orchestral or choral sounds so maybe one is less surprised. I've just written a piece for a thousand amateur singers spread across the Lincoln Plaza in New York. Clearly the performance this summer is not going to happen now. It is quite a tribal piece and it is very hard to represent that sound without a thousand people, but I found some vocal samples on the computer that gave an idea and by multi-tracking myself I could give san impression of what the piece will sound like.

DW: *Do performers find things you didn't know were there?*

JD: Yes, in all kinds of ways. It isn't a choral work but I wrote a short orchestral piece for the Association of British Orchestras in 1997 and it was played by twelve different orchestras with twelve different conductors. I was required to go to all the performances and was thinking to myself, 'how different could it be'? I was amazed. There were two Russian conductors that took the piece very slowly and got much more applause, which I thought was interesting. I think for a first-time listener it is better for the music not to go by so fast. I know when I play my music I tend to rush – perhaps I speed up to try and recapture the excitement I had when I first had the idea. Perhaps in choral music it is sometimes a good idea to take things a little slower, depending on the choir, the acoustic, the organ, all sorts of things. Actually, going back to *The Passing of the Year* and being surprised, it was of course written for a very large choir and I was surprised when the Schola Cantorum of Oxford did it one to a part, and it worked brilliantly. That's why I suggested it to Voces8 more recently. The close harmonies just sound completely different.

DW: *Do you get nervous about premieres?*

JD: Not if I have heard a rehearsal – it doesn't happen so often.

DW: *What kind of advice would you give to a young composer?*

JD: Write the music you want to hear and that's all I have to say really I think. I think there are some people that can teach very well – we talked about Robin Holloway being the best teacher for me at that time – but I'm not sure every composer can bring better pieces out of others. There may be things that you can be taught, but I think you can teach yourself most of what you need to satisfy something inside.

DW: *Elgar quoted Ruskin at the end of* The Dream of Gerontius* – 'This is the best of me…'. Are there any of your pieces that you feel have got close to that?*

JD: I'm always hoping the next one might be the best!

DW: *We are recording this at a very unusual and difficult time, how are you dealing with lockdown?*

JD: Yes, I feel diffident about being too pleased with myself for being so productive during lockdown as I know how terrible it has been for performers. I think there are difficult times ahead for composers, once some kind of normality returns. I think circumstances will be different; there will be a backlog of new pieces of course. The difficult time for composers will be in the future. I should have been travelling quite a lot during lockdown, going to performances, and although that would have been tremendously interesting, rewarding and stimulating, I do gain a lot of time by not travelling! It did raise questions about a balance I perhaps haven't managed to achieve. I just wonder if I will find a different balance in the future.

DW: *What would you say are your five favourite choral works?*

JONATHAN'S FIVE FAVOURITE CHORAL WORKS

Bach *St Matthew Passion*

Britten *Ceremony of Carols*

Pärt *Passio*

Purcell *Hear my prayer*

Stravinsky *Symphony of Psalms*

Ēriks Ešenvalds

BORN 1977

DW: *Can you tell me about your musical background? Did you grow up in a musical family? What is your earliest musical memory?*

EE: My mother was a music teacher and also the soloist in a local band that performed popular music. I remember she took me to rehearsals when I was as young as four or five, and I sang along! At kindergarten I sang a few solos in concerts and, at around seven, went to the children's music school and chose to study the piano. I had piano lessons, solfeggio, choir, ensemble playing, music history, so it was pretty serious at that age and it was all free – remarkable when you think about that. I didn't get to music high school – at that time, I was 14 I think, Latvia became a free country and everything in the country changed. To become a professional musician was not a good idea – the salaries were almost non-existent. My teachers said I had a musical gift, but that it would be more sensible to keep music as a hobby and I should perhaps try and become a university professor, teaching mathematics or a science. Also, I became a Christian which of course was impossible in Soviet times and suddenly the churches were packed; we were thirsty for spiritual fulfilment.

DW: *Was there a feeling even when you were very young, because of what had happened historically in Latvia, that there was a lot of catching up to do?*

EE: Yes, and I was always rather competitive. At church there was a choir and youth ensemble. I became their accompanist and I wrote pieces for them. I think I was ten years old when I wrote my first piece. There was a short break in the rehearsal, I had my music paper and just wrote some notes down. My friend suggested I showed the piece to the conductor. I did and she played it on the piano. It didn't sound anything special of course but she said to me 'Ēriks, maybe you should compose' – a very important sentence for me.

DW: *So that was someone switching on the light for you – what did these early pieces sound like?*

EE: Well, I sat at the piano and my practical guide was Whitney Houston*! She was very popular at the time and I loved her voice and her songs. In Soviet times we couldn't buy the sheet music of course, so I just played them from hearing them on the TV and on cassette tapes – remember those? I found her songs consisted of five or six chords, I learnt those chords and that was my guide, using 'Whitney chords'! This was the beginning – perhaps rather unusual for a composer to say this, but there it is.

DW: *You have kept that respect for popular music haven't you? Music is music and it is either good or bad...*

EE: Oh yes, there is a lot of popular music and folk music that I like very much, but at the same time, I tend to be critical and not to spend time listening to bad music! There is so much amazing music in the world, of all kinds, and, as a teacher at the Academy, I say to my students 'let us listen to the very best and not waste time on second-rate music'.

DW: *One of the first pieces of yours I heard was an arrangement of a popular song,* In my little picture frame*.

EE: That arrangement was very easy to do...

DW: *Well yes, but many less sympathetic arrangers would drown the original in all kinds of technical wizardry, but in your case you treat it with respect and it is all the more effective for that.*

EE: When I was invited to arrange that song, I was given the melody line and a recording of the singer, Renars Kaupers, who was singing to a simple cello and guitar accompaniment, so the cello part became the soprano solo and the rest of the choir sing the guitar accompaniment. I wanted to keep the simplicity and innocence of the song if I could.

DW: *You attended a Theological Seminary too.*

EE: That was my escape – after High School, studying maths and physics, I wasn't sure what to do. Psychology was a popular 'new' profession in Latvia after we became free. It was well paid and so I decided to study that, but after a month I quit, I didn't like it at all. It was October and all higher education institutions were full, so my church pastor suggested going to the Seminary. I loved it for the first year but the second much less so, and it became clear this wasn't going to work either. The President of the Seminary kicked me out and I was so happy! Someone suggested I show my choral music to a Professor at the State Music Academy. He could see that I had a good music education and a good ear, and he said come back with a piano piece in a week; sit at the piano, close your eyes and see what happens. So I did, I played it to him and the Professor said 'I can see a gift but also the many gaps in your music education'. They offered me a one-year catch-up before I did the entrance exams. It was very hard work, but I did my best and got in to the Academy. So finally, I found that to be a musician was my calling.

DW: *Your teacher at the Academy was Selga Mence*, an important composer in Latvian choral music.*

EE: Yes, she is still at the Academy and is now my boss! She has written a great deal of choral music for children, often influenced by Latvian folk tradition.

DW: *Can you describe the music you were writing at the Academy?*

EE: The most important thing at the Academy was for us to concentrate on the technical aspects of composition – harmony, form, counterpoint, fugue, orchestration. There was just not enough time to write very much that wasn't connected to that. There was so much to do. When I graduated I had the feeling that I was like a painter and on my palette I had all the colours and I was now able to do a professional job, responding to whatever I was asked to do.

DW: *Then you were travelling and attending master classes given by a wide range of composers – Michael Finnissy*, Jonathan Harvey*, Klaus Huber*, Philippe Manoury* – many of whom were working in quite advanced musical languages that were very different from your own, did this all help you to consolidate your musical voice?*

EE: I was trying to learn from all of these brilliant minds. I started to grasp their philosophy rather than any particular techniques I think. I certainly didn't want to write music that sounded like them – they would have hated that too. Michael Finnissy taught one of my final master classes and when he showed us his complex scores, his big piano piece *English Country Songs* or his orchestral work *Red Earth*, I found them to be so full of emotion and, although I was writing in a very different way, they made a deep impression. All human life was there somehow. Such a wonderful composer and teacher.

DW: *I can hear how the spiritual and poetic aspects of Jonathan Harvey's music might have affected you.*

EE: Certainly, he was very quiet and chose his words carefully, but what he said was so important – a great composer. I learnt from Jonathan that you need to spend time to listen and think... Do not make fast decisions, you must allow the music to flow and hear how it flows.

DW: *There was a definite Baltic school that developed through the 90s which you must have been aware of – Pärt*, Vasks*, Tormis*.*

EE: Pēteris Vasks is now our best-known Latvian composer – fantastic, very emotional music, full of the sounds of nature and very spiritual. Pēteris is so passionate in his music. Arvo Pärt is calmer, more distant somehow, spare, but very beautiful. Veljo Tormis was much more concerned with folklore, on the surface music that appears to be simple but hides deep complexity throughout. Once the Baltic States became free the music of these composers started to become internationally celebrated. All of them to some extent had had problems with the authorities who didn't approve of the religious or patriotic/folk elements in their work. We are so lucky...

41

DW: *Although your music is fundamentally diatonic, you are sometimes quite adventurous in what you ask choirs to do – breathing, whistling, whispering,* aleatoric* *elements, to add some extra colour, not as an effect, but part of the poetic vision you are trying to achieve.*

EE: You are right, I am visualising the music – when to cry, calm down, fight, to be happy. I sing all the phrases myself; my orchestration teacher used to say to me, 'if you can sing the second oboe part and it sounds natural it will be OK, if you can't, something is wrong'. This I think is true with choral music too – I like to sing every part. I like to think about music flowing like a river. During my studies I read so many scores, discovering beautiful moments and how it was done. I started to think that singers need not just sing, they might add other kinds of vocal sounds, some can play simple instruments, perhaps recorders or ocarinas, a little percussion, nothing that will overwhelm the choir, just add another colour, to build an atmosphere for the story you are telling. This tradition comes from composers like Silvestrov*, Tormis, Denisov*, really, a second folklore school, rather different from the way composers such as Bartók* and Stravinsky* made use of folk music in their compositions. Commissions started to come – some critics started to call me a 'choral composer', and I hated that. I'm a composer, why just a choral composer? Choirs are in general more active and more adventurous, so that is why so many of us write a lot of choral music.

DW: *You sang in the Latvian State Choir – what better education is there for a composer than singing in a choir?*

EE: Oh yes, and you know, I stood in the choir and could hear all the voices. If you play second flute in an orchestra you cannot necessarily hear the whole tutti properly, but to sing in a choir was wonderful, until I got to the last two of my nine years and that was because I wanted to compose rather than sing the Mozart* Requiem again. Still, it was a fantastic education and we sang music of all centuries and styles, under so many guest conductors. I just kept learning and learning. My last concert with the choir was in Munich: Mahler* Symphony No.8, conducted by the great Mariss Jansons* and when we got to the ending, I just couldn't sing, it was completely overwhelming.

DW: *Can you say which of your pieces might be your opus 1?*

EE: I've had a few 'false starts'. I wrote an instrumental piece when at the Academy and just had the feeling that the music started to fly but then just as suddenly it dropped on the floor, and I couldn't understand why. This went on for a little while and then my wife and I went to the island of Saaremaa* in Estonia for a weekend, and I took pictures of nature, the dawn, the landscape, the sea, the sky – I wrote a cycle of pieces for cello and clarinet inspired by these pictures. This was a new approach for me. It really worked and got into the finals of an international competition – this piece did fly!

DW: *I'm right in thinking that alongside your religious faith the other thing that is important to you, and influences your music a great deal, is the natural world, or the fragility of the natural world – sky, stars, light, snow, sea...*

EE: Yes, it all inspires me. I imagine myself flying in highest orbits and feeling the freedom. I remember experiencing this as a child, being fascinated by the movement of water, the clouds, the stars, how the light reacts – this sensitivity towards nature is very important. This plays an important part in a lot of my music, including two major works – *Nordic Light Symphony* and *Volcano Symphony* – multi-media works which are for choir and orchestra, but also include recordings of the sounds of nature and films and recordings of folk singers. I had a number of expeditions with a film crew when I was writing these works. We filmed in Norway, the Arctic, Alaska, Scandinavia, Greenland, filming the natural world but also looking at history, culture, storytellers, folk singers... It was so beautiful.

DW: *You have of course set a lot of conventional liturgical texts but also have gone searching for more unusual texts too.*

EE: I would encourage commissioners to give the composer more freedom. Honestly, when I have full freedom I can fly in the highest orbits. If they say, 'second sopranos are not so good', 'basses can't sing lower than G', 'can you set this poem?', every restriction is cutting my wings shorter and shorter, which means I can't do my best. I like longer phrases, not so many commas and full stops. For instance I have tried to set Emily Dickinson* several times – her language is very powerful, but it is complicated because she speaks in narrower phrases. Sara Teasdale* on the other hand for instance just flows beautifully...

DW: *Several of your most popular pieces,* Stars, Only in Sleep, Evening, *set Sara Teasdale. Her work isn't so well-known, certainly not in the UK, but they are beautiful, direct poems, rather naive and very touching...*

EE: Yes, very direct. I found her in this beautiful library called Google! I think the first time I used her words was in *Evening* and around the same time in *Stars* that I wrote for the Salt Lake Choral Artists and Bradley Allred. The deadline for what became *Stars* was getting closer, I was getting a little worried and just Googled poems about stars and the heavens, and that is how I found the Teasdale poem.

DW: *This is one of your pieces with that extra 'non-vocal element', in this case, tuned wine glasses.*

EE: The idea of the glasses came to me when I was celebrating Christmas with my family in my home town, and after dinner, before washing the dishes, I went out for some fresh air. The night sky was so bright, it was almost as if I had never seen the depth and brightness of the sky before. So, I came back, and there were wet wine glasses in the sink and immediately that sound connected with the feeling I had just experienced. I called my wife, gave her a glass, then our eldest daughter had another glass; we built up pitches and that is how it happened. I think my music is somehow very closely related to Sara's poems – so far I have written I think fourteen or fifteen works that set her words. She paints her ideas on a canvas and only takes the brush off the canvas when the whole story has been told – there is a constant flow and atmosphere and this is how I write my music. The language is very honest and of course inspired by nature. I have often thought that if Sara and I had lived at the same time, we would have had a wonderful collaboration.

DW: *All the liturgical texts you have set,* O Salutaris Hostia, Ubi Caritas, *have of course been set many times before. Does this inhibit you in any way?*

EE: I still study music a great deal and so of course I know a lot of these settings, but I just try to think about them differently. I visualise the texts – for example 'O salutaris...' is the moment for Holy Communion, a very private, humble moment and I imagine myself taking part in this ritual. The two solo soprano parts I have always imagined being sung with great purity, not in a big, romantic, operatic way at all. That particular work was originally written just for upper voices, but then I was asked to do a mixed-choir version and it bloomed a little more. For me the string orchestra is the female choir, the wind and brass is the male choir, but the full orchestra is the mixed choir and that is what I prefer, because I can have a range of colour. I'm in huge trouble if I am asked to write for just an SATB choir – I need at least six parts. For me the harmony is the number one priority...

DW: *When you start a piece the most important thing is to find the right harmonic world.*

EE: The harmony has to have something very special – not just a good chord but something more intense somehow. I work hard on that for some time. Then comes the melody. When I compose a new piece, all of the different aspects of the piece are on my piano or on my desk. I play sections over and over again, to make sure the textures aren't too thick. It is rather a difficult process to put into words...

DW: *Do you think about the structure a long time too? In the bigger pieces, such as* Passion and Resurrection *and* St Luke Passion *of course it plays a part, but even in the four/five-minute pieces, they feel like mini-epics somehow...*

EE: Oh yes, yes, the structure of all my pieces is very important. I don't work quickly. The pieces don't come easily. It begins like a raw stone that I look at from different sides and ask myself difficult questions. I am very self-critical and with every new piece, I want to 'receive the highest marks in the exam', so to speak. I work two or three hours, go and have coffee, and come back with a fresh mind. I love to work – what I hate is that the body needs to rest...

DW: *Do you like to know the choir or the acoustic you are writing for?*

EE: Yes, I always say to the conductor, please tell me honestly about your choir, the range of voices, repertoire, strong points, weak points, this is so important. Today, even a high-school choir can be of such a high standard. There have been occasions when a conductor has given me such a glowing report of their choir, so I write a demanding piece and they come back to me and say, 'this is too hard, the intonation is challenging, we need extra rehearsals'. They are not happy and I'm not happy – I can change and work something out. As I said earlier, I don't find being given restrictions easy, but let us at least be honest!

DW: *You lived in Cambridge between 2011 and 2013 and had a wonderful title – 'Fellow Commoner at Trinity College' – can you say how that affected your music? A wonderful choir and conductor [Stephen Layton*] of course, and you must have heard a lot of English choral music during your time there.*

EE: I loved that title too. I was there for the music of course, but also I spent hours reading in the library and in the observatory too. I went to Evensong, met lots of people and it was a unique and wonderful experience. I felt that I didn't have to care about my daily needs and I could fully focus and study. I found a new world. I learnt about the tradition and heritage of hundreds of years of music in Cambridge and was just very humbled.

DW: *I'm curious about the* Trinity Te Deum *that you wrote whilst in Cambridge. Am I imagining that this work sounds particularly English?*

EE: I think it probably does. It was written for the installation of the new Master of the College, so I think it might be rather grand, ceremonial and English, in the outer sections at least, for choir, organ and brass. I was allowed to add a harp to the accompanying ensemble, so the middle section, much calmer music, is like a folk song. I imagined myself walking in the hills of Scotland. People have called me a composer chameleon, and I think this piece might be a good example of that.

DW: *When you hear a piece for the first time are you surprised?*

EE: Yes, mostly the surprises are good. Tempi are my biggest challenge in rehearsal...

DW: *Do people take your music too slowly?*

EE: Actually, more often than not it is too fast. Although in *Stars* for instance, I always want it to be conducted in two, *alla breve* – it is rather difficult to catch the right tempo, but this is true of a lot of music I think. Of course, it depends on the acoustic and if the choir has twenty-five singers, sixty singers, or whatever. I was at a performance in America of *Evening* and it was so beautiful, but I couldn't attend the rehearsals and the one polite suggestion I made afterwards was perhaps maybe to have a little *rubato** in a particular section. The conductor was very unhappy, took the score and said 'show me, whereabouts is *rubato* written' – but surely it is all to do with feeling and what happens during the performance. We composers try to express what we feel in the score but they will become cluttered if we include every tiny detail. I think choirs are unique, acoustics are unique, conductors should be unique and the music needs to fly with the performers, not be prescribed down to the last note.

DW: *On the other hand, do performers surprise you, perhaps finding things that you didn't know were in a piece?*

EE: Yes. Oh, and musicologists – they ask me all kinds of strange things – sometimes, I just don't know what to say to them. There are occasions when I hardly remember pieces anyway. I am of course grateful when people want to sing my music but really I am more concerned with what I am writing now. So long as performers make pieces their own, I am happy.

DW: *Do you think of the audience when you write?*

EE: I don't think so. To be honest I am more worried about the acoustic of the venue. That I do think about. When in Cambridge I was spoiled by some really wonderful acoustics.

DW: *Do you get nervous when you hear a piece for the first time?*

EE: Oh yes, very nervous. I tell the performers that my destiny is in their hands...

DW: *No pressure then!*

EE: I get terribly worried and my heart goes crazy. Of course I trust performers – it just feels like I'm having a new baby each time...

DW: *You teach a good deal – do you think composition can be taught?*

EE: I just need to stay open, sensitive and patient and be able to capture those important moments when a student has a wonderful idea and show them what to do with the idea. I wish all my students could be good pianists – it helps so much, but the younger generation now walk the corridors with this terrible device [he waves a laptop], just no good for composing. The computer will play anything back but it doesn't mean to say it will sing well. I say to them 'sing the second alto part, how does it sound...?' I ask them to compose practically, play the piano, sing yourself, don't trust the machine.

DW: *Elgar quotes Ruskin at the end of* The Dream of Gerontius *– 'This is the best of me'. Can you say which piece or pieces of yours might fall into that category?*

EE: The big works probably have the best of me – *Passion and Resurrection* and *St Luke Passion*, perhaps my operas, *The Immured* and *Joseph is a Fruitful Bough*. The bigger pieces have so much in them and show different facets of my musical language. The smaller pieces have one atmosphere – it is difficult to achieve huge contrasts in a five-minute piece. Now I am writing my first ballet – I'm loving it. Something new is always interesting to me and a great thing for a composer.

DW: *We are recording this at a very difficult time. How are you dealing with lockdown?*

EE: I miss travel – I need to see mountains and valleys, the different skies and the sea, the main inspiration for my music. I went to Norway in March for a premiere and stayed for few days, just to wait for the Northern Lights, but I had to rush back because Latvia was closing the border. I had to isolate at the top of our house for a while – it was scary and it is scary, thinking how it will all end.

DW: *What would you say are your five favourite choral works?*

ĒRIKS' FIVE FAVOURITE CHORAL WORKS

R Strauss *Der Abend*

Messiaen arr C. Gottwald for choir
 Louange à l'éternité de Jésus
 (from Quartet for the end of time)

Michael Finnissy *Red Earth (for orchestra)*

Morten Lauridsen *O magnum mysterium*

Santa Ratniece *Saline*

Cheryl Frances-Hoad

BORN 1980

DW: *Can you tell me about your earliest musical memories? I know there was a lot of music at home from the very beginning.*

CF-H: Yes, there was always a lot of music. My mum was playing the flute and teaching at home a good deal. I really can't remember a time when I didn't hear music around me. I started to play the cello when I was three, a very small cello of course – apparently I gave a ninety-minute concert on this cello, which must have been fun! Our car was then stolen, with my cello inside it, so I took up the recorder and the flute, like my mum, and came back to the cello a little later and made quite rapid progress in a short period of time. It was the cello that I always loved.

DW: *Which led to you going to the Menuhin School at eight years old.*

CF-H: I went to the Menuhin School when I was just eight, after playing the cello for nine months, I think…

DW: *That is certainly rapid progress!*

CF-H: Yes, it is strange to look back. I just picked things up very quickly then, but I think I've now got slower and slower as I've got older!

DW: *Were you trying to write things down very early too?*

CF-H: To be honest, I just can't remember not composing. I think my first pieces were for the open strings of the cello when I got to that stage, because that is all I could do. I didn't really speak at that time, I was so painfully shy, and so it was a good method of self-expression. I can't think of any other reason, it just happened. I have no explanation as to why I started to compose or had the urge to do it. I just did!

DW: *So the cello was your first study at the Menuhin School, but presumably you got an all-round musical education.*

CF-H: Yes, the musical education there was incredible – I got two hours on my first study, half an hour on the second study (the piano in my case) and an hour of General Musicianship and an hour of composition every week. That was in addition to having other lessons too, you know, the small matter of English, Maths and that sort of thing. I think it is probably different now but then everyone was focused on being a performer. Performing was central to everything. Composition was not taken so seriously. Singing in the choir certainly wasn't taken seriously at all! I was convinced that I would leave school at 16 and become an international soloist. I spent a lot of time in the holidays, filling in huge numbers of manuscript books – again I just couldn't stop myself.

DW: *You did study composition at the Menuhin School with Malcolm Singer*.*

CF-H: I did, and he was very encouraging. I think he realised that I was desperate to compose and so he just let me get on with it. He was very good on harmony, counterpoint: all the technical stuff too. I remember there was a book where we had to sing in one clef and play in another – all that and ear-training was invaluable really and Malcolm was incredibly good at teaching that.

DW: *An amazing musical education but very sheltered, cocooned almost.*

CF-H: Incredibly so, it just wasn't the real world at all. Two of the things I get asked all the time, one is the tired old question about being a woman composer and then, the question of did it help you to see someone do what you are doing at a high level and encourage you to succeed yourself. Firstly, I don't recall hearing a piece by a woman composer until I was about 14 or 15 and I heard, I think, a Piano Trio by Judith Weir*. But I was still spending most of my time writing music down well before then. I didn't think about it and I still don't. Also, I was surrounded by kids like me making music all the time, so neither of those questions were relevant as far as I was concerned. I was a chubby ginger kid who liked classical music, so I probably would not have survived in a 'normal' school. From that point of view, the sheltered side of the school was fine for me, but sheltered it undoubtedly was.

DW: *A big turning point came when you were only 14 and you won a competition to write a choral piece for the London Bach Choir – There is no Rose. Looking at this piece now, it is extraordinary to think that someone so young, and I guess with little or no real experience of writing choral music or singing in a choir, could produce something so confident and self-assured. Of course there are many famous settings of this text, most notably I suppose by Benjamin Britten* and John Joubert*, but you wouldn't be aware of those.*

CF-H: It is odd for me to see and hear these early pieces. I'm still quite proud of them in some ways. I'm certainly not embarrassed by them. I can't even remember how I found the text – I'm guessing a book in the school library. I don't think I even knew what the Latin parts of the text meant, perhaps I didn't even know that it was Latin. There was a misprint in the score for years because I hadn't noticed that I had taken the Latin down incorrectly. I vaguely remember writing the piece and being seated at the piano, trying out chords. There are some crazy things in it that I wouldn't do now, a bottom G for the sopranos for instance, but the piece has a certain innocence and still works, I like to think. I would have never really listened to choral music at that time – all we did was endlessly practise! I might have been aware of the Britten but can't be sure. The big thing that annoyed my mum about the Menuhin School was that I came out not knowing much music because the emphasis was on perfection, just preparing a small number of pieces, playing studies, scales and things. I think there is still a lot of 'me' in *There is no Rose* from a harmonic and melodic point of view, but how that came about I just can't say.

DW: *As a result of winning the competition your first professional performance was at the Royal Albert Hall, with the Bach Choir and Sir David Willcocks*. That must have been quite something.*

CF-H: Yes, that experience was <u>so</u> incredible. David Willcocks was wonderful – this was a four-minute Christmas carol in a big programme, but I remember going to the rehearsal and him spending a good fifteen minutes going over the score, asking me what I wanted. He involved me in the rehearsal and afterwards sent me the most beautiful hand-written card, which I still have, encouraging me to carry on and saying how much he liked the piece. He didn't have to do any of that; he treated me as a real composer and a colleague, not as just some precocious kid, and it sends shivers down my spine just to think of it. I'll never forget that. There are occasions when I don't get treated like that now let alone when I was 14!

DW: *Then came the BBC Young Musician of the Year Composition Competition in 1996 and you won that title with a Concertino for cello, strings, piano & percussion, which was given a premiere by the BBC Philharmonic Orchestra.*

CF-H: All I do remember about that piece is writing the whole thing out straight away into full score – it just flowed and flowed. I guess I had been so well trained in musicianship and ear-training that it just seemed the most natural thing to do. It really was that performance that made me come to the conclusion that this was what I wanted to do for the rest of my life.

DW: *At 16!?*

CF-H: Yes, but having said that, I got through to the finals of the next competition as well, and I dropped out! I suddenly came to the conclusion that I needed to plan my music a lot more and not just let it sort of splurge out. I couldn't write for about a year. Up to that point I was completely unselfconscious about composing, it was all completely intuitive, and when I started to think about it I dried up musically. I didn't even write the commission, an Oboe Quartet, that I won as a result of the first BBC competition. But looking back, despite the setback, composing was something that I never considered not doing, it seemed the most natural thing in the world.

DW: *You then got to study music at Gonville & Caius, Cambridge.*

CF-H: Cambridge was a terrible shock – on the one hand I had, on paper at least, a better CV than any other composer who was there, in terms of performances and competitions, but on the other, still being chronically shy and what can I say, being nowhere near as an academic as most of the people there, I found it difficult. In fact I loathed my first term more than I can say. I hated it. What got me through were all the papers that involved 'notes' – species counterpoint, harmony, fugue, ear training. I could do all that pretty well. The composition module didn't happen until my third year. Because I somehow already had a reputation, I was getting little commissions here and there and turned to choral music again thanks to Dr Geoffrey Webber and the Gonville & Caius Choir, who commissioned me to write for them. I wrote a setting of the *Nunc Dimittis*, which was hideously hard. I don't know how they even started to sing it. As far as choral music is concerned, the turning point was the commissioning of *Psalm No.1*, in 2009, again for Gonville & Caius. The university commissioned an associated composer from every generation, so Alexander Goehr*, Judith Weir, Edward Rushton*, me, I can't remember who else, and that piece went on to win a British Composer Award. I know I got other commissions on the back of that award, even without people hearing my music, which seems very odd to me! Why would anyone commission a piece from a composer whose music you haven't heard or seen?

DW: *You studied composition with Robin Holloway* in your final year at Cambridge?*

CF-H: Robin was actually very supportive but like Malcolm Singer, very much left me to my own devices. I later found out that he had recommended me for various commissions and scholarships. I can't actually pinpoint what it was that he taught me, which is odd – although maybe it isn't so odd, a lot of these things you take in without realising what is going on. Then I went to do a PhD at King's College, London and studied with Silvina Milstein* – she was a great teacher. One particular thing I remember was her telling me to think about the independence of the bass line and making sure that I gave the bass a rest, which I still think about a lot. I don't want to sound ungrateful, I had some really good teachers, but I think they knew that the best thing to do was to let me get on with what I was doing on the whole. That's one reason why I find teaching composition so hard myself I think. One regret I do have about King's is that I didn't take part in anything very much. I lived at home in Essex at the time and I just went to the seminars I had to go to –Lontano were ensemble in residence for example and I didn't get to write for them, but that was my doing rather than the College.

DW: *One thing that worries a lot of composers, the business of finding a way forward or finding a voice, has never seemed to worry you.*

CF-H: I didn't really worry about that at all. I just did what I did. I was getting these little commissions and I fulfilled those. I didn't really think about style as such. This was one area where Robin Holloway was very helpful, he didn't impose anything on me or tell me that I couldn't write in a particular way and I remember him telling me how lucky I was not to have to worry about things like that, which worried him a lot when he was young. I know nowadays – a big difference in terms of my choral music – that I am now very much more aware of the performers and I want to write things that bring out the best in them and not just think of me, me, me!

DW: *So no more twenty-part settings of the Nunc Dimittis…*

CF-H: Exactly, that piece was very much about me. With those early pieces I really didn't think about future performances or how practical the pieces were. When I wrote *There is no Rose* I remember singing every part to check it through, but I didn't do that for a while and I think it probably shows. Now, if there is a bar or two that I can't sing myself I do something about it and think of a way of making it more idiomatic or grateful to sing. The Gonville choir was so very good – I wasn't in the choir (I've never been in a choir) and didn't really go to services – so I was spoilt for a while in terms of having such talented singers.

DW: *You have often mentioned your admiration for Benjamin Britten. Is he a composer you still feel close to?*

CF-H: I do, although I'm not sure I'm influenced by him particularly. I don't consciously take inspiration from anyone, but yes, I think Britten is still for me a major figure. Apart from the sheer compositional craft, I also admire the fact that he was able to compose such a wide range of music, for such diverse levels of ability, giving young people and amateurs the chance to perform alongside high-level professionals.

DW: *This is something you have done several times yourself – big pieces intended for large numbers of mixed-ability singers and players –* Things Grow *for example, premiered by a choir of a thousand at the Norfolk Show; pieces for Music Junction/London Chamber Orchestra,* I Am You, Brave and Strong, A Young Person's Guide to Composition *and most unusual of all perhaps,* Even You Song, *which combines elements of a traditional Evensong (with a Mag & Nunc*, anthem and organ voluntaries), with a text about travel to the moon sung by school children.*

CF-H: I think the first-ever contemporary piece I played on the cello was the tiny *Tema 'Sacher'* by Britten, and I became totally obsessed with it. That aside, in the – for want of a better expression – 'community pieces' Britten wrote, it is the combination of craft, emotion, invention and writing so idiomatically for the forces and players he had available that I admire.

DW: *If you are writing a piece along the lines of* Even You Song, *it seems like an almost impossible brief – Peterborough Cathedral Choir, a professional organist and hundreds of kids that couldn't read music…*

CF-H: I do genuinely like the practical challenge of writing mixed-ability pieces, as long as I don't do it too often! As always when you are a composer, all you have to do is write a couple of these sorts of pieces before people hang a label around your neck…

DW: *We have talked before about you being worried that you were being stuck with a reputation for writing 'community pieces'.*

CF-H: Yes, several of them seemed to come up in quite a short space of time. There is no real reason why I should have a knack for this kind of thing, but if I'm writing a piece for amateurs, be they kids or adults, an amateur choir or orchestra, I try to remember that these people are taking part in this activity for fun, or as a diversion from their day at school or being in a stressful job. I've recently written a piece for the Covent Garden Chamber Orchestra and I did make a conscious effort to give everyone something interesting to do. With *Even You Song* I really didn't want to use the children for

a tiny bit of a big piece and for them to spend the rest of the time sitting bored out of their minds, trying to wave at their parents in the audience. So the kids participate in the anthem too, which is about ten minutes long, making all kinds of sound effects. It just forces you to be creative, and of course, I wanted the anthem to stand by itself too, so it can be sung as part of an ordinary church service. One thing that sticks in my mind is going to a concert of new chamber pieces for young players and frankly most of the music was so depressing – thick harmonies, just dirges that would put the kids off for life! I just try and find interesting ways of making them feel part of the piece as a whole.

DW: *You have a similar attitude when writing for adult amateur choirs.*

CF-H: Certainly! I've been lucky enough to have had a residency with the London Oriana Choir recently and that taught me a lot. They are a pretty good choir, but you realise that these people are, I don't know, teachers, doctors, lawyers, civil servants, whatever – they have been working hard all day and could have stayed at home to watch television, but they come out to rehearse. I really wanted to give them something that they would find rewarding, challenging, but enjoyable, a piece that wouldn't make them dread their rehearsal night! It is hard to get the right balance. Sometimes I worry that I'm writing down to them and other times I worry that I'm asking too much – I think a lot about that for a long time. Perhaps after the first piece I wrote for them, *So True a Fool is Love*, whilst they did a very good job, I was able to come up with a second piece that suited them better as a result of the experience and I tried to play to their strengths, so to speak. I'm not sure I would write a piece now for a choir that I hadn't heard either in concert or a recording of some sort.

DW: *At the other extreme we should mention a couple of your more demanding choral pieces – firstly* Beyond the Night Sky, *that you wrote for the 75th birthday of Professor Stephen Hawking* in 2017 and the commission for The Cardinall's Musick,* From the Beginning of the World, *first heard at the Proms in 2015. When you are writing a piece you take on a good deal of reading and research don't you?*

CF-H: Yes, I do. For *Beyond the Night Sky* it won't come as any surprise to learn that I did an especially large amount of reading. I had lunch with a cosmologist from Caius to help me out with understanding some of the more complex ideas. I talked to Lucy Hawking, Professor Hawking's daughter, about the sort of music her father liked. I remember he loved the Poulenc* *Gloria* and Edith Piaf*, amongst other things. I was just so inspired and excited about writing a piece for Stephen Hawking – even for someone who is about as far away from being a scientist as it is possible to be, he was such a remarkable man. I really wanted to write something that was pertinent to him.

DW: *Did this mean reading* A Brief History of Time*?*

CF-H: Er... I scanned it! But I did a lot of research into him – he saw himself as being in a line coming from Newton* and Einstein*, so I read or tried to read a lot of their writing and I couldn't find anything to set. In the end I gave up and Googled poems about the universe, found a children's poem by the American poet Stephen Schur and combined it with questions from *A Brief History of Time* about the nature of the universe. I don't really use a lot of what used to be called extended techniques but I listened to space sounds from NASA and used some of those in the piece. I even thought a lot about gravity and how the chords work, gravity pulling them down somehow. I don't know how much of this comes through in the piece of course, but it is just useful for me and sets the piece on its way.

DW: *That must have been an incredible premiere – Stephen Hawking was present wasn't he?*

CF-H: Yes, Gonville & Caius Choir sang it at his 75th birthday dinner. It came at a point in my life when I was feeling a bit jaded. I had probably been writing too much, and it was truly magical that he heard it and liked it – what more could I ask for? I'm always grateful to be asked to write pieces of course, but there is a danger, especially if the text you are given is not so interesting, that one can go into 'automatic five minute choral piece' mode, if one takes on too many of that kind of piece. Sometimes I get sent a text and my heart just sinks...

DW: *In general you like to find your own texts.*

CF-H: If at all possible, yes. I don't have the confidence to write my own texts, but I especially enjoy finding ways of joining different texts together. I can generally find my way through – in the case of *From the Beginning of the World* I had a problem because the requirement was a connection with Tallis*, for the anniversary of his birth, and because of course The Cardinall's Musick have a particular reputation in that repertoire. I found it difficult to find a musical link to begin with, even though I was excited about writing for that group and that occasion. I spent weeks trying to find a suitable text, before settling on part of a German Treatise on the Great Comet of 1577 – of course I have no idea if Tallis himself was aware of this comet, but it made me think of all the great changes that happened during his lifetime, in terms of religion, the calendar, that sort of thing. There are lots of *canons** and lots of imitation, which you find in Tallis, and then there is a quote from the melody by Tallis that Vaughan Williams* used as the basis for his *Fantasia on a theme of Thomas Tallis* – I used to love playing in that piece when I was at the Menuhin School. So, all these things can come together when a new piece is on the way.

DW: *Can you say what the balance is between inspiration and technique?*

CF-H: I don't really know – I think on some days I might use technique to get me through when I'm not inspired. I don't really know what being inspired means if I'm honest. When I read texts I have musical ideas that come to me... I read and read, underline particular words, or lines that might suggest textures or rhythms, or use speech rhythms quite a lot. I say the words to myself over and over again and find a way of notating it using musical notes. I think about colours too, not synesthesia exactly, but I would never write a Christmas carol for example that was not based around E, G or F - those to me are Christmas colours! I would never write a carol in A major! I just noodle around at the piano and sing a lot when writing choral music, but at the same time I'm careful not to be limited whilst I'm at the piano. I think it is more important to make sure the lines I write are possible, so that is again how all the singing to myself comes in.

DW: *Do you think about a prospective audience when writing or people's reaction to your music?*

CF-H: I'm lucky that my musical language seems to have been pretty well-received. The language is I think, I hope, relatively accessible. I do care about the audience or rather I care about communicating. I've just written a piece for Huddersfield Choral Society - two members of the choir died from COVID-19. The poem, which has been especially written, around words suggested by the choir and is rather beautiful, really doesn't demand a hugely complex setting and I've thought about the choir and the audience in that context, trying to come up with something that is just clear, direct and atmospheric.

DW: *Are you a disciplined composer? Do you set yourself the task of writing for a certain number of hours per day?*

CF-H: I try and keep a regular schedule. I compose every day, but I did have three months off at the end of 2019, because I felt that I was getting too good at, well, churning it out.

DW: *You felt really that was the case and wanted to re-charge your batteries? The price of having a natural facility!*

CF-H: Yes, I had written a lot of music over the past few years, and just started to feel there was a potential for the way I was feeling to have an adverse effect on what I was doing. In other words, I might start doing technical things just naturally and not writing the best piece I could. It wasn't that I was unhappy with what I had written, I think I was just over-due a break. Actually, what I did was make a study of electronic music, just something different, about as far from what I do as it is possible to get – even if that resulted inme thinking a bit more about sound rather than melody, harmony and rhythm.

DW: *Does that mean that you are very self-critical?*

CF-H: I worry that my music might be too instinctive, you know: should that have been much more difficult or caused me more problems? Should I be more adventurous or innovative? But I have good days and bad days like every composer.

DW: *You tend not to revise I think.*

CF-H: No, I don't. I generally don't feel the need, even for an early piece, why would I go back and revise say *There is no Rose*, from twenty-five years ago, I'm happy with it for what it is. I have composer friends who constantly revise and on one level I'm impressed with that, but I go through so many variations when I'm writing that I don't feel the need to touch the piece when it is done.

DW: *It seems very important for you to communicate with your performer and/or listener.*

CF-H: It is the single most important thing. Otherwise there is no point to it all. Whether that is making a seven-year-old feel as if they have achieved something from playing a few notes in first position on the violin in a piece of mine, to an amateur choir, high level professionals and whoever is listening, regardless if they are 'musically educated' or not. I feel a lot of music doesn't do that. I do think this goes back, as we discussed earlier, with me being so painfully shy when I was young, and writing music was my speaking voice. I fluctuate between thinking that my piece is the most important thing in the universe and then thinking it is a job, you are writing music <u>for</u> people.

DW: *Do you enjoy rehearsals and premieres? Do you get nervous?*

CF-H: I'm very open to different interpretations of my music. Once I've written a piece, it is time to let go and I'm always curious to see what different people make of it. I often feel that I disappoint performers because I don't have pages of notes after a rehearsal. Of course I can point out wrong notes – I've got perfect pitch so I can hear that – but I try and put so much of the emotion, feeling and character into the notes and rhythms, it really pleases me when I don't have anything to say. I'm quite flexible in terms of tempo at least. I do get quite nervous at premieres. I find them quite uncomfortable. There are some colleagues who I know sort of luxuriate in premieres, but I find them quite nerve-wracking. The great thing about getting older and more experienced is that the performances tend to get better and better, and I've been very fortunate that my music is sung and played by some tremendous musicians.

DW: *Are you ever surprised when you hear a new piece for the first time?*

CF-H: Not really – with all possible respect to performers, composing the piece is the most exciting part for me. I perform them here in my composing room and of course it is wonderful to hear them live but, having said all that, I have just written a short solo piece for solo accordion and that was a surprise because I got it all wrong! I just misunderstood how the instrument works, so that is slightly different.

DW: *You don't do any regular teaching and have already said you don't find it easy. Is this because you basically think that composition cannot be taught?*

CF-H: I feel rather insecure about my lack of knowledge about contemporary music and contemporary techniques. I think I'm quite good at helping people get ideas if they are stuck but for me the most useful part of what I was taught was counterpoint and having to write a fugue a week at university.

DW: *As someone who could have quite easily gone down the performing route, do you ever miss playing?*

CF-H: Well, my cello has been sitting fifteen feet away from me for the past eighteen months. I play the piano a little. I always intend to play the cello again but I know it will be frustrating after not playing properly for so long. The problem for me is that I almost have to force myself to listen to music because, after I've been writing all day, I've sort of had enough. If I do I would listen to something in a completely different genre.

DW: *Elgar quotes Ruskin at the end* The Dream of Gerontius* – 'This is the best of me'. Can you say which piece of yours or group of pieces might fall into that category?*

CF-H: I'm really proud of the Cello Concerto I wrote for David Cohen*, *Katharsis*; in terms of choral music, perhaps that very early *Psalm No. 1*, maybe the Tallis piece, *From the Beginning of the World*, which on the one hand is full of quite complex technical detail of one sort or another but is also I think quite immediate for an audience.

DW: *Is there anything that you are particularly burning to write?*

CF-H: A Violin Concerto – one has been discussed for a while but it hasn't happened yet and I've always longed to write a big opera, but then I think does the world need any more huge operas, maybe not any more. It was always my dream to write a full-scale opera… maybe one day!

DW: *We are recording this interview at a very worrying and difficult time, how are you dealing with lockdown?*

CF-H: I'm just conscious of all the performers that are having such a terrible time. A lot of composers are probably doing pretty well at the moment, not that we know when some of these new pieces will be played or sung. I'm supposing that things will become difficult for composers later on...

DW: *What would you say are your five favourite choral works?*

CHERYL'S FIVE FAVOURITE CHORAL WORKS

Ligeti *Lux Aeterna*

Mozart *Requiem*

Malcolm Singer *Songs of Ascent*

Giles Swayne *Cry*

Judith Weir *Illuminare, Jerusalem*

Howard Goodall

BORN 1958

DW: *Can you say something about your earliest musical memories? Did you come from a musical family?*

HG: It was a musical household but I wouldn't describe it as a household of musicians. My parents loved music – both of them used to sing in the local choral society. I still have my father's copies of those distinctive Novello vocal scores that he would bring home after choir practice. He was that rare and valuable thing, a tenor. The radio was always on and my father had what was then a rather sophisticated reel-to-reel tape recorder; heaven knows how he could have afforded that. He had a big collection of 78s, still has them, and his brother Roland, who was killed in the Second World War, was very musical. He was a good violinist and went travelling around Eastern Europe to learn about folk music. My dad's father also loved music – he died in 1945 and as a child saw Brahms* and Tchaikovsky conducting their own music in London! Another uncle was a very good jazz pianist and was part of the Normandy landings – he told me that he once did a gig in a bar in France. Having played his set, another guy came on, a black Canadian pianist, who was incredible; at the end of the evening someone asked who this guy was and his name was Oscar Peterson*! We heard The Beatles* as much as *Messiah** and a lot of Rachmaninov*; it was more or less a crime to say one loved Rachmaninov in the '60s. My dad loved Couperin – so I was encouraged to play that on the piano, all sorts of quirky things like that.

DW: *Then you went as a chorister to New College, Oxford, which I'm guessing is the place you heard all the traditional English choral repertoire?*

HG: Well, yes, although it should be said that David Lumsden*, who was Director of Music, did rather plough his own furrow as far as that was concerned. Almost everyone else in the Cathedral world at that time, was still singing Stanford*, Wesley*, Blair in B minor*, Dyson in F* and all that stuff, ad infinitum, perhaps Howells* was the modern music they sang. David Lumsden took the view that a very small amount of that went a very long way. I think we did Stanford in C once the whole time I was there and that was for a joint event at Eton College – I thought it was fantastic but

61

Lumsden thought it was rubbish! What he wanted to do in the mid '60s was Tudor polyphony. At that time, if you wanted to sing Byrd*, Tallis*, Tomkins*, Palestrina*, you had to get editions done, so they were made just for us by academics in Oxford. The chapel was waiting for an organ to be put in, so we only had a small instrument and all that music worked well. I can date my obsession with pipe organs from singing in that joint Evensong with Eton Chapel too – that amazing neo-Gothic, over-the-top instrument did the kind of thing I'd never heard before. I can still smell that organ loft now and it was terribly loud – I loved it. When I was about eleven we got the new organ at New College and I started to have lessons on that – at that time that instrument was very shocking, quite harsh and it had a continental edge. My fellow choristers included the composers Francis Pott and Simon Phipps and the conductor Simon Halsey*, and we all thought that doing music all day and every day was the norm. My first choral commission was from New College Choir when I was ten or eleven years old, an Introit I think, and they did sing it – I was fanatically composing in all of my spare time!

DW: *So when you left and went to a 'normal school'…*

HG: It was a rude awakening – I got they were interested in other things but as an arrogant 13-year-old, I couldn't understand why the choir just couldn't sight-read everything. It drove me crazy – we sang *If ye love me* by Tallis and it took weeks to get it right. Looking back, I was just being uncooperative and arrogant of course, but it was just so different. I think my teenage rebellion resulted in forming a band whilst I carried on with studying the classical repertoire.

DW: *So the band started whilst you were at school, from about the age of 15.*

HG: I was the keyboard player. It eventually became 'Half Brother' – in classic rock style, the personnel kept changing and it carried on all the way through to Christ Church, Oxford, and there I met Rowan Atkinson* and Richard Curtis* on my first day. They asked me to do the music for their revues. The band came too and Rowan became the percussion player for a while. We finally released an album and two singles, won a talent contest in the days before X Factor but, of course, not on TV – the album was a flop, the band fell apart and I went on to do other things.

DW: *It is interesting that you went in that direction partly because of frustration.*

HG: It was partly that but I always did like a 'mixed diet'. I was still in the choir and orchestra at school, played the organ and wrote music that wasn't pop music. I did the traditional music degree at Oxford, which was about as traditional as you could get - harmony, orchestration, counterpoint and all that – but I wanted to do other things too. It isn't unusual now but it was a bit more unusual then.

DW: *You have always said how important The Beatles were to you and how significant you think they are in the history of twentieth-century music.*

HG: Yes, I do. I've made TV programmes about this and they were the people that showed the popular music sector that all other forms of music had immense value and they invited this music in. They were not the only people that did it but they were the most famous and the most broad, so millions of people got to know about this other genre that they were interested in. As far as culture is concerned, you have to understand that it is 'effect' – this is what influences composers. Bach* was influenced by Vivaldi* because he came across it – it doesn't matter that there was another composer who was a contemporary of Vivaldi who did the same thing, because Bach picked up Vivaldi! I'm unapologetic about The Beatles – they are one of the big reasons that tonality survived in the 1960s – tonality was so unfashionable. Leonard Bernstein* knew about this at the time. Wilfrid Mellers* wrote a book about it and people thought he was crazy. There were all sorts of bi-products of their curiosity – they were interested in experimental music too. I mean Stockhausen* was on the cover of their Sgt. Pepper album. Classical music got itself all tangled up and people wanted to hear old music rather than the new. Up until perhaps the 1930s concert programmes had new music and people wanted to hear it, but that changed dramatically after the war. In popular music being new is good news.

DW: *So you think the cutting edge so to speak, began to terrify audiences.*

HG: Even as late as the 1980s there would be a fear of new music, certainly amongst choirs. I remember writing a piece for a choir and I was messing around with organ registrations or something. It was before I'd been on TV and nobody knew who I was - someone came up to me and said this piece is awful, I can't deal with it. When they performed it, not only they, but the audience really enjoyed it. I went through this experience quite a lot at the time, writing a new piece and people thought it was going to be awful. 'Experimentation' cast a long shadow for a long time, but having said that I do believe that experimentation is legitimate as far as music, sculpture or any kind of art is concerned. I don't say it shouldn't have happened – it just had an effect. Boulez* was telling his students that if people liked what you are doing then you are doing something wrong and that was what many believed for a time.

DW: *At New College you were put through all the academic rituals – history, harmony, counter point – did you feel you learnt a great deal?*

HG: I was lazy in my first two years as I was busy doing comedy revues and going to the Edinburgh Festival. The history part I liked. The technical side, harmony, counterpoint and theory, for most people is no help at all. For me orchestration and stylistic composition was incredibly useful, it was a transferable skill. As an example, one of the things you had to do was complete a string quartet in the style of Mozart* or Haydn*. They would give you twenty bars and you would have to finish the movement. It's like a crossword, there are various things you have to know, so you won't do things that those composers wouldn't do; but the second part of the task is that you listen to Mozart and Haydn and find out what it is that makes them sound like they do. That skill I was able to put to work for my first job after leaving Oxford – I wrote the songs for the satirical news programme 'Not the Nine O'Clock News'. We did a song every week, in the style of something that was a big hit in the charts at that time. So I had to listen to ABBA* or Iron Maiden* and write something as if I was them – not copying them, but writing something on their style that might have been another one of their songs. That is much harder than it seems. When I was teaching I would send the students off and get them to write a piece in the style of Haydn or Elgar* or whoever; it very rarely did sound like those composers, partly because you can't learn that sort of thing quickly, but also because your individuality is too powerful to 'keep down'. Actually I'm going to quote from Stephen Sondheim*, from his masterpiece *Sunday in the Park with George*: 'Stop worrying that your vision is new, let others make that decision, they usually do'. Worrying about being original is a waste of worry, because it is difficult not to be original. There is a difference between writing a piece 'like' Elgar and writing a piece in the way Elgar might have written it.

DW: *You didn't stay on at Oxford to do a composition degree.*

HG: I could have stayed on and done a BMus in composition, but it seemed to me, talking to the postgraduates at the time, all they wanted was to spend a year trying to sound like their teacher, in this case, Robert Sherlaw Johnson*. I think the best way to teach composition is to make students understand how other composers do things. I would still say everything I write sounds like someone else – my wife says it sounds like me, but I just can't hear it. I can't hear that my music has a style, only what it sounds like.

DW: *You mention Sherlaw Johnson – were there any teachers you particularly found inspiring?*

HG: I must admit I didn't go to many lectures! Once I started working hard I was reading a lot of books and found that most of the lectures came out of the books. I did however meet my now wife at one of the lectures so that was worth going to! It wasn't that I didn't want to know, it was just that the lectures seemed to be a slowed-down version of the book. There were some brilliant people – Hugh McDonald* was wonderful on Berlioz and my own tutor Simon Preston*, was a hugely inspiring, charismatic individual, as both a lecturer, organist and choir trainer. I got on terribly well with him and he was a big influence and very supportive. I once agreed to play drum in John Gardner's *Tomorrow shall be my dancing day** at a carol service. I

had to be in the organ loft. I rolled up, had a terrible headache from the previous night and it was the most terrifying half hour of my life. Preston was demonic when rehearsing the choir but the choir were amazing and sounded like nobody else. His recording of *Symphony of Psalms** has never and probably will never be equalled – they sing it as if their life depended on it. It had such energy and a style of singing Latin that then spread everywhere, not the mellow warm embrace that he and others had learnt from the 'Mother Ship' – King's, Cambridge. Actually, in terms of influences on my choral music, I would say *Symphony of Psalms* was number one! If I could write a bar as good as anything in that piece I would be a happy man. You can trace everything back to Stravinsky, I think – we all lust after it. It was Preston's recordings of Stravinsky*, Poulenc* and even Lassus*, that really had an effect on what I write and the choral sound I love.

DW: *Choral music aside, you have spent a good deal of time writing musicals. Was* The Hired Man *the first one?*

HG: All that goes back to New College. The Head of Music was Paul Drayton* – a good composer too – he wrote a musical on 'The Hobbit' with Humphrey Carpenter*, to which Tolkien* himself came. We all performed it and of course it was breathtaking that Tolkien was there. When I was 15 and at a comprehensive school, I wrote three musicals for the school and completely got the bug. Then at Oxford we put it on at the Edinburgh Festival (Richard Curtis did the libretto). After that I came across a book by Melvyn Bragg*, *The Hired Man*. I met Melvyn, told him I wanted to write a musical based on his book and he thought I was mad – he humoured me and I did it. Then Melvyn plugged me into key people that would help me – I knew nothing about putting on a show in the West End –all kinds of people, like Trevor Nunn, Ken Russell. I went to play to them and they made helpful suggestions. Eventually we put it on at the Nuffield in Southampton, then the Haymarket, Leicester. Lots of rewrites! It couldn't happen now. Completely by accident, Andrew Lloyd Webber*, who I will always be grateful to, came to hear it and thanks to him we got it on in the West End. It only lasted five months but it kind of got into the repertoire and put it on the map and has been done all over the world. It was an incredible act of faith on his part and we have been friends ever since.

DW: *Writing the musicals and going on to write music for television or film -Blackadder, Red Dwarf,* The Vicar Of Dibley, *etc. – do you find yourself having to put on a different hat, so to speak, than the hat you would wear for* Eternal Light *for instance?*

HG: I would say I'm not conscious of it – because after all, two of my best-known TV themes, Dibley and Mr Bean are choral! I was allowed to use my choral gene because I knew the people that wrote those programmes very well and they didn't say no. If that hadn't been the case they would I'm sure have said no way! Composing for me is the same energy – or lack of it! The job is the same – what I'm thinking about is the mood I am creating, what is the emotional content I want to achieve? Obviously, there are key differences. In the commercial sector you are not your own boss, you are writing for the director or the star and if you can't write things twice, ten, twenty times and get something they think is right, then you can't be a professional composer! There is a difference in length too. If I'm writing a Requiem or a Passion or any big piece, the whole piece is in my head during the process of writing. I have to concentrate very hard and I don't like to listen to anything else and get distracted.

I escape to my house in France, sit in a room and get the structure clear in my head; doing a theme tune you can spend a couple of hours on it in the morning, come back to it the next day or the next week and get it in shape. It is just the scale that's the difference not the genre.

DW: *Are you always on the lookout for texts? We talked about this when you wrote* The Gravity of Kindness *for me last year.*

HG: Yes, I note things down and put them to one side – one day I might use that. I carried the text for your piece around with me for some time. Some poetry is wonderful as poetry and doesn't lend itself to be set to music and I think part of it is to do with how dense the ideas are within individual lines. I would say T.S. Eliot* is probably one of the most difficult for that reason. I think you have to separate yourself from poetry you like, Shakespeare Sonnets for example in my case, and sometimes it is so hard to set to music. It is partly due to the pace of the music too. I like setting other languages, mixing languages, as I like the ear of the listener to be moving around and not just stuck on one aural landscape. Like a lot of composers I like Latin – I like the neutrality of it. One of the challenges for living composers I think is trying to capture the reflective spiritual power of a lot of sacred music with words that are not sacred.

When we listen to the *St Matthew Passion*, we are aware that the writer of that piece had a very sincere spiritual mission – the story he is telling means a lot to him. When you hear the critical moments, you are hearing not just great music but music that attempts to mean something, and matching that level of meaning with secular words is a challenge. A lot of modern poetry is trying to have fun with the language and that way you lose some of the emotional impact.

DW: *When you came to write* Every purpose under the Heaven *was that a particular challenge?*

HG: I think the problem with the King James Bible oratorio was that I slightly prefer Tyndale*. The King James was written by scholars who knew their Latin and Greek – there is something raw in Tyndale that I love. The question is, how do you get metrical symmetry; it is mostly prose, how do you create what music needs, so I borrowed what Handel did with the Jennings text in *Messiah* and repeated phrases – a simple technique but really effective and it gives you what music yearns for and creates symmetry. Then for my Requiem and Passion settings, I wanted to find poems that said the same thing, and also, frankly, if you translate the phrases from the Latin Requiem for instance it is not that great a collection of things to live your life by. I know I'm saying the unthinkable when you consider the great Requiems of Verdi*, Fauré* and Mozart, amazing pieces of music, but they are basically saying there is going to be a hell of a lot of punishment coming your way and could you please let this person who has just died go through the minimum amount of pain possible and help save them, because we realise that we are miserable creatures. Well, I don't go along with that – I'm on Voltaire's side who said after the Lisbon earthquake 'what did the infants do, why should the innocents suffer'? They were not born bad, nobody is born bad, we may do bad things, but it is just about giving power to priests and bishops to give us a get-out clause and I couldn't in all conscience write a Requiem where those words meant anything. So I took it apart and found the things that express the human condition and express comfort, whether you have a faith or not. So I went to find other texts that expressed beautiful Latin phrases – give us peace, light eternal, I have to believe, Lamb of God take away the sins of the world. I'm not pretending I'm the only one doing this, far from it, but that's the way I see it. We are living in different times and we have to write these pieces as we are now.

DW: Eternal Light *has been a massive success and has obviously communicated something very special to a great many people – something like 600 performances now.*

HG: You never know what people will like. It had a good start – it was a dance piece first of course, it had 80 performances in the first year with Ballet Rambert. A lot of choirs sang it on that tour and it just snowballed. Had I known it was going to be sung by so many choirs, I would have made at least two movements, the second and the eighth, rather easier. The reason being I detect when I go to performances that hours have been spent on these movements, perhaps at the expense of some of the other music. I've tried to think of a way of re-barring the music – the unaccompanied movement (the eighth) is rather easier I think. I've seen choirs learn that from memory and just go for it; the difficulty is when you add those off-beat strings in the second movement, the counting is hard! But it is what it is. It is a fantastic thing to have a piece done like that and I've learnt that every performer and audience member takes something different away from the experience. I don't like to second-guess that when I'm writing – what will be will be.

DW: *So you don't necessarily think of your audience when writing?*

HG: I don't think you can – second-guessing an audience is dangerous. It has to make sense to me: why is it this speed, why these instruments, why this text? I think this has made me more serious about what I'm writing, I'm much more an editor of my own first drafts now and I've learnt from doing musicals not to be precious about things.

DW: *Do you find it easier to write as you get older, more natural?*

HG: Not more natural – I think what I wrote in my twenties is a little raw but I ran with it at the time. Now perhaps I can get the effect I hear in my head more easily but I'm alert to being too facile. I'm worried about writing a piece too quickly. I'm tougher on myself I would say. I might start a piece, get so far and then realise it isn't any good and start again; that happens quite a lot. I look at early pieces that aren't so well known and shudder sometimes.

DW: *But you wouldn't go back and revise. You are a different composer now.*

HG: I wouldn't normally – although I added a song to the *The Hired Man* recently. I always wanted to do this but never got around to it. It was odd; I had to put myself back into the shoes I was wearing in my twenties but it worked. I think it fits.

DW: *Do you enjoy rehearsals and premieres? Are you ever surprised when you hear a piece for the first time?*

HG: I love rehearsals and hate public performances. I love dress rehearsals of musicals but as soon as the public is in… It isn't anything to do with the people performing, whoever they are, it is just my state of mind. I automatically think people are hating it or what if something goes wrong. The communication between performers in rehearsal I have always and will always love. I don't think I would say I was surprised – you shouldn't be, not by the music, but I'm surprised by the effect it has on the performers. I'm often still surprised to find that what the performers find tricky is often not what I would have thought would be the case. One of the things I learnt from musical theatre is that getting an effect from an individual is so much easier than it is from 50-100 people to do that together – that is an extraordinary delicate art of choral writing, or, more to the point, directing or recording. Getting lots of

people to think the same thoughts together is very hard! One thing that does surprise me when I look at a score, perhaps of a piece I know aurally, is how straightforward it looks on the page compared to what I do! I actually mean composers in 'my category' – Lauridsen*, Rutter* or someone like that – and I sometimes feel I should find an easier way somehow. So maybe I am in the middle of my career rather than towards the end of it – one of the things I'm still learning.

DW: *How do you decide what commissions to take?*

HG: Part of it is timing of course – I'll try and find a way if I can. People often ask too late, thinking perhaps it is a quicker process than it is. Often the discussions within organisations, fund-raising, making decisions, takes time and gets in the way of course. A lot of people that ask me I know, or I know the choir and they jump to the front of the queue!

DW: *You enjoy conducting your own work.*

HG: Yes, but the only observation I would make is that my admiration for people who do it all the time has only risen exponentially from having to do it myself.

DW: *Elgar quotes Ruskin at the end of* The Dream of Gerontius*– 'This is the best of me…'. Can you say which piece of yours or group of pieces might fall into that category?*

HG: [Very long pause…] It is hard to disentangle best and most liked. I often equate result with effort and challenge. When I listen to the score of my musical *Bend it like Beckham* the challenge I set myself with that was Everest-like – how to make Punjabi music come into a western musical without it being patronising, touristic and naff – it was a long, difficult process, and the fact that it works musically is something I'm immensely proud of – the most difficult thing I've ever been asked to do. Not quite the answer you are looking for, so perhaps I would say *Psalm 23* which worked as a theme tune and is a choral piece that lots of people like to sing and listen to. I would suggest that making it do both of those things is hard. I think balancing popularity with anything that has any kind of weight is much harder than it looks – but there again I would say that wouldn't I? A few weeks ago, during lockdown, the Choir of Notre Dame Cathedral, on the anniversary of the terrible fire, sang *Psalm 23*. They recorded themselves at home and showed images of the burnt-out building and it moved me more than I can say. I wrote this little piece a long time ago, I have no connection with these people, they are singing in a foreign language and I was just so humbled and flattered that they chose my piece. I thought that was something to be proud of.

DW: *What would your advice be to young composers?*

HG: Two things really – don't look for contacts and networks from an older generation. When I was young I forged working relationships with people my own age, who were equally unknown, we created the work ourselves. I set up a network with my friends and it ended up finding a place. Secondly, create contacts with people that do things you don't – team up with a director, artist, poet, producer, whatever. Find a non-musical reason to do what you do – there isn't any point on teaming up with another composer. My most successful large-scale choral piece was a collaboration – *Eternal Light* – a collaboration with a choreographer and dance company.

DW: We are recording this interview at a very worrying and difficult time, how are you dealing with lockdown?

HG: Well, I can compose! A lot of my colleagues aren't doing that because they don't know when or if it will be performed and I can understand that. How is the structure of our industry going to survive? I'm straddled across two different worlds, the worlds of both choral music and music for the theatre, both of which have been hit disastrously. The economic damage will last for months and years – these are cataclysmic circumstances that everyone in the world will feel and of course we have the added problem of Brexit, which is suicidal. We have a double problem in this country. The whole thing is going to change in ways we can't yet imagine.

DW: What would you say are your five favourite choral works?

HOWARD'S FIVE FAVOURITE CHORAL WORKS

Byrd *Great Service in C*

Duruflé *Requiem*

Grechaninov *Passion Week Op. 58*

Ēriks Ešenvalds *The Long Road*

Stravinsky *Symphony of Psalms*

Adolphus Hailstork

BORN 1941

DW: *Can you tell me about your first musical memories? Did you come from a musical family?*

AH: My mother would like to sing around the house but that was about it. I started playing the violin in the Fourth Grade at school, after passing a musical aptitude test that was given in New York State. Then I got into choral music by singing at Junior High School and also I sang in a church, very High Church, the Cathedral of All Saints, Albany, New York, and I stayed there until I left High School. That was a foundational experience for my musical career because I learnt to read music, took organ and piano lessons. I began composing in High School and that's how it all started.

DW: *Is it right to say that the music you sang as a boy soprano in that church has had an effect on everything you have done since?*

AH: Absolutely – we did everything. We sang Tallis*, Byrd*, Stanford*, Vaughan Williams* – most of the great English music. We sang Anglican chant, even Gregorian chant* sometimes. The Cathedral was very High Church, so high it was close to being Catholic – all the smells and bells as people say – everything but the ruffled collar!

DW: *Do you remember the first occasions that you were making up pieces of your own?*

AH: I've got notebooks that go back to 1957, but I was probably writing just before then, so when I was about 14 I guess. My first piece was a choral piece and I remember conducting that in High School, although I can't remember the title… And I wrote orchestral pieces at school too. I had the most wonderful teacher, Gertrude Howarth, who said 'Adolphus, if you write it, we will play it' and that was it. So I've been writing music for over sixty years – I'm probably finally getting it now!

DW: *You went to Howard University, which is a historically black private university in Washington D.C. and studied with Mark Fax*, who was quite an important figure in Afro-American music?*

AH: Yes, a quiet but very thorough teacher who I was very lucky to have. He worked as a pianist for silent films, was a theatre organist too and was in charge of gospel music at an Afro-American church. He was Director of the School of Music at Howard. He certainly gave me a very good grounding in harmony and counterpoint.

DW: *Then you went to the Manhattan School of Music and studied with Vittorio Giannini*, who is sadly rather forgotten now, and David Diamond*. There is at least one other composer in this book that studied with Diamond and tells of him being pretty outspoken and, well, difficult!*

AH: Yes, Giannini was an Italian/American. He had lots of distinguished pupils and was himself probably what would now be called a neo-romantic. I was with David Diamond most of the time and yes, he could be pretty blunt and get to the point very quickly, but that was good for me. One occasion I brought something in and was trying to justify it in some way or another and I remember Diamond snapping back, 'well, who says? Who says you have to do it that way?' It was then that he said 'let me give you the keys to the kingdom of creativity' – I always will remember that lesson.

DW: *I suppose now and indeed even then, in the 1960s, both of your teachers were looked upon as very conservative composers – beautifully crafted music, but at the same time not music that was keeping up with the musical developments of the day.*

AH: Oh yes, very definitely. I like Diamond's work in particular. I would regard myself as a conservative composer, whatever that means now, I hope with a decent craft.

DW: *I think in between these two experiences you followed a great many other American composers and studied for a summer with Nadia Boulanger* at the American School at Fontainebleau, in Paris.*

AH: Yes, I got a fellowship and had lessons with her for about nine weeks – just a spectacular training in how to use the mind. I tell people it was a lesson in training the polyphonic mind – you had to be able to tap, sing, play the piano and read in all sorts of different clefs at the same time. It was frightening and she was a pretty demanding teacher but you came out a much more disciplined musician than you ever were before.

DW: *What about the question of finding your own voice? I suppose in America, as is the case anywhere else, you might have been expected to write in a very particular way...*

AH: Certainly, a gun to the head situation. We had a class one day and a teacher walked in, and said, 'Adolphus, we just can't accept this, you can't write like that'. She said it with such ferocity, it seemed as if she was saying 'if you want your degree from this school, you need to change'. She didn't define what 'modern' meant and if I had not been so intimidated I would have challenged her on this, but I just didn't have the gumption to stand up for myself then. It was not a case of helping people to find their own way, a sense of independence; rather, you must do it in this way, otherwise you are worthless. This was before I met Diamond, who wasn't really bothered about such things. It was a tough time in some ways. Gradually, I worked my way out of worrying about things like that.

DW: *I suppose for you it was a case of working your way out of that, but also coming to terms with your cultural heritage as an Afro-American, be that jazz, blues, gospel music, etc...*

AH: I did start coming of age at a time when all hell was breaking out in the US. This was the time of Vietnam and Civil Rights. That had a huge impact on me and I didn't want to reject Afro-American culture, but I hadn't at that time figured out how to use it in what I was doing. I'd written a couple of musicals in college and used elements of jazz in writing those. I had sung in a Gospel choir, soaked all that up, but the question was how to combine my culture with the European tradition that I had been studying for so long. When I got out of the army in '68 and I went to Michigan State University to do my doctorate, the black students were having meetings to find how they should react and relate to all that was going on, and we decided that we would take whatever talent we had to 'serve the cause'. I asked myself 'what could I do?' I had not grown up in segregation, so was not as sensitised to it as these kids from the South, but when I discovered what they had gone through, I decided I would attempt to do what I could. I had learnt that if Gregorian chant was the foundation of Western music then Spirituals could be regarded as the foundation of Afro-American music. I was also impressed with Dvořák* saying at the end of the 1890s that spirituals and indigenous Indian-American music could be the foundation of an American musical language.

DW: *What you are trying to do is make a link and put these two musical traditions alongside each other, contrasting them, juxtaposing them...*

AH: Yes, I admit to that, sometimes I write exclusively one or the other and then sometimes I juxtapose or blend them in the same piece. I like to call myself a cultural hybrid! That's really the best description I think.

DW: *With that in mind, it is clear whereabouts pieces such as the* Spiritual Songs *for unaccompanied choir come from. I was going to call them arrangements of well-known Spirituals, but they are rather more than that – they seem to be free fantasias or elaborations on the original tunes...*

AH: Exactly, fantasias, that is the right word – they aren't just an adaptation of tune and accompaniment.

DW: *But then I hear a hint of gospel music in your* Songs of Life and Love, *which includes a beautiful setting of the Yeats* poem 'He wishes for the Cloths of Heaven'.

AH: Yes, I probably do inhabit both worlds in those pieces. I'm glad you mention *The Cloths of Heaven*. It seems to be a piece that appeals to a lot of people – such a beautiful poem.

DW: *Then the* Seven Songs from the Rubaiyat *seems to be more concerned with another American tradition, coming from Copland* perhaps.*

AH: Oh yes, those piece are quite early and were written as a lark! Actually I was watching television and out they came, but yes, they are perhaps more connected directly to what might be called an American tradition.

DW: *Do you feel that you are part of an American tradition?*

AH: I read in an article that there are two major lines of American compositional thought in the last century. One was the Copland line, at least the Copland of the popular ballets like *Rodeo* and *Appalachian Spring* and the other was a more experimental line, coming from Schoenberg* (who came to live in the US), and Americans like Ives* and later avant-garde figures such as Cage* (who was a Schoenberg pupil of course). I certainly belong in the first group. My primary instrument was always the voice and I think that makes one lean to a more conservative mode of expression. I still hear the sound of the cathedral and cathedral music, that whole English tradition, ringing in my head, so perhaps it is an English tradition living alongside an American one. All that has an influence on the melodies I write, the chords I choose and the speed of my harmonic rhythm. It is always song that comes first for me. I don't really want to follow the dominant culture into twelve-tone oblivion! It is a dream of mine to come to England and hear a piece of mine in a great cathedral there.

DW: *We should talk about texts – do you spend a lot of time thinking about texts that you will set?*

AH: Well, I have always been interested in language. I love words and the thoughts that are encapsulated in those words – it is important to me. I sometimes even slice up different texts or combine them to get the effect I want.

DW: *Can you say what it is in a text that jumps out at you?*

AH: I actually teach a class on this so should be able to answer! Sometimes it is descriptive text, sometimes declamatory. I want to evoke energy. I think that is the most important element for me. Every Sunday I work on a choral piece and here on my desk at the moment is Psalm 100 – 'Make a joyful noise unto the Lord' – the level of energy is the thing, so something bright and arresting. 'Serve the Lord with gladness...' – a B statement, something quiet and reflective; 'Enter into his gates...' – more energy. I love the bright vowels in this text and as soon as I read the first line I started to have musical ideas. That is the way things tend to happen.

DW: *It is interesting hearing you talk about that Psalm because one of the things that stands out in your music is the rhythmic vitality and energy.*

AH: I would say a fluid approach to rhythm is important. You know I don't start out with a groove! There are two influences probably – one is the singing of chant when I was a boy soprano and also I think my cultural heritage which led to a lot of 'co-mingling', lots of rhythmic patterns happening simultaneously. That is probably more apparent in my orchestral pieces. When I started to conduct choral music myself, I found that my singers loved to dance with their voices, so I try to reflect that in what I do.

DW: *We have talked a little about how you absorb aspects of your cultural heritage in your music but you do engage a lot with what one might call 'Black History' and indeed more contemporary events that relate to your life in America now. I'm thinking of orchestral pieces like the* Epitaph for Martin Luther King, *your big cantata* Set Me on a Rock, *which was written in memory of the victims of the Katrina Hurricane disaster – is it right to say that you are trying to bring 'Black History' to life?*

AH: Absolutely it is. My first big choral/orchestral piece I wrote in 1985, *Done Made my Vow* is very much based on Afro-American history. It is important to me – I mean, what am I doing here? There is a whole audience out there that I think should have music that reflects their experiences and struggles.

DW: *Bringing ourselves very much up to date I think you have just finished your fourth symphony, which I believe is a big choral/orchestral requiem for George Floyd*, who was murdered by a policeman in Minneapolis in May 2020, and called* A Knee on the Neck.

AH: My friend and frequent collaborator Herbert Martin sent me a libretto within a week of that murder happening. He was so furious, as indeed I was, and so I've been working on this piece for the past few months, and channelling my fury into my music. We have been having some terrible times lately and one just wonders when will this end. I happen to think that artists can be statement makers -we are more than entertainers – and it is right to address what is going on in the world, whichever art one is making. You know composers can have feelings too!

DW: *Do you think that dealing with subject matter like that has had an effect on your career or the way people see you?*

AH: I'm not sure. As an Afro-American composer just to be seen is at least a start. Right now all of a sudden, orchestras, chamber groups and choirs are starting to lift their heads out of their cultural sand and remembering that there are Afro-American composers. This happened once before when they had a holiday to remember Martin Luther King*. I was fortunate to be coming along just at that time and I'm fortunate enough to still be alive at this time, when there is a lot of interest in what I have been doing for the past sixty years. The truth is that conductors and performers can build up whole careers and only look at the European mainstream or music that grows out of that tradition. It is just so unimaginative.

DW: *Are you a disciplined composer? Do you try and work a certain number of hours per day?*

AH: Every day, yes, I do. I'm approaching my 300th piece.

DW: *So with that in mind, it would seem that deadlines are not a problem for you.*

AH: No, I've never missed a deadline. Ever. Right now I have a piece to finish by December. This is another commemoration of another tragic event in American history, one which many have forgotten, the massacre at Tulsa, when a white mob, pretty much authorised by city officials, attacked black residents and businesses. It is the 100th anniversary of this massacre next year. I had a commission for a piece for mezzo-soprano and strings, again setting a poem by Herb Martin. I asked for some extra percussion because I wanted to raise a little hell!

DW: *Are you a self-critical composer?*

AH: Yes, my goal is to leave a body of music that is not only hopefully attractive but strong enough that people will want to perform it again.

DW: *So a legacy is important to you.*

AH: Yes, it is, very – even more so as I approach my 80th birthday. Marcus Aurelius said in his Meditations, 'Do not allow yourself to care about how you are thought about after you are gone' – he is right, but on the other hand, we spend a lot of time worshiping masters of the past. None of us are Beethoven or Mozart of course, but I wouldn't mind leaving just a few pieces that might be worthy of being tucked into the canon somehow.

DW: *You still get up in the morning and want to write. It is still something you have to do.*

AH: Yes, my mind won't wait that long! I'm always thinking about music. I just love to write, it is what makes me feel alive.

DW: *Do you revise? Perhaps you revise as you go along.*

AH: That is exactly what I do. I seldom go back and revise pieces once they are done. Having said that, there is a piece I've been working on for a decade now, a piece called *Earth Rise* – it is supposed to bring two choirs together, a white choir and a black choir, they sing separately and then join forces physically, by inter-mingling. Not ideal for present times but there it is. I wasn't happy with the ending, it was a little drawn out and lacked energy. Just this past week I came up with a solution, something that had never crossed my mind – I've just got to cut! Two of a composer's best friends are a pair of scissors and an eraser. The whole piece is about 25 minutes long but the ending can save it or kill it off, so I've made a cut.

DW: *Are you ever surprised when you hear a piece for the first time?*

AH: Yes, if I've done a lousy job of orchestrating! My first orchestral commission, *Celebration*, I wrote for the American bi-centennial. I wanted to have a lot of noise at the beginning, complete with bells and lo and behold at the first rehearsal you couldn't even hear the bells, because the orchestra was so loud. One just has to learn! But, on the whole, things generally work out and the surprises are good.

DW: *Are you ever surprised at what performers find in your music?*

AH: People tell me, after doing more than one piece, 'you have a habit of doing such and such'. I never notice these things.

DW: *So there are Hailstork fingerprints that you don't recognise yourself?*

AH: Exactly. I just don't know. I don't like the 'what is your style' question? I don't think any composers think about that.

DW: *Do you enjoy rehearsals and premieres? Do you still get nervous?*

AH: Premieres are about what 'they' will like, as in the audience. The first rehearsal is far more nerve-wracking for me, making sure that everything works the way I had imagined in my head.

DW *Do you think about the audience when you are writing?*

AH: Well lately, I've been thinking about this a lot. They have a series of concerts here in Virginia, outreach concerts for the Afro-American community. They take place in a black church, and I've been observing what they react positively to, which was never my stuff of course. I love the challenge of thinking 'I wonder if I can reach these people'. I wonder if I can write a piece that would affect them. Remember, I went to a black college and how to implement the black vernacular into what I do, we have already said, has always been interesting to me. I didn't grow up going to a black church, so this particular aspect is something I have never really investigated. I've just finished a

Piano Quintet, and I made them 'rock' a bit in the third movement and going back to the Fourth Symphony, I'm hoping that there is a melody in the last movement that this audience or type of audience can respond to. That was a long way of saying that I'm not an indifferent, abstract sort of composer and communicating is very important to me.

DW: *We have talked a little about you dealing with a good deal of tragedy in your music but do you strive for a feeling of hope too?*

AH: Yes, that happens at the end of the Fourth Symphony too. The last movement is called 'Still crossing that bridge' – I thought I was going to end the piece jubilantly but the music had other ideas, and the piece ends with a coda I called 'A time for healing' – I think what we need right now is music that brings people together. 'A time for healing' is like a prayer.

DW: *You have been teaching at Old Dominion University, in Norfolk, Virginia, for many years, so one assumes that you do believe that composition can be taught.*

AH: Elements of craft can be taught – but not talent.

DW: *Do you have any advice to a young composer?*

AH: Learn your craft and be true to yourself. Keep studying. I'm still studying – I have just been studying *Sancta Civitas* by Vaughan Williams – the score is here on my desk.

DW: *What a wonderful piece!*

AH: It is. I happen to love Vaughan Williams and I wish his music was heard much more frequently over here.

AH: *Do you write at the piano?*

AH: I try to do most of my early work away from the piano. When my wife and I go on trips, I sit in the hotel and write music and I can't wait to get back home to see what it sounds like.

DW: *Elgar quotes Ruskin at the end of* The Dream of Gerontius* *– 'This is the best of me…'. Can you say which piece or group of pieces of yours might fall into that category?*

AH: I'd say the First Piano Sonata, maybe the Second Symphony. In terms of choral pieces, *Whitman's Journey*, an hour-long piece setting practically all of Whitman's* 'Leaves of Grass', for baritone, chorus and orchestra. I was happy with that work.

DW: *We are recording this interview at a very difficult and worrying time. How have you been dealing with lockdown?*

AH: Well, I think composers are the least affected at the moment. Actually, it is the life-style I have always lived, being at home composing – really I don't have a problem with that. The world has adjusted to my life-style, although of course I recognise that this is a bad time for so many.

DW: *What would you say are your five favourite choral works?*

ADOLPHUS' FIVE FAVOURITE CHORAL WORKS

Bach *Mass in B minor*

Britten *War Requiem*

Handel *Messiah*

Holst *The Hymn of Jesus*

Vaughan Williams *Flos Campi*

Gabriel Jackson

BORN 1962

DW: *Can you tell me a little about your earliest musical memories? Your father was a clergyman at the cathedral in Bermuda?*

GJ: Yes, he was. My dad was ordained in Bermuda, so his first job was at the cathedral, in a fairly lowly capacity of course. He told me much later on that at that time, it would be the early 60s, there was still a kind of apartheid – there was a black choir and a white choir: one sang in the morning and one in the evening. Kind of shocking now, but there it is. We came back to England when I was three, so I don't have any memories associated with being there particularly.

DW: *But your father was very interested in music.*

GJ: He was actually quite a good pianist and even had aspirations to become a professional musician at one point. I remember he was good enough to play Chopin* Ballades, quite well. I also remember very serious hi-fi equipment – there was a lot of music that I heard, not so much drifting as blasting through the ceiling, when I was supposed to be asleep, but I had no idea what this music was until much later.

DW: *Did you have piano lessons?*

GJ: I did, from about the age of six I think, but I was more fascinated by the way music looked as much as the sound. I used to write down random collections of notes on paper and get my Dad to play it.

DW: *Then you got into the choir at Canterbury Cathedral at eight years old and you came under the influence of the organist and director of music Allan Wicks*, who, I have always got the impression, was perhaps the most important influence on your musical life.*

GJ: I think he was actually, but I also think anyone who was lucky enough to be taken under his wing would say the same thing. He was an extraordinary man, so charismatic and cultured, such a brilliant musician. Unlike a great many of his contemporaries working in cathedrals at that time he was very interested in the musical world outside the cathedral. I remember him telling us about the first performances of Tippett's* opera *The Knot Garden*, which he went to see; he was one of the first British organists to play Messiaen* and he gave what I think might have been the UK premiere or at least one of the earliest performances of Stravinsky's* *Canticum Sacrum* when he was at Manchester Cathedral in the '50s.

DW: *I remember you telling me years ago that you sang the Tippett* Magnificat and Nunc Dimittis *and what a deep impression that made on you.*

GJ: Yes, and that was a very rare performance, even in the early 1970s. It certainly wasn't a new piece then, but nobody really sang it as it was considered far too difficult. I thought then that it was amazing. I don't think it gets sung very much even now.

DW: *And this is where you heard a lot of early English music for the first time that has since become very important to you?*

GJ: We did a good deal of that – very little Victorian and Edwardian repertoire thankfully, which was and is the main repertoire of so many cathedrals, but more Britten*, Tippett, Lennox Berkeley*, Alan Ridout*- who had quite a close association with the choir at one point – that sort of thing.

DW: *I think you were having composition lessons from Ridout at this time.*

GJ: Yes, he was actually quite a good teacher for a kid and introduced me to all sorts of different repertoire. Then I went to the Junior Department of the Royal College of Music [RCM*]. I didn't do the whole Junior Department thing; I just studied composition with Richard Blackford*. We decided that it suited us both better for me to come into London and have lessons privately during the week, rather than make the trip on a Saturday. I used to lie about the time of my lesson so I could get out of school, get an early train and have a mooch around London, which was terribly exciting! With Ridout I was very definitely writing sub-Ridout, but Richard really got me writing properly – he was quite systematic. I remember he got me to write a piece for four percussionists that had to focus on one particular rhythm; he was rather good and I learnt a lot from him.

DW: *Then it was to the Royal College of Music as a full-time student?*

GJ: That was at Richard's urging actually. My parents and the school wanted me to go to Oxford, so they took a bit of persuading. It wasn't just a case of sending me to the RCM; Richard was very clear that I just had to study with John Lambert* who had been his teacher.

DW: *John Lambert is not particularly remembered as a composer these days, but certainly he is remembered as a teacher. He had a pretty impressive student list – Oliver Knussen*, Simon Bainbridge*, Gary Carpenter*, Jonathan Lloyd*...*

GJ: Yes, John seemed to teach everyone, later on Mark-Anthony Turnage* and Julian Anderson* too, even Barrington Pheloung* who wrote that famous music for 'Inspector

Morse' – he was the doyen of British composition teachers.

DW: *He was a pupil of Nadia Boulanger*?*

GJ: I think he saw himself as a sort of British Boulanger, which he was really. He taught an awful lot of very distinguished and successful composers. What is interesting is that there is no 'John Lambert School'- we have all gone in different directions; all of the composers we have mentioned have a very particular soundworld.

DW: *Was he an inspiring teacher?*

GJ: I think he was, but when I've thought about it, I'm not entirely sure what it was he did. He didn't teach techniques or anything like that, we basically talked – about music of course, but all kinds of things, artistic and otherwise and he was always very encouraging. I wrote a piano piece and John as usual made all these encouraging noises; then some time later we were talking and I told him that I didn't think the piece was good, that it didn't work at all and he agreed! I said to him, why on earth didn't you say something and his response was 'because I wanted you to work it out', which in itself was a very good lesson.

DW: *You were writing a very different kind of music then that doesn't have much to do with what you are writing now?*

GJ: Yes, a slightly unsatisfyingly, watered-down modernism that was around a lot at that time. I wasn't really aware of composers working outside that field. Maybe I knew a little Steve Reich*, but I didn't know about the English experimentalists like Gavin Bryars* and Howard Skempton* – that interested me later.

DW: *Can you say what prompted such a dramatic change of direction?*

GJ: It was a very definite decision that I wasn't really happy with what I was writing. After college I got a few commissions – they were not unsuccessful but I was dissatisfied somehow. Then I wrote a children's musical of all things, for my old school in Canterbury. It was quite sophisticated, aspired to be Sondheim-esque in some ways and I was struck by the reaction of the audiences who seemed genuinely moved, and not just because they were watching their offspring perform. I realised that it was possible for me to affect listeners in a different way and why couldn't I or shouldn't I do that with all of my music.

DW: *You have always been very clear about your musical enthusiasms and dislikes – certainly fifteenth and sixteenth-century English music: Tallis*, Byrd*, the Eton Choir Book* etc., but then there is a big gap until we get to probably Rachmaninov*, which we will talk about shortly. Has there always been this big hole taking in what for most is a hugely important slice of musical history?*

GJ: That certainly used to be true, but I think there is a slightly smaller gap now.

I certainly love the high baroque. One of my greatest experiences as a chorister was singing the Monteverdi* *Vespers* which again was very rarely done then. I'm sure it was very 'unauthentic' but I think that everyone who sang in that was very affected by it. I wasn't ever interested in eighteenth and nineteenth-century music really, although I find it less of a problem now.

DW: *You probably remember us doing a pre-concert talk together at the Presteigne Festival some years ago. You had to pick some favourite pieces and we had to talk about them. I think we broadly agreed on a lot of the choices you made; some proved, shall we say, a little controversial...*

GJ: Yes, we had the slow movement of Rachmaninov's Second Symphony didn't we and part of Sondheim's* *Sunday in the Park with George*?

DW: *We rattled a few cages because we said that Sondheim was the greatest living American composer.*

GJ: I'm still convinced about that – he is a great composer, even if he were only responsible for the music, let alone the words, which are remarkable enough. There is this debate that people have about composers of musicals – are they composers or songwriters? Sondheim is most certainly a composer – that incredibly sophisticated modular construction that I think started in *Sweeney Todd* where the accompaniment figure in one song becomes the foreground in another – just wonderful, so sophisticated.

DW: *We are equally enthusiastic about Rachmaninov. I imagine it was considered not at all the right thing to do at the RCM in the '70s and '80s.*

GJ: Oh yes, it was considered very odd! Ridiculous really...

DW: *What is it about his music that interests you? I know we talked about that amazing clarinet tune in the slow movement of the Second Symphony that just goes on and on...*

GJ: Well, it is that kind of thing really. There is a sort of ecstatic quality to Rachmaninov and indeed of all the music I love – an ecstatic melancholy I suppose you would call it. It is certainly in all those pieces from the Eton Choir Book, endless roulades of notes, florid and ornate, suspended in this timeless atmosphere. Stravinsky too, those amazing codas in the *Symphony of Psalms*, the apotheosis in *Apollo*, the bell sounds at the end of *Les Noces*. I don't like neurotic music – Elgar I'm sorry to say, Mahler too – I don't like neurotic art of any sort!

DW: *And that explains your love of Tippett rather than Britten.*

GJ: Oh yes, I think Tippett is the greatest British composer since Byrd. I admire and like a lot of Holst* and Vaughan Williams*, but it is always Tippett for me – again, as in a lot of Tudor music, a wonderful profusion of notes and great generosity of spirit, that ecstatic quality that sounds like no other composer.

DW: *In the '90s when you were finding your voice, this was the time when Tavener*, Pärt*, Górecki* were becoming more well known and they had an effect on you too?*

GJ: Yes, Tavener wrote a two-hour Orthodox Vigil Service and what was revelatory for me was that it showed how much you can make out of very little. That was very important to me. In the scheme of things I think Górecki might be the most remarkable composer of them all.

DW: *Aside from what one might call the 'classical' side you have often spoken of your love for R&B*.*

GJ: Yes, it is important. I don't try and imitate it in any way. I love the semi-improvised melodies that float over ostinati, the voicing of chords too in the songs that have backing singers and the voices in very close position. Yet again, a big part of black American singing is the ecstatic quality too.

DW: *Looking back can you pinpoint a piece that might be your opus 1?*

GJ: Very clearly – I wrote a piano piece for Thalia Myers* in 1987 and it had a key signature!! Then it felt like a very radical thing to do – a piece that didn't modulate in a conventional way and made up of blocks – the key-change, when it happens, is very sudden, which is something I do now...

DW: *In terms of a choral piece, perhaps O sacrum convivium?*

GJ: Yes, probably, in 1990 I think.

DW: *That piece echoes what you said about the piano piece: blocks of sound that don't develop in a conventional way, and an abrupt, startling key-change, which is certainly a Jackson finger-print?*

GJ: Yes, it has all these chords in very close position too – that probably was the beginning. I wanted to keep in touch with the liturgical world that had been so important to me as a child and as I didn't sing any more the only way to make a contribution to that culture was to write for it – although writing choral music didn't really become a big thing for me until around 2000 oddly enough.

DW: *You've said that writing music is simply 'making things'?*

GJ: I've always said that writing music is putting contrasting objects next to each other. I'm not interested in self-expression. A lot of the music I don't like is actually about the composer and I don't want to know how somebody feels! If you work with words one obviously gives some kind of expression to the words. I suppose a bit of self-expression comes from you as <u>you</u> are doing it, but for that to be your primary aim is a bit odd to me.

DW: *I know you are interested in conceptual art and powered flight in particular. Are there ways that these interests come into your music?*

GJ: Yes, but to try and translate some of these things into music is not really being inspired by them, but using them to generate material. Generating durations and structures from something else, it is that kind of response really.

DW: *Perhaps a piece like the* Airplane Cantata *has a closer relationship with the subject matter?*

GJ: Yes, that piece uses texts about early aviation. I have a pianola* accompanying the choir. The short heyday of pianola, which I think of as a machine, coincided with the first powered flights and it is good at creating 'machine like' sounds, it just seemed to be quite a nice fit. I try to have a reason for making every decision as far as things like that are concerned.

DW: *You have also written choral pieces that see the choir accompanied by a cello, a saxophone, an electric guitar...*

GJ: Yes, if you are going to do that I think you should have a reason. The piece with electric guitar, *Ave Regina Caelorum*, was commissioned by The Sixteen, the International Guitar Festival and King's Place. They wanted me to write a piece for choir and guitar, and I thought it would be necessary to amplify the guitar anyway so I might as well use an electric guitar which would open up all sorts of different colours. The piece becomes almost about that instrument rather than using it as a sort of vague accompaniment.

DW: *I've noticed that even when you use the organ in your choral pieces, it has a pretty independent role – it doesn't just support the choir.*

GJ: I was an organist and I have never understood what the point is of just doubling the choir. The organ is a fantastic instrument for exploring different colours and if you are writing a piece with limited rehearsal or even a choir that might not be very confident, you can put all the difficult stuff on the organ and make things easier for the choir. There are lots of wonderful organists around who one can use so the idea that difficult organ parts are a problem, a criticism that has been thrown at me from time to time, is absurd.

DW: *Is it too simplistic to suggest that your music is for the most part optimistic and positive? It is full of images of light, bright colours and energy…*

GJ: It is and I love creating the effects of light and texts with images of dazzling colours. I find it very difficult to set texts that are dark...

DW: *Even in the Requiem that you wrote for the Vasari Singers it isn't a bleak vision, but a much more hopeful, comforting, even optimistic one.*

GJ: Yes, but that piece didn't set out to do that actually. We decided to take out the even-numbered verses from the traditional Mass for the Dead and replace them with texts from other religions and cultures that talk about what happens after death – there is an Australian Aboriginal poem, a poem from Japan, one by a native American chief. As it turns out, all the texts have the same view of death as the Christian one, that it isn't the end, but a gateway to something else, something filled with hope. We did take out the 'Dies Irae', not because of what it said particularly, but because it was an even-numbered verse.

It all happened by chance. I have to say that when I wrote the Passion (*The Passion of our Lord Jesus Christ*) I found the crucifixion scene really very difficult to write.

DW: *Well, yes, I mean there is no getting away from the unrelenting terror and horror of that. Was that why you used that particular instrumental accompaniment that includes piccolo/alto flute, soprano/alto saxophone, bass clarinet, instruments capable of extremes of pitch and dynamic?*

GJ: Yes, originally I had the idea of trying to create an imagined idea of what music might have been like in biblical times, but then I realised if it was imagined nobody would know what it is anyway – I abandoned that. So yes, these extremes of colour and register – there is a piccolo doubling alto flute, no flute, bass clarinet, very high and raucous sax writing – I definitely wanted those raw sounds. The crucifixion was <u>so</u> hard to do. I wrote it over and over again, and it got more and more reduced and exposed, mostly one vocal line with a sparse accompaniment.

DW: *But that is why it is so effective, because perhaps musically illustrating something like that, one perhaps expects, paradoxically, to let all hell break loose – to just do the opposite is unexpected.*

GJ: I hope that is true, that it is a telling way of doing it, but on the other hand I'm not very good at letting all hell break loose anyway. I wouldn't know what to do.

DW: *Alongside the basics of the story in this piece, you include Latin hymns, Edmund Blunden* and at the end T.S. Eliot*, the last of which can't have been easy to arrange – the Eliot estate are notoriously difficult when it comes to giving permission for his texts to be set to music.*

GJ: The piece was commissioned by Merton College, who requested a Merton connection, so that resulted in me setting Blunden and Eliot, but it was always my wish to have texts that contrasted in style, period, atmosphere, which is what I like to do all the time. It was a bit of luck with Eliot. He went to Merton and I think they just found a way in, to clear the use of 'Little Gidding', otherwise that might not have happened. Even so, it wasn't easy to get permission and took over a year to finalise. I should say that it was Simon Jones at Merton who chose the texts in the first instance, although I did suggest that it might be interesting to have a Blunden war poem for 'Gethsemane'.

DW: *A lot of the composers I've talked to have said that even allowing for the problems in getting permissions from the estate, they perhaps wouldn't go down the Eliot route as he is so hard to set.*

GJ: Oddly enough I didn't find it so hard. I mean I'm not sure I understood it completely! People apparently laughed at Britten when he said that he didn't understand 'The Death of St Narcissus' when he set that, but I think you can respond to the images of the language without fully understanding it. Eliot is full of the most fantastic images and words that sound wonderful...

DW: *The end of the poem is actually a perfect fit for the end of the Passion isn't it?*

GJ: It is and I did want something to happen after the Crucifixion that wasn't the Resurrection – so 'Little Gidding' talks about circularity, endings and beginnings, and about events in the Passion of Christ being in the eternal present, not as historical events. It seems to me to be a perfect way to bring the piece to a conclusion.

DW: *We should mention the composer that you always say is your favourite composer, Thomas Tallis, because this leads us onto another important piece of yours,* Sanctum est verum lumen, *which was a direct homage to Tallis wasn't it?*

GJ: Yes, it was written for the Tallis anniversary in 2005, the quincentenary.

DW: *Without getting too controversial, as I know these things can provoke a lot of angst-ridden debate amongst experts in that area, your piece is in the same key as most people think* Spem in alium* *should be performed in now and has the same number of bars?*

GJ: That's right – very diplomatic! It is in the same key and it does have the same number of bars, but believe it or not that was a complete accident, it wasn't planned at all. Everything I did can be found in the Tallis because everything you need to know about writing in 40 parts can be found in that piece. I don't think anyone can really write 40-part polyphony – I mean Tallis didn't – you just use different combinations of choirs and voice parts. There has to be a reason for it being in 40 parts, you have to invent things that need forty voices, it isn't any good just writing for SATB otherwise there isn't any point. A lot of it is to do with antiphonal effects, choirs overlapping – like the Tallis my piece moves across the choirs and has a big silence. I have a *heterophonic** 'ad lib' section too, which is just an extension of the canonic effects in *Spem* – it is just a canon that isn't synchronised.

DW: *You use those 'ad lib' sections in quite a lot of other pieces, sections that I should say are carefully notated in terms of notes, but just uncoordinated in terms of rhythm?*

GJ: It is quite a good way to create different kinds of textures. If I wrote that conventionally it would be <u>so</u> complicated, it would be impossible.

DW: *But this creates its own problem doesn't it, because choirs are used to having people like me telling them to keep together?*

GJ: Well, yes – they have to get used to it. I tell a choir in rehearsal if you think about it too much it sounds like a mistake – it sounds as if it should be together but isn't – just be a little more confident.

DW: *You have had close relationships with many choirs – the BBC Singers, The Crossing, Merton College, Vasari Singers, Polyphony, cathedral choirs, some wonderful choirs in Latvia and further afield – when you are writing a piece do you have the sound of a particular choir in mind?*

GJ: I do if I know the choir certainly. I also like to imagine them in the venue, if I know the building, which I do quite often. Even if you don't know the choir it is good to know as much as one can about them or the acoustic they will sing in, their strengths and weaknesses, female or male altos, or a mixture, the different sounds that boy and female sopranos make, all kinds of things.

DW: *And you can focus in a particular choir's strengths or avoid what you might perceive as any weaknesses – the Choral Symphony you wrote for the BBC Singers for instance is an extreme example of laying down a challenge to a virtuoso chamber choir.*

GJ: Yes, that piece is an attempt to write a piece that was difficult even for the BBC Singers! I remember one of the Singers tweeting before a performance: 'we are just about to sing Gabriel Jackson's *Choral Symphony*, a terrifying and exhilarating prospect', which is kind of what I wanted. Because the Singers have the skills they have there is something very exciting for the audience to hear a choir mastering huge difficulties – people enjoy virtuoso piano music for the same reason!

DW: *Choral Symphony is an extreme of course, but a lot of your music sounds and looks more difficult than it actually is.*

GJ: I think it does, some pages can look as if there are an awful lot of notes! What I try to do is to have perhaps difficulties of one sort at a time, so if the rhythms are hard I make the pitches more straightforward or vice-versa. But I think if you sit and think about things for a little, most of my pieces in reality aren't so hard. I remember somebody in one of the cathedral choirs once said to me at an early rehearsal, 'have you ever heard of rests?' Then afterwards, when we talked, he had decided that the piece wasn't so difficult after all.

DW: *Are you a disciplined composer? Do you write set hours every day?*

GJ: I'm really, really bad at that. I'm quite lazy by nature. I can and do work very hard, but...

DW: *Is it starting a piece that is the problem?*

GJ: Yes. Once things are moving it becomes easier and I'm quite happy working very late, three o'clock in the morning or something; I do that quite a lot.

DW: *Are you self-critical?*

GJ: [Long pause] I certainly try to do my best and don't think any old thing will do but I also try not to put too much pressure on myself. I always think because of the way I write, working in these blocks of material, I can take things out and replace those sections with something better later on.

DW: *You don't revise at all?*

GJ: No. It depends on the piece – sometimes I can hear something and think I wish I had done that differently but then again I can hear something and think, actually, that's quite good. Not unusual for a composer I'm sure. I mean I don't want to be like Boulez* and endlessly revising all of my life.

DW: *Are you taken by surprise at a premiere?*

GJ: Not really – the surprise usually happens at a distance, some years later, which is rather nice.

DW: *Do performers find things in the pieces that you didn't know were there?*

GJ: Sometimes. A lot of time it depends on the performance really. There have been occasions when a really good performance has shown me that a piece might be better than I thought.

DW: *I think it is probably true to say that your music can't really survive a bad performance. It isn't that the pieces are too difficult but just if they are not done well it sounds as if they are not done well, if that makes any sense.*

GJ: I think that might be right. Of course, it might be my fault if a piece doesn't work but not always! No names but…

DW: *That's a disappointment!*

GJ: Seriously though, on the whole, I've been very lucky and I've heard really very few bad performances.

DW: *You haven't been tempted to conduct yourself?*

GJ: Er, no! I mean I can't conduct, I just can't! I'm not sure that a lot of composers make the best conductors on the whole and I don't want to be another one of those. Of course there are exceptions, not least Pierre Boulez and Olly Knussen* of course; in the choral world, John Rutter* and Bob Chilcott* for instance, James MacMillan* too, but it isn't for me. I'll stick to composing.

DW: *Do you think about the audience when you are writing?*

GJ: I can't deny that I do occasionally think, oh, they are going to like this! I don't in general, you can't. I was asked a lot when I was writing the Passion, was it difficult when you thought about the Passions of the past, most obviously Bach – well, if we thought about that nobody would write anything, a string quartet, or a symphony or anything else. You can't please everyone and there is no point in worrying about it.

DW: *You have never had an official teaching position but you have been involved in a lot of composer workshops and masterclasses with choirs like the BBC Singers and The Crossing - what do you find are the biggest problems for young composers when it comes to writing choral music?*

GJ: I still think the biggest mistake is writing for voices as if they were instruments, particularly when it comes to pitch, composers not really thinking about how singers find the pitches in the first place. Singing is more difficult than playing an instrument anyway because you have words to think about too. Extremes of the vocal compass can be a problem – a composer might have read in a book about how high a soprano can get and how low a bass can get and, taking that as gospel, they spend pages hovering around those registers. People wouldn't write at the very top of the range of the clarinet for pages on end, so why write it for singers?

DW: *So with that in mind can you distil into a couple of sentences what your advice to a young composer who wants to write choral music might be?*

GJ: Move around the voice, don't have people in the same place all the time. Sing every line – if you can't sing it don't ask the choir to sing it! That goes for rhythm too. You don't have to make a nice sound but if you can't be accurate don't write it. I've had occasions when I've asked a composer to demonstrate what they want and when they do that it has nothing to do with what they have written – then I ask them, what do you want, what you have just sung or what you have written?

DW: *Is there anything that you are burning to write?*

GJ: Yes, I'd love to write an opera, not on a large scale, but a chamber opera. I've never wanted to write big pieces for symphony orchestra particularly. I love the sound of the symphony orchestra but think they are perhaps not for me. I would quite like to write an Orthodox Vespers, not using traditional chants like Rachmaninov did, but just using that form.

DW: *Elgar quotes Ruskin at the end of* The Dream of Gerontius* – 'This is the best of me…'. Can you say which piece or group of pieces of yours might fall into that category?*

GJ: [Long pause] I'm pleased with the *Airplane Cantata* and perhaps *Sanctum est verum lumen*, the 40-part piece.

DW: *We are recording this at a very difficult and worrying time. How have you been dealing with lockdown?*

GJ: I found it very, very difficult to concentrate at the start of lockdown. In the months prior to that I was finishing my big piece for the Three Choirs Festival, which as it turned out of course was postponed until next year. I suppose eventually I got into other things, a new piece for choir and small orchestra. More than anything it is the weird uncertainty of how things are going to go forward too.

DW: *What would you say are your five favourite choral works?*

GABRIEL'S FIVE FAVOURITE CHORAL WORKS

Górecki *Beatus Vir*

Howells *Hymnus Paradisi*

Stravinsky *Symphony of Psalms*

Tallis *Gaude gloriosa Dei mater*

Tippett *Canticles (St John's Service)*

Sir Karl Jenkins

BORN 1944

DW: *Can you tell me about your earliest musical memories? Your father was a musician I think and a great influence on you.*

KJ: He was, yes. My father had a day job as a teacher in a secondary-modern school; he was the Deputy Head and taught music and art, which was a creative combination. At weekends he was the organist and choirmaster at the Methodist Chapel in Plenclawdd, a small Welsh village on the Gower peninsular which is where I grew up. I was born towards the end of the war in 1944 and it was a little time afterwards that my father started to build up a collection of 78rpm records, about 20minutes per side, so you could fit on a short classical symphony, but for Bruckner you would need a whole collection of records! He taught me piano, which I didn't really take to but was useful later on of course, and music theory which I later did as part of my Boy Scout exam! – 'musical proficiency' I think it was called. Music was always in the house and then we had a very good music teacher at junior school. We were taught *sol-fa/solfege**, which was popular in Wales at the time as many choirs used it to sing even big pieces. My father transcribed the whole of the Fauré* *Requiem* into sol-fa, which was quite something. There were three chapels in our small village and they each used to put on oratorio concerts – *Messiah**, *Elijah**, that kind of thing.

DW: *To me the sound of a Welsh chapel choir or indeed any Welsh choir is a little less polite than a lot of English choirs, quite raw in some ways, and I wondered if that had been an influence on you?*

KJ: Yes, it can be quite raw and tribal in some ways and I would say it has had an effect on what I write – certainly that kind of singing comes into *Adiemus* for example. I didn't sing very much myself as a boy. I did learn the recorder in junior school, and then took up the oboe at the local grammar school which had a fantastic music department. That was sort of a predetermined decision as the fingering for the two instruments is similar. I was certainly in school orchestras but don't remember doing so much singing.

DW: *I know you have written pieces that refer specifically to your Welsh background –* Dewi Sant *for instance, or the piece you wrote in memory of the victims of the Aberfan disaster,* Cantata Memoria – For the Children *but do you feel yourself to be a Welsh composer?*

KJ: No, not really. It sounds rather pompous but I feel myself to be a global composer. It sounds very grand and extravagant, but I do use a lot of devices, instrumentation and rhythms derived from other cultures…

DW: *No, it doesn't sound pompous – some composers are very clear: they do regard themselves as English composers, or American, or whatever, but I just wondered what you thought.*

KJ: No, I don't feel particularly Welsh as far as my music is concerned. My upbringing reads like an opera plot – one of my grandmothers was a cockle picker and seller and she met a Swedish sailor off a ship. They eventually married and she tragically drowned some years later out in the estuary with other cockle pickers. I'm not a Welsh speaker - I can read it and I've set it a good deal, but only in the sense that I did Latin O level* too - that doesn't make you any kind of scholar.

DW: *Was it always assumed that you would become a musician? You went to Cardiff University to begin with.*

KJ: I always thought I would be a musician of some kind, although at the same time it was never pre-planned and I wasn't sure what I would do exactly. I often call myself a musical tourist – my life has been a series of happy accidents that happened along the way. I suppose the big turn around came in my early teens when I heard jazz for the first time and fell in love with that. Jazz was rhythmically exciting, had lots of flair, was tonal, and I didn't really feel the same way about what you would call contemporary 'serious' music.

DW: *When you were a student in the sixties, you were expected to write in a particular way and possibly considered a bit inferior if you didn't.*

KJ: Yes, that was true and is still the case a lot of the time! I had this duality. Before I got to university I had played the oboe in the National Youth Orchestra of Wales, which was the first such orchestra to be formed anywhere in the world back in 1945 – it was a great thing. Then at university we did a very academic music course: harmony, analysis, fugue, form, counterpoint, history. I think the course content came from Tovey* in Scotland originally, and I played jazz on the side. The composer Alun Hoddinott* was Head of Department at Cardiff University. He was a huge figure in Welsh music at the time and he oddly enough went to the same grammar school that I did and had the same teacher.

DW: *The point is that, listening to the music you write now, it all becomes clear what a diverse musical education you have had. The serious academic side, the church, jazz, it all gets mixed together...*

KJ: It does. The church side is kind of interesting – it was very much part of that Welsh non-conformist tradition. I've never had anything to do with the English church tradition, which is completely different. So many singers and composers came through that.

DW: *You then went to the Royal Academy of Music [RAM*] in London – was that as an oboist or composer?*

KJ: I never really studied composition as such with anyone. The RAM was a post-graduate year; Leonard Brain*, who was the brother of the famous horn player Dennis Brain, taught me the oboe. I think it was my last year at Cardiff and my first at the Academy, so 1966, there was a Jazz Summer School in South Wales. This was a very new idea then and a number of musicians would come from London to teach and play. I went along and there was a bandleader called Raymond Collier who asked me to come and see him when I came to London, so I did. I remember shortly after that the Aberfan disaster happened – I never would have thought that fifty years later I would write a piece about that – anyway, I was out into the world and doing lots of different things.

DW: *So you were basically a jobbing musician, an oboist. Were you writing at all in these years?*

KJ: The only what I would term 'classical piece' from that time was the piece I wrote for my BMus Finals at Cardiff University, a set of *Three Psalms* for chorus and orchestra, which I can't remember. I suppose there is a copy in the university library along with everyone else's graduation pieces, but I wouldn't advise anyone to take a look. Jazz composition followed alongside the playing and that is really what I did for the next twenty or thirty years. It was a learning experience. I took in a lot of different compositional styles, influences, got to know a lot of world music and it wasn't until I was about 50 that I started to do what I'm doing now.

DW: *When you were in the bands 'Nucleus'* and 'Soft Machine'*, I'm assuming it was a classic band existence – travelling, recording and performing and being on the road for most of the year?*

KJ: Yes, it was. We went to America, around the UK and Europe, and that was my life until the demise of 'Soft Machine' in the late 1970s I suppose. A lot of travelling, setting up, performing and taking down again!

DW: *And then you went in a different direction and set up a music production company and started to write music for advertising.*

KJ: It was pretty much a case of 'needs must' really. The band had finished and I knew that I didn't want to go on the road again, so together with Mike Ratledge we formed a company to deal with music production, arranging, anything that came along. Mike was very clever and knew a huge amount about computers and the like before most people did. He built a sequencer and goodness knows what else. We had different skills to bring to the table. Writing music for advertising sounds like the lowest possible thing to do, but at that time Alan Parker, Ridley Scott, Tony Scott, who became celebrated film-directors, were doing commercials and production values were high and the scores we did were very filmic. It was a very good discipline. One had to be precise, pithy and get the music out quickly and of course we had none of the technology people have now. The downside was that there was always somebody telling you what you had to do. There was always a boss – a director, a producer, someone from the ad agency, whatever, and I didn't like that very much; it became rather suffocating. I did however learn a great deal – apart from the quality of the work, I was able to discover and use a lot of indigenous music, music from the Middle East, Japan, South America, which stayed with me when I went into the world I work in now. I looked at all sorts of exotic percussion instruments, different kinds of drums, tambourines, different kinds of woodwind instruments, all kinds of things.

DW: *All this ultimately led to* Adiemus *in 1995.*

KJ: It did – that was where I was heading. There was always a huge problem in the UK as to what *Adiemus* was or is – is it an oratorio, a cantata, some kind of tone-poem? -but it never bothered me as I've always resisted barriers and categories. Perhaps it should have bothered me, I don't know – I did what I did. The title is a little confusing anyway. The piece is based on an invented language – I hesitate to call it that really; it is just a series of phonetic sounds – a bit like a scat singer, but much more controlled and organised. At the time I didn't know there was a Latin word 'adeamus', which means we will draw near or let us approach. The record company were not so sure about the title for a while and asked me to read the lyrics I used for the piece, but that didn't help very much as the text didn't mean anything. But then they decided they liked the word 'Adiemus' and the whole thing became a concept, it become the band, the singers, a series of pieces, a brand name I suppose.

DW: *Do you think that* Adiemus *allowed you to find your own voice, it was maybe an opus 1?*

KJ: Yes, as I explained earlier, I am a musical tourist and I think this was when I arrived, found that this is what I could do and that it was different to anyone else, up to a point, and that it had integrity which was important to me. It was important for me that the piece had integrity – the problem with that horrible word 'crossover' is that it often just throws disparate elements together – it's a lazy description actually, and I didn't want to do that. I never use the word crossover.

DW: *The interesting thing about the vocal writing in* Adiemus *is that you treat the voices very much like instruments. As you have said, there isn't a text – if there had been do you think this would have got in the way? You are more concerned with rhythmic and coloristic effects really.*

KJ: The initial reason I wrote like that was because I was under pressure to finish the piece. Part of it was originally a demonstration tape for an advert Delta Airlines wanted to air. Then the more I thought about it the more the idea appealed because it took away the need for the text to convey any particular ideas. That is how it all started and it developed into something of its own and has stood the test of time. It was written twenty-five years ago now which is a little frightening!

DW: The Armed Man *would seem to be a natural successor – perhaps a rather more conventional piece in that it is essentially a Mass.*

KJ: It is a Mass really. I was considering what to do next. There had been a few follow-up songs or sections to *Adiemus* and it had become pretty popular, but this would be in 1998/early '99 – the Music Charitable Trust and the Royal Armouries approached me about writing a Mass for Peace. Guy Wilson, who is a military historian and at the time was Master of the Armouries, which is the UK's national museum for arms and armour, put together a text for me, so I didn't have to start to do that. He presented it in general terms and there was a lot more than I eventually used in the piece. The texts included poetry by Swift*, Tennyson*, Dryden*, Kipling*, also a section of the Indian epic the Mahabharata*, and a poem by Sankichi Toge*, a Japanese poet who survived the bombing of Hiroshima, although he died from leukaemia some years later. I also quote a medieval folksong *L'homme armé* in the first and last movements, which itself was used for a lot of mass settings in the Renaissance, by composers such as Josquin* and Palestrina*.

DW: *So all these texts are combined with the Latin Mass, in the manner of the Britten* War Requiem* *really, although he just used one poet, Wilfred Owen*, of course. Is* The Armed Man *an anti-war piece in the same way? Several of your pieces might be seen as pleas for peace?*

KJ: Yes, it is really an anti-war piece I think. I'm not a pacifist as such myself – you know defending the civilised world from Hitler was necessary of course despite the terrible cost and outcome – but senseless wars, that is a different matter. When I was writing the piece the daily newscasts were full of the Balkan crisis, which was an appalling tragedy and really an avoidable crisis and so *The Armed Man* is dedicated to the memory of the victims of the Kosovo crisis. Subsequently I went to Kosovo and did a performance of the piece which was a very special thing to do.

DW: *It is kind of incredible that* The Armed Man *has been performed in many parts of the world, something like three thousand times?*

KJ: Yes! I'm told it has been in the UK charts for seventeen years. It was meant to be for people of faith and no faith. There have been a few problems with the Muslim Call to Prayer, which is also part of the text…

DW: *There are places that it can't be done or do people try and replace it with something else?*

KJ: It causes problems now and again. There are probably places that one would expect a problem, the Bible Belt of the USA for instance one would not be surprised about, but there was a problem in Holland of all places, which was surprising. This was after the assassination of the Dutch film director Theo Van Gogh*. He had just completed a controversial film and he was murdered by someone who objected to the film's message. Most bizarrely, it was going to be done in the Dom in Berlin, the choir started to rehearse it and then the church authorities learnt about the Muslim Call to Prayer and asked if the piece could be done without it and the answer is always no! That apart, I get a lot of letters and emails from people that have been affected by the piece in some particular way which is always gratifying.

DW: *You said that the texts for* The Armed Man *were selected for you, but since then you have selected your own.*

KJ: Yes, I've done most of that myself after *The Armed Man*. I started doing a sequence of sacred choral pieces, a *Requiem*, *Stabat Mater*, *Te Deum*, but adding texts from other sources dealing with the same subject matter. So in the *Requiem*, alongside the Mass for the Dead I brought in some haiku poetry dealing with perceptions of what happens after death. The *Stabat Mater* has texts in Hebrew, Greek, Latin as well as English. I include a text by my wife Carol Barratt* (who is also a composer), two poems by the Persian philosopher Rumi* and part of the Epic of Gilgamesh*, so alongside the story of Mary grieving at the cross, there are other expressions of grief from other cultures.

DW: *And similarly you use instruments from these different cultures in the orchestra too.*

KJ: Yes, percussion instruments from the Middle East and an Armenian duduk, which is a sort of ancient wooden double-reed instrument in the *Stabat Mater* for instance. In an ideal situation one would want these instruments, but of course it isn't always possible and so I offer alternative parts for more conventional Western instruments too.

DW: *You are particularly known for music for voices – is this an accident or is it really your favourite thing to do?*

KJ: It is my favourite thing to do. I feel that my choral music has a certain gravitas on its own terms. When I'm writing orchestral pieces, I find that I am more consciously searching for a voice perhaps. My orchestral music, particularly the concertos are more quirky I think. Actually a concertante piece I wrote for the LSO for their 125th anniversary is called *Quirk*, for flute, piano, percussion and orchestra. That was quite a gratifying commission because the soloists from within the orchestra chose their own composers and they chose me! I've written a concerto for David Childs, the euphonium player, there is a Harp Concerto for Catrin Finch and an Organ Concerto for Jonathan Scott and the Hull City Hall organ. I've just written a concerto for the saxophonist Jess Gilliam, which was supposed to be premiered recently but COVID put a stop to that unfortunately. With no texts these pieces start off very differently of course. The slow movements are relatively straightforward, songlike, meditative, but the outer movements I try to make a little bit 'oddball' in some way.

DW: *Can we talk a little about how a choral piece starts? You find the text and then what happens? Do you sit and improvise at the piano to find an atmosphere?*

KJ: I do sit down at the piano and find ideas – some I keep, some I get rid of, simple as that. If it is a multiple-movement piece like *The Armed Man* or the *Requiem* I don't necessarily start at the beginning. I go through the text and see what jumps out to me. I only work on one piece at a time and I write straight onto the computer. I was already 50 before I became computer literate and learnt the Sibelius system. I've always been a bit behind the times with that sort of thing I'm afraid. Now it seems I have to update my system but thankfully my son is a media composer and he helps me out.

DW: *I think I read somewhere that you don't believe in inspiration.*

KJ: No, I don't. You know, I got asked not so long ago what I did for a living. I said I was a composer and they said, 'how wonderful, you can't get depressed'! I do actually, like everyone else, whatever their field of work – there are good days and bad days. I tend to think of composing as intuition – whereabouts I go with a piece is due to craft that one develops over time, a long time in my case. I always tell people about some of the greats, the 'jobbing' composers: Bach* who wrote a cantata for every Sunday, Mozart* and Haydn* writing because they were asked or in some cases ordered to. Since my advertising days I have no fear of deadlines and I have never missed one. It's like turning up to do a job – you can't sit around all day waiting for inspiration to drop down. The old golfing adage says 'the more I practise the better it gets', at least that is the theory. I just try and write something every day.

DW: *It seems from talking to you that the most important thing for you is to communicate. Do you think about the audience when you are writing?*

KJ: Absolutely, communication is the key, but I don't necessarily think about the audience when I'm working. I write for myself and hope that people like it. I never second-guess or knowingly dumb down, but if I didn't communicate I wouldn't compose. I read of composers who have shelves full of symphonies that have never been played and I just couldn't do that.

DW: *Are you self-critical? You don't think it gets easier.*

KJ: I am very self-critical. I think the craft part, orchestration, that kind of thing, gets more straightforward as time goes on. I can only be my own best critic. I don't think anyone can tell that something is going to be successful – they may say they can, but I don't believe them.

DW: *So does the success of* The Armed Man *for example still surprise you?*

KJ: It does, very much. I sometimes feel that some of my most popular works might not be my best but I didn't expect the reaction *The Armed Man* got.

DW: *Are you ever surprised when you hear a piece for the first time?*

KJ: No. More often than not I'm conducting the premiere or often the recording comes first now, which is a very fortunate situation. I have conducted the premieres of most of the choral works – actually thinking about it, a good number of the orchestral works too, although Sir Colin Davis conducted the premiere of *Quirk* with the LSO. Oddly enough I didn't conduct the premiere of *The Armed Man*. Grant Llewellyn did that at the Royal Albert Hall, but I've done it a lot since then.

DW: *As far as conducting your own music is concerned, do you find you have to stand aside from it in any way?*

KJ: I think what I do as a conductor is fairly second nature now. I'm always careful about tempi and even now have a metronome of some kind with me at rehearsal. Some of the individual movements of pieces have tricky rhythms and so I like to give a couple of beats in so that it stabilises immediately and doesn't float around too much. Again, I just do the best job I can.

DW: *Are you surprised with what performers bring? Do they ever find something that you didn't know was there?*

KJ: Not really, performances can be bad or amazing! I think I'm pretty laid back as a conductor so orchestras are relaxed. Choirs vary of course – some are terrific, some [long pause]…

DW: *A little rough around the edges?*

KJ: Yes, that's it – very diplomatic. It isn't so much a case of performers finding things but I can be taken aback with how good some groups are. I did a concert with the State Orchestra and Choir of Armenia recently and I don't know what I was expecting but they were stunning. I think the most important things for me are energy, spirit and some kind of emotional connection with the music, whoever is singing or playing.

DW: *Do you ever revise?*

KJ: No, I tend not to. There are bits of *The Armed Man* I have thought about looking at, not so much the music, but some details of orchestration that I think could be better. It could be notated better perhaps, but there it is.

DW: *Is there anything you would really love to write?*

KJ: I've thought about an opera for some time, but it might be too late now. If someone had come and asked me for that it would have been a great thing to do. I mean it would take me at least two years to write, there is nothing wrong with that, but time is getting on! I'm not sure there is anything else in particular. I've been fortunate to have some amazing singers perform my music – you know, Kiri TeKanawa, Bryn Terfel – no composer would be unhappy about that.

DW: *Do you think composition can be taught? What would be your advice to a young composer?*

KJ: I think that a trained musician with good academic knowledge can learn to construct an architecturally sound piece in any genre. Take serialism for example: tone row, inversion, retrograde, retrograde inversion can be as tightly woven as a snug woollen glove. However, to my mind, memorability and thus longevity is more elusive and unusual. One so-called critic said that as a composer I was 'emotionally manipulative', but what a great compliment to pay a composer! Much like the best of the jazz improvisers, I think when it boils down to it, such ability to communicate is intuitive. As to advice – write what you want to write and not what anyone tells you to write, whoever they are. We all use the same twelve notes in the west and there is great beauty in the blues, as well as in a Mahler* Symphony.

DW: *Elgar quotes Ruskin at the end of* The Dream of Gerontius* – 'This is the best of me...'. Do you have any thoughts about that with regard to your own music?*

KJ: [Long pause] No! I couldn't be sure how to quantify – as I said before, I think the successful pieces are perhaps not the best of me. Maybe if pushed I'd say the *Stabat Mater* but then I sometimes think the newest piece is the best. Last year I wrote a *Miserere* for Polyphony and the Britten Sinfonia. Stephen Layton* was conducting and it sounded amazing. I was rather proud of that. Polyphony are an incredible choir.

DW: *We are recording this at a very worrying and difficult time – how have you been dealing with lockdown?*

KJ: Yes, I find the whole experience very unsettling. We have a busy family life and I've been here in London most of the time. I've finished a piece; I've had a UK tour postponed three times up to now, just in the past few months. A big worry of course is getting an audience in with social distancing. People are going to feel vulnerable for some time I think. It is odd, maybe I'm being naive, but I wouldn't have thought that music would be so badly hit in a situation like this and of course if we leave this to politicians...

DW: *What would you say are your five favourite choral works?*

SIR KARL'S FIVE FAVOURITE CHORAL WORKS

Bach *Mass in B minor*

Fauré *Requiem*

Mozart *Requiem*

Palestrina *Missa Papae Marcelli*

Stravinsky *Symphony of Psalms*

Libby Larsen

BORN 1950

DW: *Can you tell me something about your earliest musical memories? Was it a musical household as a child?*

LL: Yes it was, in a very US Midwestern way.

DW: *This was in Wilmington, Delaware?*

LL: Yes – no professional musicians, but just a family that loved music. We had a piano in our home and we were all required to take piano lessons from the age of seven. I wanted to start at three, but this was the way things worked and I had to wait until I was seven. We had a stack of records on the record player, this would be in the late 1950s, and any one of us could add anything we liked to that stack. My home life became a mixture of piano lessons and records. My mother loved Broadway and straight boogie, my father loved Dixieland Jazz and my sisters were into the pop music of the time. I really loved early Russian piano music that I was learning at the time. The common factor was Burl Ives* - he was a popular actor and folk singer of the '50s and '60s and every Saturday morning we would have family breakfast and sing-a-long to Burl Ives, so I guess we had all kinds of music in the house. I went with my sisters to a Catholic school in Minnesota - this was before the Second Vatican Council* of course – and the music in school was a discipline of learning. Every child in First Grade learnt how to read and write music, so by the time we got a little way up the school we were ready to sing Gregorian chant*.

DW: *It is evident listening to your music that all these diverse and seemingly unconnected facets of music have remained with you. It is possible to deduce that from looking at some of your titles* – Blue Fiddler, *the Piano Concerto* Since Armstrong, Barn Dances, Licorice Stick, *etc...*

LL: Definitely. It was a healthy mix of music in our household and by the time I got to high school I was writing pieces down that I heard in my head that reflected it. This mixture of styles and influences is a conscious decision on my part, to try and invigorate the eclectic culture I live in through the music I compose.

DW: *Can you remember anything about the pieces you were writing when you were at high school – piano pieces and songs I assume?*

LL: Primarily, but I was singing in a rock band and singing close harmony so I was writing for those groups too. When I was at school we had a rather restrictive policy - girls couldn't cross over to the boys' side, that kind of thing – and so I became good at inventing 'performance art pieces' that involved a certain amount of interaction! All the music I was creating then and now, the key ingredients were and are energy and action.

DW: *Your music is always rhythmically alive, even in slower tempi...*

LL: I particularly love what Mozart* does in his Adagios. You look at the page and there are so many notes, but when you play it there is such a wonderful sense of natural flow that makes the rhythm essential to the way the melody works. I can't think of music without thinking about the rhythmic profile. As a kid I couldn't sit still and I still can't!

DW: *Was it always assumed that you would become a musician? You went to the University of Minnesota.*

LL: I did; my two older sisters did too: it was prescribed by my parents. When I went to the university I had no real intention of becoming a musician. I knew that I loved math and music equally and I came to think that I might either be a Theoretical Economist or a Coloratura Soprano! Nobody ever pointed out to me that the music I was writing was an art that could be developed, or a craft that could be worked on. I loved music theory in particular, looking at construction and architecture, but didn't really think that I could compose as a lifetime activity or career.

DW: *Once you were set on the musical road, your main teacher was Dominick Argento*, an important composer of opera in the US.*

LL: Yes, also Paul Fetler*, who was a Hindemith* pupil. They were very different. Fetler was interested in clean lines, principles of unity and variety, and musical architecture. Argento was a literary man and much more theatrical and conceptual, so the balance was perfect. He was very active and prolific when I was in college and those were the glory days for Minnesota Opera and the Guthrie Theatre – sitting in on rehearsals and performances was a wonderful apprenticeship.

DW: *We tend not to hear very much of Argento's music here in Europe, but the operas in particular were very successful at one time in the US and they have great flair and a true sense of theatre. He really knew how to write for the voice.*

LL: He certainly did and I think their success was a result of great collaboration between artists here in the Twin Cities*, it really was a school of life. To be around a piece like Argento's opera *Postcard to Morocco* when it was being put together and rehearsed was extraordinary and I learnt a lot.

DW: *Both Argento and Fetler, it is reasonable to say, were from a fairly traditional European background that transferred to America. You couldn't call them innovators in the way that Ives*, Cage* or Reich* are or were. Did you feel that you were always part of this American/ European tradition?*

LL: It is true that Argento and the composers involved with the opera and many of the choirs at that time here in Minnesota were primarily interested in extending the European model. There were a couple of more radical composers, Conrad Sousa* for instance, but I thought at the time that it makes good sense to tell a story in music in a less expressionistic, what I suppose one would call traditional way. I wanted to communicate what it is like to be alive now, in a language that can be absorbed and doesn't really have a frame around it. On the other hand I can tell you that when I studied Argento's music in detail I was always a little disappointed that he insisted on a lot of conventional structures, you know, a traditional quartet finale in the operas for instance. I wondered if the distance of opera was valuable, a form that is not so natural to the culture. I could say the same about *fugue** for instance – we didn't invent that; when composers step into a fugue, that again is creating a distance somehow. I have always wondered what kind of rhythms are innate to the spoken language too. In all of my choral and vocal music I really love to set 'American English' texts – it yields an entirely different kind of rhythm to 'British English'. I worry very much about forcing a rhythmic language on a text that is rather alien to it.

DW: *My next point was really that – I think your music sounds as if it could not have been written in any other country. That is probably due in some way to the texts that you choose to set. I know you have chosen texts by Dylan Thomas* and George Herbert* too, but when you work with Walt Whitman*, Emily Dickinson*, Willa Cather*, Elizabeth Bishop*, or whoever, you feel that you can't help but sound American.*

LL: No, you can't and without quoting a single folk tune!

DW: *You also relate to major American historical and cultural figures. There is a big choral piece about Eleanor Roosevelt* for example, or the choral cycle* Seven Ghosts *that celebrates Charles Lindbergh*, George Washington*, Harriet Beecher Stowe*, Louis Armstrong*, amongst others. This culture and heritage is a big inspiration for you.*

LL: It is. I'm not trying to honour it as such – you can't honour a culture like mine that is in flux all the time – I'm trying to speak through it.

DW: *I get the impression that it was relatively easy for you to find your own voice; it was clear early on which direction you would go.*

LL: It was really, quite early on. I felt the pressure to write a different music when I was thinking of going on to Graduate School. Argento, Fetler, and another composer/tutor at Minnesota University, Eric Stokes*, were all writing music they wanted to write. Out here in Minnesota, away from the East and West coast, this was OK...

DW: *If you had gone on to study in New York or San Francisco, for example, things might have worked out differently?*

LL: Without a doubt. The peer pressure would have been intense. I also thought, look, I'm not going to get in anywhere. In the early '70s there were still questions about what school a woman could go to – certainly not Yale, not Harvard, not Brandeis – it just wasn't happening. Also, the intense pressure to write in a particular way and suffer judgment if you didn't. I thought that I knew what I wanted to say, I wanted to say it here in the mid-west in the first instance and be involved in the full process, be with the music, and the performers, and the audiences.

DW: *It was that that lead you to set up the Minnesota Composers Forum* in Saint Paul, Minnesota, with the late Stephen Paulus*, that still runs today.*

LL: That was it in a nutshell! There were a group of about twelve of us at the beginning. We bound together in a very special way and built on each other's energy, working with local musicians, and found ways of creating performance opportunities outside the usual academic setting. We were and are concerned about giving support to all kinds of composers, irrespective of their age, gender, ability, backgrounds or anything else.

DW: *Is there a piece that you feel might be your opus 1?*

LL: Not really, it wasn't something I thought about particularly. It sounds wishy-washy but it just happened. I was with people that wanted to perform the pieces, so it wasn't predetermined at all. It was a much more collaborative atmosphere that depended on the energy of the performers as much as anything else.

DW: *You have written a lot of music, but there is a noted bias towards the voice, in opera, choral music, art song and song-cycles.*

LL: Yes, for me it is the original instrument. All voices are different, every one breathes differently, speaks differently; the variety is endless and I never find it less than inspiring.

DW: *You have said how important it is for you to communicate. There is a noticeable habit that you have of engaging with important topics. Not in a political way particularly, but to take two examples,* Mass of Earth *deals with environmental-related issues, probably some time before it became fashionable, and then the Second Symphony, a choral symphony,* Coming forth into Day, *which I think is basically a Symphony for Peace?*

LL: I need to engage with things outside music. I often worry that music itself is often not given the opportunity to connect the world to itself. I can't help but try to engage with what is happening. I'm not trying to preach or prescribe, just trying to feel, and am grateful when there is an opportunity to do this. Right now I'm writing a *Duo for Clarinet & Viola* for the leader and Music Director of the Minnesota Orchestra, OsmoVänskä*, a tarantella for our times, to dance the poison out! I'm weaving things into the music that the performer might think, 'so, that is what she is saying', rather than just dealing with yet another new piece!

DW: *The Second Symphony is interesting in that it was partly inspired by the widow of President Sadat of Egypt* shortly after her husband's assassination.*

LL: Yes, she had witnessed that terrible event, obviously very close at hand, and had a mission to raise money for a library in memory of her husband. The conductor Phillip Brunelle*, who has worked extensively in Minnesota especially, brought us together and saw the chance for us to create a piece, fulfilling her mission of cultural tolerance and peace, and it seemed to me that a Choral Symphony could at least realise that mission and energy and her will to try to change the world. What amazed me was her real and remarkable courage and it made me understand why the form of the symphony was ideal to try and express these deep and important thoughts.

DW: *We have mentioned your love of American texts. Do you spend a lot of time looking for texts to set?*

LL: I do. I love to read. I read everything – novels, biographies, history, newspapers, everything except texts and tweets – life is too short for that. Crafted words are interesting to me and I store things away. Sometimes I write my own texts, under a pseudonym, but mostly I like to collaborate with fine writers, living and dead. Just recently I've come across a wonderful living writer, Eleanor Wilner*. I've been kicking myself that I hadn't come across her work until recently, but I found a particular poem, tracked her down and now we are collaborating. It is so interesting to do that and gives a whole new level of meaning to the creative process.

DW: *It is vital for you to convey a meaning behind the text, I think, and to strive for clarity, to make sure the words are heard.*

LL: It is very important to me. I try to work with the words in a way that they can be understood both phonetically but also in some kind of natural flow. Rhythm is probably the most important thing and then trying to create a melodic contour that allows the listener to be in that moment where you anticipate what might come musically but you also remember what happened earlier in the piece.

DW: *So when you have your text what is the first thing you do?*

LL: I read and read the text over and over again, hear the way I am reading it and then question that! What is there in the text that I need to discover rhythmically? Then I look for different kinds of rhymes and look for a melodic content. By then a tempo has suggested itself and how the text is going to deal with meter.

DW: *Is the structure of the piece in your head early?*

LL: Only a general structure. The piece is whole in my head but the structure is not complete. The little forms within the architecture then find their way in. I work in a big living-room space and sing the lines. I am very keen on trying to physicalize the music, moving around the house, even running up and down the stairs.

DW: *You have often used unusual instrumental accompaniments in your choral pieces -* Alaska Spring *with string quartet; pieces with brass, wind quintet;* Double Joy *with handbells;* Everyone Sang *with harp and percussion. I'm guessing most of these choices are tied up with requests from the commissioning organisation?*

LL: Sometimes, but I do ask for things now and again. I might ask for a solo oboe if that is what the piece seems to be looking for, but yes, commissioning groups ask me for a piece with quartet, or marimba, or something...

DW: *So when you get a request like that, I mean choir & marimba, do you ask yourself, what on earth am I going to do with that?*

LL: Oh yes! I'm likely to get a lot more prickly if someone insists on a text. I don't like people prescribing texts for me to use at all. Please leave that to me!

DW: *Can you say what the balance is between inspiration and technique?*

LL: Now, that is a big topic, enough for a book in itself. I really passionately believe that the technique should be razor sharp because the music should come from instinct and be served by the technique. I'm in love with instinct and it will often tell you things that you don't want to know.

DW: *You obviously work with a great many American choirs – do you think that American choirs have a particular sound?*

LL: I always think that there is a certain kind of brightness that comes from an American choir. Perhaps it is to do with the fact that American English is consonant heavy, not a case of a vowel following a vowel. Sometimes it might sound ragged but it also energised which as we have already said is so important to me.

DW: *Are you inspired by the sound of a particular choir when you know you are writing for them?*

LL: It is less the sound and more the spirit...

DW: *So when a perhaps less-able group sings your music, one that is less-technically accomplished than perhaps VocalEssence or the King's Singers, both of whom you have written for, then the joy can be just as great.*

LL: Absolutely! For me it is about the spirit of the piece rather than the technical delivery.

DW: *Are you a disciplined composer? Do you try and work a certain number of hours a day?*

LL: I try! There are periods of my life when this has been easier than others of course. As those other creative artists that are or have been mothers will understand, it isn't always straightforward. I do actually have music in my head all the time – I mean all the time - so it's just a case of finding the time to write it down and trying not to let too many things get in the way.

DW: *Do you find that the older you get the easier it is to write music?*

LL: In many ways yes, because my brain is 'in shape'. But with so many years of composing -maybe it is a sign of the times – it has become more difficult to cast off banal ideas and say, 'that isn't good enough'. The facility to compose is there all the time – this takes years.

DW: *Are you surprised when you hear a piece for the first time?*

LL: Not any more, and that kind of worries me too. There is part of me that celebrates the fact that, yes, that is how I imagined the piece to be and that is fine. Another part of me worries that there are other things to be said that I didn't put on paper...

DW: *But you don't revise particularly.*

LL: No, I tend not to.

DW: *Are you surprised with what performers find in your music?*

LL: Yes, many times, perhaps more often with instrumental pieces. I'm surprised to hear things that I wasn't aware I was putting on the page at the time. Working with performers who are so deeply inside the music, they hear a completely different profile. I'm frequently humbled by the dedication of performers. It is probably just my own ego at work when I think I know the piece better than anyone, but more often than not this is not the case at all. I would much rather rehearse than be at a performance. I don't actually like being at performances very much.

DW: *Are you trying to guess people's reaction as they listen?*

LL: Yes, I am. My biggest thing is communication. When I'm in a hall at a premiere, or any other performance for that matter, my ears are open far too wide. I'm completely self-centred and have no idea if the piece is communicating or not. Rehearsals, especially when there is a good deal of time, are great, but performances, they happen and people have to judge there and then. This can be very worrying.

DW: *If you hear a piece you wrote twenty years ago is it a similar experience?*

LL: What is interesting is hearing a new generation of performers. One recent example was my First Symphony, *Water Music*. The Minnesota Orchestra played it in the 1980s and they played it again last year (2019). There were three members of the orchestra that played in the premiere and a whole new generation made it into such a different piece. Everything that I put on the page bubbled to life – it was wonderful. Then a group in Canada recently played my chamber piece *Four on the Floor* and I rehearsed with them virtually. These people are younger than my daughter and the technique was incredible. The tempo marking that I wrote at the time was fast enough so that I have heard performances fall apart, but they asked me if they could play it slightly faster, and could they play it!! I realised that their sense of speed is totally different – again, maybe an age thing.

DW: *Do you think about the audience when you are writing?*

LL: Yes, I do. They are an important part of the whole process. It was a problem in graduate school because of the whole Milton Babbitt* thing, 'Who cares if you listen...?' - that kind of tyrannical attitude – but the audience is part of the energy of the piece; I have no doubt about that. Valued judgment of one sort or another is not on my mind but shared communication is. I imagine that anyone that takes themselves to a space for listening to music is one way or another going to listen even if only to snippets and I just want to catch their energy.

DW: *You have never held a teaching position as such – do you think composition can be taught?*

LL: I haven't held an official teaching position by choice. I think the fundamentals of composition can be taught or developed, but you can't teach ideas. Maybe I'm too jealous of my own time. I've had students over the years and they find their way to me; I've enjoyed that, but they already have the basics.

DW: *What kind of advice would you offer to young composers?*

LL: There are so many composers that you really have to have a passion. A lot of people can build a tree house, but to build a skyscraper, that needs a different rigour...

DW: *Is there anything that you are burning to write?*

LL: *A Piano-Concerto-for Our-Times* – for mixed keyboards, voice and orchestra, with some technological enhancement. There are so many musical and cultural issues I am burning to compose into music. When I composed my first and only Piano Concerto for Janina Fialkowska and Minnesota Orchestra in 1992, our world, technologically speaking, was precariously balanced on the fulcrum of its past and future. Think of it! No web browsing, no file sharing, no YouTube, no streaming, no virtual reality, no real-time interactive capacity – none of the technological infrastructure which sustains us now and fires our creativity and sense of community, I burn to incorporate and synthesize this seismic change into the form, flow and performance techniques of my new *Piano-Concerto-for-Our-Times*.

DW: *Elgar quoted Ruskin at the end of* The Dream of Gerontius *- 'This is the best of me...'. Might you be able to say which pieces of yours might fall into that category for you?*

LL: A gruelling question but I will say the Choral Symphony I composed in collaboration with Jehan Sadat* in 1986, *Coming Forth Into Day*. It was a Pulitzer* finalist and feels special to me. For smaller, more crafted diamond-setting kind of works, I would say either *Shall I compare Thee to a Summer's Day* from *A Lover's Journey* or *Beneath These Alien Stars* from *The Settling Years*.

DW: *We are recording this at a very difficult and unusual time – how have you been dealing with lockdown?*

LL: Well, like most composers I guess the time has been pretty productive for me as I'm not travelling. One thing I have been able to do is think very clearly about pieces I would like to write and hope to have opportunities for. I've also learnt how much I love to be around people in person. I'm so lucky to live where I do – I can work in solitude and be gregarious too, but I miss people. Once all this calms down I want to work with as many people as I can to make as much music as I can. The other thing is, I've bumped up against truth in my own work and sometimes that hasn't been fun - enough time has gone by for me to deal with that. I feel that I have been writing into a void somehow - I've never done that before and never want to do it again; a major part of the process is missing – we are going to make it!

DW: *What would you say are your five favourite choral works?*

LIBBY'S FIVE FAVOURITE CHORAL WORKS

Bach *Mass in B minor*

Folksong *Polegnala e Todora(Love Song)*

Gregorian Chants: *Veni Creator Spiritus*
Subvenite Sancti Dei, Occurite Angeli
Domini (Requiem Mass)
In Paradisum (Requiem Mass)

Richard Smallwood *Total Praise*

Tormis *Rauaneedmine (Curse upon Iron)*

Morten Lauridsen

BORN 1943

DW: *Can you tell me about your first musical memories? Are you from a musical family? Your mother was an important influence on you I think.*

ML: Absolutely, she played the piano and played in dance bands when she was in high school. We had a piano at home, she would play 'stride-piano' with simple tunes over the top and I was in seventh heaven, so I asked if I could take piano lessons and I started those when I was eight. I really wanted to make music with others too and so my father insisted I learn the trumpet and went out and bought one. I remember that I wanted to play a string instrument and my father said that he wanted me to play a 'man's instrument' and so that was that. Anyway, I played the trumpet through high school and got to be a decent player. I'm still grateful for those music lessons all those years ago. In high school we could take choir or band. I chose the band, first trumpet, but I did sing in a church choir which was very important to me too.

DW: *When it came to thinking about going to university your parents were less than enthusiastic about the prospect of you studying music.*

ML: They weren't supportive of that at all. Between high school and in my first year at Whitman College, a fine liberal arts college in Washington State, I took no music lessons at all. I had spent a summer fighting forest fires and then I got a job as a lookout and was at the top of a tower by Mount St Helens for ten weeks by myself, aside from when a ranger would bring my supplies. I had my trumpet for company and I played it for the coyotes at night, but this was a great opportunity to do some serious thinking and I came to the conclusion that music needed to be a much more important part of my life, certainly more than just a hobby. Of course, I didn't know which direction I would go. I didn't want to be a performer and so I went back to Whitman and took every music lesson I could – theory, aural skills, piano, history. I sang in the choir. Then I plucked up the courage to talk to my parents and told them I wanted to transfer and expand, to do something seriously with my music.

DW: *And this led to you going to the University of Southern California in Los Angeles.*

ML: I went to have a meeting with the Department Chair, who was Halsey Stevens*, a formidable guy, a respected composer and author of the first real book about Bartók*, which is still published I think. I told him that I wanted to transfer and take a class in composition. He said that was fine and asked to see my portfolio and of course I hadn't written a note at that point.

DW: *Really! So, at that point you hadn't written anything at all?*

ML: No, well, maybe the beginnings of some pop songs, but nothing serious. Unsurprisingly, Dr Stevens wasn't impressed, but I played one of the Brahms Rhapsodies on the piano, he was pleased with that and he fired me a bunch of questions. After a long pause, he offered me a place in a beginners' composition class as a junior, to see what happens and so this is what I did. Within two years I wrote a Trumpet Sonata that was published and still gets played, and wrote my first choral piece, a setting of Psalm 150, gave a full final piano recital and then they gave me a scholarship to study for a Master's degree. I studied with Stevens and then with Ingolf Dahl*, another very formidable academic and composer – the conductor Michael Tilson Thomas* was a student of his at the same time. The university then gave me a teaching job so I could do my doctorate, again studying with Halsey Stevens. At the end of that they broke the rules of the university: they were not allowed to employ their own graduates, but they made an exception and offered me a place on the faculty. I ended up staying for over half a century. I have just this past year retired.

DW: *I believe you even succeeded Halsey Stevens as Chair of the Composition Department. He really changed your life by taking a chance on you didn't he?*

ML: Yes, I did and he did change the course of my life. I was able to repay him a little – for the last ten years of his life the poor man suffered terribly with Parkinson's disease; it was just awful, and he asked me if I would go to his studio, find pieces that he had begun when he was healthy and finish them for him in his own style. I finished a Viola Concerto, some songs and piano music and a choral piece. He heard everyone before he died and could never tell whereabouts the seam was between the two of us and so that was a great way of repaying the faith he had in a very green kid from Oregon who came to learn. I keep in contact with his children to this day.

DW: *I read somewhere that in your early days at USC you were teaching theory to the students of Jascha Heifetz*, one of the most famous violinists that ever lived.*

ML: Yes, can you imagine? He had his master classes at USC and he used to turn up and sit in my class, surrounded by his private students.

DW: *I think perhaps you see yourself belonging to two American traditions. On the one hand the art-song-writing tradition of Aaron Copland* – even more so, Samuel Barber*, Ned Rorem* – but then on the other hand the tradition of Broadway and the Great American Songbook, people like Richard Rodgers* and Jerome Kern*.*

ML: Fundamentally I'm a lyric writer. I have always admired composers who can construct long, memorable, beautifully-crafted melodies. You certainly find that in Schubert*, Schumann*, Brahms*, who I admire very much, but absolutely in the composers you mention. One of the great loves of my life, and in my next life I might go in this direction, is the Broadway stage. Those musicals, this is timeless music: Rodgers, Kern, Cole Porter*, they have left music for the ages, these beautifully constructed melodies, wonderful lyrics. I've always strived to construct meaningful, memorable melodic lines and this of course was very unfashionable at the time. As a student in the 60s and 70s, if you were writing tonal music of any kind you were 'dead meat' as far as academia was concerned. I think you can hear the influence of Broadway in a lot of my music – look at *Sure on this shining night*, look at *Dirait-on* or *Prayer*. The long lines in *Lux aeterna* were a combination of these kinds of influences and the great composers of the Renaissance that have been very important to me.

DW: *I've often thought listening to your song* Where have the actors gone*, that you could have written a good musical.*

ML: That's a good example, yes. Of course that has nothing to do with actors really. I wrote that piece when I was exiting a relationship; it was my goodbye to that and I used the idea of a play closing down to reflect my own personal experience. That seemingly simple tune is still carefully constructed, going down a step each time the refrain comes back. I've always been fond of that piece. You are right – I could have gone down the musical route, film music too – I had an approach from Sony about scoring and writing for films, but at the time I was running the university department, had my residency with the LA Master Chorale, was trying to write my pieces. Even if I did have the time, I just can't write huge amounts of music in a short period of time, it isn't the way I can work. Still, one of the things I'm most proud of is establishing the school for advanced study of composing for film at USC. I hired Jerry Goldsmith*, Elmer Bernstein*, David Raksin*, and that has been a huge success.

DW: *The composition of film music and for that matter choral music was until relatively recently considered as pretty inferior to writing 'serious music' wasn't it?*

ML: Oh yes. Of course it is a prejudice that shouldn't exist but it did and probably does. It shows a great lack of education on the part of the people that say that sort of thing. We even had a Dean at the university that gave me a hard time because I wasn't writing more orchestral and instrumental music. My response was that choral and vocal music have always been important to me and combine my two greatest loves - singing, the most personal thing of all, and poetry. It is what I do well and why I will continue to write it. Yes, I took a lot of flak, you know the sort of thing: 'you are writing melodies, recognisable chords and the like'. The composer George Rochberg* told me, after his son died, he found he could not express himself as he had been doing – he was certainly a card-carrying serialist – and he started writing melodically, music with tonal centres, and so many of his 'academic' friends dumped him when he started to do that. It's just ridiculous.

DW: *You have in some ways paved the way for a lot of younger composers, probably given them the courage to go in a particular direction. Several that have been interviewed in this book have listed pieces of yours as being very important to them.*

ML: That's nice. I keep getting emails from people saying, 'Have you heard this piece, it sounds just like you...'

DW: *Oh, there are certainly imitators too. I think your first two acknowledged pieces from the mid-1960s are solo vocal cycles –* A Backyard Universe *and* A Winter Come.

ML: Yes, I mean no composer has ever made a nickel from writing art songs...

DW: *Oh yes, Ned Rorem, who has written hundreds of them, has told me that more times than I care to remember...*

ML: Indeed! It is a rather rarefied form. I had written these songs and had set up a meeting with Peer Music and played a tape of *A Winter Come* to them. They decided that they would like to do an anthology of songs that they had in their catalogue and included a couple of mine from *A Winter Come*. I remember being in New York for some performances and to see that volume of songs in the great music shop, Patelson's, which used to be just across the street from Carnegie Hall, with Ives and Rorem and so many others, was such a great thrill. They are early pieces but I'm still fond of them and wouldn't change a note. That was my first association with Peer Music, in 1987. Since then they have sold almost two million scores of mine. The next thing they took was *Madrigali*, one of my more challenging choral pieces. At that time choral music didn't play a big part in their catalogue, but they said that they were not about to see the piece go to anyone else and so after that came *O magnum mysterium*, *Les chansons des Roses* and others. I've had letters from composers saying, 'we see your career took off when you turned 50'. I wrote *Les Chansons des Roses* when I was 50. One guy said, 'I'm 49, I'll give it one more shot!'.

DW: *So it is right to say that you are a late developer?*

ML: Yes, I took a while to find a voice, but I built up a body of work over the years, and then suddenly it took off.

DW: *We could spend hours talking about texts because I know this is so important to you. Is it that first reading of a poem that hits you and demands to be set?*

ML: Yes, exactly. I still read poetry every day and have spent a good portion of my life looking in bookshops! It has to be an immediate visceral reaction. That happened with *Prayer* for example – I brought several books of poetry by Dana Gioia* right here to my shack on Waldron Island and read them through systematically. One of the last that I read was the one Dana wrote when his baby son passed away from SIDS and it just touched and grabbed me in such an incredible way: an extraordinary poem, I just knew that I had to try and set it. A lot of the poets I set aren't so well known and I hope that I have got a lot of people reading too!

DW: *You have set texts in several languages, not just English and Latin, but French, German and Spanish too – you wouldn't think about setting these texts in translation? In the score of* Nocturnes *there is a translation of the beautiful Neruda 'Sonnet of the Night' by your son, but it is the sounds of the original language that interests you.*

ML: I'm not a linguist at all but I get together with people that are fluent in these languages and have them read the texts over and over, so I can hear the inflexions, stresses and just the sound of the words. I have to try and capture that sound in my music. I don't think I would ever set anything that wasn't in the original language. The Neruda setting is a case in point – the translation is there to help conductors and singers, but it would be a completely different piece if it wasn't in Spanish. All this takes a lot of extra time, but I have to get it right.

DW: *Something that might not strike the listener or performer immediately and is a matter of compositional craft is how tightly constructed your pieces are. It isn't just a case of finding the right melody or chord – often pieces grow out of the smallest ideas.*

ML: You bet! I take an initial small idea and see what I can do with it to unify the piece, expand it and develop new ideas out of the original seed. I learnt that initially from Bartók, how in the Fourth Quartet for example he constantly manipulates and varies a tiny musical idea through the piece. I want to get a sound at the very start, so with *Dirait-on* I knew that I wanted to make it sound like French popular song so chose a chord that was much loved by Debussy and Ravel, a triad with an added second, and everything, the tune and accompaniment grows out of that. In *Madrigali* there is what I call the 'Fire-chord', out of which so many musical ideas develop through the cycle. In the *Mid-winter Songs*, on poems by Robert Graves*, the first thing you hear, are the words 'Dying Sun' – four chords and a 'scotch snap' rhythmic idea; there are lots of major seconds – that little motif is what the whole piece is about. As you say, all this might not be apparent straight away to the listener, but it is all part of the art of being a composer.

DW: *We have to talk a little about* O magnum mysterium, *which by now must have been sung thousands of times and recorded countless times too. It was inspired in the first instance by a painting I think?*

ML: I was looking for a pathway to write this piece. Of course the text has been set many times and listening even just to the setting by Victoria*, I thought, 'who am I to set this?'. The same thing happened of course with *Sure on this shining night*, following on from the iconic setting by Samuel Barber. I came across this painting, 'Still Life, with Lemons' by Francisco de Zurbaran*, objects placed with great care on a table against a dark background. These objects have such deep meaning and yet are so overwhelming in their simplicity. This became my approach to the new piece, the most basic kind of materials, simple chords and a melody, but to use them to have a profound effect on the listener. I worked on that five-minute piece for six months. I got stuck on the question of portraying the suffering of the Virgin Mary and her sorrow at the death of her Son on the cross – how can I do that in this very direct setting? Then lying in bed one night it came to me, a note that doesn't belong, so that is the G sharp that the altos sing, the only note in the piece that is 'foreign' to the main key of D major. It creates a sonic spotlight on the word 'Virgo' – 'Virgin'. *O magnum...* was the first piece I wrote as Resident Composer with the LA Master Chorale and I sent it to Paul Salamunovich* their Music Director. I remember having heard the first rehearsal, I went out and sat in my car for a very long time. I heard the piece in my head of course, and played it on the piano, but to hear it sung by 120 voices just struck me as something very special.

DW: *Despite the success of the piece it is not an easy piece to bring off.*

ML: It isn't. I've heard so many wonderful performances but some conductors just don't get it! Many have done wonderful performances: Dale Warland* did it beautifully, Stephen Layton*, Suzi Digby* does it beautifully.

DW: *When we worked together in London some time ago, I know I was somewhat appre-hensive about conducting the piece in front of you, and I asked you then, do people take it too slowly?*

ML: It is partly that but they forget the flexibility and the fluidity of the piece. It just drives me nuts when *O Magnum...* or *... Shining night*, are done absolutely 'straight'. I try to put as much information as I can in the music, but there has to be a spontaneity about it; it has to flow, push forward a little now and again, hold back at other times – all these things that come straight out of Gregorian chant. It is so important.

DW: *I remember sitting with you at a performance in Cambridge and you were still very affected by it...*

ML: Yes, it happens. I remember going to some little college in Iowa once. I must have heard *O magnum...* thousands of times, but they did it so beautifully and sensitively, it just made me weep.

DW: *These pieces,* O magnum..., *Sure on this shining night,* Dirait-on *– they have become almost iconic in a very short period of time and have been performed heaven knows how many thousands of times all over the world. Obviously this gives you pleasure, but at the same time you must feel a huge amount of pressure when you are writing. Are people expecting you to write* O magnum... *number two?*

ML: Always! Sure, of course! But the positive side to that are the letters and emails I get saying how these pieces have changed people's lives. I go through so much angst writing these pieces. I throw away far, far more than I keep until I get what I hear in my head, feel in my heart and soul and quite honestly it takes a lot of digging to do that. You know I'm 77 now, and I expect it every time I start a piece and every time I say to myself, 'here we go again…' – but once I get the chord or the right melodic idea I'm on my way.

DW: *I know you have authorised what on paper look like unlikely arrangements of some of your pieces –* O magnum… *is available in an arrangement for wind band for instance.*

ML: Yes, it does sound a little unlikely, but the wind-band arrangement by H Robert Reynolds is so idiomatic, and he took such care with the original, that I'm very happy with it. I made a version of *O magnum…* for solo violin and orchestra for the violinist Anne Akiko Meyers. That took some doing, keeping the essence of the piece and giving her sixteen-million-dollar fiddle something to do! I think it worked out very well.

DW: *Having heard choirs from all over the world sing your pieces, do you notice any particular variations in their approach?*

ML: I do know that it is pretty damn hard to top British choirs. It is just so much part of their upbringing early on. The two albums I did with Polyphony and Stephen Layton completely blew my mind, just incredible. Suzy Digby is doing great work with ORA and there are so many others in Britain.

DW: Lux aeterna *has similarly become incredibly popular – a very personal piece for you I think.*

ML: Yes, it is for those of us who are left behind. I was writing it when I heard my mother was dying. I set out to write a popular piece. It was for the LA Master Chorale, who are a very good choir of course, but I wanted *Lux aeterna* to be sung by a lot of choirs and didn't want to make the piece too demanding from a technical point of view. It is a piece with a message, celebrating eternal life and illumination, be that spiritual, intellectual, or whatever. A piece about death, yes, but hopefully an uplifting, hopeful piece about light shining on those we have loved for ever. That is what I was holding on to when my mother was dying and it

was comforting for me too. I was thinking of Paul Salamanovich all the way through, hence the influence of chant and renaissance music, that was his specialty, and again, there is the flexibility and fluidity in the flow of the piece. Paul Salamanovich contracted the West Nile virus from a mosquito bite and was in a coma for months. I visited him in hospital once I returned from my summer on Waldron Island. His wife and his nurse were in the hospital room. I went up to Paul and whispered in his ear – 'Paul, your composer is here. Please wake up and get well. We will go on stage again and you will conduct *O Magnum Mysterium* and *Lux Aeterna*'. Each time I mentioned those pieces his right arm, still attached to tubes, raised and he made conducting gestures. Up to then he had not moved for months. He was conducting my pieces while still in a deep coma!

DW: *You have spoken about being on Waldron Island, off the coast of Washington State, and the need for isolation when writing your music.*

ML: Going back to the start of our conversation, being at the top of that tower on look-out, I learnt how essential it is to be alone, with one's own thoughts. This is why I grieve for the younger generation who can't get away from those awful cell-phones for more than five minutes. It is so distracting – they don't read books or write letters anymore – nobody seems to have quiet time and it is so important. I found that being set by the seashore, in a shack with no running water and electricity and a beaten-up 50-dollar piano, well, that resulted in *O magnum mysterium*, only hearing the sound of the sea, the waves and the birds. Some composers, many good friends of mine, can work anywhere, hotel rooms, on trains, wherever, but I know I do my best work when I can dig down and I can only do that when I have peace and quiet.

DW: *Do you enjoy rehearsals and premieres? Are there nerves before a premiere especially?*

ML: There are always nerves to a certain extent. I don't believe any composer who says they don't get nervous. I do enjoy rehearsals – when I visit different groups I have a lot to say about these pieces and I like to explain how they came about, as you remember from us working together. I've been blest with some really wonderful performers. I always urge conductors to spend a lot of time with the text before they start worrying about the notes, to see how the whole thing is put together. It is always obvious to me when a conductor hasn't even read the poem that I've set!

DW: *Are you a disciplined composer? Do you work every day?*

ML: No, I don't! I should be more disciplined perhaps, but I can tell you that once I get onto a piece, then I work around the clock. Starting a piece is the hard thing.

DW: *It goes without saying that you are extremely self-critical. With the success of the pieces we have talked about you are no doubt inundated with commissions.*

ML: I quit counting after 600 requests and that was several years ago. Out of all that I have accepted maybe a dozen or so but I generally say no. I don't like any time-pressure and I will never accept a commission that insists on a particular text, because that is very personal to me. I did take a commission this last year, but I shouldn't tell you anything about that quite yet... There are composers who just write too much and the music sounds like it, but sometimes they are trying to make a living and it is difficult. I was very fortunate that I had the university position to back me up; not everyone has that luxury of course.

DW: *Are you still surprised when you hear a piece?*

ML: Sometimes, yes. I like that, providing it isn't a negative surprise!

DW: *When you are writing do you think about the audience?*

ML: Very much so. I try to think of everyone involved in the piece – singers, conductor, audience. I want my music to have an effect on the listener, to move, exhilarate. Of course there are different audiences and there are actually, despite what people think, different sides of me, depending on what I am doing. The Lorca settings (*Cuatro Canciones Sobre Poesias de Federico Garcia Lorca*) are very edgy texts that demand similarly edgy music. I try to make each piece or collection of vocal settings so different; the contrast between the *Mid-winter Songs* and *Lux aeterna* for instance is profound really. With *Madrigali* I wanted to bring in the characteristics that I found in Monteverdi* and Gesualdo* – the harmonic drama, the word-painting, intricate counterpoint. That was a challenging piece to write. I like to take each new piece in a new direction. Of course I think about the singers too; I sing each line through to myself. If I can't sing it then I ask why.

DW: *I know altos are grateful to you!*

ML: Yes, they write to me and say thank you for our interesting lines...

DW: *You have just retired from USC after over half a century on the faculty, so it might seem a very strange thing to ask if you think that composition can be taught.*

ML: It's a tough thing with so many different students, but I try to get to the essence of what a particular student might be and try to guide them as best I can. I'm always telling them to listen! I was so fortunate in my teachers – we talked a little about Halsey Stevens. My other main teacher, Ingolf Dahl, was a greatly-respected figure in California in the 1960s. He taught a legendary class on Stravinsky* (who he was close to) that I took - just a renowned figure who scared the hell out of everyone! I still remember my first lesson with him which was completely terrifying; he threw everything at me – questions, keyboard skills, reading in multiple different clefs, score-reading, history – he did this with everyone and many couldn't take it.

DW: *You have often said yourself, if you want to be a composer you need to have a thick skin.*

ML: Oh yes. You have to be tough and listen to yourself, believe in yourself but back it up with craft and don't worry about fads and fashions.

DW: *That would probably be your advice to a young composer.*

ML: Exactly.

DW: *Have you anything that you are longing to write?*

ML: Lately I've been focusing on vocal duet versions of some of my pieces – soprano, baritone and piano. I've done *Sure on this shining night, Dirait-on, Prayer, Yaeresmia* and *Contre Qui, Rose* – I just love that genre. I'm working on some of those.

DW: *Elgar quotes Ruskin at the end of* The Dream of Gerontius* – 'This is the best of me…'. Can you say if there is a particular piece or a group of pieces that might fall into that category for you?*

ML: Perhaps *Madrigali* – even one of my earliest pieces, the vocal cycle *A winter come*; I go through such a long process, revising and revising again. When I finish I hope that it is the best I can do as far as that particular piece is concerned. I think all the works from the 1990s stand up well. All are my favourites.

DW: *We are recording this interview at a very difficult and worrying time. How have you been dealing with lockdown? Perhaps, for you, life isn't so different.*

ML: As it happens I retired from USC just at the right time, they are doing so much online and I wouldn't enjoy that too much. I'm very lucky to be here on the island - I couldn't wish for a better place to be, but of course it is just horrible, actually catastrophic. I have so very many friends that are out of work. There are no performances of course - terrible! Here we have had these appalling fires in California, COVID so badly handled with all these deaths – it is one of the lowest points for this country that I can ever remember. We just have to hope...

DW: *What would you say are your five favourite choral works?*

MORTEN'S FIVE FAVOURITE CHORAL WORKS

Brahms *A German Requiem*

James MacMillan *Seven Last Words from the Cross*

Monteverdi *Books of Madrigals*

Pärt *Berliner Messe*

Stravinsky *Mass*

Paweł Łukaszewski

BORN 1968

DW: *Can you tell me about you first musical memories? I think you are one of only two composers in this book whose father was a professional composer.*

PL: I was born in Częstochowa, a city in Southern Poland. My father, Wojciech Łukaszewski* was a composer, also a teacher and Director of the Music School in Częstochowa. My mother taught there too. My father studied with two important Polish composers, Tadeusz Szeligowski* and Tadeusz Paciorkiewicz* and in the mid 1960s with Nadia Boulanger* in Paris. I began to have piano lessons as a small boy. I soon took up the cello. My parents decided that this would be more sensible as the world needs many more cellists than pianists and I studied that later at University alongside composition.

DW: *With this sort of background it is perhaps unsurprising that you became a composer or at the very least a musician of some kind.*

PL: I think it was always going to happen. My father died at 42, I was only ten years old, and I almost felt that I was carrying on his work in some way. I started music school when I was maybe five or six years old, a small group for kids, before primary school. Then came the Musical Gymnasium and a diploma.

DW: *Were you writing music too?*

PL: Yes, the musical atmosphere was very important in my home – I saw a lot of scores, manuscript paper all over the house, conversations between my parents about music and musical life – I was only very young but remember this so well. My younger brother, Marcin*, also became a composer. I spent a lot of time looking at all my father's scores, letters to and from other composers, and I began to write some small piano pieces. I think those were my first compositions.

DW: *Częstochowa is a very important city in Poland, almost the spiritual capital and the Jasna Góra Monastery* is such an important place. I remember visiting there with you a few years ago and, although I am not a Catholic, the Black Madonna of Częstochowa had a very profound effect on me – it is astonishingly atmospheric and striking.*

PL: Yes, it was and it is still very important to me, and still affects my music. We say that the Black Madonna is Queen of Poland. She is the Polish equivalent of perhaps Lourdes in France and the monastery is a place of pilgrimage for Polish Catholics. 1980/1 was also the time of the Solidarity movement in Poland, which I know many people in the West will remember too. We lived close by. I was in the Music School and remember seeing the Military Police around the monastery on many occasions. It was a strange mixture of these two worlds.

DW: *This was after the appointment of a Polish Pope, John Paul II*.*

PL: Yes, Cardinal Wojtyla was made Pope in 1978 and I saw him many times when he came on pilgrimages to the Częstochowa monastery. Later on, in 1987, I was in the Choir of the Academy of Catholic Theology in Warsaw and we sang the premiere of Górecki's* Totus Tuus at the military airport when the Pope arrived. Actually we sang it twice, and it has since become Górecki's most famous choral piece. Then in 1980, Penderecki's Polish Requiem* was heard for the first time, which was a very significant event in Polish musical life. The 'Lacrimosa' was dedicated to Lech Wałęsa* and was written for the unveiling of a statue at the Gdańsk Shipyard that was erected in memory of those that were killed in anti-government demonstrations. The Polish Requiem became a sort of turning point in Polish contemporary music.

DW: *Poland was still under Soviet control until you were around 20.*

PL: Yes, but on the whole I don't think life was quite as difficult for us as it was in some other countries, the then Yugoslavia, Czechoslovakia, East Germany for example. I was in Warsaw at the University when democracy came in 1989 and it was of course a hugely important historical event. The first elections after communism in 1989 – I remember that very well too.

DW: *In the '80s sacred music was suddenly flourishing in Poland?*

PL: I think the turning point was the election of the Pope. Then Polish composers began to write more sacred choral works. Górecki wrote a few works before then, in the 70s, with his Euntes Ibranter Flebant and Amen. His famous Third Symphony (Symphony of Sorrowful Songs) came in 1976 and again the Penderecki* Polish Requiem. In Częstochowa at this time they had an important choral festival at which I heard many major premieres, a lot of very good choral music.

DW: *Then you went to the Chopin University in Warsaw to study composition with Professor Marian Borkowski*.*

PL: Yes, but first I was a cellist and then studied composition later after three years as a cellist.

DW: *In the '60s/'70s Poland was one of the major centres for new music, what we now call the 'avantgarde'. In the west at that time we knew of Penderecki* and Lutosławski *, but I* *don't think composers such as Górecki and Kilar* were terribly well known outside Poland until there was this extraordinary change of aesthetic and direction. Can you say perhaps why this happened?*

PL: In the '60s most of the new music came from Darmstadt*, composers such as Luigi Nono*, Karlheinz Stockhausen*, Pierre Boulez*. Then came the Warsaw Autumn Festival*. The first festival was in 1956, founded by two composers – Tadeusz Baird* and Kazimierz Serocki*. This naturally featured the work of many Polish composers, including the names you mention. I think the turning point so to speak was once again the election of the Pope. I can't say how important this was for every facet of life in Poland. Composers started to think in a very different way, looking to write music that was new and fresh, not only music that was felt to be 'contemporary' and technically advanced but music that was spiritual and had 'something inside', one can say – music that did not just experiment for the sake of experimenting. This continued of course after the fall of communism, a time of new spirituality for Poland.

DW: *As a young composer did you find it difficult to find a voice because of these dramatic changes or did you always feel more at home with a more spiritual approach?*

PL: When I was a student we studied a lot of twentieth-century music of all kinds, but somehow it was just another way, and was not really a call for me to write like that. This music was and is interesting to study, but it is somehow not for the people and for me – finding a spiritual course was much more important. I found this in choral music more than anything else. It felt natural for me to go in this direction. I knew this when I was very young. I would also mention Gothic architecture as an important influence on my work – the acoustics of wonderful cathedrals. I think about space a great deal when composing. We actually have different words in Polish for pieces and works – I very much wanted to compose 'works' – significant works in the manner of *Der Abend* of Richard Strauss* for instance. My *Tenebrae* settings and *Lamentations* are works of this kind, rather beyond an average church or parish choir perhaps.

DW: *You have used elements of what one might call the 'avantgarde' in some of your more advanced works such as the* Tenebrae Responses, *the* Lamentations *and* Veni Creator *– some* aleatoric* *elements: whispering, chanting, clusters, vocal glissandi, very dense textures.*

PL: Yes, but these techniques are not at the forefront of my mind when I am composing.

DW: *You are not using these modes of expression for effect? The text or the message of the music demands such an approach?*

PL: Yes – because I need to say something in particular that the text demands. There has to be a good reason for me making use of those techniques.

DW: *When you were developing as a composer I know you felt close to Górecki, but also to Arvo Pärt* and I think John Tavener*.*

PL: I remember the ECM CDs of Arvo Pärt being issued – the *Berliner Messe, Te Deum*, for example. This was something very fresh and new for me. Tavener was a little after that – not a lot of people knew Tavener in Poland, they perhaps knew the old composer...

DW: *So, John Taverner*, 1490 to 1545?*

PL: Yes, but in Poland the twentieth-century Tavener is even now not so popular, but for me he was very important, a milestone and example for me when it came to writing sacred music. I think Górecki, Pärt and Tavener are my three pillars perhaps. I also very much admire Morten Lauridsen* from the USA and Pēteris Vasks* from Latvia for the honesty and spirituality of their music.

DW: *Which of your works might you consider to be your opus 1?*

PL: I think my setting of the *Ave Maria* from 1992. I was still a student and it was written for the choir I sang in, the Choir of the Theological Academy. That for me is a significant piece and has since become very popular. After that perhaps the *Two Lenten Motets*. Before these two works I had used Polish texts, but I always knew that Latin texts were my way forward as a composer.

DW: *I know that the Polish sacred tradition has been important to you, the Polish folk tradition too? I wondered if I heard a little of that in your music?*

PL: I think folk tradition less. After the Second World War there was a lot of music written based on folk music and folk texts...

DW: *I suppose because that was prescribed by the authorities, early works by Panufnik*, Lutosławski* for example?*

PL: Yes, that's right. The sacred tradition is different – the Latin and Polish Catholic Tradition that is, especially after the Second Vatican Council. We had the Polish language as part of the liturgy but for me Latin was more important.

DW: *Can you say why? It would seem natural to set words in your first language.*

PL: It is very international, the language not just of the Catholic Church but of Christianity.

DW: *So the vast majority of your choral works set Latin. There are one or two Shakespeare settings...*

PL: Yes, not only from the Bible, but also the Book of Enoch, an important text about angels. I also set a text by Cardinal Newman*.

DW: *You have described what you do as 'renewed tonality'. Is that the best way to describe your compositional approach?*

PL: I think for me this is the solution to the question of how to compose sacred choral music in the twenty-first century. That is, taking elements of traditional harmony and tonality, but without following rules as such. So one might use parallel fifths, not following conventional modulations between chords. I compose in a tonal language but without rules, which is surely interesting for any composer. I still believe that there is so much still to say in the field of tonal music.

DW: *You have written a great deal of choral music, but also chamber music, an Organ Concerto, a Piano Concerto and orchestral works. Can you say how different the approach is? Do you regard those as almost sacred too?*

PL: It is different. I have composed a lot of chamber music – a Piano Trio, two Piano Quintets, three String Quartets – it is another way of composing. I was a cellist and played as part of a piano trio for many years and so played a great deal of repertoire – Mendelssohn*, Schubert*, Schumann* and Beethoven. I played in and with orchestras. I played the Schumann Concerto...

DW: *You must have been a good cellist...*

PL: Maybe I was. It was an important part of my life for a long time. I played a lot of cello repertoire with piano too – Brahms*, Rachmaninov* and so on...

DW: *So you love this repertoire and you want to contribute something yourself.*

PL: Yes, I think it is like singing in a choir. I know something about playing this music myself, from direct experience. The biggest help when composing choral music is to have sung in a choir. You can see what works, what is good, what is bad, if something is too high or low, how dynamics work, tempo. You can both see and hear this whilst you are performing – also taking part in rehearsals, how different conductors work, it is all helpful. It is the same when playing an orchestral instrument. I can tell you that members of my own choir (Musica Sacra Choir at St Florian's Cathedral in the Praga District of Warsaw), may not be professional composers or even in some cases professional musicians, but they still know which notes are good and which are bad! I will never forget playing Mahler's* Eighth Symphony in the cello section of an orchestra - it was just fantastic, being in the centre of that. I think my orchestral/instrumental music is more difficult perhaps but still I hope idiomatic. I think it is easier to write instrumental music; you don't need to worry about the text of course. Some years ago I started an experiment, to re-compose, reimagine, some of my shorter choral pieces for the piano. Now they are *Nocturnes* for piano, with no text of course and without titles too. This has been very interesting.

DW: *It is clearly important for you to carry the deep meanings of these texts to the listener, so you think very carefully about how to convey this and make them as clear as possible.*

PL: Yes, often I start from one word – Alleluia or Domine or Ave or Beati – one small word. It is important for me to find one special chord or interval to convey that word, a particular colour or feeling. I have to decide which words or lines are significant at a particular time and why at that moment. For composition of course I do not just worry about notes and rhythms but structure too. Quite often I find the text suggests a structure to me. In a Mass of course, structure is not so important – people know what a Mass is – but for the bigger choral/orchestral works such as *Via Crucis* and more recently *Ascension*, that I wrote for David Hill* and Yale, it becomes very much more complicated. For these pieces I must think about a particular structure, special points, where to place the climax. If not, I have just a series of movements that don't go anywhere.

DW: *A lot of your music is fairly calm and restrained.* Via Crucis *is slightly unusual in that it has a fairly apocalyptic climax but on the whole do you imagine your music to be a calming influence, a comfort perhaps?*

PL: I imagine it as a prayer for average people – of course the best place for this music is a church or a cathedral, but this is not always possible. I am thinking not just about the music but also the acoustic, the space and the atmosphere. Still, I hope the music has the same effect wherever it is performed. I composed *Via Crucis* twenty years ago. I think I might do it differently now.

DW: *You would? So what is your reaction when you hear your early works?*

PL: Sometimes I feel uncomfortable, maybe not for the whole piece, but in some places I look and ask myself, 'why did I do that'? Perhaps I prefer more recent works such as *Tenebrae* and *Lamentations* but these works are more difficult for the audience and the choir too.

DW: *We talked about* Ave Maria *being a very successful piece. What strikes me about the piece is the simplicity, not simple music, but it is so very direct...*

PL: I don't compose for musicologists or music specialists but for people and for God of course! Music doesn't need to be complicated all the time.

DW: *Is it more difficult to write music that is perhaps more direct in expression?*

PL: Yes, it can be much more difficult – it is important to compose music that is not so complicated for perhaps non-musicians, for prayer or just for thinking and contemplation.

DW: *I'd like to talk a little about the* Requiem, *which again is a very direct piece, not so demanding for the choir or the orchestra, written especially I think with amateur choirs in mind. It is in the tradition of Fauré* and Duruflé*, a comforting and consoling Requiem, written for the Presteigne Festival here in the UK.*

PL: I love a lot of Requiems – Berlioz*, Brahms, Britten*, Ligeti and the Verdi*. Many I have sung in myself as part of big choirs, they are wonderful, but I am more interested in the Fauré, Duruflé, and also I like the John Rutter* *Requiem* very much. For me these works are a better way of understanding what a Requiem is about. The Second Vatican Council* decided to cut the 'Dies Irae' from the liturgy and we have replaced it with 'Alleluia'. We need more light after death, light from heaven, not anything from anywhere else. We need hope! It's a question of what is important, the 'Dies Irae', with a lot of brass and drums, or the one tolling bell I have in my *Requiem*. I decided on the smaller solution – this for me was a good way. Also, whilst I was writing the work a lot of people close to me had died – my uncle, the composer Wojciech Kilar, Cardinal Glemp* (Primate of Poland) – and each movement has a dedication. I was thinking about the *Requiem* for maybe ten years, but the sad deaths of these people helped me find a way. I have been asked if I could compose another Requiem – but maybe a Requiem can be the last piece...

DW: *Best not to go down that road – look what happened to Mozart.*

PL: Yes, but he was so young...

DW: *Can you say how you start a piece once you have a text? When you look at a blank sheet of paper is it a struggle to find your way into a new piece?*

PL: I compose with my computer, not with manuscript paper...

DW: *Do you use a piano?*

PL: Never. All I need is my computer and headphones; the computer and the mouse are for me paper and pencil. I think it is important to take the time and not write, so considering ideas before actually going to the computer. When you are writing there is no time to think.

DW: *The piece is in your head before you start?*

PL: I think of blocks or patterns, transpositions of chords – it is so difficult [long pause] - it is my kitchen; I'm not sure how to explain...- it would not be any easier in Polish!

DW: *Some composers just find it difficult to talk about what goes on – maybe it takes away the mystery. Can you say something about the balance of inspiration and technique?*

PL: It is dangerous to have more inspiration than technique, inspiration without what goes on in the composer's workshop is not so good. I tell my own students this. I'm not sure I am a good teacher. I just try to instill in them so much from the history and literature of music. We must know how to make something and come to a decision. Sometimes coming to that decision is not so easy. In the end you can find yourself. You know, when I'm driving my car, I prefer pop music!

DW: *You do? A kind of release, to get everything out of your head that would hinder your own composition?*

PL: Yes, it is a problem with the brain, or at least my brain. Do you know of a great book by Oliver Sacks*, *Musicophilia -Tales of Music and the Brain*? This is important for me. A book about music being around us all the time and the effect it has on the brain, how we act and how we think. Lutosławski hated music around him, in shops, restaurants, cafes, elevators – typical places we have music all the time. This isn't freedom, to have music enforced on us wherever we are. I don't listen to very much music. Of course I spend a lot of time studying scores I will conduct and when I am teaching but for me it is important to reset the mind, draw a line under the music you hear, before writing music of your own.

DW: *Are you disciplined when writing music? With your work at the University it is probably difficult to find the time.*

PL: I have my choir, the University, the competition – I am Artistic Director of the Musica Sacra International Composition Competition which is based at the Cathedral - different associations, travelling – but I can find the time. I'm now at my summer house in the east of Poland and it is fantastic, I compose from 6 am! I like to begin work very early. Composing is not only when you sit in front of an instrument or computer - you are thinking about it all the time. I certainly think about composing when I am conducting and when conducting I look at scores with a composer's eye – the two feed into each other. I don't often conduct my own music; it just isn't something I particularly enjoy, perhaps I know my music too well. My choir sings a lot of contemporary music from the UK – Karl Jenkins, John Rutter, Paul Mealor, Bob Chilcott*.

DW: *Your music is sung all over the world. Are you aware of the different qualities of choirs say in Poland or the UK or the USA?*

PL: I love British choirs – Tenebrae, The King's Singers, Gesualdo 6, Trinity College Choir, Polyphony – they are wonderful and such great conductors. After these experiences, I did have problems sometimes with some Polish choirs, but of course the Polish Chamber Choir is wonderful, Camerata Silesia too. I have great support here at home really and in America too, but I have been spoilt, British conductors understand my music better than anyone I think. I wonder perhaps if German and Polish choirs do not understand the harmony so well or the huge energy that can exist between chords, which are so important to my music. For this reason, Tenebrae and Nigel Short were just amazing when they made my recent CD, 'Daylight Declines'. They just seemed to know all about harmony, everything happened so naturally.

DW: *Does it become easier to write music the older and more experienced you get?*

PL: It is not so easy now. I'm convinced that it was easier when I was young. Of course you know a lot more music when you get older and that is part of the problem. As I told you it took me years to finally write a Requiem even though I had wanted to do so for so long. I'm not an innovator, not always looking to do new things. I compose because I want to. Hopefully it will mean something to someone. It is a way to be human, I can pray with my music. If my music encourages people to slow down and contemplate a little, this would make me happy.

DW: *Do you think about the audience?*

PL: Not so easy to say but I think of me! It isn't for the audience. I don't compose with a certain audience in mind. Many years ago a famous Polish composer Józef Świder*, said to me, 'you must compose easier music if you want a lot of performances and to be loved by choirs' – but I don't want to be a pop star! I compose for me, as part of my relationship with God and also I think for Poland. Polish history is very difficult and partly because of this we don't have that much choral music. Chopin was wonderful of course but did not write choral music. Moniusko* is our great romantic opera composer, but the choral music is not so good, nowhere near as good as Mendelssohn* or Brahms*. We have the Szymanowski*  *Stabat Mater*, which is wonderful, but then nothing of significance really until we get towards the end of the last century, not really until the Penderecki *St Luke Passion*. I just want to write for Poland too and find something to say with these special texts. I would like to say that I love Poulenc* very much too, not just the big pieces but the shorter Motets and the Mass.

DW: *They are very hard to sing well...*

PL: Yes, and he sets Latin in a French way – the accents are sometimes strange. The relationships between the chords or rather the lack of a relationship I find fantastic –

this is what I mean by renewed tonality in my music.

DW: *When you hear a piece for the first time are you surprised?*

PL: Quite often. It depends on the choir. I need a conductor who understands not only the notes but what is inside and why I set the text the way I did. Sometimes this is a wonderful surprise. I remember I had just such an experience when David Hill conducted the premiere of *Ascension* at Yale. The rehearsal was good already and I had little to say, the concert just got better and better. This is a wonderful thing for a composer.

DW: *Do you enjoy rehearsals and premieres? Do you get nervous?*

PL: Very nervous. Not because of a problem with performers but a problem with me; sometimes I don't remember the piece because the premiere is so far ahead of the time. I finish the composition and I have to think, 'what was I doing?'.

DW: *You write mostly to commission – is there anything you are longing to write?*

PL: I would much like to write an opera. I have a libretto about John Paul I, who was Pope for just 33 days in 1978 before dying suddenly, and Patriarch Nicodemus. It is assumed the Pope died of natural causes but at the same time there has been some controversy about this. Patriarch Nicodemus himself died suddenly in Rome, during the installation of the new Pope. Nicodemus was thought to have been part of the negotiations between the Vatican and the Orthodox Church that authorised the Eastern Orthodox participation in the Second Vatican Council. In return the Vatican promised not to condemn communism during conciliar assemblies. All this would make a wonderful opera.

DW: *The Vatican might not be too happy...*

PL: True – the Orthodox Church too!

DW: *Elgar quotes Ruskin at the end of* The Dream of Gerontius * - 'This is the best of me'. Are there any works of yours that you might be moved to say that?*

PL: For me probably the Third Symphony, *Symphony of Angels* – I have been very much inspired by the world of angels. Everyone has a Guardian Angel and my Symphony is dedicated to my angel. Perhaps my *O Antiphons*, I can't really say, this is a very difficult question.

DW: *Do you have any advice for young composers?*

PL: To compose music which is important for them, not to please others, the public or the critics. Now it is possible to compose in any style. Certainly for Polish composers this was not always the case, especially during the Warsaw Autumn Festival. Of course

Penderecki and Kilar went their own way and a different direction in the 70s but they were already 'stars'. Kilar wrote lots of film music for Polanski* and Coppola*. Penderecki was conducting and celebrated in many parts of the world and money was not a problem. For others it was more difficult. It is not easy but you must be honest above all. For me writing music is like looking in a mirror!

DW: *You told me some years ago that if you write choral music in Poland you are looked down on. Is that still the case?*

PL: I don't think so, not now. It certainly used to be the case. It is less of a problem now. Amongst the younger generation I see many great things, a lot of good choral music, very fresh and new, very encouraging.

DW: *We are recording this at a very unusual and difficult time, how are you dealing with lockdown in Poland?*

PL: I compose for myself and spend time with my family in our house in the country. I have been writing a lot, a big Symphony – maybe sixty minutes, an experiment; perhaps it isn't good, I don't know, I can't tell at this point – the piano pieces I mentioned and a Flute Sonata. I am just trying to keep busy – it is such a difficult time.

DW: *What would you say are your five favourite choral works?*

PAWEŁ'S FIVE FAVOURITE CHORAL WORKS

Morten Lauridsen *Lux Aeterna*

Arvo Pärt *O Antiphons*

Rachmaninov *All Night Vigil*

Szymanowski *Stabat Mater*

Tavener *Eternity's Sunrise*

Cecilia McDowall

BORN 1951

DW: *Can you tell me about your first musical memories? Did you grow up in a musical family?*

CM: My father, Harold Clarke, was a professional flautist and principal flute at the Royal Opera House, Covent Garden. He was one of the first players to run a flexible chamber music ensemble and, as a result, the house was always full of music and rehearsing musicians. Julian Bream* used to perform with him, John Williams*, Heather Harper*, Janet Baker*, and my father would practise of course. The oddest thing about that was that I'd just hear the flute line at home, then I'd be taken to a concert at which he was playing and hear the whole orchestra. That is really how I got to know a lot of the repertoire – from the flute part! My mother sang in the Bach Choir in London and my father played in the orchestra. I was taken to choral concerts from about the age of five and one of my earliest memories was being taken to hear the *St Matthew Passion* at the Royal Festival Hall at Easter. Even now, I can still remember the experience of being there, but again, I got to know that piece from the flute part first!

DW: *Were you encouraged to have instrumental lessons?*

CM: No, my father didn't really encourage me to think about becoming a musician. By all means learn an instrument for fun, but I think he felt that a musician's life was so unpredictable. My mother was a teacher and wanted me to follow her into teaching.

DW: *Did you sing in a choir at school?*

CM: I did sing in the school choir. It was a religious school and many of the services took place in Westminster Abbey – we sang in the organ loft. This was the time when Simon Preston* was the organist and we were all completely dazzled by him, he seemed to be so charismatic. We had an association with the Abbey and we would sing as the Ripieno choir in the Bach* Passions for example.

DW: *Were you writing anything down at this stage or improvising?*

CM: Yes, I was often doing what my mother would call 'messing about' instead of doing some proper practice. Later she looked back and decided that maybe she should have been a bit more encouraging. There was a very strange local teacher who had studied something called the Yorke Trotter Method, also used by Trinity College Junior Department in London, and the idea was that you learn everything through the ear, learning music like a language. Every Saturday we went to this teacher, she gave us snippets of music and sent us away to compose the rest of the piece. I did that from about the age of seven. The painful moments came when we had to play them. She had a wild garden and we were encouraged to sing to the flowers – very New Age!

DW: *You went to study music at Edinburgh University.*

CM: Yes, when Kenneth Leighton* was there. I studied strict Palestrina counterpoint with him – not my favourite thing to do I must admit, though I would enjoy it much more now. After that I studied with Joseph Horovitz*, a little with Robert Saxton* and perhaps the longest with Adam Gorb* who is now Head of Composition at the Royal Northern College of Music in Manchester.

DW: *That's quite a diverse collection of teachers – can you say what you might have learnt from each?*

CM: Joseph Horovitz was particularly thoughtful and helpful with orchestration and at that time I needed all the help I could get. They each gave me something different I think. Robert Saxton was much more interested in the intellectual process of composition. Adam Gorb taught me about pushing boundaries and just encouraged me to think in a lot of different ways. When I look back, I think I must have been rather arrogant, because I thought then that one didn't need composition lessons, it is just something one can do or not. To some extent I think I still feel that – you have to have that creative impulse but you can be guided along and shown different paths and techniques.

DW: *Was there any pressure to write in any particular way at the time? Did you feel that you were really not supposed to write diatonically?*

CM: I did have the feeling that I should be writing something of a more intellectual nature. I think I could have done that but I just felt that it wasn't the right thing for me. What I always want to do is to try and communicate with the listener. I'm not so interested in writing music that is just for me.

DW: *Is there a particular piece that you are able to say that is my opus 1, that really is me?*

CM: My first 'proper' choral piece was commissioned by the soprano Gillian Humphreys of the Concordia Foundation for the London Musici, conductor Mark Stephenson and the Pontypridd Male Voice Choir. This was a Christmas cantata in five movements, *Every winter change to spring*, and I remember that the entire fee for the work – which was generous – was devoured by the costs of copying by hand both the full score and parts... No computers back in 1991. Shortly after this work, my father suggested that I wrote some 'tuneful' pieces for his flute students. They were subsequently published and have been on the Associated Board* list for a number of years now and have been described as 'useful pieces'. For a time I was known only by these little flute and piano exam pieces.

DW: *You have written in most genres but how is it that choral music has become such an important part of your life? Is it by accident or design?*

CM: I think it is a combination of factors. I just love the voice and what it can do. I think it is such a personal instrument. I always sang a lot in choirs and vocal ensembles and I think that takes one into a very special world. What I find interesting is to try and write something that would appeal to all parts of the choir, not just the top part, so to speak. Whatever I write, I sing it through to myself, just to see how it lies and what the line is like, but I'm just as interested in the inner parts, to try and make them as interesting as I can too.

DW: *What do you think the challenges are when you are writing for different levels of singers? You have, alongside your work for high-level professional groups, written a lot of music for amateur choirs.*

CM: I'm always aware if writing for amateur choirs to try and write something that sounds more difficult than it really is. I like to try and find a way of putting note-plants for a singer to hang on to, something that I hope won't fall apart so easily. Of course with professional choirs one can take a few more risks. I remember writing something for a particular choir and being astonished when a singer told me that it looked simple but it was quite hard. One never knows how it is going to be accepted.

DW: *In conversations we have had in the past you have mentioned Benjamin Britten* a good deal. I know you admire his music and wondered if you felt part of some kind of tradition?*

CM: Definitely. I feel indebted to the past, right the way back to the Renaissance. Britten for me was such a master when it came to writing for choirs, he just seemed to know what would work. For me the past serves the present.

DW: *You take your inspiration from so many different fields – theatre, visual art, science, dance, the natural world. One of your most recent large-scale works, the Da Vinci Requiem, celebrates Leonardo da Vinci who I know has fascinated you for many years.*

CM: Yes, Wimbledon Choral Society and their conductor Neil Ferris commissioned me to write the *Da Vinci Requiem*, to commemorate the 500th anniversary of Da Vinci's death in 1519. Before I started work I remembered that my parents had a copy of *The Notebooks of Leonardo da Vinci* somewhere in their house. In 1946, soon after these translated editions were published, my mother gave them to my father as a wedding present. She knew that my father had an enduring fascination with Leonardo and his scientific view of the world. As a child I loved poring over these large dusty tomes, filled with the most extraordinary sketches. Looking for connections between Leonardo's philosophical writings and the Missa pro Defunctis [Mass for the Dead], became a curiously enriching line of enquiry. Leonardo's position on religion and faith has always been ambiguous. Many have tried to impose their views on his beliefs, but who can say what currency they have? Vasari, the 16th-century art historian, amongst other things, wrote about Leonardo's approach to religion: 'He formed in his mind a conception so heretical as not to approach any religion whatsoever... perhaps he esteemed being a philosopher more than being a Christian'. However, Vasari omitted this rather provocative statement in a second edition of his *Lives of the Painters*. Ultimately, it's the essence of what Leonardo says, how his ideas on life and death marry so well with the Requiem Mass, which intrigues.

DW: *So you combine these writings with the traditional movements of the Requiem.*

CM: Yes, I set the Introit, Kyrie, Lacrimosa, Sanctus, Benedictus, Agnus Dei and Lux aeterna, from the Requiem Mass and extracts from the notebooks to form a seven-movement piece in the shape of an arch. I used other texts too – for the second movement I found an unusual but apt text by Dante Gabriel Rossetti* entitled *For 'Our Lady of the Rocks' by Leonardo da Vinci*. Rossetti wrote the poem sat in front of the painting in the National Gallery and focused on the darker implications of Leonardo's painting – 'Mother, is this the darkness of the end, the Shadow of Death? And is that outer sea infinite, imminent Eternity' – and in 1848, a year of revolutions and turbulence in Europe. The soloists and chorus all come together in the

last movement of the work, the Lux aeterna – light, bright, luminous, the Leonardo text focuses on flight : 'Once you have tasted flight, you will forever walk the earth with your eyes turned skyward...'. In the closing bars all voices drift upwards, folding into silence, an illusion to Leonardo's concept of 'The Perspective of Disappearance' ['La Prospettiva de' perdimenti']. It was a fascinating exploration, aligning Leonardo's insights, both artistic and philosophical, with such a profound and ancient text.

DW: *I know you read a great deal and spend some time matching texts to the circumstances of each commission.*

CM: I find this to be amongst the most interesting parts of the process – looking for the right texts. I do like to have a conversation with the commissioner to see what was wanted – sometimes texts are suggested. Recently I was asked by the Liberal Jewish Synagogue to write a piece and I was a little worried as I knew nothing about Hebrew and how the stresses and accents work. The commissioners were very understanding and asked me if I had any questions for them. I said that I didn't understand why they chose me and the reply was that they could trust me to ask so many questions about pronunciation and stresses – they were constantly feeding me the information. I also enjoy commissioning poets. It is rather wonderful to be able to discuss ideas with a writer, to find a new word if something is awkward from a musical point of view.

DW: *A number of your pieces deal with problems of our own time, climate change and the environment for example in your cantata* Five Seasons, *or war-torn Syria in* Everyday Wonders: The Girl from Aleppo *– do you feel that it is important for a composer to engage with these issues that have contemporary relevance? Also, I imagine that such pieces have an added relevance if you collaborate with a living poet.*

CM: I feel, as many of my composer colleagues will do, that there is much to be said musically which has the potential to resonate with our times. *Five Seasons* was commissioned in 2006 by the Bournemouth Sinfonietta Choir to 'celebrate the organic landscape' and I visited five organic farms in the UK with a poet I had worked with several times before, Christie Dickson. This presented an extraordinary insight into farming life: the joys, the sadness and the loss, and the incredibly hard work at all times of the year, all underlined by financial insecurity and unpredictable weather. We called the cantata *Five Seasons*. The fifth season refers to 'la saison en enfer' or 'season in hell', which is in two parts, each exploring the extremes of man's relationship with the land and the animals in his care, at any time of the year. The second section opens out to suggest the hidden consequences of man's mismanagement, where gain has been put ahead of long-term concern for consequences and the present has been severed from the past. And of course the possible cause of our present pandemic carries ominous similarities.

DW: *And you worked with Kevin Crossley-Holland* on* Everyday Wonders...

CM: This piece addresses the disturbing and still continuing migration of those displaced by war. The National Children's Choir commissioned the work and it was they who suggested the challenging subject of 'children in conflict'. Kevin had met Nujeen Mustafa at the Emirates Airline Festival of Literature in 2017 and then stayed up all night reading Christina Lamb's compelling account – *The Girl from Aleppo* – of Nujeen's journey from Syria to Germany with her remarkable sister Nasrine. He knew that he wanted to shape her story into a choral text for our cantata. Working with Kevin on this subject I did feel carried something of deep significance. Through the story of one exceptional, wheelchair-bound, young Kurdish refugee, I feel that I began to understand more of the terror, distress and helplessness experienced by those driven from their home by the horror of war. As a composer I felt it important for the music not to obscure the text in any way but allow the words to tell the story, from despair, though hope and ultimately (and surprisingly) joy. The prevailing mood of Nujeen's story is embodied by the final line of a chorale that bookends the cantata – 'singing the song of life itself'.

DW: *You have also taken the lives of remarkable individuals, in particular remarkable women, as the starting point for your choral works.*

CM: I have on a number of occasions suggested to the poet Sean Street* that I wanted to write a piece about a particular person. I've given him a text, spoken by this person, and he has put that text into context – so he has encapsulated the words that have been spoken by a historical figure and written text around them. Recent pieces have been to do with figures from science – Rosalind Franklin – a piece for the BBC Singers - who discovered the double helix, which led to the discovery of DNA, and the one I'm writing at the moment is a piece about Clara Barton who founded the Red Cross in America – but she also nursed soldiers in the Civil War – and all these have words spoken by these women and put into context. I wrote *Standing before God* which is about the life of Edith Cavell, to go on a CD – a collection of pieces to commemorate World War One. I was certainly aware of Cavell of course, had often looked at the statue outside St Martin-in-the-Fields in London and read the inscription – 'Patriotism is not enough, I must have no hatred and bitterness towards anyone'. I felt that she was perhaps not remembered enough – she had a state funeral, and this can be seen on YouTube – a story of such courage and resilience against impossible odds. She was a nurse in Belgium when the Germans invaded, she hid 200 allies and she managed to get them to Holland. Many wrote letters of gratitude to her, the Germans came across these letters, and they charged her with treason – the US, rather than the UK, made diplomatic overtures to help her, but the Germans executed her on May 12th 1915. I gave Sean the words she spoke: 'I have seen death so often, that it is not strange or fearful to me, standing as I do before God...' – he then goes on to describe her final moments...

DW: *Have you ever been beaten by a text and thought I just can't set this?*

CM: I don't think so – not yet! It can somehow be moulded into something...

DW: *Once you have the text, can you say how you begin a piece?*

CM: I need to make sure the text is right, reading it over and over again – then comes the hard work! There is that awful moment when you feel you can't put it off any longer. I just find it never gets easier – there are times when I think that it would be lovely to just slip into something, but then at the same time I feel that would be dangerous, because one would write the same piece over and over again. I think it was Hans

Werner Henze* who said 'the next piece you write should always be like the first you have written'. I think these days it is much more difficult for a composer to find the language of a piece.

DW: *You have as one would expect made a number of settings of well-loved liturgical texts, as have most composers of course, but you have also set perhaps even more iconic texts in perhaps an unexpected choral context, such as 'I know that my Redeemer liveth' and 'Some corner of a foreign field'. When dealing with a text that has been so famously set by Handel in a solo vocal context for instance, do you feel a certain pressure?*

CM: On the whole I try not to think too much about this. I just like to try and bring something fresh and new in my own way.

DW: *When you are faced with a blank sheet of manuscript paper – you still work like that- is composing still a pleasure?*

CM: Oh yes, I need the freedom of the paper at that early stage – once it is on the computer it becomes much stiffer and less easy to manipulate. The beginning is always the hardest thing but when I get into a piece it sort of writes itself – you generate the material and there is so much you can do with it, without looking for new material. I like it when I get towards the end. I can then shape it – it must be the same for painting, writing a book, writing a play, that angst and the awful abyss at the beginning.

DW: *Deadlines are a big part of every professional composer's life, do you find them a challenge?*

CM: I'm haunted by deadlines – but they are a necessity of course. Rossini said that the reasons impresarios are so bored is that they are exasperated waiting for composers to deliver their music.

DW: *Do you ever revise?*

CM: Once I've written a piece on the whole I tend to leave it, I don't do massive revisions. I think it is irresistible to feel the need to revise but you just can't keep doing that.

DW: *Are you ever surprised when you hear a piece for the first time?*

CM: Perhaps the greatest surprise can be to hear a piece released or performed at a different tempo from the one that I had in mind. If it is a rehearsal, then there is a possibility to assess the efficacy of the speed with the conductor. And of course the venue acoustics affect the tempo significantly.

DW: *Do performers find things in your music that surprise you?*

CM: Sometimes a conductor might have different voices or different instruments stand out in the texture which can give added insight into the work. I think what is fascinating for any creative artist is to discover how other artists do it and what similarities or differences there are.

DW: *Do you think of the audience when you are writing?*

CM: Yes, to the extent that I try to express something which may have a resonance with the listener.

DW: *Do you enjoy rehearsals and premieres?*

CM: Composing is so solitary I love rehearsals. It is interesting and so rewarding to hear the piece come to life. There is always a feeling of tension from my own perspective, which is nothing to do with the performers. I do enjoy premieres on the whole.

DW: *What advice would you give to a young composer?*

CM: Keep listening to music old and new. Keep improvising and keep writing – there's always scope for change once the notes are on the page. Composition is intensely personal and it's not always easy to take criticism from others but it can be helpful keeping an open mind to different ideas. It's a balance one has to find between being receptive and yet being sure that what one writes is the best it possibly can be and to be secure in that knowledge. Holst's alleged remark perhaps carries some weight: 'never compose anything unless the not composing of it becomes a positive nuisance to you'. That does suggest the need for having a real passion to write music. However, young composers today are very astute and seem to find ways of being played and being heard.

DW: *Elgar quotes Ruskin at the end of* The Dream of Gerontius* – 'This is the best of me...'. Can you say which piece or group of pieces of yours might fall into that category?*

CM: If I were to choose a work of larger proportions then probably the *Da Vinci Requiem*. Or small-scale pieces: *The Lord is Good, Standing as I do before God, O Oriens*.

DW: *We are recording this interview at a very difficult and worrying time – how have you been dealing with lockdown?*

CM: As a large family, spread across England and Scotland, we were fortunate that none of us caught the virus. But we all shaped our lives, as everyone has, to minimise the risk. On a personal level these lockdown months have been challenging as I needed to make 40-mile round trips each week to keep my 101-year-old mother and her carer in 'essential supplies' and, at the same time, endeavour to keep my mother in good spirits. My mother has since died but we were all so grateful that she was able to be in her own home rather than a heart-breaking care home situation. As a result of this, at the start of lockdown I found it difficult to concentrate on work. Knowing the outside world has become an unhealthy place, and with access denied to concerts, museums, exhibitions, meeting friends and with underlying concern about my mother's health, it was a distracting time for me.

Professionally, the realisation that concerts would be cancelled/postponed, and that travel would be impossible and recent commissions transferred to a date in one or two years' time gradually became apparent. To begin with there seemed some hope that some engagements would survive, but ultimately my residencies in the US, Sweden and Germany, workshops in the UK, festivals and concerts, were all swept aside. Although my commissions have fortunately stayed in place – just a matter of completing them! - I, like everyone else, have been so aware of the devastating impact the 'new normal' has had on my fellow musicians. Just awful. I think the pandemic has made me think much more about the world in which we live and how our politicians have handled and continue to handle events.

DW: *What would you say are your five favourite choral works?*

CECILIA'S FIVE FAVOURITE CHORAL WORKS

Bach *Mass in B minor*

Britten *War Requiem*

Tallis *Misereri, nostri*

Harvey *Come Holy Ghost*

James MacMillan *Seven Last Words from the Cross*

Sir James MacMillan

BORN 1959

DW: *Can you tell me something about your musical background and your first musical memories? I think your grandfather was an important influence in your musical education.*

JM: The most musical member of my family was certainly my grandfather, who had been a coal miner in Ayrshire and, like many coal miners, had played in brass bands. He was a euphonium player in the colliery bands and must have been playing in the 1920s, '30s and '40s; he also sang in his local church choir. In Scotland the mines were located in Ayrshire, Fife or the Lothians and a lot of the great brass players in British orchestras in the '80s and '90s started their musical careers in these bands, the trumpeter John Wallace* for instance, for whom years later I wrote my trumpet concerto *Epiclesis*. My mother had played the piano at school, but she wasn't as keen as I turned out to be so my grandfather was happy when I came along. Like a great many British schoolchildren of that generation I was given a little plastic recorder when I was about nine and that in time led to my grandfather taking me to my first band practices and he got me my first cornet. In my teens I began to sing in the school choir and that was a very important development for me.

DW: *It was your school choir that introduced you to liturgical music?*

JM: Although I was and am a Catholic I went to a largely non-Catholic school and in Scotland that tended to mean a very Protestant school! We had a really dynamic Head of Music who was very interested in Catholic liturgical music, so the choir would sing Palestrina*, Lassus*, Byrd*. I certainly remember singing the four-part Mass of Byrd, as well as Bach* and Telemann* and more recent music too. He in turn had been a pupil of a rather legendary figure in Scottish church music, George McPhee*, who was and is director of music at Paisley Abbey. He has been there over half a century.

DW: *I think I read somewhere that there was a turning point when you visited St Mary's Cathedral in Edinburgh and heard liturgical music in that particular acoustic?*

JM: Yes, that was a little earlier on. My parents used to take me to Edinburgh on holiday in the 1960s. On a Sunday morning we would go along to St Mary's and before I probably even knew what a church was I certainly remember this incredible sound that I couldn't quite understand, long before I became aware of music as a life force. It would have been Arthur Oldham* that was choirmaster at that time. He was one of the very few pupils of Benjamin Britten*. The choir were very well known at that time and used to sing regularly at the Edinburgh Festival. Important conductors like Giulini* used to ask for them all the time for the big oratorios they conducted.

DW: *It was clear from an early age that music was to be your life.*

JM: I think so, yes. It was always all I had wanted to do. It was my music teacher at school and George McPhee that had directed me to the music of Kenneth Leighton*, and so I eventually decided that I wanted to study with him at Edinburgh University. He was a marvellous teacher, especially when it came to the technical aspects of composition and orchestration. I know many think of Leighton as quite a conservative composer, and he was in some ways, but he had studied with Petrassi* in Italy and he got to know a lot of the most interesting contemporary music. I remember him showing me scores of composers such as Dallapiccola* in particular. I found those four years enormously fruitful.

DW: *I know the term 'underrated' is thrown around a lot but I do think that is the case with Leighton, a combination of a sort of Yorkshire grit and no nonsense with a deeply spiritual and emotional compositional voice.*

JM: I think so too and I don't think it is any surprise that his choral and organ music is still popular amongst church musicians, but there is a lot more to him than that, some very fine piano music and an opera about St Columba.

DW: *Then after Edinburgh you want to Durham to study with John Casken*.*

JM: Yes, another Yorkshireman! John had fairly recently come back from studying in Poland. He and other British composers like Nigel Osborne* had made a point of going to Poland, mainly because of figures like Lutosławski* and Penderecki* who had made the country a real hot house for new music, where so many interesting things were happening. Polish composers were developing their own voice, which was perhaps moving away from the more soulless nature of some of the European avant-garde. Certainly when I heard pieces like Penderecki's *St Luke Passion* and his *Magnificat* I was bowled over by it and could understand what the attraction was of studying in Poland. John was a great teacher and very good for me. It is extraordinary really – when John was eighteen he had offers from universities to study music and from art school too. He could have easily become a professional artist – he has always painted and his music has that kind of visual quality. When I was studying with him, he was writing *Orion over Farne* which is a very beautiful, impressionistic orchestral work.

DW: *I think it is true to say that it was perhaps a slower road for you to find your own voice, at least when compared to some of your contemporaries, composers like Mark-Anthony Turnage*, George Benjamin*, Steve Martland*.*

JM: That is exactly right. The composers you mention developed very early and knew what they wanted to say in their early twenties or even early teens, whereas I felt as if I was being incubated a bit more. My orchestral piece *The Confession of Isobel Gowdie* was probably the first piece that was more publicly known and I was writing that around my thirtieth birthday. I think that had an impact on my choral music too, because I had moved away from that world, mainly to focus on orchestral and chamber music. Lots of us were writing pieces around that time for groups like Gemini, Lontano, Capricorn, the London Sinfonietta of course – the nature of that particular aesthetic was very much geared to instrumental work and developing a way of writing in a very virtuosic way.

DW: *You wrote a setting of the* Missa Brevis* *in your teens I think and this has been published quite recently?*

JM: Yes, I wrote that when I was at school. I found it in a drawer and discovered that I rather liked it, so I sorted out a few little corners and Boosey's have published it. The 'Sanctus' was certainly sung by the school choir. I wrote quite a bit of choral music at school and when I was at Edinburgh University, but after that I did rather put it aside for a while.

DW: *Was it a sort of battle for you to make your peace with modernism and find your own way?*

JM: I think so, yes, and if you notice, the great modernist composers of the mid-part of the twentieth century were quite reticent in the way that they approached choirs, either ignoring them altogether or only writing for them in an incredibly virtuosic way. A lot of the composers came from countries that have allowed their choral tradition, if they ever had one to begin with, to disappear. It is less the case in Germany, but in France and Italy, Catholic countries of course, any choral tradition had been pretty much abandoned. Even Messiaen* only wrote that beautiful little setting of *O sacrum convivium* for example – the *Trois Petites Liturgies* too of course, but that is a concert piece – so composers like this turned their backs on the choir. Going further back to an earlier generation, when Schoenberg* and Webern* wrote choral or vocal music, they treated the voices like instruments; there is no real sense of there being a natural and idiomatic treatment of the voice. This was a problem for me because I knew that I did not want to abandon choirs and that I had to find a way back somehow.

DW: *There are a couple of choral pieces that come around the same time as* Isobel Gowdie - Cantos Sagrados *from 1989 and* Catherine's Lullabies *(1990) – both of which are rather politically-inspired pieces.*

JM: Yes, the *Lullabies* were actually written to celebrate the birth of my daughter but they aren't peaceful in any way really, rather more concerned with how human love can overcome the most terrible oppression and tragedy. *Cantos Sagrados* is still sung quite a lot. It was originally for choir and organ, then the conductor Christopher Bell* asked me for an orchestral version for the National Youth Choir of Scotland and recently made a very fine recording of it. It is quite a tough piece, not easy to sing, and it combines sacred texts with poems about political oppression in South America. Going back to what I said earlier about finding a way back, the crucial step for me was to find a way of writing sympathetically for voices and not just to use them as substitute instruments.

DW: *I sense that the music of Messiaen is quite important to you, another composer whose faith was central to what he did, but then, after the fall of the Berlin Wall, came all these others, until then hidden figures -Pärt*, Gubaidulina*, Górecki*, Kancheli*, Ustvolskaya* - who were important to you.*

JM: There was this perception in the modern music world, as was the case in many of the other arts, that religion was old-hat and old-fashioned and that a concern for these things, be it sacred music or the liturgy, was not where the 'cutting edge' of modern art should be. I certainly felt that when I was developing as a composer and that was perhaps another reason for me being reluctant to engage with choral music. But with the collapse of the Soviet Union, these composers – some of whom paradoxically came from countries with a very profound and important choral tradition that had been kept alive against all the odds, like Estonia and Latvia for instance – these composers were quite brave and forthright in the way that they tackled religious subject matter. Many of them clashed with the state and were persecuted of course. When their music started to come through, in an odd way it felt as if we were getting permission, along with Messiaen as you say and Jonathan Harvey in this country; it became less 'old-hat' to follow one's particular instincts.

DW: *It is reasonable to say I think that most of your music now, be it choral or anything else, has your faith at the centre of it in some way. Speaking as a non-Catholic and indeed not being particularly religious at all, I still find myself very affected by a piece such as* Seven Last Words. *I know a lot of people are taken with your work in this way and they certainly wouldn't claim to have a particular faith.*

JM: It never really bothers me what people think about these things, but music seems to be a sort of meeting point for those who love music and those who have many and diverse views about religion. You find that people will talk about music and the effect it has on their lives in spiritual terms and I think there is a truth about the nature of music and that it does open the door on the metaphysical or a door onto or into something much bigger than we are. Some might say that was religious or a God-orientated thing, but others not.

DW: *Once you went back to writing choral music there were and are pieces for virtuoso chamber choirs of course, works like* O bone Jesus *or later on* Sun-dogs, *but you also turned your attention to writing pieces for amateur choirs.*

JM: After *Cantos Sagrados* choirs started asking me for pieces, but the choirs that were asking were groups like the BBC Singers, or the Choir of King's College, Cambridge*, where one can write up to their strengths. In the '90s I wrote a piece for the BBC Singers called *Mairi* which is on the one hand quite modal and Gaelic sounding but on the other it is fiendishly hard. I then became aware that other choirs, often good ones, wanted to do this music, but it was just too difficult for them and that was a turning point because I realised that if I wanted to engage with that bigger choral world, I had to find a way of writing music that they wanted to perform and that was within their capabilities. I began to modify some of the technical things I did, the ranges, the leaps of individual lines, the chromaticism, certain rhythmic complexities, in order to suit these voices better. The *Strathclyde Motets* for example were a conscious effort on my part to create a body of work that would be useful for good amateur choirs. They were written for the Strathclyde University Chamber Choir, who are actually very accomplished. Alan Tavener* conducts them, who I have worked with a good deal, and he noticed that the first Motets I wrote were pretty simple, but as the choir got to know my style, I started to write more difficult pieces because I knew the choir could sing them! As a result there are a couple of the Motets that are quite hard, *Pascha Nostrum*, for instance, but on the whole it did teach me to think about what was possible for amateur choirs and the fine choral tradition we have in this country.

DW: *I think perhaps the secret that you have unlocked is in the first place the skill of making something sound or in some cases look complicated, when actually it isn't, which leads in a piece like* O Radiant Dawn, *to a perhaps over-confident choir sounding quite accomplished.*

JM: This is something I have thought about a great deal over many years. That little piece *O Radiant Dawn* is now one of my most performed pieces and sung by lots of different choirs. Actually, although it is one of the *Strathclyde Motets*, it wasn't written for Alan's choir. It was written for my little volunteer choir at St Colomba's Church in Glasgow, when I ran the music for a while, and they were complete amateurs – most didn't read music – they found it quite hard, but we got there in the end and they enjoyed singing it. I was able to use them as a sort of experimental petri dish as it were, to see what might be possible.

DW: *Once you have a text for a piece can you describe what happens next?*

JM: I try not to use the piano, especially when writing for voices. It isn't really helpful apart from checking the odd thing here and there. The sense of each line has to be more instinctive somehow. I used to sing myself, so it has to feel right on the voice. I don't necessarily sing it out loud but just feel it internally. I think writing in silence is a good thing – it trains the ear. If you aren't using a piano or computer you are training your inner imagination which can only be of help.

DW: *Do you think your experience of being a conductor has helped you as a composer?*

JM: Very much so. The whole experience of conducting generally has been enormously helpful to me. I never expected to conduct as much as I do; I didn't really take it seriously until I was in my thirties, by which time most real conductors have built up the beginnings of their career. I didn't do any of the training and just fell into it. As I've worked with amateurs and professionals it has impacted on what I write – I look at things I wrote in my twenties that I probably wouldn't do now because of that experience.

DW: *We have spoken a little bit about how you have taken what you can from the more experimental side of recent music, but also in some ways stepped aside from it. As a conductor you still engage with a wide range of music, including more challenging areas of the repertoire too.*

JM: I do. I've never developed the kind of ideological stance that some composers have about their style or aesthetic. I've enjoyed the plurality of British music and actually think we are far more open than some of our European contemporaries, especially in places like Germany and France. The ideological restrictions are or were very much set in these countries and I've found myself conducting a whole range of new music from Maxwell Davies* and Birtwistle*, through to Tavener* and Jonathan Dove*. I'll happily do all that. I even conducted the 'Darth Vader Theme' from *Star Wars** when I was in India with the BBC Scottish Symphony Orchestra! I don't think Max would ever have done that...

DW: *I don't think he would have done although I would have paid good money to see it... Alongside your work as a composer and conductor you have done a good deal of work to encourage amateur music making in your own community, particularly by setting up The Cumnock Tryst, your music festival in Scotland that enables amateurs and young people to both hear and perform alongside high level professionals.*

JM: Yes, I rather took my lead from what Benjamin Britten had done in Aldeburgh and what Max had done at his St Magnus Festival up here in Scotland. I was always impressed with what they did and the fact that they wanted to write music for and involve different members of the local community. We started a Festival Chorus, and they have sung standard repertoire as well as pieces of mine; we had performances by local ensembles, folk groups, local brass bands – all sorts of things.

DW: *And a recent large-scale piece of yours,* All the Hills and Vales Along, *was written for the Festival Chorus to sing alongside a local brass band, a group of professional string players and, at the first performances, the tenor Ian Bostridge*. This is an example of you having to make use of what might be available in one particular situation, however unlikely the ensemble might sound.*

JM: Yes, this is an oratorio that sets poems by a little-known Scottish war poet, Charles Hamilton Sorley*, who was killed at the Battle of Loos in 1915. The strings can be a string quintet or a fuller string orchestra, but either way I really wanted to write something that would both connect with a local audience and a work that would be both challenging but hopefully enjoyable and rewarding for a wide range of local musicians.

DW: *There have been arguments for hundreds of years about the place of music in church and I know that it is one of your great passions to provide high-quality music that might be sung both by choirs, such as the* Strathclyde Motets, *and by congregations, in your unison Mass settings such as the* St Anne's Mass *and* The Galloway Mass.

JM: For many years I was actively involved in the world of church music and advocating for the things you describe. I've rather given this up though and I've made a decision not to write any more congregational music. It is the same in other denominations, but certainly in the Catholic Church, this subject has turned into a battleground between musicians and others. Musicians are accused of being reactionaries or elitists when they try and bring high standards of music making into the church. It has been going on just recently in the Anglican Church in Sheffield and also at Westminster Cathedral in London -there is a certain element of the clergy that places no value on what musicians can offer. They think it gets in the way of 'their mission', when in actual fact it could be one of the main arms of the Christian message to help establish truth, unity and beauty as part of the life of the church. There is so much bad feeling and rancour about the whole subject that I decided to keep away from it and we moved away from Glasgow about five years ago. I'm glad I'm not involved in those discussions any more.

DW: *This might seem an odd question to ask a composer, as composers spend a lot of time thinking about musical sounds, but one of the many things that strikes me about one of your most frequently performed works,* Seven Last Words from the Cross, *and indeed your more recent* Stabat Mater, *is the use of silence – it seems to be such an important part of the musical experience – also, the extremes of dynamic, intensity, music of almost overwhelming violence but of profound serenity and hope too.*

JM: I think it was Alfred Schnittke* that used to talk of 'silent tones' in his music. He was always adamant that those moments, where it appeared as if nothing was happening, were part of the fabric of the music as much the notes and that they allow a moment of reflection for the listener, a place for them to consider and ponder on what has just been played or sung. It is the same for me but there is also something dramatic about the use of silence; it isn't just John Cage* that has the monopoly on silence, you can hear it in the work of the great Renaissance composers too, the way they would use the huge spaces they were writing for to highlight the silences in their music. Haydn* was certainly aware of silence, both in his orchestral pieces and in his own setting of the 'Seven Last Words'. As far as my *Seven Last Words* is concerned, the silences are very carefully written into the music.

DW: *In the final movement, 'Father, into Thy hands I commend my Spirit', the silences after those fortissimo chords certainly give time for the sound to travel...*

JM: I find it interesting watching conductors rehearsing these movements. They can't always be bothered to observe them in rehearsal of course, it seems like a waste of time, but when they come to a performance they are so vital. I always make a point of asking them 'just remember to be very strict with what appear to be empty bars, even though they may seem very, very long'. It can cause a bit of a panic if the piece is being broadcast; if the silence is too long people can think the signal has disappeared!

DW: *With both of these works, so much intensity which you have to release at some stage, and I would imagine you have to think very hard about the structure – the danger of creating a succession of slow movements...*

JM: With *Seven Last Words* it is, like Haydn, basically seven adagios. One does think when about to write, 'how on earth is this possible whilst maintaining a connection with the listener'. The movements have to be very different – the same with the *Stabat Mater*, four different movements all projecting a similar mood. I mean there are some faster sections but it is basically one single thrust of about fifty minutes. It can be daunting but you just have to be looking for constant variation, different combinations of voices and instruments, use of solo or smaller ensembles from within the choir, different expression, that makes the music feel as if it were evolving and changing. The *Stabat Mater* is a strange text to set and there is a lot of it! It has an odd sort of rhythmic tread too, which might put people off. I'm always looking for new ways of exploring the cruci-

fixion narrative and this is the crucifixion through Mary's eyes, which makes it so different from *Seven Last Words*, the Passion settings. Of course both *Seven Last Words...* and the *Stabat Mater* are for choir and strings; there was just the right distance between them, about twenty years, so I was able to look at them in very different ways.

DW: *And the extremes of violence and serenity – this is music that reflects the times we live in of course, but there is also a feeling at the end of these pieces of serenity, redemption, even hope. Are you conscious of that?*

JM: Yes, and I'm very conscious that my music needs a spectrum to explore the differences between extremes – extremes of violence and serenity. I think that might be the difference in my approach and in the approach of some of the composers we have mentioned. Tavener and Pärt for example tend to avoid violence in their music and I've never been like that. I suppose I am in some ways more traditional. The inheritance of a more discursive music, the presence of symphonic music and sonata form in my memory, plays a part for me; setting up certain oppositions within the same sound space is important to me.

DW: *There was a performance of the* Stabat Mater *recently at the Sistine Chapel in the Vatican.*

JM: Yes, The Sixteen and the Britten Sinfonia went over to Rome to do that. A wonderful experience of course, but nobody was really sure what the acoustic of the chapel would be like until we rehearsed. It was a bit of a worry, but one could feel the delight and relief from the performers that it was possible to make a good sound in that space.

DW: *Do you feel yourself to be part of a musical tradition?*

JM: I think so. I haven't a problem with that at all. The last century saw a good many composers doing everything they could to break their connections with any kind of tradition. They often had political, philosophical and aesthetic reasons for that, but I always think that tradition can be kept alive without the composers being backward looking and that it can inform the present.

DW: *You mention that you are interested in looking at ways to set the narrative of the crucifixion, which leads us on to your Passions – is it your intention to set them all? We already have the Passions according to St John and St Luke.*

JM: I think I would like to do the remaining two, in very different ways – actually my Passion settings are getting smaller. *St John* is for huge forces: two choirs, two soloists and large orchestra; *St Luke* is a little smaller: two choirs, no soloists and chamber orchestra, and I'm thinking that *St Mark* might be choir, organ and a couple of soloists and *St Matthew* maybe just for voices.

DW: *I don't think there is really any question that the name Bach* would not come up when composing a Passion, but it also inspires perhaps to approach the composition in very different ways. How did you come up with the idea in the* St Luke Passion *of the children's choir collectively taking on the role of Christ?*

JM: I don't remember if I planned that particularly, but the idea of children singing the part of Christ at the crucifixion is quite shocking in many ways. Christ is the focus of such terrible violence, but the effect disembodies Christ in a strange way and makes him one of humanity. You get the innocence of Christ coming across and I was able to divide the children's choir into three, which gives scope to pursue the Trinitarian aspect part of it too.

DW: *With all the other things you do, it isn't so surprising that you haven't held a regular teaching post for some time. Do you think that composition can be taught?*

JM: Yes, older and more experienced composers can open up directions for younger colleagues, and still not get in the way with technical matters too much. I haven't been able to do too much teaching for one reason or another although that might be changing as I have a visiting professorship at the University of St Andrews. There isn't a music department as such, but I'm associated with something called the Institute of Theology, Imagination and the Arts, which is basically the Divinity Department, which is a bit frightening as all my colleagues are theologians! Still, I think they are quite keen to have the likes of me involved as we are practising artists and we think about things differently. We are developing new courses and I might be teaching composition there. I sometimes go into local universities and conservatories on conducting trips too and it is fascinating. Also, I mentor young composers a good deal and have just finished my third stint with the London Philharmonic Orchestra, developing new works and leading to performances and recordings. I've done that with The Sixteen and the Genesis Foundation* too.

DW: *Is it true to say that choral music is not considered an inferior thing to write now as it perhaps was when you were a young composer?*

JM: Yes, I've noticed that too. When I was a student nobody really considered writing for choirs for some of the reasons we have discussed. That was before the time of this incredible flourishing of really good British choirs, which is still going on today. Back in the '80s The Sixteen and the Tallis Scholars were singing to small audiences. Now these choirs sing all over the world to packed cathedrals and they mix early music with new works to a willing and curious audience. I certainly didn't see that coming in the 70s and 80s and it means that many more composers are paying more attention to choral music, which is rather inspiring.

DW: *One of your more recent works is for one of these very choirs, ORA – a work to be sung and recorded alongside* Spem in alium*.*

JM: It was an amazing experience writing for 40-part choir. To be honest, when I was asked, I was initially rather worried, but I love that period of music and was able to find a way. It was an intellectual exercise and it really whetted my appetite for multi-part choral music – it was a bit like doing a very complicated crossword! I felt rather bereft when I finished it. There is a moment in my recent Fifth Symphony *Le grand Inconnu*, when the choir divides into twenty parts and so keeps the Tallis experience alive a little. I'm sure this is something I will come back to more and more.

DW: *Are you a disciplined composer? Do you try and work a certain number of hours a day?*

JM: I do try. Of course this year has been very productive and I seem to have got through a lot of things, due in no small amount to the lockdown of course. I've had a little break from composing too, planning ahead, reading a lot. I've never really had an extended break from composing for a while and it felt just right to give myself a sense of refreshment. The question is what do we write at this time. A lot of what I have written is choral music. Just this morning, a score arrived from my publisher and it was my new *Christmas Oratorio* which is a huge piece, a full evening piece, that was supposed to be done later this year – but when will that be done? It is worrying when we will be able to come back to choral music. Maybe this is the time to write chamber music!

DW: *Do you revise very much?*

JM: Not really once they are submitted to my publisher. I tinker away at things when I'm writing. I have a marvellous editor at Boosey's who is very strict about things and that is sometimes a sort of revising process. That is when a lot of revisionary thought is done.

DW: *Are you ever surprised when you hear a piece for the first time?*

JM: Yes and no. I think writing music is a bit like an old photograph that you used to have to take and be developed, before digital technology took over. You used to get back that black and white negative. Suddenly, when you hear it, it becomes a colour photograph and that is the surprise or a shock, usually a pleasurable experience.

DW: *In that case, do performers ever find things in your music that you didn't know were there?*

JM: All the time. They have insights into the expression, the pacing and the communication of the music that sometimes I don't feel. I suppose it is that next stage in the communicative process that is so vital – a composer relies on the interpretation for the music to come alive and one relies so much on the musicians.

DW: *Do you think about the audience when you are composing?*

JM: I think what I have in mind is an ideal listener, someone who is as hungry and thirsty for a new musical experience as I am. It can be difficult to find that kind of listener in the orchestral world sometimes – they know what they like and like what they know. I think what a composer needs is someone who is open-hearted and open-minded.

DW: *As we have already suggested, would you agree that choirs and audiences for choirs are rather more sympathetic to the new?*

JM: I have certainly found that. As I said earlier, I think audiences think that if a choir sings a piece by a living composer alongside Josquin*, Palestrina* or Tallis* or whoever, it must be worth engaging with. When my *St John Passion* was performed in Scotland for the first time a few years ago the promotion of the programme was being done by the orchestra and I checked a few weeks before about sales of tickets and it wasn't good. So I passed on my list of choral contacts, choral conductors and choral societies that I knew in the central belt of Scotland and of course they hadn't been contacted and didn't know this was happening. The orchestra did promote the concert to these organisations and when it came to the performance it was packed – packed by an audience of choral singers, conductors and enthusiasts, which was quite telling I thought. That wouldn't have happened had it been left to the standard orchestral audience.

DW: *Does writing music get easier the older you get?*

JM: I think you build up a fluidity that is valuable and it feeds the engine of daily work. One learns how to take the silences and the absences of progress. I think a lot of younger composers worry about composer's block. It is an important preparation time that is just as important and necessary as developing creativity. It is almost as if the inspiration goes underground or into the subconscious, it bubbles away...

DW: *You still believe in this word inspiration?*

JM: Oh yes, one has to be motivated and for me I read a lot and inspiration comes from what other people have to say about our existence and what we are.

DW: *You might have already answered this, but I wondered if there was anything that you are longing to write? Would this be the remaining Passions?*

JM: Yes, perhaps. Now I've written two I'm very keen that the four works are well spaced out and very different. I'm not ready to do *St Mark* quite yet. Perhaps I need some years to think about new ideas and perspectives on the Passion to percolate a little. I've got to be patient in that regard.

DW: *Elgar quotes Ruskin at the end of* The Dream of Gerontius* – 'This is the best of me…'. Is there a piece of yours, or a group of pieces, that might lead you to make a similar statement?*

JM: I try not to think about that if I'm honest. I'm making a series of radio programmes about four composers and the impact of religion on their lives – Tallis, Wagner*, Elgar* and Bernstein* – so quite a diverse group of composers. This quote of Elgar came up and of course he was quite young when he said this. Maybe it was a way of inspiring himself to match *Gerontius*, but hopefully it didn't invalidate everything that happened afterwards. I wouldn't like to get myself into that situation – there are certain things I'm proud of but I wouldn't want to say something was my best piece in case it was downhill from there! It might even become a source of anxiety for me, something that I have to match. Maybe this period of self-reflection that I've talked about and sense of beginning again could give me a new direction – we will see.

DW: *We are talking at a very difficult time- you mention that you have been quite productive which is positive but there are terrible negatives too of course.*

JM: I think every musician is feeling this, a sort of existential angst! There is this worry: 'is that it?' – that is the most pessimistic outcome but there seems to be delay after delay.

Other countries seem to be doing better than us, but one does think, 'when does this all end?'. For performers much more so than anyone else of course – it is so terrible. One has to just try to imagine that one is writing music for the future and it trains the mind. I suppose one is always writing for a time when one is not here, but perhaps the situation we are in focuses the mind on that even more.

DW: *What would you say are your five favourite choral works?*

SIR JAMES' FIVE FAVOURITE CHORAL WORKS

Bach *Magnificat*

Beethoven *Missa Solemnis*

Byrd *Mass for Four Voices*

Elgar *The Dream of Gerontius*

Schnittke *Concerto for Choir*

Jaakko Mäntyjärvi

BORN 1963

DW: *Can you tell me about your first musical memories? Did you grow up in a musical family?*

JM: Yes, in the sense that both of my parents had amateur music making as part of their lives. My father played in dance bands and indeed still does play 'old-time jazz' to this day. My mother less so, though she learnt the piano at school, so it was a musically-informed home. As far as I know there aren't any professional musicians on either side of the family. I learnt the piano at 'gun-point' from about the age of ten as many middle-class kids do, but it didn't really catch on until I was 13. We spent a year in the USA and I suppose you might call it deprivation therapy, we didn't have a piano there, and I suddenly realised how much I missed it. I honestly can't remember when the impulse came to write music, perhaps in my late teens, when I was at secondary school.

DW: *Did choral music play an important part in your musical education?*

JM: It didn't really become a serious pursuit until I went to university in Helsinki. I was born in Turku, a city on the southwest coast of Finland. I did a little group singing of course at school, but at university I came into contact with a pretty good student choir, the Savolaisen Osakunnan Laulajat Choir. I began to really enjoy that and realised that this was something I wanted to take further. In hindsight, it is odd that it happened that way – I remember hearing big choral pieces when I was still at school, like the Beethoven* *Mass in* C, the Bach* *Christmas Oratorio* and *Messiah**, early on, but it didn't seem to spark any interest then.

DW: *You studied linguistics at the University of Helsinki.*

JM: Well, to be precise, I applied to study musicology and English. I'm technically bi-lingual -although my parents are Finnish-speaking we spent three years in English-speaking countries when I was a teenager and young enough to assimilate the language. Studying English was therefore an easy option! As it turned out, after a year, I got bored of musicology, and decided to do a degree in English instead. At the same time I got a place at the Sibelius Academy to study what I thought was composition but turned out to be music theory, so I did the two things in parallel which is something one wouldn't be allowed to do now. Actually, I never graduated from the Academy. I studied music theory and choral conducting to a fairly high level but by the time it became necessary for me to put in a huge effort to graduate I had moved on to other things. In short, I have a Masters degree in English but no degree in music!

DW: *I read that you were an orchestral timpanist and played with the Helsinki University Orchestra too.*

JM: Yes, that just happened by accident. It just seemed like something that would be fun to do, and it was, but oddly enough it didn't translate into a burning desire to write for the orchestra. I've often wondered about this – maybe it was just the combination of the human voice and the social aspects of choral singing that drew me into that world, but either way nothing was planned at all. It could also have been something to do with the fact that as I was studying English we did a good deal of text analysis and poetry appreciation, looking at how to understand things expressed in literary terms, so maybe it was that combination that worked for me.

DW: *Text for most composers is a vital consideration, but for you it really is at the forefront of your mind all of the time.*

JM: Yes, most definitely, the text is of paramount importance to me. In fact, I can only think of one single exception that I came up with the music before I had found and studied a text. I spend a lot of time with the text before thinking about music.

DW: *And these text choices reflect a wide range of reading in several languages, Finnish and Swedish of course, but English, Latin, Basque...*

JM: I just don't like to repeat myself and so I use texts that stop me from doing that.

DW: *You have spent a good part of your life not only conducting choirs but also singing in them – the Savonlinna Opera Chorus, Sibelius Academy Vocal Ensemble and the Tapiola Chamber Choir for instance. This must mean that you are particularly mindful of the practicalities when writing for a choir. Several of your pieces make considerable demands on singers, the* Stuttgart Psalms *[Stuttgarter Psalmen] for instance would stretch even the best choir, but the writing is always idiomatic, and the music is grateful to sing.*

JM: It is certainly a huge advantage to know the instrument from the inside and that is why I write almost exclusively choral music. It is the instrument I know best and there is always a healthy demand for music for that instrument, so there has been no need for me to branch out into anything else. There are one or two exceptions. I was commissioned to write a work for organ solo a few years ago. I accepted the invitation and was curious to see how it would turn out. Let us just say that I won't be writing another organ solo. Choral music is still what interests me the most. I've been working to commission now for something like 20 years and try to write to the strengths of the group, I like to know something about the group I'm writing for, the context of the performance, what might be in the rest of the programme, even though these decisions rarely have anything to do with the future life of the piece in question. Having said that I like to write to the strengths of the choir, I also have to be careful that I don't take this too far and when writing for a virtuoso group I don't make the piece impossible for anyone else. I don't see the point of writing a piece that will only get sung once. I need to have a deadline really – things that I sketch out on my own rarely get finished unless I can fit a commission around the idea. If someone were to ask me for an instrumental piece or, God forbid, even an opera, I'm not sure how I would respond. It would depend on my mood at that time I suppose.

DW: *So that means that if you are writing for a virtuoso chamber choir you sometimes have to reign yourself in a little.*

JM: Exactly. For example, when I was commissioned by the King's Singers, even though I knew they were very good, I was careful to write a piece that would still have a chance with a less-able group. Although the opposite did happen with the *Stuttgart Psalms* that you mentioned. They were commissioned by the Bach Akademie in Stuttgart though I did know that the premiere would be given by the Uppsala Chamber Choir in Sweden and that the conductor would be Stefan Parkman. Stefan is a fantastic choral conductor and I must say that I allowed myself to get a little carried away, wanting to provide a challenge to him as well as the choir. The pieces turned out to be a big, almost thirty-minute sing and I know they had to spend a long time on them. I might not have made the work as difficult as I did had I known a little more about the choir, but in the end, they did very well and even liked the piece too. On the whole, I do tend to be rather more careful in situations like that.

DW: *That is surely half the battle won isn't it, when a choir works hard on a piece, but they feel all their effort has been worthwhile? It isn't always the case in my experience.*

JM: This is something I try hard to achieve – I certainly don't want choirs to feel that my pieces are a battle of any kind. I can only try to write music that I will enjoy and just hope that others will feel the same way – if they do, then this is a welcome bonus. I like to think that the music I come up with and like to hear is at least idiomatic and 'singable' even if it isn't terribly easy sometimes.

DW: *As far as composition goes, is it right to say that you are to a large extent self-taught? We have said that you studied choral conducting and musicology but not composition.*

JM: I'm very much self-taught. I sometimes say that I have never had any formal training in composition, although I did follow a short course at the Sibelius Academy, taught by Olli Kortekangas*. He was a modernist figure in the '80s, about ten years older than me I think, but he had a rather broader outlook than most and has written a good deal of choral music, so was more sympathetic than some would be. I had lessons with him over one semester, about ten weeks. Apart from that I have had no real compositional training as such and have learnt as a result of experience.

DW: *Were there any particular composers that you felt close to as a student that you feel might have had an influence on your music?*

JM: Certainly Einojuhani Rautavaara*, one of Finland's most important composers – he wrote a lot of choral music and had a very pragmatic approach to commissions, making sure that his music fitted the occasion and/or the groups for which it was written. I admired him a lot.

DW: *When you were a student on the 1980s, in common with a lot of the composers I have talked to, writing choral music was not perhaps the most obvious thing to do and even considered rather second-rate.*

JM: There are two considerations here I think – one, when I was a student, there was a movement here in Finland, of young musicians and composers to promote contemporary music, as there wasn't a great deal of it being programmed at the time...

DW: *This would be composers such as Magnus Lindberg*, Esa-Pekka Salonen*, Kaija Saariaho*...*

JM: Yes, very much, and they had a point. They were very active in promoting each other's work and getting performances. The flip side was that in a country with a relatively small population like Finland, there is room for only one received truth at the time. So what happened was, that as far as classical music was concerned, this became 'the word'. You were not a real composer unless you wrote in this way, regardless of whether you wrote choral music, opera, music for orchestra, or anything else. There was a sort of feud between older, more established composers of opera especially and these younger people, because there was a Finnish opera boom in the '80s, odd that it might sound now...

DW: *Yes, the operas of Sallinen* and Kokkonen* were staged all over world...*

JM: Those two in particular, also perhaps Rautavaara. JoonasKokkonen's opera *The Last Temptations* was and is the most performed opera by a Finnish composer. These operas were disparaged by these angry young men and women who thought they were terribly dated and not at all interesting. So, all this had a slightly toxic effect and people like myself, who were still interested in what one might call more traditional music, felt a little lost and that we didn't have an outlet. This might well be another reason for me beginning to concentrate on choral music, which is less insular and inward-looking. The other consideration is that choral music in Finland and in the Baltic States, with whom we have a close connection, was so firmly associated with political movements, the struggle for independence in particular, and a search for national identity. It carried the stigma of being 'ideologically loaded', either nationalistic and patriotic in some way or sacred in the context of the church. And it became difficult to see how choral music could be treated as something viable and serious on its own account. It has been a slow development for the public at large.

DW: *But the remarkable thing is that now choral music is very popular and generates a huge following both in concert and recording terms.*

JM: I have a feeling that there have always been people that have come along to a choral concert and been amazed at what a good choir can really do and what choral music can be. I think it is a public relations problem – I've witnessed more recently audience members coming in and being struck not only by the standard of performance but also by the breadth of repertoire too.

DW: *I think you have described yourself as an 'eclectic traditionalist'. Listening to your music, it is clear that you have drawn on a huge range of musics – folk, jazz, Orthodox Church music, plainchant, elements of Renaissance and Baroque music, what might be called more contemporary vocal techniques – all playing a part in your musical language.*

JM: I've always been conscious of influences coming in and influences going out. I'm hoping that the materials I use do not give the impression of just being pasted in or slapped onto a structure in some way. There are a lot of what you might call 'Easter eggs' in my music, things that people might recognise if they are familiar with the original source. One of the most obvious ones, which I put down to youthful arrogance, comes at the end of *Come away death* from my *Four Shakespeare Songs* – the final cadence, going from F sharp to F major, is also the final cadence in the Britten* *War Requiem...*

DW: *That is something that I should have noticed but I must admit that I didn't... Now you point it out of course I recognise the connection.*

JM: Perhaps it is not the kind of distinctive cadence that would lead you to make the connection, but I was working with a group once that had been involved in the Britten and they recognised it.

DW: *I did notice in that piece in particular, along with some of the other Shakespeare songs, that there is, for want of a better expression, 'an English feel' to the music.*

JM: One of the things that has surprised me over the years is that, at the time I wrote those pieces, I had never heard the *Three Shakespeare Songs* by Vaughan Williams*. People find that hard to believe now but it is absolutely true. This was pointed out by someone who didn't want to programme my pieces because they felt that they were too similar to the Vaughan Williams which I can sort of understand.

DW: *That is carrying the connection a little far, I wouldn't have said the songs were similar really, just that there is a definite 'English atmosphere' – these things are rather difficult to describe without getting very technically involved. The other remarkable thing about the first set of Shakespeare songs, the* Four Shakespeare Songs, *is that they are in effect your opus1, your first acknowledged choral piece.*

JM: Pretty much – there is a set of three part-songs setting Finnish texts that come just before that, which are nice enough but not so memorable. The *Shakespeare Songs* are the first 'real piece' I suppose.

DW: *What is extraordinary is that the songs are so incredibly confident and assured in so far as command of the genre is concerned, so imaginative...*

JM: They were written in my second year at university so I would have been 21 when I started to compose them. I find it both gratifying and worrying that these pieces remain my most often performed works.

DW: *Well, they are very popular and for good reason. It might in retrospect be seen as quite daring to take on such well-known texts as 'Come away death' and 'Full fathom five', that had been set by so many composers, not just British composers of course.*

JM: To be honest, I had no thought of them having any wider exposure than for the student choir in which I was singing and for whom I wrote them. Going back to what we talked about before, these were a very big and challenging sing for that particular choir at the time and pushed them as far as they could go, but again people liked them and so they came off rather well at the premiere. The choice of text really had a practical origin too, as they came from the plays that I was studying as part of my English degree, so my two worlds at least, were connected.

DW: *Speaking of influences, I'm not sure you quote folk music particularly – a piece like* El Hambo *is a sort of mad fantasy on a certain type of folk music, but it is an important part of your musical personality I think.*

JM: Oh yes. Maybe quote is too strong a word, but I do use elements of the ancient Finnish folk tradition, which would certainly be identifiable to Finns. There are quite a few pieces that set texts from folklore and musically to some degree involve elements from the performing tradition too, songs that used to be sung or chanted in particular ways or use certain melodic formulae. I'd say this was partly due to a boom in folk music that began in the mid-'80s, with the establishment of a Department of Folk Music at the Sibelius Academy, along with the Department of Jazz. People started to realise that one can do new things in a folk idiom rather than just playing museum pieces over and over again, creating new sounds, writing new texts in the same poetic idiom, and going in different directions. I think all that has filtered into my music, particularly the curious parallels between folk music and minimalism, this idea of gradual change or extending a moment, repetition that isn't really repetition, that sort of thing. An example would be a folksong with several verses that would get rather boring hearing the same thing over and over again, but just making tiny changes and inflexions creates gradual change over time. There are so many more interesting things going on in folk music than the rather stereotypical image might suggest.

DW: *You have said that you consider yourself to be fairly traditional as far as your musical language is concerned, but you do make use of what one might call more advanced techniques when you feel the text calls for such things – these are noticeable in the Shakespeare songs, which fittingly take on a theatrical flavour as the singers become witches around the cauldron - you occasionally use chant, free rhythmic passages, ask the singers to clap or stamp, and there is some very unnerving use of whispering in one of the* Stuttgart Psalms.

JM: You are right – it is more of a textural thing for me. It isn't that I don't appreciate choral music that draws on these techniques, it is just part of the toolkit that I can use when appropriate. In the second of the *Stuttgart Psalms* for instance there is a section that sort of morphs from chanting on one note to whispering – half of the choir sing and have a diminuendo and half the choir whisper and have a crescendo. I'm quite frugal with using these kinds of things. I'm rather interested in micro-tonality but haven't yet found a way to introduce that into what I do. The only piece in which I came close to this was the opening of the Magnificat in the *Trinity Service* – the soprano solo that begins and ends the Magnificat I imagined as an overtone melody. It should have a flat tritone and a flat seventh, but eventually, as I didn't want to drive the soloist crazy and as the rest of the piece wouldn't work in the same way, I wrote a more conventional melody.

DW: *Trinity College, Cambridge, have just, at the time of writing, issued a disc of your choral works, that includes not just a Mag & Nunc*, but a full Evensong, complete with anthem, psalms and responses. A genre that seems inescapably English I suppose...*

JM: It would have been a daunting proposal had this been dumped on me at the beginning of this recording project. The choir did work on this disc for two years. Sometime after the first recording sessions Stephen Layton* had the idea of me writing a completely new piece for the disc and initially we discussed a Mag &Nunc but it sort of took on a life of its own and I wrote an entire Service. By that time I had been to several Evensongs at the College and so saw the way they do things. Stephen tends to programme a very diverse collection of music even in the context of something as traditional as Evensong, so I was pleased to have the challenge and I was aware that what I came up with did not necessarily need to sit within a particular English tradition.

DW: *I wanted to ask you about humour in your music. There are a number of pieces that seem to tread a very delicate line, on the one hand making an audience smile, but stepping back before it becomes facile in any way.*

JM: I'm conscious of it in so far as I can't afford to be too silly, which is really what you just suggested. I do enjoy doing that – overt slapstick is one thing...

DW: *Maybe ironic is a better word...*

JM: Ironic or witty maybe? One can have certain allusions of things that people may or may not recognise.

DW: *For instance, the tiny cycle of pieces that you call 'Announcements', that set, well, announcements: 'We regret to announce...', 'Under health and safety regulations...', etc.*

JM: Yes, those texts are something that people are used to hearing all the time anyway, so setting them to music just highlights them in a different way, pointing out that one can set anything to music: recipes, instructions, regulations, whatever – not a pairing that one might expect. Another level is what I called earlier on the 'Easter Eggs' – there are things that I hide in my pieces, lifting things from one place and putting them somewhere else. These work on varying levels of subtlety – quotes or allusions that only I know about but others that are more recognisable. I have come to the conclusion, that having something recognisable in a piece makes a connection with the audience. I wrote a piece that sets 'The Famous Tay Whale' by William McGonagall* that ends up with the whale being caught, and I quote a fragment from Wagner's *The Flying Dutchman**. Humour works on many different levels.

DW: *But the humour is always affectionate – in* El Hambo *for instance you are poking gentle fun at a certain kind of folk music and a not very good folk band...*

JM: Yes, the piece should have three beats in the bar but actually has five, giving a lop-sided effect. As with the other similar piece, *Pseudo-yoik*, I've often made the point to performers that these are not meant to be comedy pieces. The audience might well find them amusing and that is fine, but this doesn't mean that the performers have to demonstrate that they find it funny too. I'm often reminded of what Eric Morecambe* said to André Previn* before that famous television Christmas special: 'On no account must the audience see that we think this is funny…'. In effect, comedy is a serious business.

DW: *We have talked about texts – what happens once you have the text: do you improvise, do you use a keyboard?*

JM: I have a bad habit of proof-reading by synthesiser. Actually, that isn't the whole truth. I make a habit every so often of writing by hand, the old-fashioned way, just to keep up the practice. I do use a keyboard sometimes, but these days I know to quite a large extent in my head what is going to happen before I start a piece. In an alarming number of cases, the first thing I put down to fill a gap often turns up in the finished piece.

DW: *Looking through your catalogue, you have written a setting of the* Stabat Mater *but that apart you seem to have avoided Masses, settings of the Requiem, Te Deum, that sort of thing.* Canticum Calamitatis Maritimae [Song of Maritime Calamity], *inspired by the MS Estonia disaster of 1994, is a sort of mini-Requiem perhaps?*

JM: It is in a way, yes. As to the Mass and the Requiem, one just feels the rather heavy weight of tradition on one's shoulders in a rather negative way. There is quite a high threshold. Also, I don't like to repeat myself and I don't enjoy repeating things that have been done a million times in the past. I have used shorter liturgical texts that have been set God knows how many times – 'Tantum ergo', 'Ave verum corpus', 'Ave Maria', for example, but as to the bigger statements, I think it is the weight of tradition. I would never even contemplate writing a string quartet, however much someone offered me!

DW: *Are you a disciplined composer? I know you have two professional lives really – you are a Finnish-English translator and a composer – do you still manage to compose every day?*

JM: No, I don't deliberately divide my time between the two activities. I tried it at one time and it just doesn't work. I'm not the sort of composer who can rent a villa in Italy for three weeks and go off to write. I work best on several things, for short periods of time. Even within one working day I can work on three different translations and then go back to music, or vice versa. I tend to have periods of activity, especially if the deadline for a new work is uncomfortably close... It is difficult to quantify as I have musical ideas rolling around in my head long before I write them down.

DW: *Are you ever surprised when you hear a piece for the first time?*

JM: Is it terribly arrogant of me to say no?

DW: *Not at all – I've had several different answers to this question.*

JM: I can't recall that I've ever been completely surprised by the end result and by now I have a large enough body of experience to know what any given texture will sound like. I also have a reasonable degree of tolerance when it comes to performances of my music. To begin with I don't have perfect pitch, so if something goes flat but hangs together somehow, in tempo, then it can still work. I may notice this happening, but it doesn't worry me very much. I do provide metronome markings in my pieces but these are a guide – the only time it does bother me is if a piece is clearly faster than I have imagined it. I may come around to accepting it but the first impression is that the performers don't believe in the material and are trying to get to the end as fast they can!

DW: *Are you surprised at what performers find in your music?*

JM: Sometimes yes. The *Stuttgart Psalms* are a case in point. I carefully worked out all the metre changes and relationships between the tempi. I noticed that when Stephen Layton rehearsed the work with Trinity College Choir for the recording he did something slightly different – initially I wondered about it, but on reflection decided that it really improved the energy levels, so I am always interested in what performers bring.

DW: *It is one thing conducting your own pieces of course, but you have often sung in performances of your works as a chorister too – is it difficult to step back in these sorts of situations?*

JM: Yes and no! I have been guilty of conducting my own music at a different tempo to the one indicated in the score and I've had this pointed out to me. My first response is that I'm the composer and I outrank you! But, more seriously, this is of course to do with the choir I am working with, the acoustic of the venue, the mood of the day, etc. If it sounds better at a different tempo I am inclined to go that way. As far as other performers are concerned, I do trust them to do what they think is right at that time. If I'm singing in a choir that is performing my own stuff, I'm in performer mode and so tend not to have a running commentary as to what is going on, unless something goes widely off-track. I know several conductors have felt rather uncomfortable when conducting my music if I'm singing in the choir – it is bad enough having the composer there but having him singing too?!

DW: *Do you hear huge differences in the sound that choirs make around the world? For instance, do choirs in Finland sound very different to choirs in the UK or the US?*

JM: There are certainly noticeable differences between American and European choirs – American choirs I think have a more 'soloistic' approach, regardless of whether they are singing in a choir or not. I don't like to talk about vibrato too much as it is there all the time in one form or another, but I think American choirs have what might be called a fuller sound in general. Whether that is positive or negative depends on the choir and the singers in it. Honestly, I'm not sure that the differences are so huge – people in this part of the world are always a bit perplexed when people talk about the Scandinavian choral sound, because as far as we're concerned it doesn't exist. There are perhaps a small number of national characteristics that you will hear in choirs from Norway, Sweden, Finland, the Baltic states, but I do think that western choral music on the whole is pretty homogeneous. The underlying tradition is not that different from one place to another.

DW: *There is such a rich choral heritage in Finland, most of which is not heard outside of Finland I suppose because of the problem of the language.*

JM: It is sad really because paradoxically Finnish is actually one of the easiest languages to pronounce – the grammar is murder, but the pronunciation is easy because it is basically one letter one sound, with very few exceptions. If you are used to singing in Latin you are halfway there anyway. Again, it is a PR problem; everyone seems to think that Finnish is an impossible language, but really, singing in a foreign language that you have no knowledge of at all is always a problem. As an English-speaking choral singer, if you are faced with Italian, German or French, then you have some notion of what is going on, but if you come across Finnish, then the initial reaction is that you don't have a clue.

DW: *You have held firmly with Sulasol, your publisher in Finland. I read that you consider yourself to be a hopeless self-promoter, but I wondered that with your success there might be some surprise that you have not been 'snapped up' by a bigger publishing house.*

JM: I am the worst self-promoter in the world! I do ascribe whatever success I have had to the efforts of my publisher, in particular Reijo Kekkonen. Sulasol is the publishing arm of the largest national choral association in Finland and Reijo is responsible for the huge expansion in publishing. He had sung some of my music, the *Shakespeare Songs* in the first instance, and he asked me if he could publish them rather than the other way around. He is just exceptional at what he does and knows exactly the right piece for the right person or occasion.

DW: *Are you self-critical?*

JM: Oh yes, very much so. That is partly the reason that a lot of my first ideas often end up in the finished piece – that and the necessity of a deadline. I do worry endlessly and if I didn't have that I would never finish anything.

DW: *The act of composition gets easier with more experience.*

JM: Easier in so much as it is more straightforward to arrive at the finished product. Being able to accept the finished product has not got any easier. One thing I did decide rather early on was that once a piece was out and published, I would not go back and revise it.

DW: *That's my next question…*

JM: No, unless there is something really drastically wrong, I don't do that. Sometimes I have been asked to do an arrangement or adaptation of a piece and I'm open to do that, but nothing more than that.

DW: *Do you think of the audience when you are writing?*

JM: In a sense, yes. Going back to the 'Easter Eggs' again, I like to put in the occasional reference to help the audience along, but it would be very dangerous to do this too much.

DW: *I'm not sure you have held a regular teaching position – we have said that you were pretty much self-taught, but do you think that composition can be taught?*

JM: There are certain elements that can be taught and it is good to get feedback, or more particularly, learn how to take feedback! I suppose the flip side of my not having a proper composition teacher is that I have been asked to teach and I've always said no. It is not something that I would be comfortable with. I've said that I would be prepared to offer comments with my 'performer's hat' on but not wearing my composer's hat. I don't know if that makes a difference or not but there it is. In any case I wouldn't be interested in teaching composition.

DW: *But surely for a young composer to have comments from an experienced conductor and singer is just as useful?*

JM: Possibly, but if you are teaching composition there always seems to be an underlying philosophy that you are wanting to impart, or an approach that you are wanting to communicate or even impose. There are things about my process when writing music that I can't even explain to myself!

DW: *Do you have any advice to young composers?*

JM: The scene has changed so much since I started out. I suppose it is all about networking these days. You can't imagine that you are writing music in your studio and not telling anyone about it – certainly as far as choral music is concerned there is a very powerful grapevine, and people recommend pieces to one another. *El Hambo* is a good example – it was commissioned by a choir in Finland, then performed in Sweden, then at the ACDA* conference in America – that piece just travelled around to begin with because conductors told each other about it.

DW: *Is there anything you are particularly longing to write?*

JM: Pretty much anything at the moment as I haven't written very much at all this year. These odd circumstances we are in have not helped of course; one becomes very lazy. Choirs have slowly started rehearsing again but for how long? I've been terribly lazy and unproductive and haven't really felt the urge to write anything new to be honest.

DW: *Elgar quotes Ruskin at the end of* The Dream of Gerontius* – 'This is the best of me...'. Can you say which piece or groups of pieces of yours might fall into that category?*

JM: I'm not sure I can single out one piece. There are some pieces that have been less successful than I had hoped, both in terms of what I feel and any afterlife they might have or have not had. Maybe the *Four Shakespeare Songs*, even though they are on the cusp of more enthusiasm than technique, they have done rather well. *Canticum Calmitatis Maritimae*, which, after a slow start, has done well particularly in the US - that isn't an easy piece at all either. Also *Die Stimmer des Kindes* – a piece commissioned by a vocal group here in Finland, a male ensemble with counter-tenor, but that has been taken up elsewhere and I know it is the piece that got me commissions from Chanticleer and the King's Singers so I must have done something right and I'm quite pleased with the piece.

DW: *We have touched on this a little already, but we are recording this interview at a very worrying and difficult time – how have you been dealing with lockdown?*

JM: I have the kind of personality that without obligations or deadlines I don't write! I'm not entirely sure how I would respond at the moment anyway. There are a few sketches around for pieces I would like to write at some point, but I also have a phobia of not mentioning details of incomplete ideas... I've spent the time I would have been writing music watching YouTube videos basically! Actually, I have done a YouTube documentary about *Spem in alium** called 'Spem in alium – a mystery in 40 parts'. I wrote my own 40-part piece some years ago, *Tentatio*.

DW: *What would you say are your five favourite choral works?*

JAAKKO'S FIVE FAVOURITE CHORAL WORKS

Berg arr. Clytus Gottwald *Die Nachtigall*

Rachmaninov *All-night Vigil*

Rautavaara *Die erste Elegie* (I could have chosen several of his pieces)

Tallis *Spem in alium*

Eric Whitacre *Water Night*

Paul Mealor

BORN 1975

DW: *Can you tell me about your first musical memories? Did you grow up in a musical family?*

PM: I was born in St Asaph, North Wales, and both of my parents were and are amateur musicians, but good ones. We were a brass band family. My dad played the tuba, my mum the flugelhorn, my elder brother was a very good improvising pianist – something which I still can't do, but wish I could. Music was around the place for fun, there was never any hint of pressure, but it was always there. Then when I was nine, something extraordinary happened – I had a religious experience. I've spoken about this before and lots of people have written to me to say that something similar had happened to them. I fell into a river near my home, couldn't swim and started to drown. There was nobody about and after a while I stopped fighting and surrendered to what I thought would be death. I suddenly felt an incredible warmth come over me, which made me feel if this is what death is like, it can't be so bad, but it was an amazing feeling I hadn't felt before or since. Eventually, I was lucky enough to be dragged out by a passer-by and resuscitated. I told my dad what had happened and the only thing he could think of to do was to take me to St Asaph Cathedral to talk to the Dean. I remember walking into the Cathedral and the choir were rehearsing two pieces – Orlando Gibbons'* *See, see, the Word is Incarnate* and John Rutter's* *What Sweeter Music*. I was completely mesmerised; I had never heard anything like that before and said to my dad this is what I want to do! Shortly after that I had an audition for the choir and by a stroke of luck I got into the choir and I sang in the cathedral choir from the age of nine.

DW: *So the sort of music you were singing at St Asaph's, the acoustic of that building and the atmosphere, quite apart from the religious experience you mentioned, have all affected everything you have written since?*

PM: Absolutely. The amazing cathedral – it was just so beautiful, quite apart from the choir itself, an incredible experience for a kid of nine to be singing in that building. Also, my father is of Polish-Russian descent – our name was originally Milerovsky – and his mother, my grandmother, used to play a lot of music from the Russian Orthodox tradition which made a very deep impression on me.

DW: *That's where those low bass parts come from...*

PM: I think so. I can't think of any other reason for them to be there. Hearing all that Church Slavonic has stayed with me.

DW: *Whilst you were in the choir you started having private composition lessons from William Mathias* who was a hugely important figure in Welsh musical life at that time.*

PM: It was all by chance – my other grandmother, my mother's mother, lived on Anglesey close to where Will lived and she spoke to him about me. He had just retired from the University due to ill health and, alongside the hope that he would have the time to write the music he wanted to write, he was looking for a 'new project' of some kind and that's what I became! I went to see him every couple of weeks or so and he taught me harmony, counterpoint, orchestration, all the things one would never think about at that age. He was very jolly and easy to work with, especially for a kid. Having someone to talk to about music who was sort of child-like himself was wonderful. His wife Yvonne was a mother figure and looked after everyone. I remember at that point he had an old BMW or Mercedes – it was orange! I used to love being driven around in that and often, as I was going in for my composition lesson, Aled Jones* would be coming out of his singing lesson with Yvonne, who had been a professional singer.

DW: *Mathias is an interesting figure, rather under-performed these days; you say he taught you harmony and counterpoint, but do you remember anything in particular from his teaching?*

PM: He was a huge Mozart* fan, as I became subsequently, so we looked at and listened to lots of that – Beethoven* and Sibelius* too; not so much Bach* surprisingly. I think he was trying to teach me about structure, although perhaps I wasn't aware of it at the time. What do you do with an idea? Lots of people can think up a melody but then what do you do? He would explain this is what Mozart and Sibelius did, that sort of thing. I always wanted to find out what Will was writing but he was reticent about that. Maybe he was worried that at such a young age I'd try to sound like him, which certainly didn't happen. When Will became too ill to teach, I worked with John Pickard* a bit, another Mathias student, and he was completely different, teaching me to think much more symphonically.

DW: *The pieces you were writing at nine, ten years old, were they influenced by anyone in particular?*

PM: Well, thankfully, I think only one or two have really survived, or there may be others in my mother's cupboard. Sort of sub-Vaughan Williams* really – I loved Vaughan Williams and still do, but I think I was trying to find a Welsh 'folk sound' of some kind at that time. Also, I was very interested in brass instruments. I played in a brass band and wrote several pieces for them.

DW: *Then you went to York University, which has always had a strong composition department, but, listening to your music now, people might be a little surprised because it is reasonable to say that York was known for a pretty advanced kind of musical thought?*

PM: That's the reason I went. John Pickard said that I should experience something different, something out of my comfort zone. Also, it wasn't Wales – I mean I love Wales and am proud of being Welsh but at that point I'd spent my whole life there and wanted to go somewhere else and York is such a lovely city. At that time, most of the faculty at the university were composers – Nicola LeFanu*, David Blake*, Roger Marsh*, Richard Orton*, Wilfrid Mellers* – a whole gang of them, all so different, and it was such a vibrant place to be. I applied, got in and was there six years! I threw myself into everything. Anybody who was anybody used to come and give lectures and it was close to the Huddersfield Contemporary Music Festival which was then at its peak, so we saw, heard and talked to Ligeti*, Stockhausen*, Boulez*, Steve Reich*, Xenakis*, an incredible time. I studied with Nicola and she was very good, not pushing me down a particular path, but just quietly encouraging. I wrote atonal music and some aleatoric music and it was performed. A lot of it was pretty terrible but we got so many chances to hear what we were doing and therefore had the chance to learn from our failures. I certainly learnt more from my failures than my successes. The further I got on and as I started my PhD it became clear to me that that just wasn't the kind of music I wanted to write – there are people who could do it much better. There can't be any doubt that as I got back into writing more diatonic music, I found it had been coloured by what I had heard and written at York. I was writing slightly more angular lines, more adventurous in colour and timbre, grittier harmony perhaps and in those six years I went to Denmark and studied with Hans Abrahamsen* and had sporadic lessons with Denmark's greatest composer since Nielsen*, Per Nørgård. Then I went to Sweden and worked for a while with Magnus Lindberg* and Bent Sørensen*.

DW: *An incredibly diverse collection of teachers.*

PM: All very different. One is never quite sure what one learns until much later. I had a great time with Lindberg, who has, as far as I know, written very little choral music, but rather these huge, multi-layered orchestral pieces. I learnt a lot about dealing with texture, timbre, orchestral colour and I'm sure that this has fed into my choral writing as well as orchestral music.

DW: *Do you think coming back to the choral world, that choral music was regarded as a sort of poor relation? Young composers wanted to write big orchestral pieces, pieces for specialist new music ensembles, that kind of thing, and if they wanted to write a choral piece it would be for a group like the BBC Singers, and they would come up with a piece that about three choirs in the world could sing.*

PM: I think it is still true now. A lot of composers think when asked about what they have written, and they say a big orchestral piece, there will be a much more positive and admiring reaction than a sort of shrug of the shoulders if they mention a choral piece. I feel you have to think much more deeply, and if you are lucky enough to have a group as good as the BBC Singers that is great, but writing for a local choir you have to learn how to adapt what you do for them, not write down for them but create something that challenges but does not scare them, something that can be put together in the time they have to rehearse. I think those restrictions are really great skills to learn, whatever you are writing. A lot of young composers don't understand what choirs do, how they work and the technical difficulties involved. That is not meant to be a criticism as such, they just haven't been taught. There again if you write a lot of choral music – I know Judith Bingham* talks about this – you get called 'just a choral composer' – 'JUST a choral composer'! One wanders down a path that is attractive to you but also tries to write what you are asked to write.

DW: *Was it perhaps the* Stabat Mater *where you felt that you had found your own voice?*

PM: I think it was the first big piece. Just before then I wrote a little Ave Maria that I was pretty happy with. I was exploring lots of other choral music at that time too, and finding a lot in both old and new music and reminding myself about the Russian choral sound I loved so much. I listened to lots of music. I'm not sure I was so concerned about finding my own voice as much as finding the courage to write what I wanted to write in my own way and not having people telling me that it wasn't the right thing to do. The Stabat Mater is a very personal piece too, a big 25-minute piece, I wrote it as my grandmother was dying and there is a lot of her in it somehow. She loved singing in amateur choirs and there is a solo in the second movement that is inspired by her singing. It's a move away from childhood to becoming a young man I think. I just wanted to get it right, to make sure it was exactly what I wanted to say. Even in the Stabat Mater, there is a lot I would do differently now of course.

DW: *What happens if you have to conduct it? – do you need to be slightly removed from it, as though it had been written by someone else?*

PM: You do. If you are a conductor of your own piece you have to do that I think. I get caught with the *Stabat Mater*, it is quite an emotional piece for me even now, but I wouldn't change it. There is no point in going back to re-write history. I think it was Shostakovich* who basically said, I got it wrong but I'll get it right in the next piece. Perhaps I really 'arrived' as much as one can with *Now sleeps the crimson petal.*

DW: *You won't be surprised to learn that I wanted to talk about that piece or rather what it became* – Ubi Caritas. *You must be a bit tired of discussing this now but it had such an important effect on your life.*

PM: World-changing! I was lucky. The *Stabat Mater* had been performed a bit and got my name around, then shortly afterwards came *Now sleeps the crimson petal* which is in a cycle of four settings of poems about romantic, ecstatic love and it was the title piece that got picked up by the Duke and Duchess of Cambridge and it was what they chose for their wedding. We began what became quite lengthy discussions with the powers-that-be at the Abbey who thought that Tennyson's* text wasn't suitable for that occasion – two lovers lying naked in each other's arms. So, all this went on for quite a while and it was suggested that I re-set the piece to new words. Suddenly I had to do this very quickly as the music had to be 'signed off' by the Queen; I'm not sure to what extent that actually happened but there it is. I cleared my schedule and set the words of 'Ubi Caritas' ('Where charity and love are, God is there') in a day, sent off the score to James O'Donnell (Music Director at Westminster Abbey), they printed off the music and recorded it that night. The Queen listened to it apparently and that was that. It was a somewhat tense 24 hours as I guess it could have been rejected – that could have easily happened.

DW: *The first audience was in the millions – extraordinary exposure for any new piece.*

PM: Yes, I got asked to the rehearsal with John Rutter who had a new piece being sung too. I was almost beside myself with terror and John was so very nice and supportive. He had nothing to prove of course, where as I... At the end of the rehearsal James O'Donnell* said 'Are you ready for this?' I wasn't convinced. I didn't think there was a real tune, the piece is rather tense and has gritty harmony. I really didn't think it would be popular. It turned out that I was wrong and I had something like seventy thousand emails over the next few days about this piece. The server crashed. Then America found out who I was – they certainly didn't know who I was up to that point and that opened a great many doors for me.

DW: *That kind of success at quite an early age can be a doubled-edged sword of course. Was it difficult to manage that?*

PM: Not then, because I was up for it, had the energy and had lots of ideas. Sustaining it was the problem, and certainly over the last few years I've paid the price. I mean for about eight years it was literally non-stop, a large number of pieces every year, not all little anthems, some big pieces too; that and a full-time Professorship at Aberdeen University, together with conducting, it begins to take its toll and it certainly did. The great thing now is that I've taken semi-retirement from the university and I've cut back what I write quite dramatically. I have more free time and space to think. I'm much calmer.

DW: *Soon after the Royal Wedding came the Military Wives.*

PM: Yes, after the Royal Wedding I got asked to a lot of parties and the like and I suppose I thought I might as well go and meet all these interesting people as it wouldn't last and I was unlikely to be asked again! I went to a party at Chelsea Football Club of all places, met Gareth Malone* and he told me he was looking for a song for these women to sing, hadn't been able to find anything and would I like to write a piece. Up to that point I had never written anything like that before, so I agreed. They sent me these poignant words and I wrote *Wherever you are*. Nobody involved in this had any idea this was going to go quite so crazy. All the radio stations decided to play it but they couldn't decide how to categorise it – was it a classical piece, a pop song, a folk-song? It became number one in all the charts, was heard on TV, extraordinary really.

DW: *Of course you had to think very differently when writing this piece.*

PM: That's right, most of these women had never sung before and they had eight rehearsals to get it right. So it had to have enough in it to be memorable but nothing too difficult and above all have a good tune! It was one of the simplest things I ever written but at the same time incredibly hard to do.

DW: *Do you think that your career as a composer has suffered because of the success of* Wherever you are *in particular? I think there is still an element of musical snobbery in the musical establishment and if you get in the charts that is bound to be a bad thing!*

PM: Yes, no question, but you know I couldn't care less! Some of my favourite what we used to call 'serious' composers have written great film music, lighter songs and that sort of thing, Vaughan Williams and Walton* for instance. Beethoven wrote light songs, made folksong arrangements and wrote incidental music. Composers have always done this. It's only in the last stuffy hundred years or so that certain expectations seem to have developed. I've certainly suffered from the stuffiness of the musical world but... tough!

DW: *Do you spend a long time looking for texts? Is this is a big part of the process?*

PM: It is a big part. I'm a Christian so I love the Christian texts, the Latin motets especially, and I'm trying to set as many as I can. I'm an old romantic and so am drawn to poetry that talks about beauty, the beauty of love and nature, and quite often people send me texts. I've struck up a great working relationship with the Welsh poet Grahame Davies* whose work I adore. I've set a lot of his poems and he has written texts especially for me. We are talking about 'fire' at the moment – and how it is represented in different areas of life and in different religions, so that's the subject matter of my next choral piece. You can't write the music without really understanding the text and loving it. Many people have asked why I have set so many texts that have been set before – 'Ave Maria', 'Ubi Caritas', 'A Spotless Rose', 'The Beatitudes', 'If ye love me', and so on. I love what many composers have done with these words but I don't feel Howells* or Tallis* or whoever breathing down my neck – rather they are saying, so it's your turn now, have a go. This is what I find fascinating – it isn't a competition!

DW: *So you sit and read the text to yourself over and over again.*

PM: I do. My niece buys me these bound notebooks and I actually write the poem out. I like to see it in my own handwriting and as I read it the music starts to come through bit by bit and when I go for a walk I make little annotations – rhythm, keys, feelings, different ideas, things like that.

DW: *Have you been defeated by a text?*

PM: Yes, W.B. Yeats*. I love it, but it just defeats me every time. T.S. Eliot* too. I've been asked to a few times, particularly Yeats. I think they are already poetic enough and don't need anything added, whereas a poet like Tennyson I've always been able to find a way through. The poem has to speak to you.

DW: *So often a musical idea comes as you read.*

PM: All the time – the third movement of *Now sleeps the crimson petal* is a little madrigal, 'Upon a bank with roses sprouting', and I create this little waterfall within the choir - the structure came from the image of that water running down the rocks.

DW: *Do you feel that you are part of some English or in your case, should I say British Choral tradition?*

PM: I do because I've gone through it – I don't think you can avoid it. We have one of the greatest choral traditions in the world. I think it was the conductor Suzy Digby* who said in a lecture that the two Elizabeth ages have developed a wonderful outpouring of choral music. With Elizabeth I there was Tallis, Byrd*, Tomkins* and so many others; in the reign of Elizabeth II, a certain choral style has developed I think and I'm rather proud to be part of that.

DW: *It is clearly important for you to communicate in your music, do you think about that when writing, either your audience or performers?*

PM: I don't go down the route of saying as Milton Babbitt* more or less did, that one shouldn't care about the audience, but I mean you don't know who the audience is going to be do you? If you write sacred music perhaps the audience is God and one is helping people to get into that 'space'. I'm not saying that you need to be a Christian to enjoy the music – after all, you don't have to be a Marxist to watch Brecht, and you don't need to be a Christian to listen to Bach. I'm just trying to create a 'space' that can help people touch the divine. Well, I try! The choral music I love to listen to –Tavener*, Górecki*, Morten Lauridsen* – I think this is what these composers do, not necessarily a religious thing but certainly a spiritual one. I try to communicate what I feel about the world. The performers matter and I do try and keep them in mind. Sometimes my pieces aren't so easy, but they are doable and it does matter I think that it connects in some way, or else why bother?

DW: *We should call it a British Choral tradition because of course you are Welsh and you have lived in Scotland for two decades – does that affect what you do?*

PM: I spend half of my life on Scotland and half in Wales and I am interested in the different choral traditions – church music in Scotland is very different of course; the whole male voice choir tradition in Wales, the Gaelic singing, the Eisteddfod – I feel I'm part of all of those to some extent.

DW: *And non-musical things as well of course – visual art, literature, landscape. Some composers scoff when you mention the word 'inspiration'.*

PM: I've listened to many distinguished colleagues who scoff at the word inspiration but that's nonsense – you can't write without it. Often the music is 'inspired' by something that happens, something that someone close to you says, someone you love passes away. You hear a beautiful birdsong, and it inspires you. If they say they are not inspired, I don't believe them. I remember Roald Dahl talked about his work and said that inspiration starts at the desk. I spend four or five hours at the desk every day and you try and create something out of these ideas. Technique is vital and I can see how some composers get caught up with it, but unless you are inspired it can't work. I walk or cycle every morning, go to the beach or walk in the highlands. I love sailing, and every day I'm inspired.

DW: *Are you eager to get to the desk every morning?*

PM: In many ways I find the act of composing more interesting than the finished piece. On the one hand I wouldn't know what else to do, but on the other I have delaying tactics I must admit. I go for a walk, I come in and sharpen my pencils, arrange the paper on my desk, clean the piano, anything I can do, but it's a sort of ritual that's part of the process and once you get started you are on the way. Then, when I finish a piece, I'll take a bit of time off so I can let the piece get out of my system before starting something else. I'll go away or do something different because pieces linger with you.

DW: *Are you surprised when you hear a piece for the first time?*

PM: I'm often surprised when I hear what a group does with a piece. I've just done a CD with a wonderful young choir in Connecticut in the USA, Voce, and their conductor Mark Singleton. They sing in a very different way, sort of *sotto voce*, under the voice all the time, always hushed, and so the pieces find a new world – they speak very differently. Quite often that happens: conductors decide to do something different. Sometimes I don't like it but most of the time I find it fascinating and rewarding.

DW: *How do you feel about rehearsals and premieres?*

PM: I'm lucky enough to be able to work with people I know, which is a great honour. So I deliver the piece and like to talk to the conductor a bit before they try it out, so by the time I get there things have been ironed out. Of course composing is quite solitary but it is nice to be on the other side of things and hearing choirs rehearse, listening to their stories; they come across your piece and they have just split up with their husband or someone close to them has passed away and some piece of mine had been a small comfort. There are always stories, which of course you don't hear when attached to the desk. It fills one with hope that one is doing something right some of the time.

DW: *Your music is sung by the world's best choirs but on the other hand so many amateur choirs love your music too. Is this something you think about when you are writing, that you might get Tenebrae* singing this piece but later there might be an amateur choral society down the road singing it too?*

PM: To be honest some of the most effecting performances I've had have come from amateur choirs who have spent weeks and weeks learning a piece. There is something incredibly special about amateur singing. A huge number of what we call amateur choirs are incredibly good of course. I don't write the kind of music that can only be sung by just top professional choirs any more. Some of my pieces are more tricky than others, but I've heard them sung by both professionals and amateurs. I'm pretty sure all the pieces I've written for the BBC Singers for instance could be done by amateur choirs too.

DW: *You write totally to commission – how do you decide what to take on?*

PM: Quite often people come to me and say can we have a piece for a few years ahead, we are talking about 2025 now – I'm much more organised these days. I have a calendar. I've built in family time, holiday, time off, things I didn't think of before. Now I'm able to tell people honestly and I turn down a lot or put it off for a couple of years. I thought when I was in my 20s that if I said no, nobody would ever ask me again, but I have more confidence and you see things in a different light. Life changes, you have a bit more financial stability, you just see things differently.

DW: *You have spent a good deal of time conducting – when you are watching other conductors do you have to sit on your hands?*

PM: That's a good question. There is nothing worse than a back-seat conductor. I do less conducting now. I do big things, and a few workshops where we sing through a few pieces of mine – 'Singing Days' and so on. I love doing that. I used to run lots of choirs but now conduct only two, a big community chorus – and we don't do any of my music, we do the Mozart *Requiem, Messiah**; that kind of thing – and then a small group called Caritas who meet as and when. There have been very few occasions when I haven't been happy with conductors, but I don't interrupt them in rehearsal. I used to hate it being done to me – there is nothing more annoying than a composer jumping up to complain about a speed or dynamic every five minutes. I only ever talk to them privately if I think it's too slow or something and then it is up to them. A conductor knows or should know their group, what they can do in that acoustic, and it isn't up to me to interfere too much.

DW: *Do you think it has helped you as a composer that you have conducted choirs – this is something you recommend to your students I think?*

PM: It is vital – all my students have to have practical experience. I pretty much make them join a choir or an orchestra and conduct their own pieces. Some hate it of course! You should experience what it is like from inside the choir. Nobody is expecting everyone to be the best singer in the world but, to be part of a big chorus, this is the only way to get to know how this amazing medium works. The same applies with orchestral music; one of the reasons I took up the trombone was that William Mathias told me I should join an orchestra and I should play the trombone so you can do a lot of listening in all the bars rest and then I took up the tuba and had even more bars rest, but I could really watch the conductor and hear what was going on from within the orchestra. I also advise writing music by hand. I think a computer programme is great for making a beautifully presented score when the piece is finished of course, but turn the sound off. You shouldn't actually write 'at the computer' – the choral music 'sound' is horrible and you can't hear the words. A piano is useful. The older I get the less I use it, but it is good to have it around to check things out.

DW: *You do less teaching now but it has been very important to you.*

PM: I've been teaching for twenty years, extraordinary to say that now, but there we are, and it has changed. Now you are a sort of counsellor too in this weird world of ours. How can you create something that has relevance? The main thing is how do you take the ideas you have and take them forward, just as Mathias did with me all those years ago? I find it so rewarding, getting into their heads, into their language and I learn as much as I teach. There should be a psychological study of this. It is such an interesting thing do, quite unlike any other sort of teaching. I certainly don't want to encourage multiple copies of me, they must find their own way and I just try to help.

DW: *You mention Sibelius and I've often wondered whether there is a Nordic/Scandinavian feel to what you do, maybe a bit of Americana too?*

PM: Absolutely – I've spent a lot of time in Scandinavia and Per Nørgård was of course the only real pupil of Sibelius, so it's kind of nice to be a grand-pupil of Sibelius. I feel very connected to Sibelius, Arne Nordheim*, Abrahamsen, Nørgård, Nielsen*. In America certainly figures such as Randall Thompson*, Lauridsen again, have always interested me.

DW: *Despite all that, I think it is true to say that your 'musical voice' is instantly recognisable.*

PM: Perhaps it is but I get praise and criticism in equal measure for being recognisable. The praise says that you have created an individual voice and the criticism says you are doing the same thing all the time. For me, and this surprises everyone, every time I sit down to write I try to do something different. But I don't really – it's like having a Welsh accent, or a Liverpool accent, or a New York accent, but it isn't me. The more you fight against who you are the more pointless it becomes.

DW: *Is there anything that you would still particularly love to write?*

PM: Well, one wish I made came true recently. I've been longing to write a Requiem and I wrote one for the commemoration of the First World War. It seemed the appropriate time to do it and I felt I had the necessary experience to do it now. I've always wanted to do something with moving images and that's happening too, just at the right time. I don't want to be a TV/Film composer as such but would love to try. So many of my favourite composers did it brilliantly– Arnold*, Walton, Shostakovitch.

DW: *Elgar wrote at the end of the score of* The Dream of Gerontius *that 'This is the best of me...'. Are there any of your pieces that you feel have got close to that?*

PM: That's tricky – it always sounds a bit arrogant and hopefully I might have a bit more time to get the best of me. Maybe simple things, the little Introit, *If ye love me*, perhaps *A Spotless Rose*, Christmas carols – just the pieces that although very small, I like to get as right as I can. I think I'm a miniaturist by nature, much as I like writing symphonies and concertos, but I'm not sure there is one piece really.

DW: *Do you have any advice for young composers?*

PM: Easy – this is something I'm often asked. Simply be yourself. Now we have a refreshing pluralism/poly-stylism and one can write anything without worrying about being 'up to date' or 'old fashioned' or whatever. It may be popular, it may not be. Write who you are and what feels right to you and stuff everyone else!

DW: *We are recording this at a particularly difficult and peculiar time. As a composer it must be nice to have the space but how are you finding all this?*

PM: The two halves of the day job have been fine – composing of course has been the same as ever, the teaching on line is fine. The big problem is the lack of music making. I don't think people have quite realised what a vital part of their life going to the theatre, a rehearsal, a concert is – people are bereft. It is terrible. I like sport and love to watch rugby in particular but at the moment everyone is enthusing about sport and that's great, but it makes far less for the economy than the arts! I think governments need to wake up. I'm quite a social individual and I miss meeting friends and seeing my parents, who are getting on now and still living in Wales, but I haven't broken the rules. Unlike some, I don't need to test my eyesight!

DW: *What would you say are your five favourite choral works?*

PAUL'S FIVE FAVOURITE CHORAL WORKS

Orlando Gibbons *See, see, the Word is Incarnate*

John Rutter *What Sweeter Music*

Morten Lauridsen *Lux Aeterna*

Mahler *Symphony no.2 'The Resurrection'*

Per Nørgård *Sange fra Aftenland*

Tarik O'Regan

BORN 1978

DW: *Can you tell me a little about your first musical memories? Were your parents musical?*

TO: Intrinsically yes, my parents were musical, although they never played an instrument. We didn't have a piano at home and I wasn't ever sent to sing in choirs or anything like that. Later on in life I remembered them singing around the house and it dawned on me that they always had sung in tune and had a real sense of pitch, which was interesting. They had a big record collection – my father was really into big band jazz – Glenn Miller*, Tommy Dorsey* – that kind of thing. My mother had emigrated to the UK from North Africa in the '60s, had a tremendous collection of LPs of British rock bands - rather extraordinary for someone growing up in Morocco and Algeria – she listened to Led Zeppelin*, The Rolling Stones* and The Who*. I spent a lot of time in North Africa as a boy and heard a broad range of music on the radio: '80s pop music, also Rai music (a sort of Algerian folk music) and other kinds of North African music. The great thing was that there was never any sense of musical hierarchy, nobody ever said to me, 'you can't listen to that, it's rubbish' sort of attitude, and that has certainly stuck with me.

DW: *It is right to say that you came to music quite late, at least as far as reading music, when you went to secondary school?*

TO: I remember playing drums at primary school in a band that would accompany concerts and assemblies, but I certainly couldn't read music. When I got to Whitgift School in South London it had a very forward-looking music department and was very much about offering as many different musical opportunities as possible. I started playing jazz – there was a very good semi-professional dance band at the school. I wasn't quite good enough at the time to play in that but I was aware that it was something I wanted to do. Whitgift was a boys' school and we often joined up with a local girls' school to put on shows, so that was an attraction in itself. They put on a production of *West Side Story* and it had all the things I had grown up with – jazz, lots of percussion from all over the world – but I think I auditioned to be in the show to meet girls! Then one of the music directors of the show suggested that I might want to play the drum-kit part. I was aware when I first read the part that it was way beyond me, but that was how I started to read music. The school was so encouraging and I would put it down to that particular experience that things developed as they did.

DW: *You went to the Junior Department at the Royal College of Music [RCM*].*

TO: Yes, as a first-study percussionist. I would have been 14 and it was only then that I started learning the piano. The big thing about being at the RCM was the standard. It was extraordinary to be part of the orchestra, as a timpanist, and it was the first time that I sat in three-hour rehearsals, seeing pieces put together, and hearing it from in the middle of it all was just amazing.

DW: *Did you have any thoughts about writing pieces of your own at this time?*

TO: Around that time in the early '90s composition had become a key part of the syllabus of GCSE* music, so it probably started very basically then, using notation software and things like that. I remember discovering *minimalism** – Steve Reich*, Philip Glass* and John Adams* – thinking I can do that, and then writing really terrible imitations of what they were doing. Also, my piano teacher at the Junior Department of the College, whilst being aware that I really was a beginner, would introduce me to Ives*, Satie* – all kinds of things I had never come across before.

DW: *So from a late beginning it was a very quick trajectory.*

TO: It was. I had no intention of studying A Level*, let alone studying music at University, so it all happened very fast.

DW: *Did you study with Jeremy Dale Roberts* whilst still at school?*

TO: The school was very good. They could see that I was interested in composition, and that there wasn't anybody there to really help in a serious way, so I took lessons with Jeremy privately every few weeks.

DW: *This continued while you were at Pembroke College, Oxford, studying music.*

TO: Yes, the big decision for me was choosing between a conservatoire and a university. For me it was the idea of being part of a relatively small college with lots of people doing lots of different things that appealed to me. The degree was primarily a music history degree with some keyboard harmony and a notorious fugue paper, all rather old fashioned, but I did learn a lot.

DW: *I only remember meeting Jeremy Dale Roberts a few times. I heard great things about him as a teacher.*

TO: He was just fantastic and opened my eyes to so many things, broadening my horizons no end. The great care he took over his own, relatively small output was deeply impressive, so inspiring – such a generous, funny, lovely character and he saw little moments in your work that opened up an entirely new world. Even though we wrote in very different styles, it just wasn't an issue for him and I think that was why he was so successful as a teacher.

DW: *It was whilst you were at Oxford that you started to turn towards choral music I think. You sang in the college choir.*

TO: I only sang in the college choir because I knew that I wanted to write choral music. I had sung in huge choruses before, but this was different – the singing and choral music at Oxford at that time was so far ahead of any instrumental music that was being performed. I felt at the time – as I was still swimming around a bit, experimenting, and not being entirely sure what I wanted to do – what I needed were good performances, to see what works and what doesn't. With less than good performances one couldn't tell if it was your fault or the performers. The Pembroke choir was a ragbag bunch put together by the organ scholar, Sarah Faulkner, who did a great job. I was not a good singer, nothing came naturally to me – holding onto pitches, singing quietly, listening to other parts, breathing properly...

DW: *But these are the sort of things that are good for a composer to know…*

TO: Absolutely. There is something inspiring about being in a relatively low-pressure environment and discovering things for yourself. Jeremy Dale Roberts suggested that I should look at settings of the Responses*, so I did, but at the same time he was introducing me to the music of Ligeti*. The two things sort of collided, so I went away and wrote the most dysfunctional set of Responses you can imagine…

DW: *A Ligeti* Lux Aeterna *set of Responses…*

TO: Exactly, in about twenty parts, completely useless in every way. I showed them to Edward Higginbottom* at New College, who to his great credit didn't tell me to go away, but honestly told me that they would never be performed. He also said he felt I had interesting things to say and that I should try and turn the Responses into a short anthem so I did that. The choir performed it and let me record it. That for me was a spectacular moment, not just a performance but a really good one, and it meant a huge amount, the beginning of it all really. I went to a lot of Evensongs around the colleges and I'm not speaking of them in any anti-religious sense at all but they were basically very good concerts! I wrote a piece for Pembroke, *Locus iste* – I wanted to write a piece that I could sing with my choir but that would still have some of the textual effects I had been playing around with. That was an interesting experience, being part of your own premiere as a singer.

DW: *Might that be thought of as your opus 1 perhaps?*

TO: I think it probably is. That piece has been done a lot. It was written with the small chapel at Pembroke in mind. Then doors started to open a little.

DW: *Then it was to Cambridge to study with Robin Holloway*.*

TO: Yes, I had a holiday job at J.P. Morgan, as a banker, and there was a job for me there, but then I had the choice between studying film music at the University of

Southern California or an MPhil at Cambridge. There was a scholarship on offer for Cambridge, so I got one of those. There were two of us studying with Robin that year – one was Errollyn Wallen* and the other was me. We would meet in his rooms, in an extraordinary building where he still lives. It had been hyper-Art Deco at some point, an incredible place, and I can't imagine the number of British composers that have walked down those corridors.

DW: *How did the lessons with Professor Holloway go? He was and is known for not mincing his words.*

TO: Actually we always got on and he was very helpful. There were occasions when he was a little mean, but he just made me laugh! I've heard of other cases of course and these clearly affected people. I know Errollyn got on with him too – she was a bit older than me and more experienced and established – but we took the same kind of approach in Robin's lessons I think. What he did was to explain that musical composition is not some odd isolated activity; if you are to be a composer you need to think about literature, visual art, architecture, whatever, and that was very important to me.

DW: *You then got a Fulbright Scholarship and went to New York. This did I think have a significant effect on your musical language.*

TO: Yes, I think it definitely did. The other thing that struck me about being in the UK was that musical opportunities were incredibly centralised and I was straying away from writing the sort of music that these opportunities supported – the broadcasts, commissions, workshops, performances etc. New York was a leap into the unknown. The concert world was much more diverse, there seemed to be a greater variety of things happening in NYC or the US, and things were not controlled by one centralised organisation, be that the BBC or anyone else.

DW: *Did you feel more at home aesthetically in New York? There is I would suggest a strong American feel to your music.*

TO: It didn't feel alien. The first time I went to New York it felt as though I'd lived there for ever. It is one of those cities that seem to fit around what you want to do, and you don't feel constrained in any way. It has all the trappings of a capital city, financial and cultural, even though it isn't one.

DW: *I don't want to make this sound too simplistic, but what makes your music stand out to me is that you are completely unafraid to write genuinely fast music at a time when, in choral music at least, this is by no means so common.*

TO: I think it is partly because I came to music a little late, but also it has never made any sense to me that there seemed to be a different musical language for composers that depended on whether or not they were writing for a choir. For me pace, texture, energy are just as important, whether you were writing for choir or anything else. I feel relatively neutral about the comprehension of texts in choral music – it is very different from writing a work for the stage. A poem has its own internal rhythm, clarity and pace, and, even if I set it 'respectfully', I'm still messing about with what the poet is saying. I've always enjoyed experimenting with textures, the sounds of syllables and how the words clash together. If you free yourself from worrying about natural stresses and comprehensibility it is really very liberating and enables you to write faster music on the whole.

DW: *So the colouristic effect is as important as hearing the text clearly.*

TO: I think it is of equal importance. If you think of renaissance music, which I go back to a lot, total comprehension of the text happens at key points but it certainly isn't there all the time. One thing that people have said to me over the years, not a complaint exactly, but they have said, 'I couldn't understand all the text'. A perfectly valid comment but it just isn't at the forefront of my mind.

DW: *Can you say something about the way you join together or even blur the lines between the sacred and the secular? One of your most frequently performed works,* Triptych*, is basically a memorial piece, setting Blake*, Milton*, Islamic texts and Wordsworth*.* Mass Observation *is written with the shadow of the Mass hanging over it but sets Virginia Woolf*, Oscar Wilde* amongst others and* The Ecstasies Above *sets a very strange text by Edgar Alan Poe* that talks about all kinds of sacred things but in an almost supernatural way.*

TO: Yes, I am interested in how these worlds work together or collide – definitely in terms of what I see as the connections between the sacred and the secular and across multiple elements of both. *The Ecstasies Above* was actually a commission from a fund to support sacred music at Yale! I had one or two queries about my choice of texts! The refashioning of the sacred is what I find interesting and that is certainly what Poe does. *Triptych* is I think about life and the journey to death, with not a clear answer as regards what happens next: a piece that I hope was forward thinking and exciting, not just a series of endless reflections. *Mass Observation* is about our ambitious relationship with surveillance, our nervousness about being watched over whilst we have an utter dependence on devices that track us, and I just find looking for texts that cover this subject endlessly fascinating. Each of those works has a sense of ritual too, not unconnected with sacred music. What I'm hoping to do is take the audience, and the performers too for that matter, on a sort of ritualistic journey relating to a subject I'm hoping everyone has thought about at some time. After all, cathedral buildings where so much choral music is sung are used for secular purposes too – modern day tourism.

DW: *Are you a disciplined composer? Do you work regular hours?*

TO: Yes. I live in San Francisco now and I go to the office away from my home like most other people. I go every day, more or less 9 to 5. The only difference is that I have a keyboard, but I only use that if I have to fix something in particular. Of course I may work 9 to 5 and then throw it all away. The problem for composers is of course that the public only ever see a tiny percentage of what survives.

DW: *Are you self-critical and tough on yourself?*

TO: I am self-critical. Once a piece is done and printed I don't really go back to it and revise anything. I would rather take a nugget from a piece and develop it in another way in the next piece, rather than keep going back to something I have already done. What other people take from your work is entirely different and valid from what the composer may think. There are works of mine that I think could be revised in some small way, but they are being performed and speaking to people in their own way, so it is best to leave them. I do my best with deadlines. I don't believe any composer that says that they have never missed one – with the best planning in the world sometimes it just doesn't work! It isn't a case of being lazy or having writer's block; sometimes it slowly begins to creep on you that you are writing things that don't work and it needs to go!

DW: *How does it feel if you get really stuck?*

TO: Slightly nauseous! I take a stiff drink. You have to look at what is being thrown out and if it is something that is key to the whole piece. The best thing is to write to the commissioner or your publisher and say, 'really sorry but this is going to come in late' but, if it is something less critical, just take a break.

DW: *Is the piece in your head before you write it down?*

TO: A lot of it probably is – textural ideas especially, the relationship between voices and instruments, tempi, that sort of thing. I've found that it is probably good to end the day with something that is going well.

DW: *When you hear a piece for the first time are you surprised?*

TO: To a certain extent, but I think you get better over the years with knowing what a piece is going to sound like. As long as music is performed there is always some kind of magic; no two performances are going to sound the same, even with the same conductor, ensemble, venue. I know what is in the score of course but there is something else, more exciting, happening in a live performance. One doesn't want to curb that at all – it is what makes what we do exciting.

DW: *Do choirs sound very different to you, travelling as you do, backwards and forwards across the Atlantic to hear performances?*

TO: I think they do. What was eye-opening to me, coming to live in America, was just how good the choirs are here. I was led to believe that English choral music was so far ahead of anything else in the world and that I should prepare myself to be frustrated, but this was not the case at all. I would say the general level of average college choirs, outside those world-famous elite institutions in the UK, is higher in the US. Up and down the US there are amazing choirs who tackle new repertoire with enthusiasm, and the choirs, the bands, sport, are a fundamental and vital way of university life here. The professional choirs here are often staggeringly good too and I think it is sad that so many American choirs are not so well known in the UK

DW: *Do you enjoy rehearsals and premieres?*

TO: On the whole I enjoy them. I feel once I've delivered a piece my work is done and it is in the hands of someone else. Of course I'm happy to help in any way I can. I sometimes find it hard if a conductor is subservient to the composer's visions – you know, 'what exactly do you want here?'. My reaction is often, 'thank you, but just bring what you feel to my music: this is now a joint effort'. I love it when conductors take things in new directions and it creates a dialogue between us. I think a performance is different to a recording but still I like performers to take ownership of a piece somehow.

DW: *We are talking about choral music, but ironically, you have probably been writing less of that over the past couple of years than ever before, concentrating on opera and ballet. Was there a worry in your mind that you were being a little bit 'type-cast'?*

TO: Yes, I think lots of composers worry about that...

DW: *A price of success almost...*

TO: One of the odd things about commissioning new music (and nobody ever says this to you) is what has a commissioner to go on other than what you have written before? I've never had a commissioner say, 'we want you to write a piece like *Triptych*' for instance, but I can always sense that they have heard a particular piece or group of pieces and they are wanting something similar. Now, any composer needs to live, so choral commissions lead to choral commissions, and I'm certainly not complaining. I have actively been turning down some choral commissions recently and pursuing commissions for stage works to try and even out the balance. If you do that you have to be prepared that the only thing that will happen is that you alter your perception of yourself! The choral audience is not the opera or ballet audience and these worlds don't talk to each other. The musical world is rather provincial, so if, as I have just done, I write a full-length piece for Dutch National Ballet, actually especially ballet where you get a lot of performances straight away, that's what you become known for there. It is the strange world in which we live... of course a lot of this comes down to paying the mortgage too – an opera takes two years to write!

DW: *You have done a lot of teaching – can you briefly say what your advice might be to a young composer?*

TO: For whatever reason, in the nineteenth century composing became a profession by itself. In my lifetime it seems to have returned to be a much broader part of the musical world. My advice is to be aware that you will probably have to do other things as well – some of those things may not be musical – in order to pursue your interest in composing. In the years I have been teaching it has struck me that students have not been aware of that much music which is startling – I mean pop, jazz, classical in all its many guises, folk – so you must listen and be aware. Today the chances are that you will have to teach, play, conduct, write, be your own agent. For a long time composers lived in a vacuum, they would write the music and others would look after the performing aspect, but those days are over.

DW: *Having said that, have you ever conducted your work?*

TO: Never! I've been very lucky to make my living from composing, commissions and royalties, but I've always had a relationship with teaching and I've always loved interacting with young people that are interested in composing. I've always taken great joy from that and of course, being realistic, 90% of my income can be paid at any time, especially writing a big opera when the cheques might come in two years apart. I think the best advice one can offer is to suggest how one makes a living – making sure what there is in a contract, how to clear the rights for texts you want to set, how to negotiate fees – all that kind of thing, which many at one time regarded as the 'dirty' side of what we do! Conservatories should be preparing people for all aspects of their work. It would be very odd if law schools didn't do that kind of thing.

DW: *Elgar quotes Ruskin at the end of* The Dream of Gerontius* – 'This is the best of me…'. Can you say if there is a particular piece or group of pieces that might fall into that category for you?*

TO: I'm proud of *A Letter of Rights* which was commissioned by Salisbury Cathedral for the 800th anniversary of the Magna Carta, and is a collaboration with poet and librettist, and now, friend, Alice Goodman. It's one of those 'slow-burn' pieces which was performed once in 2015, but then took a while to gather momentum in terms of interest in it from other groups, and it has now received performances all over the world. It's a complicated, long (40-minute) cantata of sorts for chorus, string orchestra and percussion. Alice and I refer to it as our 'Magna C(ant)arta'. Really, it is a piece about poise, and I think that's what I'm most proud of – getting the balance (drama, pace, duration, ebb and flow) right. Paul Hillier, Chamber Choir Ireland, and the Irish Chamber Orchestra have now recorded it for Naxos, for release before Christmas this year [2020].

DW: *Is there anything that you are longing to write?*

TO: I'd love to write something for period instruments, or a movie soundtrack – perhaps they can be combined in some way? Essentially there is a gradually diminishing list of forms and genres in which I have not written, and thus items on this list hold a special appeal. These two are at the top of the list!

DW: *We are recording this interview at a very difficult and worrying time – how are you dealing with lockdown?*

TO: The writing part of my life has remained constant and relatively unaffected, but what has changed is the context. What I call 'writing into a vacuum'. Composers are used to the immense pendulum swing of months (or indeed years!) of writing in isolation, only to find themselves suddenly standing in front of an orchestra or choir and (hopefully!) large audiences when performances happen. It's a giddy sensation, sometimes uncomfortable, but forms a fundamental part of 'what being a composer' means. The specific combination of ongoing, and indeed incoming, commissions without performances in sight only leaves isolation. And as I watch my friends and colleagues who are performers suffer without work, and performing organisations remain shuttered, the sense of isolation only grows.

DW: *What would you say are your five favourite choral works?*

TARIK'S FIVE FAVOURITE CHORAL WORKS

Anthony Davis *Voyage through death to life upon these shores*

Lassus *Infelix ego*

Ligeti *Lux aeterna*

Kaija Saariaho *Nuits, adieux*

Stravinsky *Requiem Canticles*

Roxanna Panufnik

BORN 1968

DW: *Can you tell about your earliest musical memories? It goes without saying that music was an important part of your household, but was it always clear you would be involved in music too?*

RP: To begin with I wanted to drive ambulances! Then, when I was three, it must have been a Prom or something on television, Ida Haendel* who died a few days ago [July 2020] was playing a Violin Concerto and I announced to my mum, 'Mummy, I want a violin with a stick to make it sing …'. Perhaps she was hoping that she had a prodigy on her hands but sadly it was not to be. I certainly wanted to play but only wanted to play my music and not anybody else's. I used to find an orchestra on the radio and make up my own Concertos to play with the orchestra. It must have sounded absolutely hideous but probably looked amazing.

DW: *But you played other instruments as well. I seem to remember you played the harp.*

RP: Yes, I played the harp – it was my second study at the Academy. Later on I played the piano, but again I was only interested in improvising. I did get to Grade 8 on the flute and Grade 4 on the classical guitar, which has been quite useful as I've just had to write a big guitar solo!

DW: *Obviously there was a lot of music going on at home, lots of musicians visiting, and music was part of your every-day life.*

RP: Yes, my brother and I got taken to a lot of concerts, but I didn't really think about music as a career until I was about 16 and the school started to ask 'what are you going to do?'. It was clear that I was too lazy academically to go to university but they said 'you can sort of compose, so what about music college?'.

DW: *You wrote quite a big piece whilst still at school, a Requiem, I think.*

RP: Yes, when I was 17 I wrote a Chamber Requiem for a cousin of mine who had died in a car crash some years before. We had a wonderful Director of Music, Jonathan Willcocks*, now a well-known composer and conductor, and he decided to have it performed. It was for choir, piano and string quartet. They did it a few times. Then

I realised that I really did love composing, working with performers, and then things fitted into place.

DW: *You then went to the RAM*. Am I right in thinking it was not an entirely productive time for you? At that time there was a pressure to write in a certain way and you didn't feel comfortable with that.*

RP: Very much so. I only wanted to write the music I liked to listen to and it seemed that unless your music was hugely complex and esoteric it wasn't deemed to be very good. Now when I go in to meet composition students at music colleges, I'm so jealous, because now 'anything goes', which is great. I guess my professors were right, I should have tried to be a bit more experimental. I remember coming in one day and saying that I had written something really ugly, and the professor seemed so pleased! But I left thinking that I didn't want to be a composer after all and wasn't going to make it and I went off to work in research and production for BBC television.

DW: *It was as bad as that, you just wanted to give up?*

RP: Yes, it was. My end of college report said that I had a gift for melody but that my music was naive. I would almost take that as a compliment now but I certainly didn't at 21. I was still writing the occasional short pieces for friends and that's how I kept going.

This would be 1991/2, so it coincided with my father's death, which obviously had a profound effect on me, but also there was a developing interest in the music of composers such as Górecki* and Tavener* – John in particular with his piece for Princess Diana's funeral, *Song for Athene*, beautiful music that everyone could relate to. I think that combined with an amazing conversation I had with my father just before he died in 1991, after which I realised that life was too short not to be doing what I really wanted to do and I began to pick up the pieces again and think, maybe I can do this after all.

DW: *The music arena did change around that time didn't it? Do you think at the Academy there was a certain kind of expectation, even a suspicion, because of who you were and that fact that your father was a famous composer*?*

RP: I don't think it was a problem for the staff really. There were certainly some snide remarks from other students who would say things like 'with your name on a score, people will always look at it', that kind of thing – never mind the fact that it has to be good. Later on I heard of comments that came from the staff common room. Some of them used to refer to me as 'Little Panufnik'. Now I'd find it flattering, I love the idea of being 'Little Panufnik', but then, with so little confidence, it was very off- putting.

DW: *So, you went into BBC production.*

RP: I did. I had a wonderful three years there. The great Dennis Marks* was my boss, and I worked on Young Musician of the Year and a brilliant children's programme called

'What's that noise?' that covered every genre of music. It was a great way of learning how the music industry worked, whether that be classical, pop or whatever, and it was valuable training that has stood me in good stead as a composer.

DW: *Do you think there are elements or characteristics of your father's music in your work? I've always thought that there might be harmonic similarities, particularly in his love of the rather bittersweet, tangy combination of major and minor?*

RP: I have inherited his love of the combination of major and minor but I think I take it quite a lot further. When I was starting to write my *Westminster Mass* I was staying with an order of enclosed nuns (!), and I was working on the opening harmonies of the Kyrie, which are very bi-tonal, quite jazzy chords, and I heard his voice over my shoulder saying, 'Roxanna, clean up your harmonies'. But I thought I didn't take any notice of you as a teenager, so I'm probably not going to now! It's interesting when my music is played in Poland, people say to me, your music sounds so Polish, but I can't quite fathom out what this means.

DW: *Your Polish heritage is clearly important, but you were born and brought up in the UK, and yet this dual personality comes through.*

RP: Possibly, also, I'm not afraid to wear my heart on my sleeve, outrageously so sometimes. I think Poles are very demonstrative by nature and probably my Catholic faith has a lot to do with it, but it is quite hard to be objective. I think it is inevitable – genetically, chemically, physically, I'm partly him and there will always be something of my dad's music in mine, but it certainly doesn't worry me in any way.

DW: *You have learnt Polish I think and have recently set the Polish language too.*

RP: Well, I wouldn't say I've learnt it. I have spent thirty years on and off trying to learn Polish and I've just finished my third year at a Polish Evening Class. I still go into a Polish deli near to where I live and struggle, it is such a difficult language. Did you try and learn it?

DW: *I did a little yes. I went to Poland a few times in the '90s and I remember telling your Dad when I used to visit him that I was trying to learn Polish and he would just give me a sort of quizzical look!*

RP: I set Polish in a big recent piece, called *Faithful Journey – a Mass for Poland*, which is in English and Polish. It was a joint commission between the National Radio Orchestra in Poland and the CBSO. The Birmingham chorus were AMAZING – I didn't make things easy for them, but they worked so hard at their Polish – just so impressive. I had hoped that I could have been more help to them, but this was during my first year at the evening class. I like to think that now it would have been better, so hopefully someone else will ask me to set Polish.

DW: *Did you find that the language coloured your musical language in any way?*

RP: Only in terms of inflexion, accent and prosody – I use a bit of folk music too in *Faithful Journey*.

DW: *There is a healthy bias towards the voice in your output, whether this be choral, song or opera, is this by accident, design or choice?*

RP: It just seems to have been the way I have gone. I loved choral singing at school and we had a fantastic chamber choir – we went on tour and I've always loved singing in choirs. I think because *Westminster Mass* became quite well known and it was the piece that got my name around, I got asked to write lots of choral music. It just built from that. Some people have asked me if I have done this to separate myself from my father who very much specialised in orchestral music and wrote very little choral music but that isn't the case at all. There is also the fact that I was a 'want-to-be singer', I was a mezzo and wanted to be Carmen!

DW: Westminster Mass *was a kind of turning point for you I think. Was that the piece where you thought that this is me?*

RP: It coincided with my 30th birthday and I do remember feeling that I had done something that was really strong musically and it was a great turning point – a fabulous opportunity. It was a time that contemporary choral music was really starting to be popular. The timing just worked out in my favour.

DW: *The Mass was written for Cardinal Hume's* 75th birthday.*

RP: Yes, it was. John Studzinski of the Genesis Foundation* commissioned it as a birthday present and I wrote to the Cardinal before I started work and asked him, as it was for his birthday, was there any particular text that he would like me to include. I got quite a prickly letter back saying that this isn't for my birthday, it isn't for me it is for the choir, and then, at the end of the letter, there was a little sentence that said, but if you could please set Psalm 63 in Latin I would really like that. We ended up becoming good friends, he was a wonderful man and we just about managed to get the recording to him before he died.

DW: *The setting of Psalm 22, 'Deus, Deus Meus' that comes from the Mass was probably the first piece of yours I heard and I've come to think of that as your sound, the harmony, the way the chords are spaced.*

RP: Absolutely – also, looking back, the treble solo in that piece sounds a bit like the slow movement of my dad's Violin Concerto. Certainly, something that wouldn't have occurred to me at the time.

DW: *Looking back on earlier pieces like that from a twenty-year perspective, are you still quite proud of them?*

RP: I think so, yes. There will always be one or two that would make me shudder a bit, but I'm sometimes surprised. Last year we were recording a String Quartet that I had written when I was in my twenties and I was quite taken-a-back. You know, it was OK! Of course, there are other things that I thought I mis-judged and some things have been consigned to the bottom drawer, but we are all human!

DW: *Since then you have gone in very much your own direction and developed your interest in both sacred and secular music of different faiths and cultures. How did that happen?*

RP: It started with my Dad giving me a beautiful book – folk music and folksongs of the Tatra Mountains – with images of paper-cuts, pictures and folk art. I was so intrigued by how one can hear the music moving geographically east, the use of different modes, pentatonic scales and the like and it started me thinking of music from other coun-

tries and how someone who perhaps didn't know a great deal about music, upon hearing a particular mode, would recognise that it was from the Far East, or Pentatonic scales that they would associate with Japan and China, so I started to look into this more deeply. Then I was pregnant with my first child when the attacks on the World Trade Centre happened in New York and this depressed me very much. I started to think, what kind of world am I bringing this child into? All this hate between Christians, the Jews, Islam, and other religions, surely we could concentrate on what binds us together a little more, rather than what divides us, and so I started to look at ways that I might be able to join these beliefs and faiths together in my music in some way.

DW: *You have already spoken about the importance of your faith, but is your interest in these other faiths and how you bring them together part of some larger message and trying to communicate, trying to unify a little?*

RP: That would be nice but I'm under no illusion that what I do could help that. But I do want people to hear how beautiful the music is, because all we hear about these faiths are the differences, the obstacles and the things that set us apart. That's all there is in the newspapers and the media. Catholic chant, Islamic chat, Sephardic Jewish chant, Sufi music – as the chants spread out geographically they become more and more elaborate and are differently ornamented, but they all basically come from the same place – they are timeless and I'm just fascinated by this.

DW: *This gives your music a particular spiritual quality, is that what you hope – perhaps spiritual rather than sacred?*

RP: Yes, I hope so – it is very much about soul.

DW: *I've been thinking about your titles –* Unending Love, Love Abide, Love Endureth, *even the pieces that don't mention that word –* Celestial Bird, *the Proms piece* Songs of Darkness, Dreams of Light *– are basically about love.*

RP: Well, it makes the world go around, doesn't it?

DW: *You have said you wear your heart on your sleeve.*

RP: Absolutely I do.

DW: *And for the most part your music is uplifting and positive – there doesn't seem to be a log of angst or tension in your music. Do you think that is fair?*

RP: Yes, yes, I'd like to think so. There are times I have to put a little angst into what I write. It isn't a choral piece but in the guitar piece I'm writing now I'm thinking about immigrants crossing the Mediterranean. For us it is a place to go for a nice holiday, but for some of them it is a matter of life and death. In the opera *The Silver Birch* there was a good deal of angst.

DW: *Do you find it hard to do that sort of thing rather than be uplifting?*

RP: No, I have little pockets of darkness that I can draw on! I've been very lucky in my life, but like everyone there have been dark times and it can be cathartic to draw on those times.

DW: *We have talked about other cultures but do you feel you are part of a sort of musical tradition? There are at least two pieces that are very specific about this, the little Kyrie after William Byrd* you wrote for ORA and as far as a more recent composer is concerned,* 99 Words for my Darling Children *which sets a text by Sir John Tavener. He was an important figure for you I think?*

RP: He was. I've always loved his music. We had to do a photo-shoot together at the end of the '90s for the BBC Music Magazine and I was terrified of meeting him as he was such a hero of mine. But he was so adorable, human and really funny. He reminded me of my dad who exuded a huge amount of spirituality and profundity but at the same time had a rather naughty sense of humour. He made a huge impression on me and I admired the way that he had, like my dad, the integrity and determination to follow what he wanted to do and not what was fashionable at the time.

DW: *The 99 words are messages he wrote to his children at the end of his life – kind of a daunting thing to set to music?*

RP: It was. I heard his very brave daughter, who was about 20 at the time, read this text at John's memorial service and Suzi Digby* asked me if I would set this to music. My first thought was that I really couldn't but after a while I talked to his widow, and eventually she said yes, so that is how that happened. I wrote it for choir and cello, a sort of acknowledgment of John's wonderful Cello Concerto, *The Protecting Veil*.

DW: *What do you think the balance is between technique and inspiration?*

RP: That is a very hard question. For me inspiration is really important – words, concepts, notion, beliefs, it can be anything – once you have the inspiration, it kind of leads you there. Technique you learn along the way and you are always learning that.

DW: *For example there is a choral piece called* Four Choral Seasons...

RP: Yes, a lot of people have taken that concept and dealt with it instrumentally, but not chorally and it seemed to be a fascinating idea.

DW: *You have set a lot of the standard liturgical texts of course, but do you find looking for texts an important part of the process?*

RP: Yes, I'm very lucky. I have two wonderful ex-English teachers from my school, who help me to find texts. I'll call them up and say, as with the Seasons choral piece, I need poems about autumn, winter, or whatever and they'll send me a selection. It really helps to live with the words before writing music, analysing the texts a bit, thinking about them, and then slowly musical ideas start to emerge.

DW: *Are you someone who has the piece in your head before you put it onto paper?*

RP: No, It doesn't work like that for me. I might have a musical atmosphere in my head. I try and figure it out at the piano, start to think about pitches and see where it goes.

DW: *You set Estonian a few years ago in your* Tallinn Mass – Dance of Life.

RP: Yes, I got asked to set poems in Estonian by the Tallinn Philharmonic Society to celebrate Tallinn being European Capital of Culture in 2011, and thought it might be similar to Polish. It is a beautiful language but completely different of course: not like anything I have ever seen or heard.

DW: *So how do you start to set that?*

RP: I worked from the original text, then a basic translation, then a word-for-word translation as their word order is different, and then I had a recording of the poets reciting their work. I literally took down pitch dictation, where the stresses landed and took note of the rhythms.

DW: *And you enjoy collaborating with writers. Jessica Duchen* has written a good deal for you.*

RP: Yes, Jess is an old friend, and we do a lot together. We did an opera together, have another one planned, texts for choral works too. I love it – if I'm repeating some music and I need an extra syllable or there are too many words, it is very straightforward, I can just ask for the problem to be solved.

DW: *Are you surprised when you hear a piece for the first time?*

RP: Not really. As far as possible I'm sending things through as I'm writing, so hopefully it isn't a nasty surprise for them or me. There is a limit to how much you can do that with a choir of course but with the Seasons piece I wrote for the Bach Choir in London, I wanted to have some whistling in the winter movement and I came to a rehearsal to see what their 'whistling range' was!

DW: *On the other hand are you surprised what a performer finds in your music?*

RP: Hearing a piece for the first time is a bit like someone is reading your mind and you do feel very vulnerable. It's a bit like lying in the dentist's chair with your mouth open or sharing your deepest emotions with hundreds of complete strangers. I like to build up relationships with the performers I trust and so even that is less stressful than it might be. I even like to picture them in my mind as I'm writing.

DW: *Do you think about the audience?*

RP: Always, and how I can help them to connect with what they are hearing. I think choral music has the edge, because the audience is already connected by the words of course, especially if they are famous words, so that helps a lot.

DW: *Do you enjoy the rehearsal process and the performance?*

RP: I love both. I love the collaboration. I sometimes get anxieties leading up to premieres about things going wrong, but when I'm actually there I love it. I love to get involved in the rehearsal process and like to make sure that I have written what I've heard in my head. I used to be very shy about this kind of thing but less so now. I find it much more unnerving when I'm asked to speak to the audience beforehand, just terrifying. Far worse than the actual performance.

DW: *Well, that might be an inherited thing too – your father hated it.*

RP: Yes, he did and of course I don't even have the language barrier. Before the premiere of the Seasons piece, the conductor David Hill* was talking to me on the platform at the Festival Hall – he is so nice, but I was completely terrified.

DW: *Do you revise?*

RP: Yes, I do. I think in the past I've been a bit self-indulgent about things like pauses, breaks between movements. I'm finding I like things to be more compact now, more momentum perhaps. I used to make things very slow, but I like them faster now! Maybe that says more about me as a person or maybe it is an age thing.

DW: *It strikes me that you like to feel useful as a composer.*

RP: I'd like to think so, I'd LOVE to be useful. I often think that what I do involves a lot of navel gazing and being rather self-indulgent. I once got a letter from a teacher in a school after 9/11 telling me that *Westminster Mass* had brought them a lot of comfort and that affected me very much. I'd love my music to be a comfort, that it helps, calms and heals in some way.

DW: *Does the writing get easier or is there still a horror when you see the blank paper?*

RP: There is often that and there are days that are like pulling teeth. Generally, if I have been thinking about it, it is OK. I use the piano, my dad's piano from his study, and Sibelius software. I have this bizarre rhythmic dyslexia – I can hear a rhythm, feel it, imagine it, but I can't 'do it'. I can't dance in time; I could never conduct. I just remember the nightmare  conducting lessons at the Academy. I think John Rutter* once said that all composers should learn to conduct. I suppose I should at some point. The Sibelius playback facility helps me to discover what I hear is what I've written down.

DW: *You hear colour in a very particular way too – in choral music too, not just instrumental music.*

RP: Absolutely. I've got synesthesia. Messiaen* had it – it affects people differently. I see letters of the alphabet, days of the week, numbers, in different colours, and so it has a bearing. When I'm at the piano a D flat major chord is very warm to me, a D is dark blue, the A is red and the flats mellow it, so the chord becomes a mellow purple. A major is a bright and stringent harmony – the A is a really bright red, the E a sort of gold and the C sharp a transparent white, so that does have an effect on what I do.

DW: *Do you have any advice for young composers?*

RP: If you want to write choral music join a choir and sing one of the internal parts! Have the experience of singing those parts whilst lots of things are happening around you. It is all very well singing the tunes but be an alto or tenor, pitching the notes – very useful I think.

DW: *Is there anything in particular that you are burning to write?*

RP: I would love to do more inter-faith choral work. I'm excited to have a commission to write a piece for Yom Kippur, for a Jewish choir, and I'd love to work more in that field with singers and instrumentalists. There is another opera coming up for Garsington and I have a large-scale opera that I would love to write.

DW: *Elgar quotes Ruskin at the end of* The Dream of Gerontius* – 'This is the best of me…'. Is there a particular piece or a collection of pieces that might fall into that category for you?*

RP: I think *Faithful Journey – the Mass for Poland* at the moment. That might change. It covers so many different themes, atmospheres and things that sum up me as a person as well as a composer.

DW: *We are recording this at a very difficult time – how are you getting on with Lockdown?*

RP: From a composing point of view it has been incredibly productive of course. I haven't been able to go anywhere and my children are old enough so I don't have to worry about home schooling. I've been busy writing a couple of pieces for Lockdown premieres – a short piece for string quartet and a choral piece. That apart, I've been fighting the fight to keep church music going, which is so worrying. My son was a chorister and it made me appreciate even more what an incredibly important and unique tradition this is and we simply have to save it. Many of my closest friends are performing musicians too – it is so worrying!

DW: *What would you say are your five favourite choral works?*

ROXANNA'S FIVE FAVOURITE CHORAL WORKS

Bach *All of it!*

Fauré *Requiem*

James MacMillan *O Radiant Dawn*

Szymanowski *Stabat Mater*

Tavener *Hymn to the Mother of God*

John Rutter

BORN 1945

DW: *Can you tell me a little about you earliest musical memories? Did you grow up in a musical family?*

JR: My parents didn't know anything about the workings of the musical profession, which I think was probably an advantage as that meant that they didn't try and put me off what I wanted to do. Had they known how many setbacks a life in music can have, or how economically precarious it is, then they might have suggested that I train as a chartered accountant! When I was young, they stood back in what I realise now might have been quiet admiration, as I showed a musical gift from an early age, accompanied by bewilderment. My father was fond of music and could play the piano a little by ear, my mum had a great love of words, poetry and drama, but would have been the first to admit that she was pretty close to being tone deaf, if there is such a thing. I did once look into the family tree for signs of musicians, and all I came up with was a little documented composer called Rutter, who was a court musician for Henry VIII! Not one note of his music has survived, and I can't really tell if I am a direct descendant or not. My one regret about all this is that I never had the opportunity to play chamber music in the home with the family.

DW: *Little music in the home then but a lot at school from an early age and you had piano lessons?*

JR: I went to a now defunct nursery school close to where we lived, and every day started with assembly and singing hymns. I remember I didn't enjoy sport of any kind at all, but what I did enjoy was the singing and remember wishing, even at four or five years old, that the rest of the day could be like this. My first school report said 'John sings well, if he sings softly' – I had the makings of a vocal show-off from an early age. We had a battered upright piano in my parents' flat, which was above 'The Globe' pub on the Marylebone Road. This piano was left by the last occupants of the flat and I'm afraid to say was never tuned, which blighted my sense of perfect pitch for life. I began to doodle at the piano and as an only child, at least until the age of 10 when my sister was born, I was quite happy in a world of my own, making up little pieces...

DW: *You would rather make up little pieces of your own than practice scales and arpeggios.*

JR: I'm afraid so. I was sent along to a lovely piano teacher called Mrs Melville in Kentish Town, who spotted early on that I had all the makings of a dreadful pianist, but she encouraged me in my singing and composing. That was when I started to learn to read music at least but I remember being less than enthusiastic about some of the pieces I was given to learn and finding that I would rather make up my own, and that they were much better of course !

DW: *A lot of composers I've talked to have said that there was one particular figure that changed their lives and helped them decide that music was for them; in your case it was Edward Chapman, Director of Music at Highgate School?*

JR: It was. Mr Chapman taught in the Senior School. Before then I went to the Junior School, and was taught by a remarkable man called Martindale Sidwell, organist of Hampstead Parish Church and a well-known musician at the time. He did class music with us and taught me a lot about singing, how to breathe and that sort of thing. In the Senior School, Edward Chapman really did give me the encouragement I needed to go on and study music at university. My best friend at school was John, later Sir John Tavener*; younger contemporaries included the pianist Howard Shelley* and Anthony Camden*, oboist and Chairman of the LSO, it was really a very musical school. Edward Chapman was a pupil of Charles Wood*, a name well known to church musicians. He wrote some popular anthems, such as *Hail, Gladding Light*, and co-incidentally has a strong association with Christmas – most choirs sing his version of *Ding, Dong, Merrily on High*. I think it is true to say that a lot of the concepts and beliefs of Dr Wood, came down to me via Edward Chapman. Wood was what would be called a very conservative composer I suppose, but the music is always so beautifully crafted and well-heard. He was a great devotee of counterpoint and fugue, which I am too really; it is a way of learning how to make the notes do what you want them to do, and not let them run away. You can discipline what you write, even if later on, as Debussy said, you learn the rules and now don't use them.

DW: *That means you were a grand-pupil of Charles Wood and a great grand-pupil of Charles Villiers Stanford*?*

JR: Yes, I'm rather proud of that. The great glory at school was the Chapel Choir, which I didn't need any encouragement to be in. I didn't realise then how closely our carol service was modelled on the famous King's Service of Lessons and Carols – that was certainly the ideal in Chapman's ear, I think. There was also the big concert chorus, which most of the school population seemed to sing in, and we tackled the big works, as you would expect – Bach*, Mozart*, *Messiah**, the Beethoven* *Missa Solemnis* – I'm not sure how that worked; there was no shortage of ambition. We also sang Tippett's* *A Child of our Time*, which was quite new then of course. I think the chorus did pretty well, but it was perhaps a little beyond the school orchestra. Slightly embarrassingly for us the composer came and I remember he didn't smile very much. It was, let us say, a brave endeavour!

DW: *Most notably you sang in the first and most famous recording of Britten's* War Requiem conducted by the composer.*

JR: That was 1963 and by that point my voice had changed but I could fake an alto and get the right notes. I think Chapman thought that his 'musical boys' as he called us would benefit from being present for such a historic occasion even if we didn't contribute much vocally and of course he was right. It made a huge impression on me. It is hard to realise now just how difficult the *War Requiem* was considered then. The first performance left a lot to be desired I think and, when it came to the recording, Britten and his record company Decca wanted to make sure it would be good and relatively easy to put together in the time available. Little did I understand then quite how important this was – we were allowed to be present for the whole recording. The soprano Galina Vishnevskaya*, who was a diva and a half I can tell you, Peter Pears*, Dietrich Fischer-Dieskau*, the Melos Ensemble, the Bach Choir (directed by David Willcocks* of course, who was to be important to me later on) and the LSO. I did realise in retrospect how in control Britten was of those huge forces, I mean, just a wonderful conductor. I've heard a number of fine recordings of what is now almost a repertoire piece under a lot of good conductors, but there is still something very special about that first recording.

DW: *I think you wrote one of your best loved pieces,* The Lord bless you and keep you, *for Edward Chapman's memorial service?*

JR: Yes, I did. An awful lot of his pupils gathered for that service. I only really ever thought of that one original performance, it was the final item in the service. I do remember that I had just under three weeks to write it. That piece was written with a huge amount of admiration and gratitude and perhaps that comes through somehow.

DW: *We have mentioned Wood and Stanford, I wondered if you still feel part of this English choral tradition?*

JR: It is written into my DNA I suppose. We all have to come from somewhere. I like to think of myself as a musician and citizen of the world, whilst not lacking in appropriate patriotism. Some years ago, I was one of the adjudicators at a singing competition in America and one of the contestants sang a little song by Roger Quilter*, and I found myself in tears, thinking I was far away from home. I detest political nationalism of any kind but I can see why Vaughan Williams* wanted to look at the great legacy of English folksong and indeed church music too – Byrd*, Gibbons*, Tallis* – all this music does touch something deep within me. I'm also sure that the acoustic and aesthetic of King's College Chapel has had an influence on me too, it has a very particular acoustical signature.

DW: *What has always been interesting to me, and what is another big influence on you, I think, is the Great American Songbook. I'm convinced that the shape of your melodies comes as much from that music as anything else.*

JR: Oh yes. I think Jerome Kern* was one of the heirs of Schubert*, Schumann* and Brahms*. The interaction of words and music was so important to people like Kern, Richard Rodgers*, Cole Porter* – they knew that a tune is a wonderful way of conveying the sense of a text and carrying it straight to the heart of the listener. That was something that was becoming less important in contemporary classical music as the twentieth century progressed. I love Stravinsky*, but when he writes for a choir his music is deliberately rather objective, not really trying to convey the sense and meaning of the words. I've always thought that melody is an important part of any composer's toolkit. I've said many times, but up to the time of Wagner, no composer would have survived without an outstanding gift for melody – Mozart*, Haydn*, Schubert*, Schumann*, Tchaikovsky and so on. From the beginning of the twentieth century composers took us into new realms. I remember being very taken by Stockhausen's* *Stimmung* and the influence it had on music after that. People seem surprised that, because I do what I do, I would be interested in anything more experimental. I know that if I've got any kind of gift at all it is not for writing the more advanced kind of music – melody is far too important to me. That is why so many of my efforts have gone into little forms, pieces that mean it is still OK to write a tune, Christmas carols, anthems, that kind of thing.

DW: *There was never any particular interest in writing concertos, operas, symphonies…*

JR: I just don't think I have the strength of will to write the kind of pieces that would take months to write, would get one studio performance from the BBC and then languish on my publisher's shelf for years. Broadly you can divide composers into explorers and magpies, and I'm a magpie. I take the sounds I hear around me and make something from them. I don't think it matters if it has been done before, I'm not convinced that it is possible to write pastiche – if you have a personality at all it will just come over as being you in time.

DW: *Well, I don't think it is too controversial to say that you have lots of imitators.*

JR: I don't know, maybe, I couldn't say. I would describe myself as 50% composer and 50% songwriter. Somehow people don't perhaps expect a composer to write music that is melodic these days, with a songwriter they certainly do.

DW: *You must have felt that in the '60s and '70s you were swimming against the tide to some extent, but now I think tunes and key signatures are less shocking, especially in the field of choral music of course.*

JR: That is probably the case. It might have been the Fifth Symphony of Vaughan Williams, that I heard performed, when I was just starting out, in the William Glock*

218

era at the BBC, and the reviewers were saying 'why bring this music back, what a load of sentimental rubbish, we have moved on, etc'... Critics are now saying, what a wonderful piece, so uplifting and spiritual. When the chips are down and you are forced to think about what really matters... I don't worry about being up to date and fashionable because that which seems to be new and important today might not be tomorrow. It is great to innovate, every good composer has to look for freshness in what they do, but this doesn't necessarily mean stylistic innovation.

DW: *Stepping back, we should talk a little about one of the important figures in your musical life, Sir David Willcocks.*

JR: Of course I knew of David before I met him in person. It would have been perhaps 1961 when my great friend John Tavener took me into Kensington Presbyterian Church and he was brandishing a green book. He started playing the Willcocks descant to *O, Come all ye Faithful* on the organ and it just lit up the sky as a great descant should do. When I later went to Cambridge, in my second year I found myself in David's harmony and counterpoint class. He was under pressure from all sides and his academic teaching was done 'on the quick' shall we say. He would rush in, chalk up a Bach chorale on the blackboard, and say '...write a canonic chorale prelude on that tune'. He would then rush out, come back an hour later, gather up our pieces and say he would look at them for next week, which he never did of course. When the next week came we would play through the pieces and his comments were always very astute. 'Mr Rutter, I'm afraid this sounds a little too much like film music' was one of the comments that I got. One day, David took me aside and said 'I believe you have been composing' and asked me to bring a 'representative collection of your works to my rooms on Monday morning at 9am'.

DW: *I guess you couldn't say no...*

JR: Well, he was a military commander at one time – he won the military cross for his bravery during the Battle of Normandy – and so there wasn't really an option. I brought a collection of things I had written, including *The Shepherd's Pipe Carol*. David looked through them whilst I nervously shifted from foot to foot and he said 'Would you be interested in these being published?'. Being a published composer was so much more vital then than it is now – no internet, no computer-produced music, no way of getting your music in front of the right people. I remember getting the letter from Alan Frank, the head of music at Oxford University Press, saying that they liked a number of pieces - *Nativity Carol* was another one – and would I like an annual retainer of £25 for first refusal of anything I wrote? That began my lifelong association with OUP. At the time I wasn't planning to concentrate on choral music particularly but of course, once I was in print and my name got around, I started to be asked to do more and that is how it started. OUP were an international publisher and promoted my music in the US, which resulted in my first invitation to go there, in 1973. I was asked by a wonderful choral director called Mel Olson* if I would write a new piece.

DW: *This became the* Gloria.

JR: That was the *Gloria*. I was given very precise instructions, a very specific brief, and this is what I still advise people commissioning composers to do. Don't be afraid to say exactly what you want and what you don't want. Mel wanted a twenty-minute piece for a pretty good choir, a rather dry auditorium; they had a good organ, but no budget for a full orchestra, it would be good to have a familiar text etc... So that is how that happened and the piece almost wrote itself. In telling me what he was looking for Mel was also telling me what thousands of other choral directors were looking for and I'm everlastingly grateful for that.

DW: *It is true to say that your name became more widely known in America before it did here?*

JR: I think that is true. It doesn't often happen that way – I went from international to local really and it usually happens the other way around. Rather to my surprise, churches in the UK suddenly started to sing some of the anthems that I had written for American churches, pieces like *For the beauty of the earth, All things bright and beautiful* – that I really wasn't expecting. A strange career in some ways, but I wouldn't have had it any other way. I was just fortunate enough to be around at a time when choral music suddenly took off and choirs, both amateur and professional, improved so much. I can't tell you how different choirs sound now from when I first started out. That has been a terrific advance and another reason why choral music has taken centre stage in the world of recordings as well as in concert halls and in church. There are so many good choirs and a big audience that really want to listen to choral music.

DW: *You were Director of Music at Clare College, Cambridge, in the 1970s and I imagine it was considered rather revolutionary to have women singing the top line?*

JR: Yes, very startling, no question, especially if you were singing Byrd*, Tallis* or indeed Bach, to have young adult female singers on the top line, when next door at King's it was boys of course. It was a wonderful experience but in the end, I had to leave so that I could devote more time to composition. Out of that of course came The Cambridge Singers, which was one of the first professional chamber choirs. I had a very rewarding time with them. I think we were the first choir to make a recording of the complete Poulenc* sacred music – standard repertoire now, but it certainly wasn't then. You had better be good to record that music!

DW: *For some reason I had got it into my head that you had studied with Herbert Howells* but that isn't correct is it?*

JR: No, I didn't study with him, but I did get to know him, to begin with at a day for composers who were invited to bring pieces they had written and to receive advice from an older composer – Dr Howells – and a younger one – me. I was then asked to drive him back to his home in Barnes. He was a remarkable figure and I later commissioned him on behalf of our choir at Clare to write a new piece – he was a composer who had a lot more in him than might be assumed; there was far more to him than music for the church. Earlier in his life he was much better known for his chamber and orchestral music.

DW: *One of my favourite pieces of yours is* Hymn to the Creator of Light, *which was written in memory of Howells.*

JR: Yes, for his centenary in 1992 and the installation of a new stained-glass window at Gloucester Cathedral. I just thought of light and stained glass, and that conjured up a particular sound for my piece and of course the image of blazing light was very important in the music of Howells too. I was very fortunate to know him.

DW: *You took on the orchestration of one of Howells' most famous pieces – the 'Magnificat' from the* Collegium Regale, *perhaps the most famous of his two-dozen canticle settings.*

JR: Yes, this was for a concert to celebrate the anniversary of Howells' publisher, Novello. The concert was to be at the Royal Festival Hall and the organ was out of action, so I was asked to do an orchestration. Truth to tell it wasn't hard to score in a Howells style - somehow, his organ writing seems to suggest orchestral sounds and there are lots of clues in the two or three staves he provides. I hope the result would have met with his approval.

DW: *I know you sometimes write the texts for your pieces yourself, but can you say something about your search for texts?*

JR: The words are often harder than the music I find. For sacred pieces I always go to the Bible first, then old prayer books, liturgical books and chant; only then, if I can't find something suitable, do I write my own. For example, I was asked by the Council for the Protection of Rural England for a piece that would reflect what they do and about the sense of wonder of the natural world. I started looking in the Bible and couldn't find anything, so decided to write my own, *Look at the World* – if it fits the music and does the job, fine, but Shakespeare or Milton I ain't!

DW: *We have talked about the importance of melody for you, is it true to say that writing a memorable tune is still the hardest thing to do?*

JR: It isn't easy. Sometimes a melody is there but you just need to uncover it. It should just feel right and as though it has always been there, even if it takes unexpected turns on its way. Think of a tune like Paul McCartney's* *Yesterday* which is seven-bar phrases and of wonderful motivic consistency actually, but I don't suppose he ever thought about it like that. I've said this a lot to young composers: don't be content with the first thing that comes into your head, chip away at it, and with a bit of luck just changing a couple of notes or rhythm will transform it into something special. I read once in the memoirs of Richard Rodgers, that when someone asked him how long it took to write a good tune, he replied, as long as it took to write it down – I don't believe it! I'm sure he burnt the midnight oil to get those tunes right. I think of a great melodist like Schubert too, but in such a short lifespan that is a sort of almost supernatural genius.

DW: *Does it get easier to write, the more experienced you get?*

JR: [Throwing up his hands] – No, no! Every piece is like the first!

DW: *In your case is that because of the huge success you have had with pieces such as the* Requiem, Magnificat, Mass of the Children, *as well as the carols and anthems? Does this weigh on your mind?*

JR: You are absolutely right. I think if you develop some sort of track record, in whatever field, there will always be people that will be ready to say, he's gone off, or that isn't as good as... It was Heifetz* that said the biggest problem for him was that whenever he played, people always expected him to play like Jascha Heifetz*! – I know what he means. I think you have to take each job as it comes and do your best. The most useful advice that Edward Chapman gave me at school all those years ago was 'Rutter, write the music that is in your heart'. We are all under the shadow of not only ourselves but the shadows of the great masters from previous centuries, but, if you spend all your time worrying about that, nobody would write anything ever again. It is a cliché but everyone says that our pieces are like children, you send them out into the world and they have to do their own thing. You can't be the judge of what you do – we just do our best.

DW: *Are you a disciplined composer? Do you try and write every day?*

JR: No, I must confess that I don't. I lack the single-mindedness just to compose. I enjoy conducting, record producing; I enjoy doing my singing days where I go out into communities and promote the joy of singing in a choir. Composing is a solitary business and all of these things take me away from my desk, but I need be involved in music in different ways. I go to my little composing cottage close to where I live and can be completely alone with my thoughts, but my life is and has been made much more interesting by doing lots of different things.

DW: *When you hear a piece for the first time are you ever surprised?*

JR: Only by how well or how badly it is going! The perfect recording of the piece is always playing in my head. I think experience gives you a good idea of things like balance and the sound of any given moment.

DW: *You conduct your own pieces a great deal – if you are just present as a listener do you have to sit on your hands?*

JR: I'm not truth to tell a very good back-seat conductor. If a premiere is in safe hands, with good singers and players, I'm relaxed. If I think that might not be the case, then that is certainly stressful, particularly as one needs to be seen to be smiling at all times. On the whole I prefer to conduct premieres myself if at all possible. A bad first performance is a composer's worstnightmare, there are so many examples scattered through musical history, it tends to scarboth the piece and the composer.

DW: *Do you think about the audience as you are writing?*

JR: Only in so far as I hope not to bore them. I would never write down to an audience. There is a three-legged stool here: composer, performer, audience – the stool will fall down if one of those legs is missing. Warm applause is lovely of course, but a quiet word of appreciation means more to me I think, especially if this comes from a colleague who is a performer or composer.

DW: *You must get people writing to you all the time, not professional musicians, telling you how your music has affected them.*

JR: Yes, and that is always nice to read of course. Generally people who don't care for what I do tend to stay away! The hardest ones to deal with are messages from people that are quite confessional, people suffering from a personal crisis, a bereavement, a breakup of a relationship, all kinds of human experience. If they to say to me, your music got me through, what can I say apart from thanking them for taking the trouble to write? Quite often I'm sure it might be the text that affects people – my setting of *The Lord is my Shepherd* for example seems to affect people a good deal. If the music I write brings the message of the words over then people have heard it through the vehicle of the music I've written. You know, music and people's lives intersect in ways that none of us can hope to understand. I think this is one reason why musicians understand the transcendental, because we all live with the mysterious and unknowable every day of our life. People always ask composers whereabouts ideas come from – who can say?

DW: *I know you taught composition when you were at Clare – do you think composition can be taught?*

JR: Yes. I think you can teach technique which is the vehicle through which people express themselves. Sometimes a voice can be stifled by lack of technique, although it can happen the other way around too, we have already mentioned Poulenc, whose music I love, but I think his choral music might have been easier to sing if he had had a conservatoire training perhaps.

DW: *And your advice to a young composer?*

JR: Be yourself and the most wide-ranging composer you can be. I get people writing to me asking how they can be a successful composer of choral or church music. I always say to them, 'don't just concentrate on that, try and write anything you possibly can. Get the experience and make use of it'.

DW: *Is there anything that you are still burning to write?*

JR: I'd love to write a musical. I moved into the wrong world to do that. I do still believe in the musical theatre, but really if you want to be Lloyd Webber* or Sondheim*, you have to start off in that world very early on. The pressure and money involved in the staging of a new musical are now astronomical. Lerner and Loewe* had to beg for money to stage *My Fair Lady* and they DID have a track record, so starting from scratch must be impossible.

DW: *Elgar quotes Ruskin at the end of* The Dream of Gerontius* – 'This is the best of me...'. Can you say which piece or group of pieces of yours might fall into that category?*

JR: I think the best of me is the piece I haven't written yet. In some ways one can say that a three-minute piece that hits the mark is just as or more effective than an hour-long piece that rambles. I'm not sure I can come up with a particular piece.

DW: *We are recording this interview at a very difficult and worrying time – how have you been dealing with lockdown?*

JR: I think as a composer I'm better prepared for isolation – most of us are I think. Wearing my conducting hat it is devastating, it is like having your right arm cut off. I cannot imagine how professional performers must be feeling. Oddly enough, this time has not stimulated me to write anything new; what it has given time for is to do some tidying up and get underway a few things that I have been meaning to do for a long time and never got around to doing. I've put together two books of my short choral pieces arranged for piano solo. I would never have found the time to do that and people have been asking me for years. I've looked at an old orchestral piece of mine, a *Partita* for orchestra that has slumbered in my publisher's hire library for over 40 years and I've taken the opportunity to do a computer-set score and parts. I'm also developing a choral-learning app, again taking some of my shorter choral pieces, recording them with a small group of professional singers, and putting it out so that singers can learn their own parts. That might contribute to a virtual performance of some kind perhaps. Then, finally, I have been trying to offer words of encouragement to choirs all over the world not to lose heart – the choir that loses heart falls apart – just to encourage and say, 'this situation isn't for ever, though it might seem like it at the moment'.

DW: *Do you think that virtual performances are here to stay, regardless of how and when we get out of the present situation?*

JR: I hope what comes out of all this is the importance of being in a choir as an educational and social experience and being at one with the audience. However, I do think that virtual choirs will be here to stay and will have a part to play in the whole choral experience, especially for those that can't get to a choir for reasons of physical disability, or living in a remote area, reasons of age, being a carer, shift patterns of work, whatever the reason might be. Not the same thing as live performance of course, but virtual choirs will I think play a part long after the present crisis is over. Of course they can also bring people from all over the world together too – much needed when our society is so full of disagreements of one sort or another. That can't be a bad thing.

DW: *What would you say are your five favourite choral works?*

JOHN'S FIVE FAVOURITE CHORAL WORKS

The musical contents of the Liber usualis
   or Gregorian chant in general

Bach *Mass in B minor* (or anything else
   by him!)

Fauré *Requiem*

Billy Joel arr. Chilcott *And so it goes*

Sheppard *Liberanos, salvanos*

Howard Skempton

BORN 1947

DW: *Can you tell me about your earliest musical memories? Were your parents musical?*

HS: My father was very musical but he couldn't read music. I think he played the trumpet when he was young. He could certainly pick out tunes on the piano and his left hand would waft back and forth, sort of vamping in a rather imprecise way. My mother was artistic and had studied the piano. We had a piano in the house, my elder brother had lessons and I started having them when I was about seven. As far as I remember my first practical experience of music would have been those piano lessons, although I won a talent competition when I was seven, singing 'How much is that doggy in the window' on Worthing Pier! My brother and I put on little magic shows at home, writing plays, so I was always a performer of some kind!

DW: *You had quite a lot of encouragement from a school teacher I think.*

HS: Yes, we went to a direct-grant school that used to be an independent school in Birkenhead. The school didn't give much help with individual lessons. I think people were expected to do that outside school, but we did have a very good choir. There was a chapel and just one music teacher, Tim Lawford, who came to the school when I did. He seemed to spend most of his time practising the organ, but was a very good choir trainer. The class teaching wasn't so good because there were only a few of us that wanted to do anything; everyone else saw it as a chance to mess around. I was very committed to music and was keen to join the choir -a rather obnoxious boy who was a school prefect. Singing in the choir meant two morning services a week and a Sunday service, so I had to travel in on the bus from home and disrupt family plans, which wasn't always popular, but singing in that choir was one of the formative experiences of my musical life.

DW: *Were you composing at that time?*

HS: No, just playing. My piano teacher, a Mrs Lock, decided that I had some talent, but, as I wasn't going to be a professional musician, there wasn't any point in doing exams, so I didn't go through all that. I was allowed to go my own way. I remember playing some of the Mendelssohn *Songs Without Words*, easier Chopin, a little Debussy, but then I hit a brick wall because I didn't have the grounding or technique.

DW: *Do you remember any of the music you sang in the choir?*

HS: Yes, that was very important to me. Tim Lawford, who I kept in touch with until he died a few years ago, was not an experimental or radical figure really, but was passionately interested in the music of Britten*. We had a choral society and a chapel choir and I remember singing *Rejoice in the Lamb* as a treble and *St Nicholas*, as a tenor. When I did O-level [exams] the featured composers were Walton* and Britten and I loved that. The interest in Britten has never really stopped and I still admire him enormously.

DW: *Of course in the late '50s/early '60s these pieces were quite new...*

HS: Yes, we also did Britten's *Psalm 150*, which was even more recent then, and I remember Tim doing a lecture on Bernstein's* *Chichester Psalms* that had recently been premiered. It was just a very imaginative and lively atmosphere if you were interested. Through the choir I also got cheap tickets for what they called 'Industrial Concerts' at the Liverpool Phil*, conducted by John Pritchard and Charles Groves*, and these were a revelation. I heard Walton's *Belshazzar's Feast* which was a key experience, and then in 1964 something quite different, Webern's* *Six Orchestral Pieces* which really made me want to be a composer. I saw four operas in one week as a teenager, including *Peter Grimes* in the old Sadler's Wells production probably from the premiere, so Liverpool was a good place to be in the '60s.

DW: *We have to mention the Beatles too...*

HS: Very much so, through the radio for me, although my brother saw them live. I listened to the radio a huge amount, all kinds of music, in particular what was then the Third Programme. The Beatles* were a local group and I felt that I could understand their wit and playfulness, which is so integral to Merseyside. You know that saying, brevity is the soul of wit. This after all is what I've tried to do in a lot of my music. I'm a sort of 'Liverpool Poet' in that sense.

DW: *As you became more interested in experimental music did the interest in singing and choral music dwindle?*

HS: Not really – the voice came into play again. My teacher Cornelius Cardew* had been a chorister at Canterbury Cathedral and in the Scratch Orchestra we were writing for non-professional musicians – the voice was a common factor. Cardew's *The Great Learning* is primarily a work for voices and the voice was an important part of experimentation in this country, maybe less so in the US – Steve Reich*, Terry Riley*, Philip Glass* and even John Cage* were focused on keyboards. In the U.K. Gavin Bryars*, with whom I've seemed to work in parallel, myself and a few others, came back to the voice in a serious way. I don't remember writing much what one would call conventional choral music at this time, just open-score pieces for the Scratch Orchestra, until the 1980s.

DW: *You moved to London in 1967.*

HS: I left school and had several university interviews. I think I might have impressed people but also mystified them and I ended up doing a degree at Ealing Technical College in London. All sorts of people have been there – Rick Wakeman* I think, and Freddie Mercury*. At that time a lot of arts students were moving towards music, like Gavin again, and Brian Eno*.

DW: *You went to study with Cardew at more or less the same time – I know he was a huge influence on you.*

HS: It was my new piano teacher, Tom West, who introduced me to Cardew – he was very interested in early music, but also experimental music too and he, like a lot of English composers of the time, had studied composition with Mátyás Seiber*. I approached Cardew. I think I was a bit of a nuisance really and wasn't going to take no for an answer, but he ultimately agreed to teach me and I took pieces to show him every so often. He would be very quiet for a time, as I am when I'm teaching I think, but I would say that he was much more cutting than I would be. Sometimes he would be very doubtful about a piece – he certainly was about my piano piece *Humming Song* which I now think of as my opus 1. He accused me of writing salon music, but he changed his mind and I later found out that he had played it in America several times. I felt an immediate rapport with him, a bit like an elder brother. He was very quiet and calm, more like a visual artist really, but a superb musician and full of integrity. Cardew was a maverick but greatly respected in the musical world and he gave me great confidence for which I'll always be grateful.

DW: *After all that you worked in music publishing.*

HS: I wasn't a very good student at Ealing; I was working on my music all the time. For a year I did a bit of postgraduate teaching and when I was at a very low point financially I wrote to some music publishers because I felt that I wanted to be on the inside of the music profession so to speak. Donald Mitchell from Faber replied, interviewed me and was of course happy to know I was interested in Britten – Faber Music had basically been set up to publish Britten – so all that worked out. I wrote some left-handed piano pieces for Britten when he lost the use of his right hand towards the end of his life.

DW: *Is it correct to say that your first 'real choral piece' didn't appear until 1980,* The Song of the Years Turning?

HS: Absolutely – before that I was writing small pieces for piano and accordion. I had taken my cue from Morton Feldman* to some extent and I really admired him for the homophonic element of his work, the vertical thinking and the concentration on sonority and harmony. Feldman himself had written some choral works, without a text. The piano pieces, both his and mine at the time, had a certain 'chorale' quality. It is almost as though I was writing choral music but writing it for the piano. I started to experiment with additive rhythms in my piano pieces as well and then I became aware that there was a Welsh competition, to write a choral piece. I can't remember if I had to set a Welsh text, but in any case I chose a rather austere poem by R.S. Thomas*. To begin with I wrote quite a chromatic melodic line away from the piano, and then went to the piano and tried to create some sort of clear harmonic world to go with it. That was the technique I acquired there and then and that is what I do now when writing choral pieces. Up to that point I felt that I hadn't really found a way of setting texts, but it suddenly occurred to me that this was the way to do it and it made sense. I certainly hadn't heard any of Arvo Pärt's* choral music at that time, but like him I discovered that strong-accented syllables can be longer than weak ones. I would give the accented notes *minims** and the unaccented notes *crochets**, let the metre follow that and slot in the bar lines later. That has been the pattern I've followed ever since.

DW: *A lot of the time it seems as if the bar lines shouldn't be there at all…*

HS: Well yes, but then it would be difficult to conduct without them – it is just a practical thing. With additive rhythms it was a simple way of achieving a subtle complexity. This is something that is already there in the text – the English language has that flexibility. The problem I have with Vaughan Williams* for instance is that he seems to almost force the language into a square rhythm. The actual homophonic nature of a lot of my music owes a lot to my chorister years, singing hymns certainly but also the flexibility and flow of Anglican chant and the way it is phrased when done well – actually, the elegant way those chants look too. I was looking at these chants every day as a boy, so there is little wonder that my music looks like it does. As a mostly self-taught composer I have a sort of genetic deficiency that makes me original I think. Perhaps I'd bracket myself with someone like Peter Sculthorpe* or maybe even Messiaen* – I'm not comparing myself to them of course, but they also developed a language and didn't really change it through their career. Looking at that first choral piece I immediately see similarities with what I'm doing now – a sort of prototype and how I turn a text into music.

DW: *You have talked about 'unlocking a text' – this is what you mean.*

HS: That's right – I'm unlocking it but I want to emphasise my respect for the text. It isn't just a means to an end; I really try to focus on the feeling and the emotional content.

DW: *I think you told me some years ago that you had to send R.S. Thomas a cheque, so you could use his text?*

HS: Yes, this was in the days before I had a publisher and I contacted the poet's son in the first instance and cleared it for the performance – then I had to pay him £30, which for me in those days was a lot of money.

DW: *I think this has meant you try to find texts that are out of copyright.*

HS: Yes, I hear many stories of difficulties that colleagues get into with using copyright texts, but there are other considerations too. I'm much too fastidious – it used to enrage Cardew; he told me that in a letter – and I don't feel I have the authority to set a text unless I have the measure of it.

DW: *There seem to be particular kinds of texts that interest you – Longfellow*, James Elroy Flecker*, George Russell*, William Morris*. There is something very clear and straightforward about the texts, very direct, even naive imagery in some cases – a sort of childlike wonder perhaps?*

HS: Yes, I think I am attracted to a particular kind of verse. In 1989 I got one of my first commissions, I was already over 40, and I had a neighbour who was interested in Mary Webb*, an early twentieth-century novelist and someone who wrote very fine lyric poetry, often about people she knew. The poems have a wonderful lightness and musicality and I found that I could hear the music for them without much difficulty. So, I wrote the *Five Poems of Mary Webb* for high-voice choir. They are entirely triadic – I wanted to try and capture the childlike innocence of the words and invest everything in the melody. Of course I looked at her dates and at that time she was out of copyright! I'm not sure the second sopranos and altos have such an interesting time but I'm rather proud of those pieces. The subtle shifts between major and minor is actually something I exploited when I wrote my orchestral piece *Lento* – that piece owes a huge amount to the Mary Webb settings and to choral music in general. It has even been suggested that if Barber* can turn his *Adagio* into an 'Agnus Dei' then I could do it with *Lento*, but that isn't what the piece is about at all. Anyway, I love looking for texts, it is certainly one of the most enjoyable parts of the compositional process and I'm always eager to start reading when a request for a piece comes through.

DW: *Do you think of yourself as an English composer? Is such a thing important to you?*

HS: I think so, yes. That is probably one of the reasons I became so interested in choral music; it really took off in the '90s and I've never looked back. In 1995 I was asked to write a carol, *To Bethlehem did they go*, slightly quirky, again full of syncopations and additive rhythms, and then Oxford University Press asked me for a piece for the OUP Chamber Choir and that became *We who with Songs*, again setting Flecker, which was chosen for me, but I was drawn to try and get inside the vivid vocabulary of that text and find the emotional richness of the words. The thing about Englishness is the language. For me what is important is the flexibility I find in the landscape, the music, in the language and actually in the character – I try to find a way of celebrating all that.

DW: *As you say, the floodgates opened* – The Flight of Song, Adam lay Ybounden, *the Edward Thomas* settings and the beautiful Yeats* setting,* He wishes for the cloths of Heaven, *perhaps my own particular favourite…*

HS: Yes, I think I had discovered a way forward, trying to solve problems and finding my own individuality. I loved writing the carols especially and they seem to have done well. The commissions started to come in for more choral works. Another piece from around this time is *Rise up my love* for the Estonian Philharmonic Chamber Choir. I was writing these and other pieces under some pressure, as well as writing pieces as gifts, copying them all out by hand. I think on reflection I was pushing myself too hard and it made me ill, but I still enjoyed writing them so much. I think what is important about writing choral music is that it would be difficult to write a piece without being generous – an act of friendship as Malcolm Arnold* used to say about writing music in general. You have to be mindful of what is possible for the choir you are writing for, but it is definitely an act of friendship.

DW: *You have written a good deal of music that sets sacred texts. I think this was partly due to a close friendship with Matthew Owens* when he was assistant organist at Manchester Cathedral and continuing this association when he went to St Mary's Cathedral, Edinburgh, and Wells Cathedral.*

HS: Yes, he and the churches he was associated with performed, commissioned and recorded a good deal of my music. It has been a wonderful working relationship and my late wife and I were very good friends with Matthew and his wife too.

DW: *For a composer that has been involved in the musical world you have been, it might be surprising that you have written so much sacred music.*

HS: Well, it was simply because Matthew was keen. He was interested in the experimental world I came from early on I think. He was also conducting the Exon Singers and commissioned pieces for them. That kind of confidence in one is so helpful - any composer would say that. I've enjoyed a close association with James Weeks and EXAUDI too. Once people know that you are interested in writing liturgical music they come to you, but I know Matthew was wanting to involve composers that might not otherwise be writing liturgical music and that could be how it all started.

DW: *The thing with all of your music is, I think, that the pieces look easy to sight-read, but then the work begins – that is certainly my experience.*

HS: In the end what excites me is subtlety and refinement in music – the idea that with just a tiny twist you can achieve something very special and turn straw into gold. It is true for both composing and performing. Several conductors, including you, have told me that unless the pieces are sung well, they just don't work. My music can't survive a bad performance it seems.

DW: *I know the question of tempo is very important to you.*

HS: Yes, very important – the right tempo, but a tempo that allows *rubato**. Again it is the subtlety that interests me – just nicely poised and balanced. Intonation is another big thing for me and I think I'm aware of this when composing a piece, sometimes treading a dangerous line so to speak.

DW: *How do you decide on which commissions to accept?*

HS: I'm aware that I sometimes agree to do things and then find I don't have the time; what I will say is that I'm happy to do a piece. Of course one thing about having a publisher is that one can get a decent fee! I have always been hopeless dealing with that kind of thing myself.

DW: *Are you surprised when you hear a piece for the first time?*

HS: [Long pause] Well, rather worryingly, no. I think I'm lucky…

DW: *Are you surprised what performers bring to your music?*

HS: That's an interesting question – I think of the performers when I'm writing… [another long pause] – I'm more surprised at the time of composing the pieces actually. Of course the magic and energy of live performance is very special. Suddenly one can be quite taken by a piece – I just hope everything is written into the music.

DW: *Do you revise?*

HS: No – I work very hard to get it right the first time. I play and sing the pieces over and over again before I admit to them being finished.

DW: *Do you think about the audience when you are writing?*

HS: I think it is true to say that with choral music the experience for the choir will be shared by the audience or congregation – again, another reason that I love writing choral music. I suppose in the case of liturgical music you have to be aware of the context, so writing Responses for example, you have to imagine the piece is part of an act of worship. It is very satisfying to do something in that way.

DW: *Do you enjoy rehearsals and performances?*

HS: Yes, I do on the whole. I might just tweak one or two tiny things in rehearsal. I'm not usually worried – the crucial thing again is the tempo and I want to make sure that the piece has the possibility of *rubato* that I talked about.

DW: *You still teach a good deal – do you have any advice for young composers?*

HS: The first thing I would do is advise them to write choral music because it isn't the first thing that they might consider. Unfortunately in conservatoires there isn't much of an emphasis in writing music for choirs, as they often don't have choirs, but I would certainly encourage it, as there is a demand, and it is often the case that choirs are so much more welcoming than orchestras. I'm sure choral music brings out the best of me. It stretches me in every way I want to be stretched – all the aspects of composing are laid bare. There is something about working with texts that is endlessly fascinating.

DW: *When Elgar completed the score of* The Dream of Gerontius* *he added a quotation from Ruskin at the end: 'This is the best of me...'. Can you say what might be the best of you?*

HS: I think the last movement of *Rise up, my love* hits the spot in a way that surprises me – again it is the surprise at the moment of composition rather than anything else. Also, the last of the *Three Motets* (*Ave virgo sanctissima*) – I was pleased with the shape of that. Like a lot of my pieces, it begins with a single line and flowers outwards. I sometimes listen to it and think I don't know how I did that. I like the ending too, although for some there isn't really an ending, but that's the point: the best endings don't close a piece down, they open them up!

DW: *Is there anything you are burning to write?*

HS: The pieces I am burning to write are those pieces for friends that I've somehow been diverted from writing. I've hoped for a long time that I'll have the chance to compose some settings of the poems of James Stephens, an Irish writer of delightful lyric verse, whose work is likely to come out of copyright at the end of 2020. I see 2021 as a year for choral music, thanks again to Matthew Owens who wants some music for Belfast Cathedral. He was recently appointed Director of Music there.

DW: *We are recording this interview at a very difficult time – how are you dealing with lockdown?*

HS: I've been quite impatient I'm afraid – I've found that I should have had more time but... I'm copying a big choral piece, setting texts of pupils at the school that commissioned it, but beyond that I've got to write an accordion piece for the RAM* and more choral pieces. The point is, of course, there is more time and although I've had a productive routine in the past, the disruption of that routine has slowed me down a bit. The lack of live music is very worrying. I suppose the thing about composing is the proof of the pudding will be in the eating as far as these particular pieces are concerned, when they are eventually performed.

DW: *What would you say are your five favourite choral works?*

HOWARD'S FIVE FAVOURITE CHORAL WORKS

Britten *Ceremony of Carols*

Górecki *Totus Tuus*

Kreek *Psalms of David*

Messiaen *O sacrum convivium*

Walton *Belshazzar's Feast*

Will Todd

BORN 1970

DW: *Can you tell me about your earliest musical experiences? Where you born into a musical family?*

WT: I was born in Durham. Dad taught at the University in the English Department and my mum comes from a mining family who lived in Easington, the village that they used as the setting for the 'Billy Elliott' film*. I suppose you could say that it was an educated household from a working-class background. Everyone had an interest in music – my two elder sisters played instruments, my dad played the piano in a rudimentary way, twelve bars blues! Most important of all was that everyone listened to music constantly – folk, jazz, rock, orchestral music, musical theatre, choral music and in particular opera, which my parents loved. I got to realise that lots of my friends liked one type of music but I have always had very eclectic interests and this comes from that time. My parents were not judgemental about art of any description – they would say it didn't matter if someone said that this was a second-rate book – who cares really; that is meaningless. Of course, you don't think about that as a child, but now I realise how lucky I was and I think one has to be careful judging any kind of art and saying that something is good or bad.

DW: *You played the piano by ear from very early on?*

WT: Yes, when I was very small. I didn't have piano lessons until I was about twelve. By that time I had learnt 'my technique', which meant of course that I was in permanent conflict with my lovely piano teacher. We are still great friends but she had a hell of a time getting me through Grade 8 – my fingers were all over the place. The Bach* 48 Preludes and Fugues are on my piano now. I probably learnt one for Grade 8 or something, and of course I've never played them since, so the project this year is to play all of them and I'm loving it.

DW: *Some of them are really hard aren't they!*

WT: They are really, really hard! Despite me wanting to do my own thing I had a wonderful piano teacher. One learns from classical technique regardless of if that is your primary interest or not. I played the violin, the saxophone, I was heavily involved in the

County Music Service, when such amazing things existed, playing for local productions of musicals, anything and everything you could as a teenager.

DW: *I'm guessing your composing at that stage was all done by improvising at the piano?*

WT: Yes, playing and singing at the piano. I also had composition lessons from the choirmaster at our local parish church. I joined the choir and that was how I learnt to read music. The choirmaster, David Higgins, was a pretty good choral composer too and at that stage it was inspiring to see that a composer was a 'living person'; he taught me harmony and counterpoint – a really good teacher; I owe him a lot. He would say, 'here are some rules but sometimes it is OK to break them' – very encouraging for an adolescent, not to see red pen all over the place. The O level and A level exams at that time didn't really include free composition – it was a bit dry – so at school composing felt a bit like a secret activity.

DW: *What did they sound like, these early pieces, when you wrote them down?*

WT: I was given a manuscript book when I was about eight and I became obsessed with writing things down. I got really exercised about trying to work out how to write down complex syncopated rhythms. I was trying to build the Taj Mahal with bits of broken wood! I was writing four-part psalm settings for the church choir – lyrical, quite chromatic – and at the same time a few pop songs and ballads. I tried to write orchestral music and discovered the miniature scores of Beethoven* and Brahms* Symphonies, which fascinated me. Rachmaninov* and Sibelius* I loved too.

DW: *This eclecticism certainly comes through in what you do now.*

WT: Very much so and I've had to some extent learn to accept that. The church choir were amateur of course but good enough to sing a couple of services a week. We did what I thought then were modern settings, you know the Darke in F* sort of thing, John Rutter* of course, and *Carols for Choirs** which I adored. Actually, one of my proudest thoughts is that now I see John as a friend and colleague and yet, when I was a boy he was this far-off mythical figure! He is a wonderful person and musician.

DW: *And then Bristol University. Was there a conflict in what you were doing at this time, with these eclectic tastes, and what was expected of you?*

WT: Oh yes, by that time I was a pretty confident jazz player on sax and piano, but then leaned much more towards the piano. I had a great time at Bristol, but my university years were a constant period of conflict with my tutors, not in an unpleasant way at all, but I was interested in such a wide variety of things and they had definitely more modernist leanings. There was a big pressure on all of us to write music that was 'cutting edge'. I was quite good at some of it and I'd get high marks but I knew I wasn't really in control of it and although I was pushing things around the page as it were, it didn't mean much to me as a composer. There is a lot of atonal music I love but I don't want to write in that style. In some of my operas there are high levels of dissonance for dramatic reasons, but the jazz/cross-over things I was doing as a student – I wrote a piece for jazz ensemble and chamber ensemble – it didn't go down well. I think nowadays things would be different. It was expected that you would be either a modernist or write what one of my passionately modernist colleagues would call, in a broad Yorkshire accent, 'tonal slush'! I don't look back at all this as bad, it is part of the never-ending cycle of aesthetics and it helped me find my way. The big thing at University was music making - music of all kinds – and I took full advantage of it.

DW: *Do you find that you have to put yourself in a different box if you are asked to write a little anthem or carol, such as* My Lord has Come *or a jazz piece?*

WT: You do a little, because the realities of being commissioned are that someone will have heard or sung *My Lord has Come* or *The Lord is my Shepherd*, liked it and that is their 'blue-print' for asking you, so one has to find out in initial conversations what they want. If someone wants a piece that mixes choir and jazz ensemble I can move into that world. I don't have any problem with that now but it is odd, I read reviews of my 'classical pieces' and the writer will say, it has these lovely jazz harmonies in it...

DW: *But your two worlds constantly collide and one can see how they influence each other...*

WT: Yes, and there aren't many good things about getting older, but one of those things is that I don't worry about that now, as long as I think 'those chords' are in context and fit with what I'm doing. If they are helping to make the 'story of the piece' then by definition they must be right and it doesn't matter if it is a big 11th chord or an open 5th, it will work. Actually, going back to *My Lord has Come*, I think it works because it stays in four parts which allows it to be sung by all kinds of choirs, but originally it was in six or seven parts. Knowing there was a chance of it going in *Carols for Choirs 5*, I stripped it back to four parts. I often say to students who come to me with pieces in eight parts, this sounds great, but it is pretty hard to sound bad in eight parts and can you get a better result by reducing it and so ensuring that so many more people will sing it?

DW: *I wondered if there was a particular piece that you can point at and say that is my opus 1?*

WT: A few years ago I began to think about this – I began to curate my own catalogue and I must confess I found it quite hard. There is a setting of *A Boy was Born* when I was 18, just a four-part piece and I look at it and it holds up. There is a certain naivety but I think some of my earlier accompanied pieces are less good perhaps.

DW: *There are a lot of big pieces from your earlier years – you called them Choral Symphonies.*

WT: Yes, *Midwinter, The Burning Road* and an Oratorio, *St Cuthbert* – the choral symphonies are I hope still powerful and strong enough to hold their own. The first, *Midwinter* was written in 1992. I've rather enjoyed that form, an extended choral work that you wouldn't exactly call a Cantata or an Oratorio, and they all have a symphonic structure that is carefully worked out in a symphonic way. *Midwinter* is monothematic and even has a twelve-tone theme that gets worked through. I like in bigger works to think like that; even *Mass in Blue* has a symphonic structure really.

DW: *Are you conscious of being part of the English choral tradition? Those pieces seem to be very much in that line.*

WT: I think so – when I was a kid in Durham I often heard big pieces in the Cathedral – Elgar* oratorios, Tippett's* *A Child of our Time*, Britten's* *War Requiem* – and I sang a lot of British music liturgically. I still love the Elgar symphonies and especially the symphonies of Vaughan Williams* which cover such a huge range – there is a composer who has become known to a large extent for doing 'one thing', you know, the English pastoral piece, but he is so much more than that.

DW: *Yes, but your* Mass in Blue, *which is by far your most successful piece, has had the same effect and you have been put into a pigeonhole I think.*

WT: You are very much put in a pigeonhole. It is the double-edged sword of any kind of success. I realised this with a *Te Deum* that I wrote after *Mass in Blue* and I wanted it to be quite different, but somehow it didn't quite work, I was half-mimicking the Mass and half not. In *Passion Music* that I wrote recently, I took a large part of the structure of *Mass in Blue* for the simple reason that it worked well for your average choral society - there are times for creating new models and some times not. When I pick up the latest Lee Childs* thriller I want it to be at least a little like the last one I read without being repetitive – in *Mass in Blue* something is working. It is certainly right to say that some of the music in the symphonies is much more chromatic and dark – *The Burning Road* is really quite angular.

DW: The Burning Road *is about the Jarrow March and St Cuthbert is of course a Northumbrian Saint – you obviously feel a strong pull to your roots.*

WT: Yes, I was obsessed on every level about the area I grew up in. My mum was a good local historian, was full of stories and I got a good sense of the region. It took me a long time to really leave. A lot of my early pieces were trying to encapsulate these places.

DW: *You are obviously passionate about music in society, doing outreach works, working with young people, amateurs...*

WT: For sure, it started very early on – again involved in County Music guided by professionals. For a long time amateur music making was the thing that occupied me and was my musical experience. I still observe problems that exist between a wholly professional world and the amateur world. There is a sort of gap in the musicianship of elite choral singers being involved with amateur groups. Maybe this is changing, but I wish there were not these differing degrees of ivory tower. I think a lot of what I have done has been judged negatively because the pieces work for amateurs. I would say if you are truly going to be valuable you should be able to write for the Royal Opera House and a children's choir in Norfolk! Let's be honest, bad music can sound great when sung by good musicians, but it doesn't work the other way around. We don't encourage composers in conservatoires to get their hands dirty and write a piece for three-part choir and thereby discover great joys in that. If you stand in a village hall for the afternoon, maybe the singers aren't so good, but you can have a really wonderful time; you can also stand in front of a high-level chamber choir and have a really bad time! There are all sorts of layers where I believe amateur music making contains the real and sheer joy of music making

DW: *To* Mass in Blue *– it has had hundreds of performances now.*

WT: Yes, we used to track the number of performances but it isn't possible. I've sometimes woken up in the middle of the night, in a cold sweat, thinking imagine if I hadn't written *Mass in Blue*!

DW: *You must be delighted that the piece has done so well, but, on the other hand, do you feel 'why don't they sing another of my pieces'?*

WT: I can honestly say that I always enjoy performing it because of course, with all the improvisation, no two performances are quite the same. I do different things depending on the acoustic, the size and ability of the choir; there are different versions as you know - for jazz trio, a larger band or orchestra – and you play differently because of that. It was first performed by Hertfordshire Choral Society in Cambridge in 2003; a friend of mine came and I said to him beforehand that I thought it was a good piece but that nobody would like it and I've been proved spectacularly wrong I'm pleased to say. Why was I so wrong? What I hadn't understood at the time was that somehow in the Mass I just used my choral skills and my blues skills and didn't think too hard about the dividing line between the two. It was a huge milestone for me and I learnt to use the skills you have and not to worry too much about them living side by side. There was an earlier version that was much more complex as though my University tutor was standing over my shoulder. I played it through with my wife Beth, who has sung solo in most of the performances I've done, and we both thought that it didn't flow. Every time it settled in an interesting groove, I would stop it, as much as to say, 'I'm a contemporary composer and I can't do that'; but ultimately I chucked all that out and the piece became so much more honest; I think that is why it works.

DW: *But it creates certain problems – if you have a conventional choral society, of a certain type or even dare one say, of a certain age, trying to get them to relax into the idiom is not easy.*

WT: I think this is interesting – one part of all this and the 'jazz repertoire' in general is that the choral parts and accompaniment are written out in painful detail. In the Mass, the choral parts are there of course, but the accompaniment includes a rhythm section and although there is notation you generally have musicians with some sort of experience in the field – they play the groove and not necessarily all the notes. So underneath that choral sound you always have an engine room of jazz going on. I've always noticed at the afternoon rehearsal, choirs will say: now we hear the

band, we see what is going on and we can relax and sing; 'you know, we are not worried about semi-quavers tied to semi-quavers over the bar, off-beat rhythms; we are just singing'. People become less self-conscious, but whenever I'm involved I always say at the afternoon rehearsal 'the time for getting all these notes in place has gone – we are doing this in three hours, just have fun'. It's lovely to hear a great choir sing it of course; yes, it does get some rough performances, but it survives.

DW: *The big thing is that they have got to think about rhythm in a completely different way, or maybe not think about it.*

WT: Whenever I do workshops I always say 'a lot of these rhythms are easier if I sing them to you and then you sing them back as a question and answer'. In jazz arrangements that is always the problem – how can I write out what I want. I think you write it as accurately as possible but there will come a point of overload, where even good choirs will struggle.

DW: *Was this one of the reasons that you started to be involved so much with your Trio – a bit like Steve Reich* forming his own ensemble because he felt he was the one that knew what he wanted?*

WT: It was certainly true in the early days – quite quickly we were doing 10-15 a year and we could always slot in somehow. I used to perform a lot and then in my late twenties I got terrible performing nerves and I gave up playing in public; but, when the Mass came around, I thought that I really had to do it. I was terribly worried about the first few performances but since then I haven't looked back.

DW: *The other important side to your work is opera* – Alice's Adventures in Wonderland *has been particularly successful.*

WT: I really wanted to write for the stage from a very early age. I started to work on what was an awful version of 'A Christmas Carol' with my dad when I was about ten! No music exists thank God! I find working in theatres and being part of the mechanics of theatre just so exciting. When it came to '*Alice...*' it wasn't my first stage piece – I knew by then about collaboration with singers, directors, designers, lighting people, to get the best possible show and to be prepared to make changes and cuts on the hop. I think composers are a bit self-indulgent sometimes, not taking enough notice of the listener, not exactly making it easy for them, but you certainly mustn't strive, especially in the theatre, to make things confusing. I'm lucky in that I can write quickly – any opera/theatre composer will tell stories of how helpful that is, be they Puccini* or Sondheim*; the smart composer for the theatre is ready to adapt.

DW: *Again, as a jazz musician you have to think all the time about pacing, how long a section should be, adapting a solo or chord progression – all these things collide.*

WT: Yes, you are right – having that sense of adapting is hard for some, but not for me - it is something I'm used to.

DW: *You often write your own texts for choral pieces. How did that come about?*

WT: When I was younger, I used to set psalms, liturgical texts, then love-sick ballads as an adolescent to my own texts. I wrote a lot of poetry too. I read a lot. When I went to university this didn't happen. I looked for texts, then I started collaborating with writers. Ben Durwell has written several texts for me – we learnt a lot of difficult things about collaboration which has benefitted us later on. In more recent years I've written a lot to texts myself. *My Lord has Come* is an example and that gave me confidence, so when I think it fits I'll write them myself. A good text is the difference between a successful piece and an unsuccessful one.

DW: *How does a piece start? Do you start with a melody or harmony or is it a case of sitting down and improvising to get things started?*

WT: Yes, I improvise myself into all these pieces. For *My Lord has Come* I thought about that drone that it begins with, echoing around Durham Cathedral, then that plainsong melody and how that worked in that acoustic. Atmosphere is very important. There might be a rhythmic pulse or a melodic shape. I sketch on big sheets of paper and it's very messy! I've learnt there is no point in leaving the piano until I have what I call my 'click moment' – as soon as the click moment comes we are there, even if that is only the first phrase. I have faith in an idea that I know will work. Because of this there tends to be a high failure rate!

DW: *So you throw a lot away.*

WT: Oh yes. I might have still gone with one of those bad ideas when I was younger, but I know now that there is no point because I will regret it later. Even under a lot of pressure it is always best to wait until I get a good idea, often something very simple, but something that convinces me.

DW: The Call of Wisdom *that you wrote for the Queen's Diamond Jubilee Service is a case* *in point – just one simple idea to start the piece off.*

WT: Yes, what happened with that was that originally the text was much longer and the piece started with a big, bright, fanfare idea. What survives was going to be the slower section.

DW: *So you began to channel your inner Royal Occasion William Walton* mode.*

WT: Exactly and I just thought, hold on, there will be any number of fantastic fanfares in this service and the piece is about the youth choir – we want people to be drawn in - so I slashed off the front! The simple idea worked.

DW: *Are you very self -critical?*

WT: Yes, most of the time I think I have never written anything decent. I never take anything for granted. I've had to be less self-critical I think as time has gone on – partly a question of deadlines, but also, when I get my 'click moment', I'm more often than not right and go with it. In the past I'd get that moment, start fiddling around with it and mess it up, so I've learnt to leave it and trust my ears. I have to try to ensure that it is the very best I can do before sending it off to the performers.

DW: *So when you hear pieces you have written twenty years ago…*

WT: Mostly, it is OK. It is sometimes difficult – a bit like reading an old love letter! Slightly excruciating, but that is who you were at that time.

DW: *When you hear a new piece are you ever surprised?*

WT: Earlier on yes, hearing a big choral/orchestral sound that you had written was intoxicating, but devastating when you got it wrong and drowned out the singers. To be honest, if I'm not playing or directing I'm not so keen on going to hear my pieces. I like to be involved but just sitting and listening I find difficult.

DW: *Having said that are you surprised what performers bring?*

WT: Yes, we all go to performances that aren't so great – that can be a little disturbing, but more often than that the piece comes to life in a way you had not imagined. The energy that performers can bring can be quite something. I often say to performers that when I write this stuff out I'm writing out energy for you to give back.

DW: *Do you think about the audience when you are writing?*

WT: Over time I've learnt that less is more. I think you want to make the listening experience clear for the audience – how long can you interest them? When I'm writing I do think, 'if I was in the audience would I be enjoying this?'

DW: *What about teaching? You mentioned that you get people sending you music.*

WT: Yes, I've done a little teaching of different kinds. I taught jazz piano and jazz studies at Surrey University which I loved. I only stopped because time became an issue. Often I turn up to talk to composition students and I've realised you are in front of a mixed group – they could be writing in so many different ways – so I break it down. Simply, to begin with there is no piece, then there is a performance – this is true whatever you are doing and everyone has a very personal experience. I think the thing to do is offer lots of practical thinking. For instance, 'this is nice, but very hard, you need to be aware that if Tenebrae aren't singing this it isn't going to work. That doesn't devalue it as music but how could you do something to make it more straightforward without losing the power. Does it need to be as long?' People love writing long slow choral pieces that are never so easy to sing. There is a finite amount of time that choirs have to rehearse and I like to try and get young composers to think creatively about those parameters and not see them as the enemy – a real opportunity to strip the music down.

DW: *Do you think choral music is a poor relation for young composers?*

WT: I do. It certainly shouldn't be but it is. The great fallacy is that writing choral music is easy and it isn't easy at all. It is far easier to write for the BBC Symphony Orchestra than it is to write a successful four-part piece – there is nowhere to hide! There are some people one can't teach because they can't benefit from what you are trying to say, especially at a high academic level; you want to talk to composers about their emotions, because ultimately I don't see why you would create anything if you didn't want to express something and/or communicate. Part of the power of music is its vulnerability – the power of the simple gesture. That's why you can hear a very complex piece of music and not be affected at all, but hear an old guy in a bar, singing the blues...

DW: *If you were giving advice to a young composer...*

WT: It depends who they are. What kind of music are you trying to write? I would tailor my advice but to try and work out how to do something in a simple way, particularly with choral music, ultimately I just do my best to be encouraging.

DW: *Elgar quotes Ruskin at the end of* The Dream of Gerontius* – 'This is the best of me...'. Is there a particular piece or a collection of pieces that might fall into that category for you?*

WT: I struggle to be confident about the pieces I have written – all of them have, in my mind, faults. I am always grateful for works which resonate with the audience – in that sense *Mass in Blue* is the best of me. However people close to me always say my *Requiem* for voices and electric guitar is 'The One'. I, however, find it 'challenging'. I actually feel that *Passion Music* is probably 'The Best Of Me'.

DW: *We are recording this at a very difficult and worrying time – how are you dealing with lockdown?*

WT: People like me are very fortunate to have pieces booked in that I can work on. For people further down the food chain it is far more difficult. Any other formal things that help a young composer will get scarce, which is awful. I think creative artists are struggling to understand their existence – this isn't brand new on COVID because many of us are worried about the environment and perhaps COVID has shown up our fragility more starkly. I find myself thinking what piece do I write, what text do I use? I'm always slightly sceptical about writing within and about a crisis because I'm not sure what I think; music needs time to think, but I'm sure that eventually there will be lots of pieces about COVID-19!

DW: *What would you say are your five favourite choral works?*

WILL'S FIVE FAVOURITE CHORAL WORKS

Batten *This is the day that the Lord hath made*

Jonathan Dove *Seek him that maketh the seven stars*

Ireland *My Song is Love Unknown*

Stanford *Beati quorum via*

Walton *The Twelve*

Errollyn Wallen

BORN 1958

DW: *Can you tell me about your earliest musical memories? Did you come from a musical family?*

EW: My parents told me that when I was a baby, and this would have been in Belize where I was born, I never cried, I was always singing. One day they woke up to hear me (aged between one and two years old) singing 'When I fall in love, it will be forever'…

DW: *That Nat King Cole sang…*

EW: Yes, exactly. I can't imagine how they recognised a baby singing that. My father had a beautiful voice and loved to sing around the house, sometimes songs he wrote himself, you know, popular 'crooning' songs. It took me a while to sing myself because I believed that was my father's domain really. My mother was extremely musical too, but neither of them had any real idea of the professional life of a 'classical' musician; I think it rather bemused them when I went down that road.

DW: *It was when you moved to London that you started to have piano lessons.*

EW: Yes, from the age of nine I had unconventional piano lessons with a series of teachers, that, what can I say, were perhaps not so well-versed in the repertoire. I remember my sister and I went to one teacher for a while and we were exclusively playing what I now realise were Edwardian parlour songs. I went to boarding school at 13 and it was then that I was introduced to Associated Board Exams* and my training became a lot more traditionally rigorous. Before I went to boarding school in Sussex. I'd developed a huge appetite to play absolutely anything and used to go to the local library, completely unsupervised of course, to see what I could find, and I remember bringing back Humperdinck's opera *Hansel and Gretel* and sight-reading my way through that. This would have been my introduction to opera apart from placemats with photos of a production of *Carmen* we had at home in Tottenham. My teacher, Miss Pearse, in Sussex had us singing madrigals and other choral music, but I always felt that playing the piano was a good way to discover things. I didn't have pushy parents at all. I made these discoveries myself.

DW: *And dance played a large part in your musical education too.*

EW: My sister and I were sent to dancing lessons, as were lots of kids then – we did tap, modern stage, national dancing, ballet, all involving different kinds of music. One day a pianist came in to play for us and played Chopin*, and I remember being mesmerised and went home to try and find it on the radio. That's how I discovered Radio 3. In Tottenham we had a great primary school teacher, Miss Beale, who taught us all how to read and write music at the age of nine, no fuss about it, just treating it as the most normal thing in the world. She would encourage me to write pieces for the class – my first piece was 'Frogs and Toads'. I found this poem and I got everybody to sing and play different instruments, even though at that time I couldn't read and write music that well – it was my first proper composition and we performed it in a school concert.

DW: *I think your original intention was to study to become a professional dancer. What was it that changed your mind and made you go down the music route?*

EW: I had such a passion for ballet music and when I was around 12 my dancing teacher said I should go to a ballet school, but my parents said that they hadn't seen any black ballet dancers and they didn't want me to be disappointed, so the answer was no. I was completely devastated and heart-broken, to the extent that for several years I couldn't bring myself to watch any dancing at all. To make myself feel better I just started to play the piano non-stop. Then I went back to dancing when I was around 17/18 at The Urdang Academy in London followed by intensive courses at the Dance Theatre of Harlem in New York. There was a course being started at Goldsmiths' College that combined music and dance, but after the Dance Theatre of Harlem it felt like a step backwards and I sensed that music was pulling me more and more towards it. I was practising the piano ten hours a day. They were very difficult times, and it took a while for me to find the right thing for my temperament. I began to feel that as a musician or composer you were more in control of your own fate, rather than being faced with endless auditions that working as a professional dancer would involve.

DW: *The influence of movement and dance has stayed with you because rhythmic energy is central to your work as a composer?*

EW: Yes, it has. Dance for me is not just about rhythm but also about making gestures and lines in space and the control of flow and textures. One of my dreams as a young girl was to be dancing on the stage of Sadler's Wells and years later, *In our Lifetime* was performed there by the London Contemporary Dance Theatre (an existing musical work which was choreographed by Christopher Bruce) and I was taking a bow on stage. It was only then I realised that my dream had come true – I was on stage and dancing through my music! I was so thrilled by that. For me still any piece I write is a physical reality. I'm always conscious of movement and the way the phrases work. I had piano lessons with an incredible woman called Edith Vogel* at the Guildhall...

DW: *I had a few lessons with her too – she was completely terrifying!*

EW: She certainly was! What fascinated me about her though was her understanding of the importance of rhythm and leading me to appreciate how rhythmic structures operate in the piano works of Beethoven*, the idea of upbeats and hemiolas being so important. Edith Vogel had an equally profound influence on me as a composer as well as a pianist. She told me I was a composer, though I can't remember what work I showed her.

DW: *After Goldsmiths', you went to King's College, London.*

EW: Yes, I studied with Nicola LeFanu* and David Lumsdaine* back in the days of hard-core serialism. I did steep myself in contemporary music and had been listening to predominantly contemporary music for years. At that time, even though my fellow students and I were working hard, there was a sense that a life in composing was only for the 'anointed few'. There was little discussion of vocal or choral music as such. I suppose people just didn't write songs then. I did enjoy my MMus course and was very grateful for the training, it taught me a certain rigour, and that all came from Nicola and David, but I'm also glad that things have opened up so that different aesthetics are also now countenanced.

DW: *I read somewhere that Bach* and Stravinsky* are your two composer idols.*

EW: They mean everything to me. They both can do just brilliantly the things that I love in music with their mastery of every possible aspect of music and range of expression. They can do things on a small scale that feel to be epic and things on a large scale that breathe so naturally, and which sound inevitable.

DW: *You said that your parents were clear that they didn't want you to go down the dance route, because at the time they hadn't seen any dancers of colour. Were you aware when you were growing up that this, together with being a woman, was another battle that you might have to fight?*

EW: If I'm honest I've always been proud of my background because it was so unusual. I've always felt that music called me towards it and, it's true, nobody around me had any great expectations of me. I had no expectations myself. In a way for a developing composer it isn't a bad place to start. Some composers have had so much pressure and tension thrust upon them from an early age and I think that is harder. My first battle was realising that if ever I wanted to do anything in music, I must not ask anyone's permission, I would and need to get on with it and chart my own course. Now we are beginning to recognise women composers, composers of colour, but for me starting out without role models, the main objective was to try and reach potential I saw in myself. If there wasn't an opening, I would just have to forge one. Yes, there were many years when I wasn't taken seriously at all and was overlooked but the important thing was to keep composing, performing and getting my music performed.

DW: *The business of song writing and singing the songs yourself must have seemed somewhat 'left-field' in the '70s and '80s too?*

EW: Oh yes. I remember a well-known composer telling me early on 'you can't do that, you can't write songs like that and also perform them. You can't form a band to play your music in such a wide range of styles and I kept thinking – 'why?'.'Why shouldn't I do what I love?' This is why I feel close to baroque composers, writing music that is asked for, music that is useful, not the nineteenth-century thing, sitting around dreaming and having a vision made possible through a private income. When I left King's I was doing all kinds of things to earn a living – playing with pop bands, my own ensemble [Ensemble X] – it was such fun and was very social. Music could be fun and adventurous in so many other ways, in so many contexts, it didn't have to go down just one avenue.

DW: *You were already a busy professional composer/performer when you went to King's College, Cambridge*.*

EW: I was and I viewed that experience as kind of a sabbatical! I came across a notification of a scholarship at Cambridge to do an MPhil and write an orchestral piece and that year was the making of me really, meeting people who were so passionate about what they do, not just musicians, but people who cared passionately about economics, literature, science – it was fabulous. I was still working at commissions and I was writing a chapter of a book at the same time, but it just taught me so much.

DW: *You studied with Robin Holloway*.*

EW: I'm not sure that Robin knew what to make of me! What I wanted more than anything was to pick his brains about orchestration. He has such an extraordinary mind and just to show your music to someone like that, whatever they said, was a valuable experience. His biggest compliment to me was 'You find this easy, don't you?'

DW: *Did the experience of being close to that English musical tradition in Cambridge affect your music in any way?*

EW: Whilst I was in Cambridge I sang in a group that John Butt* (who has gone on to do great things with the Dunedin Consort) ran: King's Mixed Voices. We sang Evensong on a Monday night in the Chapel, which taught me a lot about the Anglican service (I was brought up a Methodist) and I remember singing my own songs around the place, even doing a gig in King's Chapel, probably much to the horror of the Director of Music, Stephen Cleobury*- I'm not sure he relished having 50 speakers, amplifiers, drums and electric guitars in the chapel! I had one of the best years of my life at King's. It was a bit agonising going back to writing essays, but I upped my game and enriched my life by going there.

DW: *As you mentioned King's and Stephen Cleobury, we should perhaps jump forward to more recent times and talk about the recording of some of your choral music that, at the time of writing, is due to be released. Again this is wrong, but I think people have a certain perception of you, and to hear that you had an album of choral and organ music coming out being performed by King's, Cambridge might come as a surprise.*

EW: Absolutely! I realise that people's perception of me is somewhat prejudiced, but this was a good reason to get this particular project moving. I have actually written some mighty choral pieces for large forces including orchestra – *Our English Heart, Carbon 12, Hawks and Horses, PRINCIPIA, ONLY, Rani, Queen of the Stars* (for the Queen's Golden Jubilee), *Diamond Greenwich* (for the Queen's Diamond Jubilee), but the smaller works, recently recorded by the Choir of King's College, Cambridge, are very important to me. *See that I am God* was commissioned by St Paul's Cathedral to celebrate the 20th anniversary of women being admitted into the priesthood of the Church of England. It was written for an adult mixed choir, but as I was writing I was dreaming of the sound of King's. Then there is a carol *Peace on Earth*, which originally was a song I sang myself and which is in the Errollyn Wallen Songbook, published by Peters Edition. There are a couple of organ pieces I wrote for John Butt and Thomas Trotter* – *Tiger* and *Triptych* respectively. I was originally only asking if I could hire King's College, Chapel to make the recording but Stephen Cleobury suggested that we release the recording on King's own label and I was so honoured and excited. He had conducted *Our English Heart*, to celebrate Nelson and the Battle of Trafalgar, so he knew my work, but I certainly wasn't in the inner sanctum of choral composers at all, so this was such a special opportunity.

DW: *Another choral piece on the recording is a short piece called* PACE *that you wrote for the Christmas anthology I put together a few years ago.*

EW: Yes, of course, you were responsible. Thank you, David! *PACE* took a while to get just right. I set just one word 'pace' ['peace'].

DW: *This must have been one of Stephen Cleobury's last recordings?*

EW: It was, June 2019. Stephen prepared and conducted my music with such devotion and care. With *PACE* he worked miracles, colour-coding the score for each singer so that you don't even hear a single breath. He was very unwell and had to have several breaks during the sessions to recover his energy, but it was just an unforgettable experience. I feel so fortunate that I was able to be there and to have my music directed by such a great musician. Of course, recording in King's Chapel, which has its very own idiosyncrasies was special, and we had a brilliant sound engineer, Benjamin Sheen, who is also the label manager of King's College Recordings and it made for a memorable experience.

DW: *You have written for voices a great deal, we have mentioned your songs, the choral music, and of course your operas. Does writing for the voice give you the most pleasure?*

EW: I actually love composing for everything, though I do think that if you know how to write for the voice it helps when writing for instruments too. Chamber and orchestral music feel almost like a holiday for me because I can let the instruments sing in a different way and am not bound by a text. Growing up in a house where song was so important, it is just part of me. I love the challenge of writing for different kinds of voices – highly-trained opera singers, children, amateur choirs – each kind of voice is an endless source of fascination for me.

DW: *It is perhaps surprising that you haven't written more choral music. Is this just because you have not been asked, or is it because, again, it is not what people are expecting from you?*

EW: I actually feel that I have covered a lot of ground as regards choral music, admittedly not much that can be seen as part of the 'English choral or church tradition', but there is a good deal. As I mentioned before, most of it has been on rather an epic scale, which suits me well!

DW: *Can you say a little bit about the texts you choose and how you go about deciding what might be suitable for a musical setting? I notice you have set a good deal of Shakespeare, both on a large scale in* Hawks and Horses *which sets a sonnet that gives the piece its title, and in smaller pieces such as* Full Fathom Five *for women's voices.*

EW: Aside from the music, I grew up in a family that loved to read too. It was my Uncle Arthur that got us reciting poetry almost as soon as we could read and so the sound of declaimed text is something I've been used to since early childhood. My natural inclination was at one time towards literature too and so finding the right text to set is really important to me. I used to write a lot of poetry myself and have written words for most of my songs which I sing myself. I admire all kinds of poets and songwriters. I am fascinated by the fact that once you set a single word to music, you begin to usher in a whole new atmosphere. I've enjoyed collaborating with a lot of living writers too. On the other hand, I think that some poetry is only meant to be read to yourself or read out loud, so that makes it unsuitable for music. I love setting simple, condensed texts. What is really important to me, whoever I'm writing for, is to give singers something they will enjoy learning and singing. I studied at a time when extended vocal techniques were the most important thing, but there is a real art in writing singable, direct vocal lines.

DW: *You mentioned that you have written a number of choral pieces on a truly epic scale – your oratorio/choral symphony* Carbon 12… *for instance [*Carbon 12: A Choral Symphony*], which I think is a celebration of the landscapes of South Wales and the mining industry that was so important to it. This is on a truly massive scale – soloists, massed choirs, brass band and orchestra; also* PRINCIPIA *which was one of two pieces you wrote for the opening ceremony of the Paralympic Games, held in London in 2012.*

EW: *Carbon 12…*was a turning point for me; it seemed almost beyond my grasp at times. There were so many different types of singers – the chorus from Welsh National

Opera, community choirs, soloists from within those choirs, a Welsh male-voice choir – and I remember thinking to myself how crazy this was. Then I thought, actually, this gives me a real opportunity to explore lots of different ideas and textures within these diverse groups, so I came to enjoy a bigger palette. The Paralympic pieces were less daunting because of composing *Carbon12*.

DW: *But* PRINCIPIA *again involved huge and diverse forces and had a first audience of goodness knows how many millions, many of whom probably would find the idea of listening to a 'classical' piece by a living composer unlikely.*

EW: I remember considering all of that and I was aware that all the music in the other opening ceremonies was 99% pop music. I just thought that this was my chance to bring something else. We still see contemporary classical music as a rather specialist thing and it really is time to open up! The brief was to write about scientific developments and how they affect society, human rights, goodness knows what – quite a lot to pack in to four to five minutes! I've always been interested in the sciences, not least outer space – I even wrote a song for an astronaut to sing in outer space! -and so I wrote the lyrics for that piece myself. I did write something rather ambitious, almost too ambitious, considering that the work was for amateur voices, with all the clusters at the beginning representing the stars. It was at the edge of possibility with all the time constraints that were imposed. It was broadcast to a billion people around the world.

DW: *You have loved writing for young people, songs for the 'Friday Afternoons' collection commissioned in 2018 by Snape Maltings, to follow up the famous set of songs by Britten*, and the other extreme,* My Granny Sarah, *written for the National Youth Choir of Great Britain, for which again you wrote your own text.*

EW: Yes, this is what I mean about writing for different kinds of voices, even in this particular genre. I always try and compose with the sound of very specific voices in my mind, whether this is very young children singing mostly in unison as with the 'Friday Afternoons' pieces or given the opportunity to work with a young, but amazingly good choir like the NYCGB. *My Granny Sarah* is again a memory of my Granny's voice and Belize, even though my memories are more to do with the time she came to live with us in Tottenham when I was very small. She was by this time suffering from dementia but I remember being captivated by stories about her life in Belize.

DW: *With your eclectic background, do you still feel yourself to be a British composer?*

EW: It's odd, I was thinking about this the other day. I was brought up in such an English way, coming from Belize which was a colony, and the very English culture that was loved by my family. Then at my school in Sussex, the music teacher there was a big fan of the English madrigalists and Britten, so we sang all those classic pieces - *A Ceremony of Carols, Noye's Fludde* – and I think he has been a big influence on me. Having said that, because my parents went to live in New York, I've always had a strong pull towards America too. I very much wanted to study music in the US at one point and I often wonder if my music would sound different if I had done that. Maybe I belong somewhere in the middle! Or maybe, I am the perfect example of a modern Briton!

DW: When the Wet Wind Sings *has another English connection and is also in a way a mini-epic, being a 40-part piece for the Tallis Scholars. Here you bring together fragments of all kinds of texts – Cicero, Ovid, even Elizabeth I, and again yourself.*

EW: That piece was commissioned to celebrate the anniversary of the birth of Elizabeth I. I wanted to write something about the history of the River Thames, the beginnings of slavery (which dates from the start of her reign), and it is a very transatlantic piece about travelling across water, as it was commissioned by the Greenwich & Docklands Festival, an area that has had sea-faring at its heart for centuries. It might be one of the most complicated contrapuntal pieces I've written, exploring as it does all the different textural possibilities of a large group of accomplished singers, solo and varying groups of voices against the main body of the choir. I took up smoking composing that work…

DW: *And the Tallis** Spem in alium *hanging over your head too?*

EW: I suppose there should be a certain amount of terror, but I don't seem to get scared about things like that. The Tallis is utter perfection of course, but there is no point in being worried about being in the same space as it. That piece already exists, you love these pieces, honour these composers, and come closer to them by writing your own take on what these great figures have done. Somehow you come closer to the great masters in asking how a piece like that was put together and you just try and do your own thing. It's an enormous privilege really. I'm writing a Piano Concerto at the moment and look at the baggage and heritage that comes with that genre! I always think of the live performance itself rather than getting bogged down in ideas of tradition. I'm really inspired by the film director Quentin Tarantino – he is the ultimate film fan and when you see his work you aren't just seeing his work and personality, you are also seeing his love and admiration for film-makers of the past and I think that is the way to be a composer

DW: *I know you escape to your lighthouse in the very north of Scotland to write. You find that that kind of isolation helps?*

EW: I'm a very social person – I like being with friends and love big cities. I'd never thought about having a special place to write, always thinking that a composer should be able to write wherever they find themselves and should not to be too precious about it. But I have so much music to compose now and so much thinking to do, having a quiet place where I can totally focus, with just the Atlantic Ocean for company, is a necessary thing.

DW: *You say you have a lot to write and I'm wondering how you decide which commissions to take?*

EW: Well, firstly it is a question of time and economics. As a freelance composer I probably take on too much. There is also the question of enjoying the challenge of something I haven't done before and working with people I know and admire. At the moment I'm working on three operas, but operas take SO long to put together, there are so many people involved and they are planned quite far ahead. As a result of that I mix them up with smaller projects that need to be done more quickly and that gives me the variety too. I had to turn around the new version of *Jerusalem* for the Last Night of the Proms this year in three weeks!

DW: *With that in mind, deadlines must be, if not welcome, then something you deal with relatively easily?*

EW: When I left King's, London, I started a recording studio with a partner. We wrote commercial music and so I got used to deadlines and having to turn things around really quickly in order to deliver. I do think it is important to 'show up' and do the job that someone has asked you to do, just like anyone else would be expected to do. There is the concomitant stress and anxiety with deadlines but you often can surprise yourself – deadlines force you to make decisions about things.

DW: *Do you revise very much?*

EW: I revise as I go along. I tend to build in a period of time for reflection. So with the Piano Concerto I've written the piano part and am now orchestrating – that always takes time and it is good to go back and re-consider decisions as the piece develops. I sometimes look at the pieces I wrote when I was young and think they might be a bit rough around the edges and could do with some revision, but I rather like their energy. I still think about my works long after they have been written, and some performances find me making tiny tweaks. .

DW: *Does it get easier to write as you get older and more experienced?*

EW: I think it probably does get easier. It has been hard won, but I think I've hit my stride now from a technical point of view. I've also got better at cajoling myself along.

DW: *Are you surprised when you hear a piece for the first time?*

EW: I'm surprised by the reality of the sound having just heard it in my head. I remember with the Paralympics piece for example, we had no real rehearsal for the orchestral part – the LSO played it through once and I was relieved to hear that it did exactly what I had hoped. There was just no room or time for any discussion. What does amaze me is what different performers and performances bring out of my music...

DW: *And that was my next question...*

EW: Oh yes, definitely. I learn so much about my music from a performer that is fully prepared; the more I hear my music performed well, the more I learn about what lessons to take to the next piece.

DW: *Do you think about the audience when you are writing? Or different kinds of audience?*

EW: Yes, I do. I started composing because I wanted to write the kind of music that I wanted to hear myself. You can't second-guess everybody of course. The influence of my Mum and Dad has been so profound, in the way that they loved listening to so many different types of music, so I sometimes think 'what would they have liked to hear'.

DW: *Do you enjoy rehearsals and still get nervous before a premiere?*

EW: Oh yes, I feel sick inside! The first rehearsal of any piece is terrifying. Most recently, to see *Jerusalem* come to life very slowly, we had to be socially distanced and rehearse in sections, it was only the day before that it began to make sense to everyone and that certainly made me anxious. My job is to quietly 'will' things along and to be a positive presence in rehearsals. I used to see a lot of composers that were terribly arrogant and who refused to veer in the slightest from their 'vision' and sometimes be quite unpleasant to performers, but there is always a certain amount of negotiation between composer and performer when rehearsing a new work, to try and get things as good as they can be. I still find it unnerving sometimes, walking into a room of strangers, an orchestra or choir, incredibly skilled people; so many times you know that they are making things work practically that you have written. To walk in with any kind of superiority or arrogance seems to be wrong to me.

DW: *Do you think composition can be taught?*

EW: I think you can teach attitude, patience and different ways of asking yourself questions about your work. I'm an enthusiastic person and think that writing and hearing the music you write is such a wonderful thing. I try to be encouraging to my students in a way that perhaps I wasn't encouraged myself, to bring them into the fold and not to shut them out, whoever they are, whatever their background, whatever sort of music it is they write.

DW: *What would be your advice to a young composer?*

EW: Listen, listen and listen! To develop the ear is the number one thing. Become involved in music making in as many different ways as you can.

DW: *Is there anything in particular that you are longing to write?*

EW: [Long pause] Whenever I'm composing I always think, maybe this is the time that I just get everything absolutely right! I am always aiming to write a piece of music that will connect both emotionally and intellectually.

DW: *Elgar quotes Ruskin at the end of* The Dream of Gerontius* – 'This is the best of me...'. Can you say which piece or group of pieces of yours might fall into that category?*

EW: Gosh! People tell me I have a distinctive style, but it isn't my first consideration when working. There is a song that people really love and say that sums me up – *What's up Doc?* I remember the conductor Gary (Elgar) Howarth* hearing that and telling me that Ligeti* would love that song! I don't know – you really have put me on the spot... I am very fond of my Concerto for Percussion and Orchestra, *Carbon 12, Chrome*, Concerto Grosso, Cello Concerto – all the C's!

DW: *We are recording this interview at a very difficult and worrying time. How have you been dealing with lockdown?*

EW: I'm far away from my normal musical life up here in Scotland but at the same time I feel very connected. This has actually been the busiest year of my life. As I compose I wonder about whether the works will happen as planned, there have been so many postponements and some cancellations, but I've got to carry on and do my best, because we will all be so hungry for live music – when it returns, it better be good! There has been a lot of online activity of course and I've been involved with some brilliant projects including working with Chineke!, the RSNO, the pop band Clean Bandit, Last Night of the Proms, the National Youth Orchestra of Great Britain, Royal Conservatoire of Scotland, as well as co-curating this year's Spitalfields Festival, but what I do know is that we will look back on this time and remember how much we took performing and going to live performances so much for granted.

DW: *What would you say are your five favourite choral works?*

ERROLLYN'S FIVE FAVOURITE CHORAL WORKS

Stravinsky *Symphony of Psalms*

Bach *Magnificat*

Verdi *Requiem*

South African national anthem
  Nkosi Sikelel' iAfrika

Britten *Ceremony of Carols*

Judith Weir

BORN 1954

DW: *Can you tell me about your earliest musical memories? Did you come from a musical background?*

JW: My parents played instruments at an amateur level and used to get little groups together. I think we had a relative who sang in a chorus in Scotland, but apart from that there is no great choral tradition as far as my background is concerned.

DW: *I believe you had a rather inspiring teacher at North London Collegiate School when you were there?*

JW: Yes, Margaret Semple – she certainly played the organ and we did have a school choir, but I don't remember singing in it. She certainly made me very curious about different sorts of music and didn't find the idea of me wanting to write my own music at all strange. Only a few times in my life do I remember singing in a choir, although I try to join in singing hymns when in church. I started to play the oboe and took up the chance to be in any instrumental groups I could. From about the age of 13 I played the oboe whenever I could, and I was in the National Youth Orchestra – Simon Rattle* was a percussionist in the orchestra at the same time. This was how I got most of my musical education. I'd play pieces in the orchestra or pieces of chamber music and this would lead me on to explore those composers. Sometimes I would play in orchestras that would accompany local choral societies, so in my teens I would be playing in *Messiah* or the Bach Passions. That apart, my choral experience was pretty limited really.

DW: *What drew you to composition in the first place was, I think, writing for small ensembles at school, either arranging pieces for them or writing original pieces?*

JW: Yes, I had great friends at school and we seemed to have very long lunch breaks during which we could do that sort of thing. One thing I notice now when visiting schools is that the curriculum is a lot more focused and pressurised and there seems to be a lot less time for activities of that kind. In a relaxed way that is how I came to compose.

DW: *You began having lessons with John Tavener* whilst you were still at school, who at this time was something akin to a pop star, as well as being a very successful young composer.*

JW: I think describing them as lessons might be a bit extreme. He was a colleague of my music teacher at school and at the time an organist at a big church in North London, part of a group of people who were involved in the musical life of the area. He also lived quite close to us in Wembley and I would drop around a few times after school to show him what I was writing. You are right, he was a kind of pop star, but also a very prominent young composer who had great success early on, pieces like *The Whale*, *In Alium* and the piece I particularly remember, just after I got to know him perhaps, *Ultimos Ritos* which was broadcast live from the Holland Festival. He had an extraordinary career by the time he was in his twenties. This was the beginning of the 1970s and so we spent a lot of time talking about the whole modernism question and how we slot into all that. John had spectacular ways of describing how he was distancing himself from the modernist tradition, but I do remember his enthusiasm for the later serial pieces of Stravinsky, which of course were still very recent at that time and I remember listening to those on the radio.

DW: *You were part of a whole generation of composers, well, probably several generations, that studied with Robin Holloway* at Cambridge.*

JW: Yes, I got on with Robin well and found him to be a very kind, understanding teacher and person. This was quite early on in his teaching career – I was one of his earliest pupils I think, along with Robert Saxton*. At that time there was very little compositional content in the Cambridge degree course – we were a bit on the fringe – but I did have lessons with Robin for a year and found them extremely useful and inspiring.

DW: *You got a scholarship to Tanglewood* to study with Gunther Schuller*. He once described to me what he called 'a British Invasion' – Oliver Knussen* in the first instance I think, but then Simon Bainbridge*, Steve Martland*, Mark-Anthony Turnage* and you, amongst others.*

JW: This was during my Cambridge years. I was lucky enough to get a scholarship to go to Tanglewood. Another resident teacher that year was Olivier Messiaen*, so that was very exciting too. Interestingly enough, Messiaen wrote relatively little a *capella** choral music, which I have always thought to be a great tragedy – there is that early setting of *O sacrum convivium* and the very difficult *Cinq rechants* – when you think of what he might have written!

DW: *Thinking of the era you were growing up in and developing as a composer, did you find it difficult to find a voice, with the spectre of high modernism hanging over you?*

JW: I think it was a problem for a whole generation of us. Modernism was a very strong force; looking back it had some similarities to a cult, a behaviour, and things one must do that were laid down very strictly. If one didn't do what was expected that was looked upon with some disdain. When I explain that to young composers now they find all this very surprising and so far removed from what one might experience today, when composers can write in any style they want to and not get ostracised. I can say that I learnt an awful lot from modernism and from having to make my peace with it. To be honest I find that a lot of music these days lacks the kind of rigour that modernism tried to have, but it took me about ten years after my student days to write pieces that I would say are now in my style, so to speak, and not to worry about what I, or more to the point, what other people thought I should be doing. A lot of my generation did feel that we were to some extent self-taught. A lot of the people we have talked about certainly helped us of course. Schuller at Tanglewood was remarkable and in retrospect I wish I had had more time to pick up what he had to say, but we had to some extent find our own way, making use of what we learnt from modernism and adapting it as we saw fit in our own particular cases.

DW: *We have said that you came to choral music quite late. Your first acknowledged choral work is* Ascending into Heaven *from 1983.*

JW: Yes, that's right and of course I was asked to write that piece for the St Alban's Organ Festival, so ironically it is the organ rather than the choir that plays an important part in that piece. I'd been writing quite a few organ pieces at that time, so I have always thought of that piece as more of an organ work than a choral one.

DW: *Do you think that choral music was regarded as something that wasn't so important to composers of your generation?*

JW: I don't think it was considered very much at all if I'm honest with you. If you think of the post-war generation, very few of them wrote with any regularity for choir. There is a good reason for that of course – the sort of music they were interested in is almost impossible for an average choir, even a good one. If I think of choral music of that period it is almost only the repertory of the BBC Singers that comes to mind. It just didn't really exist apart from that. I have to say to you that there is still an element of that today with a lot of composers on the contemporary scene – it isn't something that everyone wants to do.

DW: *One of your next important choral pieces is* Illuminare, Jerusalem, *which despite being very short, seems to be rather an important piece in terms of finding a 'choral voice'. It was written for the King's College, Cambridge* Nine Lessons and Carols in 1985 and has since become almost a repertoire piece.*

JW: I just wrote that because Stephen Cleobury* asked me to. I mean to write a Christmas carol at that time was rather 'left-field' in some ways. It was such an interesting thing to do and I did rather approach it as a puzzle, to try and work out how one might approach such a request. Of course as a family we had listened to the Nine Lessons and Carols as we prepared for Christmas every year, so I did have an idea of what was expected. I really don't remember any conversations with Stephen about what I should do or not do; I think this was only the second or third piece he had commissioned for this service, but then his tradition of commissioning a new piece from all kinds of different composers lasted almost forty years. I think the number one piece of advice was not to make it too long! I do remember the premiere being really very tight and wonderfully in tune, something that I was reminded of when an archive recording was issued recently – amazing really.

DW: *One of the surprising things I, along with every other conductor, has had to deal with in this piece is the pronunciation of the text, which is in a medieval Scottish dialect. The other extraordinary thing, and I'm hoping not to insult organists here, is the unexpected effect of the organ only playing for three bars, that are marked 'mysterious and urgent', I have always found that incredibly striking.*

JW: Yes, I think there is now perhaps a clearer understanding of how to pronounce the text, but it probably caused a problem or two earlier on. The organ just discreetly underlines one word, 'Illuminare' – actually, people don't always realise there is an organ part there, but it just adds a discreet bit of colour and mystery to that particular word. That really comes from my student memories, hearing the extraordinary sound of the organ pedals at King's College, which, combined with that amazing acoustic, create a very special atmosphere.

DW: *I think another interesting thing about* Illuminare, Jerusalem – *and it is probably very difficult for you to comment on this – is that listening to it now, within a couple of bars it is clear that it couldn't be by anyone else: the Judith Weir 'fingerprints' are there immediately.*

JW: I think it would be bad for a composer to be conscious of developing fingerprints or mannerisms and that it would become rather uninteresting for them as there would be a danger that things could become quite mechanical. What I can say is that at that time I was trying to develop a melodic style that somehow harmonised with itself as it were. The kind of harmony that we learnt at university, of which there was a huge amount, was more to do with the nineteenth century and I for one was trying to work out a new harmonic system of my own. I do remember it being really very hard work at the time to come up with material of that kind.

DW: *Then we come full circle because I think you were the only composer to be asked twice to write a new carol for the King's Nine Lessons and Carols. This was* O Mercy Divine, *unusually, at least as far as these carols are concerned, with cello accompaniment?*

JW: The cello was Stephen's idea – he just very clearly asked for that. The cellist at the first performance was Guy Johnston*, a very good player who had had a long association with Stephen, as he had been a choirboy himself at King's. We all knew by that time that this would be Stephen's last Nine Lessons and Carols as he was due to retire, and it seemed a nice thing to do.

DW: *You obviously had a long and close association with Stephen Cleobury and it is rather poignant that this was the last carol he commissioned. Can you say something about the qualities you saw in him as a choral conductor?*

JW: He was a very important musician in my life and supported my work a lot over the years. What he did was to look through the catalogue of pieces that had been written for other choirs and take them up. I think this is quite a rare thing in the choral world. It is for example thanks to Stephen that *Ascending into Heaven* became better known - it languished for a bit after the premiere, he started to champion it a good deal and it became part of the choir's repertoire. He was a wonderful musician. When he was conducting, at least on the face of it, he seemed to be doing very little and he used to laugh when I told him this. Stephen was not one of the great 'arm-wavers' or a theatrical conductor in any way, but had the most fantastic ears and was a very sensitive musician. I think, because he was essentially a rather private man, not everybody realised the great emotional empathy he had not only for the music but for all those he worked with. I just used to love to talk to him about music – quite apart from being in charge of the choir, he was a Cambridge Don of course, and he seemed to know so much. Thinking of the people that have gone from my life he is an example of one that I really, really miss.

DW: *I wanted to talk a little bit about texts – do you like to find your own texts or do they come with the commission request?*

JW: I tend to choose the texts. Sometimes in church contexts I get the texts given to me, certainly in works I've taken on as part of my post as Master of the Queen's Music*. For these big state occasions I'm grateful for someone, usually at the cathedral in question, who will say, 'we would like a piece lasting this number of minutes, please set this text', but I think if I had to do that all my life I wouldn't have enjoyed writing for choirs so much as I have. It is still difficult to find the texts and it can take a lot of time. Actually one can find that whilst searching and reading, some of the compositional work can be done at the same time, trying to recognise that special something that will fit with the idea you have at the back of your head. There is so much text and poetry in the world and on the whole I find that the range of words that are set in the choral world is quite narrow. That is sometimes because we are always being asked to write carols or a Mag & Nunc*, so that limits the field. I think that one of the most interesting things for choral music to do, which will help ensure its future, is to be much more adventurous with the words the choir are singing.

DW: *I certainly made a discovery when conducting one of your relatively recent pieces,* The Song Sung True, *and when hearing your even more recent BBC Singers piece,* blue hills, beyond blue hills – *both works set the Scottish poet Alan Spence [born 1947].*

JW: Exactly, there is a case in point: he is a poet I have admired for many years. In Scotland he is very well known and a sort of national poet. If I say he is a Buddhist, that maybe is not quite the right term, but he teaches meditation and there is a true Zen quality to his work. He writes mostly in haiku form and they are wonderful because they are very philosophical and clear, but use everyday language.

DW: *At the other extreme you have come back on several occasions to the metaphysical poet George Herbert*, in works such as* Love Bade me Welcome *and* Vertue. *What is it that attracts you to his work?*

JW: Herbert is a very formalist poet and his works often have a pictorial look on the page, a poem like 'Easter Wings' for instance, which on the page looks like the wings of an angel. The poems have a very graceful metre that gives some freedom and guidance, but I also like the fact that Herbert primarily uses very short words, nothing too fancy, and that gives great vocal freedom and transparency. The worst problem when one is setting a text is to have words that are just too heavy and lumpy. Opera libretti often have that problem too.

DW: *Have you ever been defeated by a text?*

JW: Well, because I generally choose texts myself the answer is probably no, but the poems I do set are a distillation of hundreds and thousands of pages that I have read over the years. I do hear and see people setting a lot of twentieth-century poetry that is very metaphorical in intent, so the poet is not making things particularly clear on the surface. I think that creates a problem in a choral situation because we can't always hear every word clearly. I go for poems that make an audible impact as much as anything.

DW: *You have said that when you wrote your* Magnificat and Nunc Dimittis *that it was interesting for you as you had no baggage, so to speak, and had no real knowledge of the Anglican choral tradition. What strikes me about that piece and about your music in general, despite your answer to my last question, is how very clear the text is – it really is possible to hear pretty much every word.*

JW: Well, this is the attraction for me in setting texts. I enjoy the texts myself and want others to enjoy them too. Again, coming out of the modernist period it was some-times thought to be wrong to have the text 'intrude' in some way. You would set up an atmosphere, then forget the text and leave it hanging in the air somehow, but if I go to the trouble of finding a text I like to make sure that it is heard. I know there are those that think that is a rather infantile attitude – you know, people can read the words if they want to, the idea of people singing the text at them appeals less, but it has been important to me.

DW: *Now you are writing choral music regularly, can you say what the joy of writing for a choir might be?*

JW: Having now written for a lot of different choirs, it is just that all these choral groups are so diverse, both in sound and social grouping, so it always makes it new. I think you could compare it with writing lots of orchestral music – you might get a great orchestra and perhaps a less good one, but the idea of an orchestra is sort of interchangeable. Choirs are really so different from a composer's point of view. What I love is that once a choir has sung a piece it will be picked up by a completely different choir – you might have written the piece for an eight-part group and then it can be sung by a 100-voice choral society, it is almost as if the piece is born again.

DW: *There is also the fact that you are trying to write music for professional and amateur choirs at the same time?*

JW: Well, lots of amateur choirs are really very good and it is pleasing to me that the boundary between amateur and professional is not so clearly drawn as it is perhaps in the instrumental/orchestral world. I think this has been a problem in that sphere in the last few decades. Ideally one would hope that all kinds of people could try most of my pieces: even some of the works I have done for a group like the BBC Singers, these could be and have been sung by non-professional choirs.

DW: *A lot of your recent choral work has been the result of your appointment as Master of the Queen's Music. Your predecessor Sir Peter Maxwell Davies seemed to make it a much more public role then it had been over recent years – was this a pattern that you were keen to continue?*

JW: Yes, Max became a prominent and striking public figure; he was so charismatic and really did say what he thought, certainly as regards important matters like music education. I've taken a lot of satisfaction from being asked to write music to celebrate important national occasions and play a role in that way. I wrote a piece for the seventieth anniversary of VE Day [Victory in Europe Day] in 2015 (*His Mercy Endureth for Ever*) and I remember one of the most moving for me was the Armistice Service to commemorate the end of the First World War. That was a very beautiful occasion that was attended by both the Queen and the German President. For that occasion I wrote *The True Light*. Then I was asked for a piece to celebrate the ninetieth birthday of the Queen, and that became *I Love all Beauteous Things*. There are probably a couple of such occasions a year. I did a new arrangement of the National Anthem for the re-burial of King Richard III after his body was found under a car park in Leicester; that service was in Leicester Cathedral and they had a great choir.

DW: *It certainly doesn't sound as though it is a problem, but I wondered if it is difficult to re-imagine what you do for these state occasions? I don't know if people are expecting ceremonial fanfares and that sort of thing – do you have to put yourself in a different place and perhaps try and avoid some of the mannerisms that we might associate with music of this kind?*

JW: To be honest I'm not sure I think about stylistic things. Often the requests come in relatively late and so the main concern is getting the piece done and making sure what one does is practical. I have noticed on these occasions that there is very little rehearsal time and one has to be totally realistic – above all it just has to work and you can't take too many risks. Most of the events are televised too, and the first performance can sometimes be the first time the piece is sung from the beginning to the end. So often with new music one might say that you need to hear a piece more than once to thoroughly get to grips with it. Well, not in this case; it just isn't the place for experimentation on the whole. Having said that, in the piece I wrote for the commemoration of the Armistice in 2018, I found myself writing a short anthem with a rather flamboyant organ solo in the middle, which as it turned out was good for the television broadcast!

DW: *There is no specific job description for Master of the Queen's Music as far as I know, but you do spend a good deal of time travelling around the country listening to amateur music making of one sort or another.*

JW: It seems to me to be an important part of the job, to get around and hear performers that might not otherwise be in the limelight, being in other places and finding out what is going on. If there is something that is binding the country together it is choral music.

DW: *Can you say what is the first thing you do when writing a piece once you have the text? What is the next stage?*

JW: A mood and atmosphere might be suggested by the text, but there is a lot of pre-thinking which is hard to describe, considering colours, ranges, accompaniment, if there is one, that sort of thing. I would say that with choral music you do of course have the words to set you off so it is important to get some idea of tempo and a rhythmic idea too – that tells you a lot. I would generally get to work on a skeleton of what the choir will sing and then the rest of it happens very gradually. Even though I've told you at great length that I'm not a singer, I do try and sing the parts through, because I have learnt that this is often the problem, particularly with the inner parts. My dear friends, the altos in the BBC Singers, have told me about some of the awful alto parts they have had to sing. So I think about that very carefully. I like to try and be sympathetic to people trying to get those pitches, which isn't always an easy thing to do.

DW: *In general it is far more difficult to start a piece.*

JW: Yes, so many of the decisions are taken early on and it does in theory get easier by the time one gets to the later stages.

DW: *I'm guessing that with all your other commitments it is difficult to commit to regular composing times? Do you find yourself often having to steal a couple of hours here and there?*

JW: That is really what I find myself doing these days. I find I get the most done in the late afternoon and if I can really focus for a couple of hours I can achieve quite a lot. Of course I have read a lot of accounts of composers' working hours and that some are very disciplined; Britten* for example was at his desk very early every day and would work for several hours at a time. I can see how one would need to do that when writing operas and I've done that myself when necessary. Another big tip is to start as soon as possible and give oneself plenty of time whenever possible. As I told you, some requests for the pieces for state occasions can come in a little late, but on the whole, I find it a much more pleasurable experience if I'm not under pressure.

DW: *Do you find that it gets easier to write as you get more experienced? Maybe easier is the wrong word.*

JW: I think you certainly feel more relaxed about technical things at my advanced age, and in some ways it is easy to foresee what might happen but that can be a restriction too in other ways. I suppose as an older composer you do, or should, have most things under control.

DW: *Are you very self-critical?*

JW: To the extent that I don't think it is acceptable to complete a piece that is not at the very least acceptable to me. This is where I do differ from some composers I know – I'm not so much interested in producing music at all costs.

DW: *You must have to listen to a huge amount of music. Does this inhibit your concentration when you get home? I know some composers who shut themselves off from music when writing a big piece.*

JW: That seems strange to me. I would have thought it makes it a little easier. It isn't a question of finding things to steal in particular but when I go and hear a choral society for instance I can come away with ideas to put into a piece – this often happens. I think the problem about being interrupted is a time and motion thing really. I suppose I am quite choosey about the music I listen to – of course now you are going to ask me what that is...

DW: *No, I won't do that!*

JW: There is something very positive about going to hear an amateur choir, it is just so life-affirming. I find it cheers me up if I'm honest!

DW: *When you hear a piece for the first time are you ever surprised?*

JW: Yes, I am often surprised by some features – the acoustic and perhaps the performers. As you will know yourself, with a large chorus you can never really tell what the balance is going to be like; perhaps that is one of the biggest problems to overcome. I would say pitch wise I do know what the pieces are going to sound like. Sometimes, when I started out, that could be a shock, but then I was writing a rather different kind of music.

DW: *I have noticed when being kind enough to come to rehearsals of your pieces that I have done, you seem very relaxed and seem to enjoy the rehearsal process. I think it is true to say that you like the performers to have a certain amount of freedom.*

JW: I think so. I do know that a composer interfering all the time just doesn't help and can have a negative effect. I often say to students in rehearsal situations, distil your thoughts into two or three sentences and say them very clearly at the appropriate time. To be honest, if I'm going to hear a new piece for the first time, I find that I am often in another world and I'm not really in a position to jump up and say that the speed isn't right!

DW: *Of course another important part of your work is opera – maybe it is a little different, but when you see a new production of an opera of yours is there any temptation to get involved with interpretive questions, particularly with opera directors?*

JW: I think it is slightly different and more complicated in that there are so many more ingredients than a choral or orchestral situation – design, lighting, costume, the set, all that apart from the music and it is difficult to get involved in it all. I think it is a much more removed situation for a composer.

DW: *Do you think of the audience when you are writing?*

JW: Probably – to the extent of 'if I was in the audience what would I like to hear?'. I don't think one can assume what the audience will be like. Something might go very well for one audience but rather baffling for another. One can never be sure who will turn up! It can't be an exact science. I try to think what the audience's experience will be. One thing I do hope is that the audience might be able to see the text I have set, either in the printed programme or sometimes these days projected on a screen. Clearly I have found there are a lot of people that feel differently about this, but it is important to me at least.

DW: *You have done a good deal of teaching and certainly a lot of workshops/master-classes with young composers who write choral music. Can you say what kind of problems you come across?*

JW: We spoke at the beginning of this interview about me not having a lot of choral experience and I think this might still be the case with a lot of young composers now. I think there is a basic lack of knowledge of the genre – problems about finding pitches, the design of the lines, a big danger of things getting too congested and clarity of register. I have found that it is often not so much very high soprano parts that were the problem but an awful lot of very low bass notes – bottom E flats are fine and you might be lucky to have someone who can sing them, but one really should not make them happen too regularly. You have to really try and make the pieces work for as many people as possible. That is what I try and recommend.

DW: *With that in mind would you have any advice for young composers?*

JW: I think simply to hear as much choral music as you can, sing in a choir or conduct one. It really is the form that practical experience will tell you so much about. If you are writing for wind quintet, I wouldn't advise that you have to learn every instrument, but choirs are so different.

DW: *Elgar quotes Ruskin at the end of* The Dream of Gerontius* – 'This is the best of me…'. Are there any pieces of yours of which you feel particularly proud?*

JW: I do enjoy hearing earlier pieces but along with probably most composers I am perhaps more sympathetic to my most recent work. In my mind would be two big pieces I've written in the last five years or so whilst I've been Composer in Residence with the BBC Singers. One is a mini-oratorio *In the Land of Utz* and the other we talked about briefly, a sort of Buddhist Cantata for choir and string quartet, *blue hills, beyond blue hills*. They are both quite substantial works of around 40 minutes and very much told through the medium of the choir. I would say those pieces are the ones I am most proud of at the moment, but this may change over time of course.

DW: *We are recording this interview at a very difficult and worrying time – how are you dealing with lockdown?*

JW: When the lockdown first started and absolutely everything got cancelled I can't deny that there was a part of me that was quite exhilarated, being given what I have never had: a lot of uninterrupted time at home. However, I quickly realised that the whole act of composition is just part of the whole picture of going out and hearing people performing music, as well as the social interaction with other musicians. I mean it has been a pleasure to do this over Zoom but in normal times we would have done this over a cup of coffee or something. That whole element I really, really miss and I think it has slowed me down a lot as far as writing music is concerned.

DW: *What would you say are your five favourite choral pieces?*

JUDITH'S FIVE FAVOURITE CHORAL WORKS

Bach *Mass in B minor*

Beethoven *Mass in C*

Handel *Messiah*

Bernard Hughes *The Death of Balder*

Tavener *Three Hymns of George Herbert*

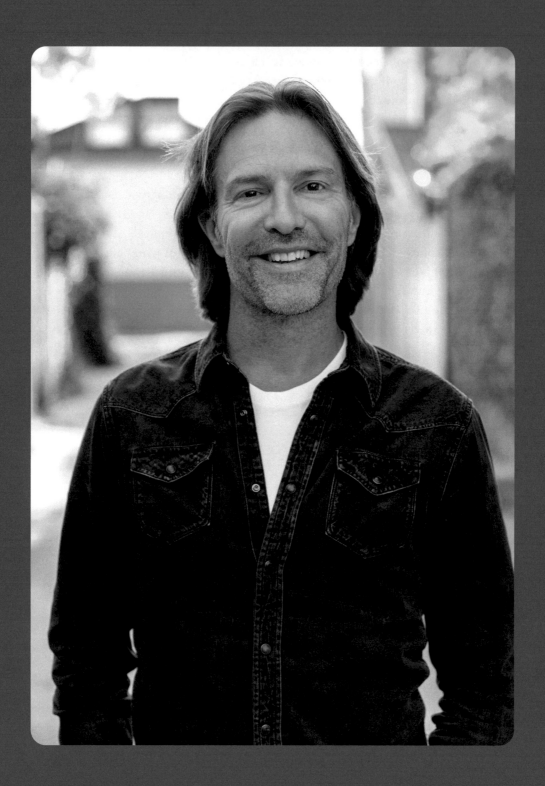

Eric Whitacre

BORN 1970

DW: *Could you tell me about your earliest musical memories? Did you grow up in a musical family?*

EW: Definitely not. We had a piano on which I would try to pick out tunes, but I have an odd memory, when I was very young, of my grandmother playing two pieces on the phonograph. One was a Bach* A Minor Invention, the other a Brahms* *Hungarian Rhapsody* and I remember these pieces got me very excited and running around the room. When I was a little older I played in a marching band but never learnt how to read music. I just listened to the guy next to me and copied him. When I was fourteen I discovered synthesisers and drum machines and started to write hundreds of pop songs. I always used to say that I wanted to be the fifth member of Depeche Mode* – I still do.

DW: *But you took a decision that you wanted to study music at university – presumably you learnt to read music before then?*

EW: No, thinking of it now, it is amazing really. I was 18 and went to the University of Nevada in Las Vegas, just because it was the largest school in the State. I had no real idea what I wanted to do. If you had asked me then I might have said that I wanted to go into astrophysics; I've always been interested in that but the truth is that I just didn't have the math for it. I auditioned for a music scholarship without being able to read music. They asked me to play something on the piano from my repertoire and I didn't know what repertoire meant, so I just improvised something. There was a man called David Weiller*, who is still at the University. He heard me play and hauled me into his room, gave me some sight-reading and found out I couldn't do that either. I guess he must have seen something in me, as he then asked me to join his big chorus. The first piece we sang was the Mozart* *Requiem* and it changed my life. As a result of that I became totally obsessed with choral music and then between the ages of 18 and 21 had proper music lessons, studied harmony, theory and everything else and wrote my first 'official' piece at 21.

DW: *This is one of those strange situations where one man changed your life.*

EW: Yes, actually, David changed my life more than once. Firstly by having me sing in the choir, and then by programming the first piece that I wrote for him, a setting of the English poem 'Go, lovely rose'. There was a sort of long-standing tradition at the

273

school that they would do a different setting of that text every year. The choir sang it at a choral convention, it was heard by a publisher who asked me, 'is that piece published'? I'm not even sure I knew what that meant, but that is how it all started. David also had me conducting the choir when I really had no business to be conducting at all, and recommended me to be assistant conductor at a Summer Stock Theatre Company in Massachusetts. They did operettas and musicals. I had no idea what I was doing…

DW: *So you learnt on the job?*

EW: Well yes, but unfortunately so did everyone else. I don't know what my life would have been like without David Weiller.

DW: *In that case,* Go, lovely rose *is your opus 1.*

EW: That's it, the very first one, now one of the *Three Flower Songs.*

DW: *Then it was to New York and the Juilliard School – you studied with two very significant figures in American music, David Diamond* and John Corigliano*?*

EW: Yes, two of my pieces, *Cloudburst* and *Water Night* were getting around a little already, and then I went to the Juilliard for my Master's Degree. My first year with David Diamond was very difficult as he made it patently clear that he really didn't like what I was doing and made it even more clear how unschooled and uneducated he thought I was.

DW: *He had quite a sharp tongue I think didn't he?*

EW: He certainly did. He was infamous and I could fill a book with Diamond quotes. Looking back, my favourite was about a piece of mine called *Ghost Train*, a piece for concert band that had already been published and performed a good deal. David looked at it and said, 'Well, it's effective but I certainly wouldn't call it music'.

DW: *Not so encouraging...*

EW: In general the Juilliard was not what I thought it would be. I think I was hoping it would be something like 'Fame', people dancing on tables and such, but it actually felt like a high-class, hyper-competitive finishing school full of very ambitious people. Having said that, John Corigliano was one of best teachers I ever had and Mary Anthony Cox, a legendary teacher at the Juilliard, taught ear-training and theory there for forty years and was wonderful. I met some life-long friends so it wasn't all bad.

DW: Ghost Train, *the concert band piece, was perhaps your first big hit and then there was a thought you might go and write film music.*

EW: Yes, at my Juilliard audition John Corigliano asked me why I wanted to come and study there and I said that I wanted to write film music, so he said don't come here! I moved out to Los Angelesand it just didn't work. By that time I wanted to write these 'whole worlds', and wanted to be in control. I didn't want to be a small cog in a big wheel at all, doing what directors or producers told me to do.

DW: *What is interesting about your work is that you have said that you were certainly not as highly musically educated as many, and yet you seemed to find your own voice from the very beginning.* Cloudburst *is quite clearly Eric Whitacre, how did that happen?*

EW: Yes, even *Go, lovely rose* is 'me' to some extent, I think. I'm 50 now and I look back on those pieces at thirty years' distance, and it is odd to me. I had no real formal training at all, suddenly there are these pieces and I think the core of my choral voice, whatever that might be, has been pretty consistent since then. Where does it come from? This will sound very Californian – I just remember listening to those first Mozart *Requiem* rehearsals and it was as if I was hearing my 'true name' for the first time, not Eric Whitacre, but my 'true name'. Being in the centre of all that just did something remarkable. Suddenly choral music fitted me like a glove.

DW: *But it can take a composer years to find the direction they want to go and find their true voice.*

EW: It can, but I have the luxury now that the only pieces that people know are the pieces that survived. There were others, plenty of disasters, and I don't know if they sounded like me but do know that they were not very good. There is an extremely polished narrative now. Looking back, I can see clearly what the influences were: certainly Morten Lauridsen* and Arvo Pärt*. The sound world of Pärt, I'd never heard anything like that before and the way that Lauridsen makes the poetry leap off the page. The poetry is as essential to the composition as the music was and this had a very profound effect on me.

DW: *Having talked about your particular sound, can you say how you get to that? Do you improvise your way into the pieces?*

EW: For me always, always, it is the poetry. Once I've found that, I read it over and over again, memorise it and then draw these plans, something that Corigliano taught me. I've made my own version of it now and I call it emotional architecture. I draw out the emotional journey of the piece first, before there are any notes. Then, as you say, I might improvise a little, walk around and think and usually there is a moment – a moment that I call the golden brick, it could be a chord, it could be a couple of notes – that will become the DNA of the piece. I think although I've got a pretty distinctive voice this is modified if the poetry demands a different sound world, so if I'm setting Cummings* or Tony Silvestri*, I have a different response. I filter them through my own harmonic world.

DW: *The structure is a huge thing for you.*

EW: Yes, again, something else that John Corigliano taught me – before him it wasn't a real concern. Now harmony is sort of secondary and the structure must work on every level. I want it to make as unified a vision as possible.

DW: *Is that true of the shorter pieces too?*

EW: Yes, the shorter pieces are easier to do of course, but I recently wrote a piece called *The Sacred Veil*, a twelve-movement piece lasting over 50 minutes and it was terribly difficult to keep it all aligned. A piece like *A Boy and a Girl* is much shorter and so there are very few choices to be made, so once there is a single governing principle it follows through. Even in those little pieces, every molecule counts and I agonise over them. I've yet to have an easy experience writing any piece come to think of it.

DW: *Are you very self-critical?*

EW: Yes, hyper self-critical. My wife is always trying to talk me down from the edge of the cliff. There are very few things that I'm proud of. I just generally see the flaws, you know, 'I almost got it'.

DW: *But you wouldn't go back and revise?*

EW: There was a period when I did that and even when rehearsing choirs I'd say, can we try this, playing with it in real time, but then I realised that isn't a good idea and the pieces are there warts and all. They are a record of who I was at the time. There is perhaps a virtue in that. Something might not be as polished as I would now want, but I made pretty bold mistakes and I've learnt to let them go!

DW: Cloudburst *is a pretty bold statement – it isn't so long, but a lot happens in a short period of time and amazingly it is your second published choral piece. I'm interested in that because of what you have said about the poetry.*

EW: Exactly, with the very first notes I wrote back in *Go, lovely rose*, the idea was that this whole piece would literally blossom like a flower from a single note, so the choir starts on a single note and then they form that cluster. I became enchanted by the idea of text painting, finding a musical gesture or a combination of notes that painted that idea. I think in *Cloudburst* I took this to the maximum level – what I did was what Octavio Paz* suggested in his text; all of the music is inside the words.

DW: *I debated whether or not I should tell you this, but I conducted* Sleep *in Austria not so long ago and afterwards someone came up to me and said, 'that's a beautiful piece, do you know if there is a version with the text in German? I'm afraid I said that I couldn't imagine anything worse, because those chords, the cadences and everything else are so tied up with the sound of the words and the vowels.*

EW: Absolutely – I'm so glad you said that. The vowels suggest whereabouts the music goes, how dense it is, the colour, and if you hang different words on to the music it just can't work. I know there are some composers that write the music first and somehow get the words to fit but I just can't imagine doing that. Singing that piece in German is something I just can't imagine!

DW: *I would say that* When David Heard *is one of your most personal pieces. In the first place it is one of the most difficult pieces of yours to bring off technically, but also I wondered when you are conducting it, do you have to detach yourself in some way, it packs such an emotional punch?*

EW: I absolutely do. I re-live the pieces when I'm conducting, so if it is a sweet piece or a joyful one that is my frame of mind at the time. *When David Heard* was written for my friend Ronald Staheli* and his amazing choir at Brigham Young University. He had performed a bunch of my pieces and a few weeks after he asked me to write something new for his 19-year-old son who was tragically killed in a car accident. I knew of other much earlier settings of this text of course, by Thomas Tomkins* for instance, but at the time I thought this is a fitting tribute. I was only 29 and now, having a son myself, I wouldn't dream of doing something like this, but there it is. I have a friend who is an actor and he calls me a method composer, that like a method actor I have to go there and actually feel whatever piece I'm writing. Not to sound over-dramatic about it, but it was excruciating writing that piece. I've only conducted it a few times because it's so difficult not to become too emotionally involved. The only way I can do it is to rehearse it in small sections, break it up and during the performance I have to get myself in the right place somehow. My recent piece, *The Sacred Veil*, with words written by my friend Tony Silvestri, is even worse. The text was written some years after he lost his wife to cancer. It is the same problem: you can't lose control when you are conducting.

DW: *When David Heard has a very short text for what is quite an extended piece.*

EW: Yes, my original conception was for a piece of about four to five minutes; then as I started to get into it I realised that you just can't tell that story in a short period of time. I'm not religious at all, nor do I have any particular connection to the bible, but I just thought of the moment a father heard that his son had died. I don't think I did it intentionally, but I think I spelt out the grief, the denial, the agony and eventually the acceptance. In order to paint that story you have to live in that world and meditate for a while. At that time I was completely obsessed with the Arvo Pärt *Passio* and I think you can hear that; it is clear that *When David Heard* is cut from the same cloth.

DW: *Ah, the power of silence too…*

EW: Absolutely, nobody does silence like Pärt. I have this theory that the silences in music are for new neuro-pathways to form. We get all this information and then we have to wait until Pärt says something. Then you wait and by the time you are finished with a piece like that, after the performance, you are physically transformed, you are a different person at the end.

DW: *Your work gets performed a huge amount all over the world by choirs of all kinds, some of the best choirs in the world and some that are less good, but the interesting thing is that one or two pieces aside, perhaps something like* The Seal Lullaby *or* Animal Crackers, *it is pretty tough to sing well. Even choirs that might not be so keen on singing new music will do their best with your pieces. I wondered how you account for that, or if you can?*

EW: I've wondered that myself but I only have 'pet theories'. The artist in me would like to think that it is partly because the approach to the music making and text is honest and vulnerable. The pieces are very emotional, so however hard they are, ultimately the journey is worth it. There is nothing worse for a choir than slogging away at a hard piece and then feeling at the end of the process somehow unrewarded. The pragmatist in me goes back to the fact that I'm not a good singer. I have the soul of a singer, but, like many composers I suspect, part of the reason I write for choirs is that I can't sing. The pragmatist in me knows that I love those tight harmonies, close shimmering clusters, but of course I know they are difficult. Having said that, I know that in *Cloudburst* for example, if I have to start on the note A and stay on the note whilst half the section move down half a step, then that isn't so difficult. In general, I just try to be practical in terms of voice-leading. Perhaps it is difficult but not as difficult as it ought to be and it sounds more difficult than it actually is?

DW: *These shimmering chords are a Whitacre fingerprint, where do they come from? Is it just a colour that the text suggests?*

EW: I think this goes back to singing in the University Choir. Tony Silvestri and I sang together and he introduced me to the Harmonic Choir, directed by David Hykes*, who was one of the earliest western pioneers of overtone singing. They made the most spectacular sounds. I couldn't get enough of it and would take a group of friends into stairwells, somewhere with a lot of reverb, and get them to build up clusters of notes – it used to thrill me. The first few pieces were an exploration of these chords. In *Cloudburst* that opening cluster – it sounded like an expression of wonder and awe; it matched in a weird way how I felt about a storm. After the first performance people were talking to me and they were using some of the same words to describe the music that I felt. Over the years I've tried to use those shimmering chords as tools to convey a very specific emotion. In *When David Heard* the text says 'When David heard that Absolom was slain/ He went up into his chamber and wept...', so the chord paints that, climbing up to the highest note, then becomes more optimistic before it collapses on the word 'wept'. Now to my ears it sounds a rather bitter-sweet melancholy, with a flicker of hope, so I'm trying to convey information both to the audience and to the singers as well. I've always felt that the right combination of notes manifests itself in the bodies of the singers and the listeners.

DW: *Do you think your music sounds American?*

EW: I didn't until I met Stephen Layton*, who recorded a disc of my music early on. I owe him a huge debt for introducing my music to the world through that disc. He wrote to me and said that, as he was reading through the score of *I thank you God…* in a music shop for the first time, he was thinking that only an American would write that opening phrase. At the time I didn't really understand what he meant by that, but then I lived in London for five years and I've now travelled quite a bit and I think there is a big part of my music that sounds distinctly American or, not to get too political, what I think America used to be! There is an inherent optimism and naivety, naivety in the best way, something that isn't cynical or jaded perhaps, that strikes me as a very American approach – bold, big gestures, without being self-conscious about it. For Americans, wearing our heart on our sleeve, especially on the west coast is our default.

DW: *You have spent some time living in both Cambridge and London. Do you think that rubbed off on your music at all? I know you love a lot of British music.*

EW: Definitely! Before I came to London, if only through John Rutter's* recordings I knew I loved that pure beautiful English sound, the bright, clear tone. There is a kind of, dare I say, stoicism to the approach that I like very much too, a gravitas that choirs find in music, in my music too. Now looking back at my time in England, it makes me laugh how English I became for a couple of years. I wrote a piece for cello and strings for Julian Lloyd-Webber*, *The River Cam*, and I mean it is Vaughan Williams*. Somehow I just took the sounds and the landscape of England and it has stayed with me. When I think of my music being performed now, I think of British cathedrals. If everything could be sung in the Lady Chapel at Ely Cathedral, I'd die a happy man!

DW: *I know you aren't a Christian but you have set a number of sacred texts and there is clearly a deeply spiritual aspect to your music that communicates to people of all faiths and no faith.*

EW: Yes, the way I like to think about it is that I am a humanist. A lot of my music is about sensuality, touch, hearing, taste, what it means to be human, to feel sorrow, joy, to be loved, to have children. I remember when I was first in college, learning about sacred music and secular music and I couldn't for the life of me work it out – isn't it all sacred? Why do Christians have the monopoly on sacred music? When it comes to spirituality I treat it as my deepest faith but it just happens to be about the human experience rather than the religious experience.

DW: *You wouldn't think of writing a Requiem or a Mass? Maybe the new piece,* The Sacred Veil*, is a sort of Requiem for you or is that reading too much into it?*

EW: No, it very much is although I didn't take the Requiem as a model. I love them as musical works but, as a way of honouring the dead, they never have made any sense to me at all. It takes the humanity out of everything.

DW: *The sound of the words in the Requiem or is it what they stand for?*

EW: Both – the intention of them too. One of the movements in *The Sacred Veil*, one of the rawest moments, is when Tony and his wife first heard the dreadful diagnosis and there is page after page of medical language, which being mostly in Greek or Latin, sounds not unlike a Requiem text. You can't possibly set that in a distant or detached way, it is so intimate and personal.

DW: *Having heard short excerpts of* The Sacred Veil *it sounds like a new direction to me, still recognisably your own recognisable language, but clearly an important development.*

EW: I didn't feel it so much when writing it but people tell me it is something new. I don't know; it is too new at the moment. If I'm completely honest about all this, I turned 50 this year, I got divorced three years ago, I re-married the love of my life, and then the gravity of the subject matter and text of the piece…

DW: *It is pretty stark and raw…*

EW: It is – it lays it out. I don't think I could have written the piece thirty years ago. I know I couldn't have. Some of the early pieces, *Cloudburst*, *A Boy and a Girl*, I think of them as little utopias, but I got to 50 and, you know, it turns out it isn't all perfect – it can be tough; people suffer, people die. I guess I reconciled with that and maybe the music started to change.

DW: *It is a big piece and so this is where your structure planning must come in.*

EW: I spent a huge amount of time on that. I decided the number three would be the defining principle, so three-note motifs, up a third, down a third, four three-movement sections – just an endless pre-occupation with three, perhaps my most hyper-structured piece.

DW: *Are you a disciplined composer? Do you work regular hours?*

EW: No – I wish I was. In general, the way it looks is that there is a deadline and then there is a slow disintegration of my personal life as that deadline gets closer! I spend a lot of time not deciding to go in a certain direction and then take the best idea I have to date. The most painful thing is locking something down.

DW: *So do you have the piece in your heard before committing it to paper?*

EW: In general I have the basic structure and an aspiration. I know what I want to do.

DW: *Does it get easier as you get older or are you more critical?*

EW: [Long pause] I think I'm much more self-aware than I used to be. I imagine with each note I write that people are going to sing this. I'm a pleaser as a personality and that isn't always a helpful place to be in.

DW: Do you think about the audience?

EW: Endlessly, but it isn't even that I want them to like a piece. I just don't understand how you can write a piece without bringing the audience along. If that wasn't the case I'd just write a piano piece for myself to play but, to make it an experience, I want them to have a communal experience, not in a pandering way but to have a dialogue with an audience.

DW: As far as the choirs are concerned, you think about the particular sound they make?

EW: Yes, even recently, writing for the LA Master Chorale, I couldn't help thinking of my eighteen singers in London. I call them my choir, but of course there are a few from The Sixteen, from Tenebrae – it isn't really my choir. These days I have eighteen of the most incredible singers, so when I'm writing an alto part I see the faces of these people very clearly.

DW: Do you think that all the conducting you've done, the practical experience, has helped your composing?

EW: No question. I have no real formal training and I think there was a time that I felt more conceptually, but now I'm much more pragmatic because I know someone like me will have to put the music together, so it needs to be incredibly clear, not just in terms of the instructions, but I go back to the structure again too. If you get that right the piece will just unfold. If you want a *fortissimo* from the choir, then write one in the right register and on a good vowel sound that will work in that way. Lots of things like that I've learnt as I've gone along.

DW: When you hear a piece for the first time are you surprised?

EW: Every time. It tends to be a combination of things, how some parts work that I agonised over or how others work that I put down at the last minute. *The Sacred Veil* is a good example – there were six rehearsals before the premiere and I'm not exaggerating when I say that a good percentage of those rehearsals were me re-writing things, so the end result was so different. Then, after the premiere, which I consider to be a dress rehearsal, I'll make changes. Maybe by the fourth performance it will go off to my publisher for the last time.

DW: Are you surprised what performers find in it? If you are not conducting a performance but are in the hall is that more difficult for you?

EW: I used to be quite possessive about the pieces. People would send me performances and without listening I could tell if I would like it by looking at the timing of the tracks. Then when I started conducting pieces other than mine, and understood all the decisions that have to be made, I became much more relaxed. Now I love to listen to performances and listen to the internal logic. If you listen to tempo and rubato you can hear immediately if the conductor knows the piece. How many times have you adjudicated a choir when what you really want to do is have a conversation with the conductor?

DW: *The tempo question is interesting. I worked with Morten Lauridsen a few years ago and he was telling me that lots of conductors take his music too slowly. Do you have that problem?*

EW: Yes, I feel the same way. People get caught up in the lushness of it perhaps.

DW: *It becomes overly sentimental.*

EW: Yes, they revel in the sound and it should always be about the forward flow. But the other thing I've learnt is that somehow the pieces become important with a capital I. You must know Lauridsen's wonderful *O Magnum Mysterium* – an almost untouchable pedestal and yet it needs to have all that visceral power it had the first time around. I've found that some of my pieces can easily become museum pieces.

DW: *Do you enjoy rehearsals? Are there pre-premiere concert nerves?*

EW: I prefer rehearsals! All the tender, funny, magical things about music-making happen then. Performance for me is different and I get terribly nervous. I tweeted once that the terror of performing never goes away, you just get comfortable being terrified. That's how it feels, but I've learnt to deal with it.

DW: *Your music affects audiences in very particular ways, certainly through the Virtual Choirs*. Are you surprised about that?*

EW: Early on it certainly did surprise me a lot. I couldn't figure it out. Now I'm just genuinely humbled by it. Again, to be really Californian, I feel like a surfer, the music and the emotion is on a wave and I'm riding on top of it as opposed to making the wave.

DW: *Of course you arrived at a time in musical history when you are allowed to do that.*

EW: Yes, I don't think I would be a 'classical' composer if I were writing in the '60s and '70s. So not only did I get lucky in that people were going back to a more harmonically neo-romantic sound in the '90s, but there was an explosion of choral singing across the world too. At least in America I have to give huge credit to Morten Lauridsen for that - he was writing music that was relevant, timeless and perfect, music that people really wanted to sing and listen to.

DW: *How do you decide what commissions to take or is it a case of your idea being offered to people?*

EW: These days I have an idea of the kind of piece I want to make. Sometimes it is just an opportunity, my orchestral piece *Deep Field* for example. I got the chance to conduct the Minnesota Orchestra and the programme was open. I asked them if they would like a new piece and thankfully they said yes. Now, if it was the other way around, certainly if someone asked for a liturgical piece, I don't think I could do that now.

DW: *Do you teach or do you think composition can be taught?*

EW: I don't really – the best lessons I had were with Corigliano. We would sit down and look through his scores or pieces by Stravinsky* and Bartók* for example. He would stop and say, look at his, see the way he does this... I wouldn't know how to begin as far as teaching composition is concerned.

DW: *You still use pencil and paper. You need that physical contact somehow?*

EW: Oh yes, that is the only way I know how. I find that however big the screen is I get boxed in somehow and I can write longer, better phrases with big sheets of paper rather than using a computer.

DW: *Is it important how it looks on the page?*

EW: Very much so. I remember early on when *Water Night* was published, it went in to Dale Warland's series*. He is a fine conductor of course, but the score came back with loads of edits, old school, just over written and I respectfully asked for them all to be taken out! That piece just needs to look a certain way. You know, Arvo Pärt's music looks the way it sounds.

DW: *Is there anything you are longing to write?*

EW: I have had this idea for years – I call it album length, so about 70 minutes – a kind of meditative music that doesn't have a climax. I've tried, but somehow it is difficult to write music that doesn't 'go somewhere'. I heard David Skinner at Cambridge talk about Thomas Tallis* and he said that his music induces a sense of twilight – l love that, choral music is good at being timeless. I don't know what this piece would sound like or look like but…

DW: *Elgar quoted Ruskin at the end of the score of* The Dream of Gerontius**: 'This is the best of me…'. Are there any of your pieces that you feel have got close to that?*

EW: I'm hoping I haven't written my best piece yet, but every time I conduct *A Boy and a Girl* I think it is the closest I've got to a perfect piece, whatever that means. Again I don't take much credit for it, I just did what the poem suggested, but I think all the notes work in that piece.

DW: *Do you have advice for young composers?*

EW: If they are setting music for voices, the poem is everything! Read, read and read until something catches your breath. Then find a single musical idea that has the same effect and make the entire piece about that idea.

DW: *Is choral music still the poor relation as far as young composers are concerned?*

EW: Ten years ago yes, but now I don't think this is the case. I like to think that choral music is more relevant than ever now.

DW: *As your Virtual Choirs have proved…*

EW: The new one has over 17,000 singers from almost 130 countries. I think this speaks not so much of the Virtual Choirs but the effect that choral music has on people of all kinds all over the world.

DW: *We are recording this at a very unusual time – how are you dealing with lockdown?*

EW: This is the longest time I can ever remember without travel, nearly five months now. That has been a gift in some ways. The challenge is that I'm finding I'm not seeing, hearing anything new, so much that feeds the soul – no music, theatre, not seeing people, no making music. I'm feeling that my world has got very small in terms of stimulation. In that sense I'm not bubbling to make something.

DW: *What would you say are your five favourite choral works?*

ERIC'S FIVE FAVOURITE CHORAL WORKS

John Adams *Harmonium*

Debussy *Trois Chansons*

Morten Lauridsen *O magnum mysterium*

James Macmillan
   Seven Last Words from the Cross

Arvo Pärt *Passio*

The Appendices

Composers' Favourites

Gathered together here are the works cited by the composers at the end of their interviews with David Wordsworth. The works have been listed by composer's surname in alphabetical order. A work's title is followed by the initials of the composer who has cited the work as one of their favourites. Where the work is in copyright, the name of the publisher is given. Composers who are listed in the References section of the book are marked with *.

Adams, John* – *Harmonium* – EWhit (Boosey & Hawkes)

Bach, Johann Sebastian* – *Magnificat* – EWall; JMacM

Bach, Johann Sebastian – *Mass in B minor* – AH; CMcD; JR; JW; KJ; LL

Bach, Johann Sebastian – *Singet dem Herrn* – BC

Bach, Johann Sebastian – *St Matthew Passion* – JD

Bach, Johann Sebastian – *Mass in C* – JW

Batten, Adrian (c.1591-c.1637) – *This is the day that the Lord hath made* – WT

Beethoven, Ludwig van* – *Missa Solemnis* – JMacM

Berg, Alban (1885-1935) (arr. C. Gottwald) – *Die Nachtigall* – JM (Universal Edition)

Brahms, Johannes* – *A German Requiem* – ML

Brahms, Johannes – *Fest und Gedenksprüche* – BC

Britten, Benjamin* – *Ceremony of Carols* – EWall; HS; JD (Boosey & Hawkes)

Britten, Benjamin – *War Requiem* – AH; CMcD (Boosey & Hawkes)

Byrd, William* – *Great Service in C* – HG

Byrd, William – *Mass for Four Voices* – JMacM

Davis, Anthony (b.1951) – *Voyage through death to life upon these shores* – TO'R (Wise Music)

Debussy, Claude (1862-1918) – *Trois Chansons de Charles d'Orléans* – EWhit

Dove, Jonathan* – *Seeketh him that maketh the seven stars* – WT (Faber Music)

Duruflé, Maurice*: *Requiem* – HG (Durand)

Elgar, Edward* – *The Dream of Gerontius* – JMacM

Ešenvalds, Ēriks (b.1977) – *The Long Road* – HG (Musica Baltica)

Fauré, Gabriel* – *Requiem* – JR; KJ; RP

Finnissy, Michael* – *Red Earth* – EE (Oxford University Press)

Folksong – *Polegnala e Todora (Love Song)* – LL

Gibbons, Orlando* – *See, see the word is incarnate* – PM

Górecki, Henryk* – *Beatus Vir* – GJ (Boosey & Hawkes)

Górecki, Henryk – *Totus Tuus* – HS (Boosey & Hawkes)

Gregorian Chant – *In Paradisum* – LL

Gregorian Chant – *Subvenite Sancti Dei, Occurite Angeli Domini* – LL

Gregorian Chant – *Veni Creator Spiritus* – LL

Gregorian Chants – *Liber usualis* – JR

Gretchaninov, Alexander (1864-1956) – *Passion* – HG (Musica Russica)

Handel, George Frideric* – *Dixit Dominus* – JB

Handel, George Frideric – *Messiah* – AH; JW

Harvey, Jonathan* – *Come Holy Ghost* – CMcD (Faber Music)

Holst, Gustav* – *The Hymn of Jesus* – AH

Howells, Herbert* – *Hymnus Paradisi* – GJ (Novello)

Hughes, Bernard (b.1974) – *The Death of Balder* – JW (Composer)

Ireland, John* – *My Song is Love Unknown* – WT (John Ireland Trust)

Joel, Billy (b.1949) (arr. Chilcott) – *And so it goes* – JR (Hal Leonard)

Kreek, Cyrillus (1889-1962) – *Psalms of David* – HS (SP Muusikaprojekt)

Lassus, Orlando* – *Infelix ego* – TO'R

Lauridsen, Morten* – *Lux Aeterna* – PŁ; PM (Faber Music)

Lauridsen, Morten – *O magnum mysterium* – EE; EWhit (Faber Music)

Ligeti, György* – *Lux Aeterna* – CF-H; TO'R (Schott)

Ligeti, György – *Magyar Etudok* – JB (Schott)

MacMillan, James* – *O Radiant Dawn* – RP (Boosey & Hawkes)

MacMillan, James – *Seven Last Words from the Cross* – CMcD; EWhit; ML (Boosey & Hawkes)

Mahler, Gustav* – *Symphony No.2, The Resurrection* – PM

Mahler, Gustav – *Symphony No. 8* – JB

Mathias, William* – *Ave Rex* – PM (Oxford University Press)

Messiaen, Olivier* (arr. C Gottwald) – *Louange à l'éternité de Jésus* (from *Quartet for the end of time)* – EE (Carus-Verlag)

Messiaen, Olivier – *O Sacrum Convivium* – HS (Durand)

Miyoshi, Akira (1933-2013) – *Ikiru* – BC [publisher unknown]

Monteverdi, Claudio* – *Book of Madrigals* – ML

Mozart, Wolfgang Amadeus* – *Requiem* – CF-H; KJ

Nørgård, Per* – *Aftenland* – PM (Edition Wilhelm Hansen)

Palestrina, Giovanni Pierluigi da* – *Missa Papae Marcelli* – KJ

Pärt, Arvo* – *Berliner Messe* – ML (Universal Edition)

Pärt, Arvo – *O Antiphons* – PŁ (Universal Edition)

Pärt, Arvo – *Passio* – EWhit; JD (Universal Edition)

Poulenc, Francis* – *Figure humaine* – EWhit (Mrs); JB (Éditions Salabert)

Purcell, Henry (1659-95) – *Hear my Prayer* – JD

Rachmaninov, Sergei* – *All-Night Vigil* – JB; JM; PŁ

Ratniece, Santa (b.1977) – *Saline* – EE (Latvian Music Information Centre)

Rautavaara, Einojuhani* – *Die erste Elegie* – JM (Boosey & Hawkes)

Rutter, John* – *What Sweeter Music?* – PM (Oxford University Press)

Saariaho, Kaija* – *Nuits, adieux* – TO'R (Chester Music)

Schnittke, Alfred*: *Concerto for Choir* – JMacM (Edition Sikorski)

Sheppard, John (c.1515-1558) – *Media vita* – BC

Sheppard, John – *Libera nos, salva nos* – JR

Singer, Malcolm* – *Songs of Ascent* – CF-H (BMIC/Composer)

Smallwood, Richard (b.1948) – *Total Praise* – LL (Boosey & Hawkes)

Sontonga, Enoch (c.1873-1905) – *Nkosi Sikelel' iAfrika (South African National Anthem)* – EW

Stanford, Charles Villiers* – *Beati quorum via* – WT

Strauss, Richard* – *Der Abend* – EE (Universal Edition)

Stravinsky, Igor* – *Mass* – ML (Boosey & Hawkes)

Stravinsky, Igor – *Requiem Canticles* – TO'R (Boosey & Hawkes)

Stravinsky, Igor – *Symphony of Psalms* – EWall; GJ; HG; JD; KJ (Boosey & Hawkes)

Swayne, Giles (b.1946) – *Cry* – CF-H (Novello)

Syzmanowski, Karol* – *Stabat Mater* – PŁ; RP

Tallis, Thomas* – *Gaude gloriosa Dei mater* – GJ

Tallis, Thomas – *Misereri, nostri* – CMcD

Tallis, Thomas – *Spem in alium* – JM

Tavener, John* – *Eternity's Sunrise* – PŁ (Chester Music)

Tavener, John – *Hymn to the Mother of God* – RP (Chester Music)

Tavener, John – *Three Hymns of George Herbert* – JW (Chester Music)

Tippett, Michael* – *Canticles (St John's Service)* – GJ (Schott)

Tormis, Veljo* – *Raua needmine (Curse Upon Iron)* – LL (Fennica Gehrman)

Vaughan Williams, Ralph* – *Five Mystical Songs* – BC (Stainer & Bell)

Vaughan Williams, Ralph – *Flos Campi* – AH (Oxford University Press)

Verdi, Guiseppe* – *Requiem* – EWall

Walton, William* – *Belshazzar's Feast* – HS (Oxford University Press)

Walton, William – *The Twelve* – WT (Oxford University Press)

Weir, Judith* – *Illuminare, Jerusalem* – CF-H (Novello)

Whitacre, Eric* – *Water Night* – JM (Chester Music)

Composer key: AH – Adolphus Hailstork, **BC** – Bob Chilcott, **CF-D** – Cheryl Frances-Hoad, **CMcD** – Cecilia McDowell **EE** – Ēriks Ešenvalds, **EWall** – Errollyn Wallen, **EWhit** – Eric Whitacre, **GJ** – Gabriel Jackson, **HG** – Howard Goodall, **HS** – Howard Skempton, **JB** – Judith Bingham, **JD** – Jonathan Dove, **JM** – Jaakko Mäntyjärvi, **JMacM** – James MacMillan, **JR** – John Rutter, **JW** – Judith Weir, **KJ** – Karl Jenkins, **LL** – Libby Larsen, **ML** – Morten Lauridsen, **PŁ** – Paweł Łukaszewski, **PM** – Paul Mealor, **RP** – Roxanna Panufnik, **TO'R** – Tarik O'Regan, **WT** – Will Todd

References

The references listed here are to names, titles and terms mentioned in the interviews and marked with an asterisk (*). References to other titles or names in the notes are given in bold.

ABBA – Swedish pop group formed in 1972. The name of the group is an acronym of the first letters of their names.

Abrahamsen, Hans (b.1952) – Danish composer, whose recent successes have included an orchestral song cycle *let me tell you*, for which he won the Grawemeyer Award.

A cappella – Literally translated from the Italian means 'in chapel or choir style' but is now taken to mean a work that is sung without instrumental accompaniment.

ACDA – The American Choral Directors Association, the professional association for American choral conductors and teachers.

Adams, John (b.1947) – American composer and conductor, particularly known for his operas, including *Nixon in China*, *The Death of Klinghoffer*, and *Dr Atomic* and for his orchestral music.

Agee, James (1909-55) – American author and poet. He became one of the most influential US film critics.

Aleatoric – Depending on the throw of dice or on chance. Relating to music or other forms of art that involve elements of random choice when it comes to pitch or rhythm or both.

A Level – UK school examination, officially the General Certificate of Education: Advanced Level, largely taken at the age of 18.

Anderson, Julian (b.1967) – British composer and teacher, admired for his vivid orchestral music that takes in a wide range of influences including the folk-traditions of Eastern Europe as well as diverse Western concert traditions.

Argento, Dominick (1927-2019) – American composer particularly known for his lyric operas, including *The Aspern Papers*, *Postcard from Morocco*, and *The Dream of Valentino*, and his choral music.

Armstrong, Louis (1901-71) – American trumpeter, vocalist, and actor, also known as 'Satchmo'.

Arnold, Sir Malcolm (1921-2006) – British composer, particularly known for his orchestral works (including nine symphonies) and film music, including *The Bridge over the River Kwai*, *Whistle down the wind* and *Hobson's Choice*.

Associated Board of the Royal Schools of Music (ABRSM) – A music examination board founded in 1889. It examines in over 90 countries.

Atkinson, Rowan (b.1955) – British actor, comedian and writer, known for television and film success such as *Not the nine o'clock news*, *Blackadder*, *Mr Bean* and *Johnny English*.

Babbitt, Milton (1916-2011) – American composer, theorist and teacher, a pioneer in the composition of serial and electronic music. He taught at Princeton and the Juilliard School for many years.

Bach, J.S. (Johann Sebastian) (1685-1750) – German composer. He is perhaps the most significant figure in music of the Baroque era alongside Handel.

Bainbridge, Simon (b.1952-2021) – British composer and teacher. He won the Grawemeyer award for his *Ard Or Incerta* ('Four Orchestral Songs from Primo Levi)' and was Head of Composition at the **RAM** between 2001-2007.

Baird, Tadeusz (1928-81) – Polish composer. After incarceration in a concentration camp as a teenager, he studied in Warsaw and was one of the first Polish composers to embrace serialism.

Baker, Dame Janet (b.1933) – British mezzo-soprano, widely acclaimed for her work in the concert hall, opera house and recording studio. Regarded as one of the greatest singers of her time.

Barber, Samuel (1910-81) – American composer. One of the most respected composers of the twentieth century, Barber wrote music in most genres with his best-known works being the *Adagio* (from the String Quartet), *Knoxville: Summer of 1915* (a setting of **James Agee**) and the opera *Vanessa*.

Barbirolli, Sir John (1899-1970) – British conductor, remembered as chief conductor of the Hallé Orchestra in Manchester, but who also had an extensive international career and succeeded Toscanini as Music Director of the New York Philharmonic, 1936-43.

Barratt, Carol (b.1945) – British composer and piano teacher. She has composed a great deal of educational piano music and has more recently turned her attention to writing poetry, libretti and choral music.

Bartók, Béla (1882-1945) – Hungarian composer, ethnomusicologist and pianist, a major figure in the history of twentieth century music. Central to his output are his six string quartets, three piano concertos and much solo piano music.

Beatles, The – English rock band formed in Liverpool in 1960. One of the most influential and successful groups of all time, famous for its innovative recordings such as *Sgt. Pepper's Lonely Hearts Club Band* (1967).

Beethoven, Ludwig van (1770-1827) – German composer and pianist. Acknowledged as one of the greatest composers of all time, through his innovations in form and expression he was hugely influential in the transition from the Classical to the Romantic era in music.

Bell, Christopher (b.1961) – Northern Irish-born/Scottish choral conductor, who has been Director of the Royal Scottish National Orchestra Chorus, the Belfast Philharmonic Choir and the Edinburgh Festival Chorus. He is at present Artistic Director, National Youth Choirs of Scotland, Artistic Director of the Washington Chorus in the USA and Chorus Director of the Grant Park Music Festival in Chicago.

Benjamin, Sir George (b.1960) – British composer, conductor, and teacher. He was a pupil of **Messiaen** at an early age and had a major public success with his orchestral work *Ringed by the Flat Horizon* at the Proms when aged 20. More recently his operas *Into the Little Hill*, *Written on Skin* and *Lessons in Love and Violence* have enjoyed international success.

Bennett, Sir Richard Rodney (1936-2012) – British composer, pianist and vocalist, long resident in the US, whose music ranged from children's songs, symphonies, choral music and opera, to film scores such as *Murder on the Orient Express* and *Far from the Madding Crowd*. He was also a much-admired jazz pianist and cabaret artist.

Berio, Luciano (1925-2003) – Italian composer and conductor, a leading member of the avantgarde, whose experimental work in the fields of vocal music, opera and electronic music has had an important influence on succeeding generations.

Berkeley, Sir Lennox (1903-89) – British composer and teacher. He was a pupil of **Nadia Boulanger** and a Professor of Music at the **RAM**, 1946-68. His many distinguished pupils included **Sir John Tavener**, **William Mathias**, David Bedford, Sally Beamish and **Sir Richard Rodney Bennett**.

Berlioz, Hector (1803-69) – French composer and conductor, one of the key figures of the romantic period. His *Treatise on Instrumentation* was hugely influential through the nineteenth and twentieth centuries.

Bernstein, Elmer (1922-2004) – American composer and conductor. He wrote extensively for film and television. His most successful film scores included *The Magnificent Seven*, *To Kill a Mockingbird*, *The Great Escape* and *Thoroughly Modern Millie* for which he won an Oscar.

Bernstein, Leonard (1918-90) – American composer, conductor, pianist and educator, one of the most significant musical figures in twentieth century music, whose compositions included music for the Broadway stage and film, including *West Side Story*, *On the Town*, and *On the Waterfront*, as well as works for orchestra and choral music, such as *Chichester Psalms*.

Billy Elliott – British film directed by Stephen Daldry and written by/adapted from a play by Lee Hall. It later became a successful stage musical with songs by Sir Elton John.

Bingham, Judith (b.1952) – See interview (page 3)

Birtwistle, Sir Harrison (b.1934) – British composer. He was Music Director of the newly established National Theatre until 1983 and has since become one of the most significant composers of his generation. His output includes operas – *Punch and Judy*, *The Mask of Orpheus*, *Gawain* and *The Second Mrs Kong* – as well as a number of major orchestral works.

Bishop, Elizabeth (1911-79) – American writer, best known for her poetry and short stories. She won the Pulitzer Prize for poetry in 1956 and is regarded as one of the most important poets of her generation.

Blackford, Richard (b.1954) – British composer, whose works include music for films and musicals, and orchestral and chamber works, and most recently a series of large-scale choral works, including *Mirror of Perfection*, *Not in our Time* and *Pieta*.

Blair in B minor – Magnificat and Nunc Dimittis in B minor by Hugh Blair (1869-1953), one of many Canticle settings by this British composer, organist, and conductor.

Blake, David (b.1936) – British composer and teacher, founder member of the University of York Music Department. He is a student of **Schoenberg**'s pupil, the Marxist composer Hanns Eisler. Blake co-founded the University of York Music Press in 1995.

Blake, William (1757-1827) – English poet, artist, and printmaker, considered to be a major figure in the history of poetry and the visual arts, whose influence stretched long into the twentieth century and beyond.

Blunden, Edmund (1896-1974) – British writer and critic, who wrote of his experiences in World War I and was Professor of Poetry at Oxford University.

Bolton, Ivor (b.1958) – British conductor and harpsichordist. He has been Music Director of Glyndebourne Touring Opera, Principal Conductor of the Scottish Chamber Orchestra and is Chief Conductor of the Mozarteum Orchestra of Salzburg.

Borkowski, Marian (b.1934) – Polish composer, musicologist, and teacher. He studied with **Messiaen** and **Nadia Boulanger**. He has been on the faculty of the Chopin University in Warsaw since 1968 and is a prominent figure in Polish musical life.

Bostridge, Ian (b.1964) – English tenor and scholar, who was awarded a Doctorate from Oxford University on the significance of Witchcraft in English public life between 1650-1750! Since becoming a full-time singer in 1995, Bostridge has had an international career in both the opera house and concert hall.

Boulanger, Nadia (1887-1979) – French composer, teacher, and conductor. One of the most significant composition teachers of the twentieth century whose pupils included **Aaron Copland**, Elliott Carter, Virgil Thomson, **Sir Lennox Berkeley** and many other important musicians.

Boulez, Pierre (1926-2015) – French composer and conductor, a dominant figure in French music and internationally as a performer, composer, conductor, and thinker, who influenced and polarised the classical music world for several decades.

Bragg, Melvyn (Lord Bragg of Wigton) (b.1939) – British broadcaster, parliamentarian, and writer. Best known as presenter of the television arts programme *South Bank Show* (1978-2010).

Brahms, Johannes (1833-97) – German composer and pianist. The Hamburg-born Brahms was one of the great Romantic composers, renowned for his symphonies, concertos and chamber music. Had a strong interest in folk music reflected in his Hungarian Dances and Rhapsodies.

Brain, Leonard (1915-75) – British oboist and cor anglais player. He was the brother of the famous horn player Dennis Brain and played with the Royal Philharmonic Orchestra, 1945-73.

Bream, Julian (1933-2020) – British classical guitarist and lutenist, who did much to pioneer the guitar as a solo instrument. **Britten**, **Berkeley** (both **Lennox** and Michael), **Tippett**, **Walton**, Takemitsu, **Henze**, all wrote works for him.

Britten, Benjamin (Baron Britten of Aldeburgh) (1913-76) – English composer, pianist and conductor. One of the key figures in British music in the twentieth century, he leapt to international fame with the premiere of *Peter Grimes* in 1945. He made a significant contribution to choral music including works such as *A Boy Was Born, Rejoice in the Lamb, St Nicholas* and **War Requiem**.

Brunelle, Philip (b.1943) – American choral conductor and organist. He has been choirmaster of Plymouth Congregational Church in Minneapolis since 1969, was Music Director of Minnesota Opera (1969-86) and is the founder and Music Director of Vocal Essence, one of the most significant choral organisations in the USA.

Bryars, Gavin (b.1943) – British composer and bass player, a leading figure in the English experimental movement. Many of his early works such as *Jesus' Blood Never Failed Me Yet* and *The Sinking of the Titanic* involved his own ensemble, but more recently Bryars has written a number of operas and ballets, as well as music for the church and concert hall.

Bush, Alan (1900-1995) – British composer and political activist. He joined the Communist Party in 1935 and all four of his operas were premiered in East Germany.

Butt, John (b.1960) – British choral conductor, keyboard player and scholar. He is Founder and Musical Director of the Dunedin Consort, one of the world's leading baroque ensembles, based in Scotland.

Byrd, William (c.1539/40-1623) – English composer and keyboard player, one of the major composers of Renaissance. He produced a wide range of music for both the Anglican and Catholic church, as well as a good deal of instrumental music.

Byron, George (Lord Byron) (1788-1824) – British poet and politician. One of the greatest poets of the Romantic movement.

Cage, John (1912-92) – American composer, theorist, philosopher, and artist. A pioneer in the use of electronic music, indeterminacy in music and the use of non-standard musical instruments. Perhaps best known for his musical work *4'33"* which is performed without any deliberate sound.

Camden, Anthony (1938-2006) – English oboist, who was Principal Oboe of the of the London Symphony Orchestra between 1972 and 1986, becoming Chairman of the Board of the LSO and later holding academic posts in Australia and Hong Kong.

Campbell, Hilary (b.1983) – British choral conductor and composer. She conducts both amateur and professional choirs, including Blossom Street, Bristol Choral Society and Chiswick Choir.

Canons – A musical technique that involves a melody with one or more imitations of the melody played after a given duration.

Cardew, Cornelius (1936-81) – British experimental composer and pianist, co-founder of the experimental performing ensemble, the Scratch Orchestra. He assisted **Stockhausen** in the late 1950s but then abandoned serial composition to develop his work with experimental and indeterminate music.

Carols for Choirs – A series of anthologies (at present numbering five) of Christmas hymns and carols, published by Oxford University Press and edited at various times by Reginald Jacques, **Sir David Willcocks**, **John Rutter** and **Bob Chilcott**.

Carpenter, Gary (b.1951) – British composer and teacher. His large output includes chamber music, instrumental, vocal and orchestral works and a number of musicals. He was Associate Musical Director for the cult horror film *The Wicker Man* and teaches at the **RAM** and the Royal Northern College of Music.

Carpenter, Humphrey (1946-2005) – British writer and broadcaster, who wrote notable biographies of **J.R.R. Tolkien**, W.H. Auden, **Benjamin Britten**, Dennis Potter and Spike Milligan, amongst others.

Caravaggio, *Supper at Emmaus* – a painting by the Italian master Michelangelo Caravaggio (1571-1610) in which Jesus reveals himself to his disciples, only soon to vanish from their sight.

Casken, John (b.1949) – British composer, painter, and teacher who has taught at the universities of Birmingham, Durham and Manchester (where he was Professor between 1992 and 2008). His music takes much of its inspiration from the landscape and folk traditions of Northumberland.

Cather, Willa (1873-1947) – American writer, who was celebrated for her stories of American frontier life, including *The Song of the Lark* and *O Pioneers!*.

Child, Lee – The pen name of James Grant (born 1954), a prolific author of thrillers, particularly known for his Jack Reacher series.

Chilcott, Bob (b.1955) – See interview (page 15)

Chopin, Ballades – Four one-movement piano works by the Polish composer and pianist Frederic Chopin (1810-49), who was a pioneer in the use of the genre.

Clair de Lune – a popular piano piece by Debussy, the third movement of his *Suite Bergamasque*.

Cleobury, Stephen (1948-2019) – British choral conductor and organist. He was Chief Conductor of the BBC Singers between 1995 and 2007 and Director of Music at **King's College, Cambridge,** between 1982 and 2019.

Cohen, David (b.1980) – Belgian cellist who made his debut with the Belgium National Orchestra aged nine and has since developed an international career.

Coleridge, Samuel Taylor (1772-1834) – British poet, critic, theologian and philosopher who, with his friend **William Wordsworth**, was a founder of the Romantic Movement.

Coll Reg – Abbreviation of Collegium Regale, a collection of choral settings by the British composer **Herbert Howells**, originally written for **King's College**, **Cambridge** ('Collegium Regale' in Latin).

Copland, Aaron (1900-90) – American composer, teacher, writer and conductor, the first American composer to achieve an international reputation, still referred to by many as 'the Dean of American Composers'. He is best known for the works he wrote in the 1930s and '40s that evoke the American landscape and spirit such as the ballets *Appalachian Spring, Rodeo* and *Billy the Kid*.

Coppola, Francis Ford (b.1939) – American film director, screenwriter and producer, whose films include *The Godfather* series, *Bram Stoker's Dracula* and *Apocalypse Now*.

Corigliano, John (b.1938) – American composer, whose music for the concert hall, opera house and cinema has been widely recorded and performed. He won an Oscar for his score for the film *The Red Violin* and the Pulitzer Prize for his Symphony No.2.

Così fan tutte – An Italian-language opera in two acts by Wolfgang Amadeus **Mozart** (1756-91) with a libretto by Lorenzo Da Ponte (1749-1838).

Cowie, Edward (b.1943) – British composer, painter, writer and naturalist, whose work takes much of its inspiration from the natural world. He lived in Australia for several years, where the landscape had a profound effect on his music, and was Composer in Residence with the BBC Singers between 2002 and 2004.

Crossley-Holland, Kevin (b.1941) – British writer, teacher, and translator. A prize-winning author of children's books and best known for his Arthur trilogy.

Crotchets – A quarter note in America – a musical note with the time value of one quarter of a semibreve (or whole note).

Cummings, E.E. (1894-1962) – American writer and painter, who wrote almost 3,000 poems, as well as essays, plays and novels. Much of his work uses lower-case spellings for poetic expression.

Curtis, Richard (b.1956) – British screenwriter, director and producer, who co-wrote a number of successful television series – *Blackadder*, *Mr Bean*, *The Vicar of Dibley* – and screenplays for films including *Four Weddings and a Funeral* and *Notting Hill*.

Dahl, Ingolf (1912-70) – German-born American composer, pianist, conductor, and teacher, who taught at the University of Southern California from 1945 until his death.

Dale Roberts, Jeremy (1934-2017) – English composer and teacher. He was Head of Composition at the **RCM**.

Dallapiccola, Luigi (1904-75) – Italian composer, one of the most significant figures in Italian music of the twentieth century, particularly admired for his operas and vocal works.

Darke in F – Magnificat and Nunc Dimittis by the British organist, conductor, and composer Harold Darke (1888-1976). He was particularly associated with St Michael's, Cornhill, London, where he worked for half a century.

Darmstadt – City in Germany, the venue for important summer courses for new music in the 1950s and '60s. Still a major centre for new and exploratory music.

Davies, Grahame (b.1964) – Welsh poet, editor and critic. One of the leading Welsh-language poets, his poetry has been translated into several other languages and has appeared in many anthologies.

Denisov, Edison (1929-96) – Russian composer, long resident in France. He was blacklisted by the Russian authorities in 1979 for his musical experiments and was an important figurehead for younger Russian composers.

Depeche Mode – British electronic music band formed in 1980.

Diamond, David (1915-2005) – American composer and teacher. Central to his output are 11 symphonies and 10 string quartets. Despite early success he found his music side-lined by the musical developments of the mid/late 1900s.

Dickinson, Emily – *Answer July*, a poem by the American poet (1830-86), depicting with meter and repetition the cycle of a year.

Digby, Suzi (The Lady Eatwell) (b.1958) – English conductor and educator. She is Founder of The Voices Foundation, Co-Founder of The London Youth Choir and Founder/Musical Director of ORA, a London-based professional chamber choir.

Dorsey, Tommy (1905-56) – American trombonist, composer, and bandleader, known as the 'Sentimental Gentleman of Swing'.

Dove, Jonathan (b.1959) – See interview (page 27)

Drayton, Paul (b.1944) – English composer, pianist, and teacher, who was Director of Music at New College Choir School, Oxford.

The Dream of Gerontius – See **Elgar**

Drummond, William (1585-1649) – (William Drummond of Hawthornden) Scottish poet, the first notable poet in Scotland to write in English.

Dryden, John (1631-1700) – British writer, critic, and translator. He was the first Poet Laureate, appointed in 1668.

Duchen, Jessica (b.1965) – British author, critic and librettist. She has collaborated on operas with **Roxanna Panufnik**, Paul Fincham and John Barber, written seven novels, and biographies of Korngold and **Fauré**.

Duruflé, Maurice (1902-86) – French composer, organist and teacher, who was highly self-critical and published only a small number of works including a popular Requiem and a number of works for his own instrument.

Dvořák, Antonin (1841-1904) – One of the first Czech composers to achieve worldwide acclaim, who successfully brought together elements of the romantic movement with his own national idiom. Many of his works, such as the Symphony No.9 (*From the New World*) and the Cello Concerto, have become staples of the repertoire.

Dyson in F – Magnificat and Nunc Dimittis by the British composer Sir George Dyson (1883-1964). Dyson was a schoolmaster, a prolific composer and was appointed Director of the **RCM** in 1938, a post he held until 1952.

Einstein, Albert (1879-1955) – German-born American theoretical physicist, who developed the theory of relativity and won the Nobel Prize for Physics in 1921.

Elgar, Sir Edward (1857-1934) – British composer and conductor, the first British composer to have his works enter the mainstream symphonic repertoire. He was an acclaimed conductor of his own music and appointed Master of the King's Music in 1924. He regarded his oratorio *The Dream of Gerontius* (1900) as his finest work to that date.

Elijah – An oratorio by Felix **Mendelssohn** (1809-47), premiered in Birmingham, England, in 1846.

Eliot, T.S. (Thomas Stearns) (1888-1965) – American-born British writer, critic, and editor, regarded as one of the most significant poets of the twentieth century.

Eno, Brian (b.1948) – English musician, visual artist, and record producer. He joined the glam rock group Roxy Music as synthesiser player in 1971.

Epic of Gilgamesh, The – An epic poem from ancient Mesopotamia. One of the earliest surviving pieces of literature.

Eton Choir Book, The – an illustrated collection of sacred music written during the fifteenth century. It contains works by John Browne, Robert Wilkinson, Richard Davy, Robert Fayrfax, William Cornysh, and many others.

Fantasia on O Magnum Mysterium – An organ work by **Sir Peter Maxwell Davies**.

Fauré, Gabriel (1845-1924) – French composer, organist and teacher. His *Requiem* (Op.48, 1887) is regarded as one of his finest works.

Fax, Mark (1911-74) – American composer and teacher who taught at Howard University between 1947 and 1972.

Feldman, Morton (1926-1987) – American composer. Along with other New York composers such as **John Cage**, he was a leading figure in the development of indeterminate music, in which some elements of the composition and performance are left to chance.

Fenby, Eric (1906-97) – English composer, best known for his work as assistant to Frederick Delius (1928-34).

Fetler, Paul (b.1920) – American composer and teacher, a pupil of **Hindemith**, Boris Blacher and Quincy Porter.

Finnissy, Michael (b.1946) – British composer, pianist and teacher, whose music is often concerned with the social and political aspects of music and pushing the limits of the technique of performers.

Fischer-Dieskau, Dietrich (1925-2012) – German baritone and conductor. He is regarded as one of the greatest singers of the twentieth century and was equally active on the concert stage and the opera house.

Flecker, James Elroy (1884-1915) – British writer, best known for his poetry collections, including *The Golden Journey to Samarkand*.

Floyd, George (1973-2020) – American rapper and hip-hop artist, who was arrested and murdered by a police officer in Minnesota, USA, in May 2020.

Fugue – A compositional procedure involving voices entering successively in imitation and developing the principal theme contrapuntally.

Gardner, John (1917-2011) – *Tomorrow shall be my dancing day* – A popular carol by the British composer, setting an archaic text.

GCSE – General Certificate of Education. UK school exam taken by most pupils at the end of year 11 (aged 16).

Genesis Foundation – UK charity established in 2001 to support emerging talent in the creative arts industries.

Gesang der Jünglinge (*Song of the Youths*) – A seminal electronic work by **Karlheinz Stockhausen**, often described as the first masterpiece of electronic music.

Gesualdo, Carlo (1566-1613) – Italian composer, Prince of Venosa. Notoriously murdered his first wife and her lover. His madrigals and motets employ an intensely expressive chromatic language.

Giannini, Vittorio (1903-66) – Italian-American composer and teacher, composer of seven symphonies, operas and vocal works in a neo-romantic idiom.

Gibbons, Orlando (1583-1625) – English composer and keyboard player, a master of the English madrigal school, an important link between the Renaissance and Baroque periods.

Gilchrist, James (b.1966) – English tenor, particularly admired for his performances of the Bach Passions and English song.

Gioia, Dana (b.1950) – American writer and Chairman of the National Endowment for the Arts in the USA, 2003-09. In December 2015 he became Poet Laureate of California.

Giulini, Carlo Maria (1914-2005) – Italian conductor, whose international career spanned over half a century. He was Music Director of the Los Angeles Philharmonic (1978-84) and had long associations with several great orchestras and opera houses.

Glass, Philip (b.1937) – American composer and pianist. A pioneer of minimalist music, alongside **Steve Reich** and **Terry Riley**. His prolific output spans the opera house, concert hall and film studio. His highly successful and at times controversial operas include *Einstein on the Beach*, *Satyagraha*, *Akhnaten* and *The Perfect American*.

Glemp, Cardinal Józef (1929-2013) – Archbishop of Warsaw between 1981 and 2006.

Glock, Sir William (1908-2000) – British pianist, critic and administrator. He became Controller of BBC Radio 3 and Director of the Proms and was responsible for introducing a great deal of music by the European avant-garde to the UK.

Goehr, Alexander (b.1932) – German-born British composer and academic. A central figure in the post-war **Manchester School** of composers, along with **Birtwistle** and **Maxwell Davies**. He was Professor of Music at Cambridge University from 1975 and has taught several generations of prominent composers including Thomas Ades, **Julian Anderson**, **Sir George Benjamin** and **Robin Holloway**.

Goldsmith, Jerry (1929-2004) – American composer and conductor, best known for his film music. He won an Oscar for his score for *The Omen*. His other successful scores included *Chinatown*, *Planet of the Apes*, *Logan's Run* and five films in the *Star Trek* series.

Gorb, Adam (b.1958) – English composer and teacher, particularly known for his music for wind bands, but he has made contributions to many genres. Gorb has been Head of Composition at the Royal Northern College of Music since 2000.

Górecki, Henryk (1933-2010) – *Totus Tuus* (*Totally Yours*) – a sacred choral work by the Polish composer, written to celebrate Pope **John Paul's** third pilgrimage to his native Poland.

Graves, Robert (1895-1985) – British poet, known especially for his memoir, *Good-bye to All That*, and historical novels such as *I, Claudius*, as well as a large number of poetry collections.

Great Learning, The – One of the four books of Confucianism, but also the title of an experimental musical work by the British composer **Cornelius Cardew**.

Gregorian chant – A form of unaccompanied monophonic song in Latin developed during the ninth and tenth centuries and used extensively by composers throughout history as a basis for their choral works.

Grieg, Edvard (1843-1907) – Norwegian composer and pianist, admired for his piano music and songs, with his Piano Concerto in A minor perhaps his best-known work.

Groves, Sir Charles (1915-92) – British conductor, who was known for his wide repertoire, particularly of British music and works by contemporary composers.

Gubaidulina, Sofia (b.1931) – Russian composer, long resident in Germany. Her music is often associated with human transcendence, mysticism and religious subject matter.

Haendel, Ida (1928-2020) – Polish born British/Canadian violinist. An astonishing prodigy, she won the Warsaw Conservatory's gold medal at the age of five. She played at the Proms 68 times.

Halsey, Louis (b.1929) – English choral conductor and composer, who founded the Elizabethan Singers and the Louis Halsey Singers.

Halsey, Simon (b.1958) – British choral conductor who has been Chorus Director of the City of Birmingham Symphony Orchestra and the Berlin Radio Choir and is at present Chorus Director of the London Symphony Chorus. He has worked worldwide as a conductor, teacher and adjudicator.

Harper, Heather (1930-2019) – Northern Irish soprano, active in both the opera house and concert hall. She became internationally known after singing the world premiere of Britten's *War Requiem*, and thereafter became closely associated with the music of **Britten** and **Tippett**, as well as being known for her performances of **Mozart** and **Wagner**.

Harvey, Jonathan (1939-2012) – British composer and academic. One of the most significant British composers of his generation, particularly admired for his choral music and for combining electronics and non-western traditions with standard Western musical forms.

Hawking, Professor Stephen (1942-2018) – English theoretical physicist, cosmologist, writer and academic, Professor at Cambridge University between 1979-2009. His book *The Brief History of Time* contributed to Hawking becoming perhaps the most famous scientist since Einstein.

Haydn, Franz Josef (1732-1809) – Austro-Hungarian composer, known as the 'Father of the Symphony' and 'Father of the String Quartet'. He travelled widely and became the most celebrated composer in Europe.

Heifetz, Jascha (1901-87) – Russian-American violinist, one of the greatest violinists of the twentieth century, who turned to teaching when an arm injury made him cut down on performing.

Heine, Heinrich (1797-1856) – German writer and critic, best known for his lyric poetry that was set to music most famously by **Schubert** and **Schumann**.

Henze, Hans Werner (1926-2012) – Prolific German composer and conductor, long resident in Italy. His vast output of operas, symphonies, chamber and orchestral music put him at odds with the more experimental composers of his generation, but he remains a key figure in twentieth-century music.

Herbert, George (1593-1633) – Welsh-born poet and priest of the Church of England. Recognised as one of the metaphysical poets, his lyrical and musical poems have been set by a great many composers.

Heterophonic – A musical texture that is made up of the simultaneous variation of a single melodic line.

Higginbottom, Edward (b.1946) – English organist, conductor and scholar. He led the New College Oxford choir for more than 35 years and made 20 recordings with the choir.

Hill, David (b.1957) – British choral conductor and organist. He has held posts at Westminster Cathedral, Winchester Cathedral and St John's College, Cambridge and was Chief Conductor of the BBC Singers (2007-2017). He has been Music Director of the Bach Choir (London) since 1998 and is Principal Conductor of the Yale Schola Cantorum in the USA.

Hindemith, Paul (1896-1963) – Prolific German composer, viola player, teacher and conductor. He became a major figure in German music between the wars and later emigrated to the USA, but returned to Europe in 1953, living in Zurich for the rest of his life.

Hobbit, The – A children's fantasy novel by the British writer **J.R.R. Tolkien**. It remains a popular and much-loved classic of its kind.

Hoddinott, Alun (1929-2008) – Welsh composer and teacher. His large output includes orchestral, chamber and choral music, as well as operas and folk song arrangements. A distinguished teacher, he was responsible for the expansion of the music department at Cardiff University.

Holloway, Robin (b.1943) – British composer, academic and teacher of several generations of composers at Cambridge University until his retirement in 2011. His music is often inspired by his own personal relationship with music of the past, particularly of the late nineteenth and early twentieth centuries.

Holly, Buddy (1936-59) – American singer-songwriter, who was an important figure in the rock and roll movement of the 1950s. He was killed in an air crash in 1959.

Holst, Gustav (1874-1934) – British composer, arranger, and teacher of Swedish/German descent. A pioneer (with his friend **Vaughan Williams**) in the collection and arrangement of English folksong, his later music also reflected his wide-ranging interests in the music and traditions of other cultures, most notably those of Africa and India. His most frequently performed work is *The Planets*.

Horovitz, Joseph (b.1926) – Viennese-born British composer and teacher. His extensive output includes music for brass and wind bands, as well as award-winning scores for television, including music for *Rumpole of the Bailey*.

Houston, Whitney (1963-2012) – American singer and actress, one of the most popular and awarded singers of her time.

Howarth, Gary (Elgar) (b.1935) – English trumpeter, conductor, and composer. A major figure in the brass band world, as well as being much admired for his championing and performances of major contemporary composers such as **Birtwistle** and **Ligeti**.

Howells, Herbert (1892-1983) – British composer and teacher. His early reputation was built on orchestral and chamber music, but he devoted much of his time to the composition of choral and organ music for the Anglican church.

Howerd, Frankie (1917-92) – British comedian and comic actor, a popular entertainer on radio, film, and television from the late 1940s.

Huber, Klaus (1924-2017) – Swiss composer and academic, a prominent teacher whose pupils included a number of important composers of recent times, such as Brian Ferneyhough and **Kaija Saariaho**.

Hume, Cardinal Basil (1923-99) – English Roman Catholic Cardinal. He was Archbishop of Westminster between 1976 and 1999.

Hykes, David (b.1953) – American composer, singer, writer and teacher. He was a pioneer of overtone singing and contemplative music that he called Harmonic Chant.

In my little picture frame – Song written by Latvian pop artist and actor Renārs Kaupers (b.1974). With his group Brainstorm his song *My Star* came third in the 2000 European Song Contest.

Ireland, John (1879-1962) – *A London Overture* – Originally a work for brass band entitled *Comedy Overture* by the British composer, later re-worked as *A London Overture* for orchestra, a musical depiction of the Edwardian city.

Iron Maiden – British heavy metal band formed in 1975.

Ives, Burl (1909-95) – Popular American singer, song-writer and actor. His two most famous film roles were Big Daddy in *Cat on a Hot Tin Roof* and in *The Big Country*, for which he won an Oscar.

Ives, Charles (1874-1954) – American composer, whose advanced musical thought was largely ignored in his lifetime, but who in the later twentieth century came to be recognised as a major figure.

Jansons, Mariss (1943-2019) – Latvian conductor, whose international career included periods as Music Director with the Oslo Philharmonic, the Pittsburgh Symphony Orchestra, the Bavarian Radio Symphony Orchestra and the Concertgebouw, Amsterdam.

Jasna Góra Monastery – An important monastery and place of pilgrimage in the Polish city of Czestochowa. The home of the Black Madonna of Czestochowa to which miraculous powers are attributed.

John Paul II (1920-2005) – Polish Cardinal who became Pope and Head of the Catholic Church between 1978 and his death in 2005.

Johnston, Guy (b.1981) – British cellist, who won the BBC Young Musician of the Year in 2000.

Jones, Aled (b.1970) – Welsh singer and broadcaster.

Josquin des Prez (c.1440-1521) – Often referred to simply as Josquin, French composer, considered by many to be the greatest composer of his generation and an important figure of the Franco-Flemish school.

Joubert, John (1927-2019) – South African-born British composer. He taught at the universities of Hull and Birmingham and wrote over 180 works.

Kancheli, Giya (1935-2019) – Georgian-born composer of concert and film music, long resident in Belgium.

Keller, Hans (1919-85) – Austrian-born British musicologist, writer and broadcaster, who made important contributions to music criticism and invented the method of wordless functional analysis, in which music is analysed in musical sound alone.

Kern, Jerome (1885-1945) – American composer and songwriter of the early twentieth century. His most notable success was the musical *Showboat*, but he also wrote a large number of songs that have become an important part of the Great American Songbook.

Kilar, Wojciech (1932-2013) – Polish composer of concert and film music. He belonged to the Polish avant-garde movement of the 1960s, but later worked in a much less complex musical language. His film scores included *Bram Stoker's Dracula*, *The Pianist* and *The Portrait of a Lady*.

King Jr, Martin Luther (1929-68) – American civil rights activist and Baptist minister, who advocated advancing civil rights through non-violent demonstration and civil disobedience. He won the Nobel Peace Prize in 1964 and was assassinated in 1968.

King's College, Cambridge – Service of Nine Lessons and Carols – A service held on Christmas Eve every year since 1918 and broadcast around the world.

Kipling, Rudyard (1865-1937) – British writer born in India whose culture and history inspired much of his work. Considered an innovator of the short story, his most famous work includes *The Jungle Book*, and *The Man Who Would be King*, as well as many well-known poems such as *If-* and *Mandelay*.

Knussen, Oliver (1952-2018) – British composer and conductor. A hugely significant figure in contemporary concert music whose influence as a champion of new music and mentor to young composers cannot be over-estimated.

Kokkonen, Joonas (1921-96) – Finnish composer, one of the most renowned Finnish composers after Sibelius. His opera *The Last Temptations* received over 500 performances all over the world after its premiere in 1975.

Kortekangas, Olli (b.1955) – Finnish composer whose large output includes several operas and much choral music.

Lambert, John (1926-95) – English composer and teacher. He was Music Director at the Old Vic between 1958 and 1962, when he became a Professor of Composition at the **RCM** until 1990.

Lassus, Orlando de (c.1530/32-94) – Franco-Flemish composer of the late Renaissance and one of the most important and prolific musicians of his time. Lassus wrote over 2,000 sacred and secular choral works.

Lauridsen, Morten (b.1943) – See interview (page 117)

Layton, Stephen (b.1966) – English choral conductor. He is Founder and Musical Director of Polyphony, and Music Director of the Holst Singers, and has been Director of Music at St John's College, Cambridge since 2006.

Led Zepplin – British rock band formed in 1968, consisting of Robert Plant, Jimmy Page, John Paul Jones and John Bonham. One of the most successful bands of all time.

LeFanu, Nicola (b.1947) – British composer and academic, particularly known for her operas and vocal music. She taught at King's College, London, before becoming Professor of Music at York University (1994-2001).

Leighton, Kenneth (1929-87) – British composer, pianist, and teacher, particularly admired for his sacred and liturgical music. He held academic posts at the Universities of Leeds and Oxford and was Reid Professor of Music at the University of Edinburgh from 1970 until his death.

Lerner and Loewe – Alan Jay Lerner (1918-86) and Frederick Loewe (1901-88), respectively American librettist and Austro-American composer of a number of highly successful musicals, including *My Fair Lady*, *Gigi* and *Camelot*.

Ligeti, György (1923-2006) – Hungarian-born Austrian composer, whose experiments in the field of electronic music, micropolyphony and polyrhythm made him one of the most significant figures of the twentieth century avant-garde.

Lindberg, Magnus (b.1958) – Finnish composer, pianist and conductor, whose large-scale orchestral works have become part of the international repertoire. He studied at the Sibelius Academy under **Rautavaara**.

Lindbergh, Charles (1902-74) – American aviator, activist, and writer, who made the first solo transatlantic flight from New York to Paris in 1927.

Lloyd, Jonathan (b.1948) – British composer who has written extensively for the concert hall. He also composed a new score for Alfred Hitchcock's early silent film *Blackmail*.

Lloyd Webber, Andrew (b.1948) (Lord Lloyd Webber of Sydmonton) – British composer, songwriter and theatrical impresario, whose musicals, including *Joseph and his Amazing Technicolour Dreamcoat*, *Cats*, *The Phantom of the Opera* have been huge successes all over the world.

Lloyd Webber, Julian (b.1951) – British cellist and conductor, who was Principal of the Royal Birmingham Conservatoire, 2015-20.

Longfellow, Henry Wadsworth (1807-82) – American writer and educator, whose lyric poetry, most famously *The Song of Hiawatha* and *Paul Revere's Ride*, is often concerned with myth and legend.

Łukaszewski, Marcin (b.1972) – Polish composer, pianist, academic and writer.

Łukaszewski, Wojciech (1936-78) – Polish composer, writer and administrator.

Lumsdaine, David (b.1931) – Australian-born British composer and teacher. He taught at Durham University before becoming a Senior Lecturer at King's College, London. Lumsdaine is also an ornithologist and his music has frequently taken its inspiration from the wonders of nature and landscape.

Lumsden, Sir David (b.1928) – English choral conductor, keyboard player and educator. He was organist and choirmaster at New College, Oxford (1959-76), Principal of the Royal Scottish Academy of Music and Drama (1976-82) and Principal of the **RAM** until his retirement in 1993.

Lutosławski, Witold (1913-94) – Polish composer and conductor. One of the first and most important Polish composers to emerge after the Second World War. His early work was influenced by Polish folk music, whilst his later music developed his methods of aleatoric process in which rhythmic coordination is subject to chance.

Macdonald, Hugh (b.1940) – British musicologist, chiefly known for his work on music of the 19th century, in particular for his writings on Berlioz.

MacDonald, Malcolm (1916-92) – English composer and critic.

MacMillan, Sir James (b.1959) – See interview (page 151)

Maconchy, Dame Elizabeth (1907-94) – Irish-English composer, particularly known for her cycle of string quartets, although her output includes a good deal of choral, orchestral music and opera.

Mag and Nunc – Magnificat and Nunc Dimittis – the Anglican service of Evening Prayer. The Magnificat ('Song of Mary') and Nunc Dimittis ('Song of Simeon') are biblical canticles and have been set to music by countless composers through the ages.

Mahabharata – one of the most important Sanskrit epics of ancient India.

Mahler, Gustav (1860-1911) – born in Bohemia, he became one of the leading composers and conductors of his generation; his symphonies were a major influence on twentieth-century composers.

Malone, Gareth (b.1975) – choirmaster and broadcaster known particularly for his innovative programmes encouraging non-singers to form or join choirs.

Manchester School – a term applied to a group of composers and performers who, while students at the Royal Manchester College of Music or Manchester University, set up New Music Manchester to promote contemporary works. The group included **Alexander Goehr**, **Harrison Birtwistle**, **Peter Maxwell Davies**, **Elgar Howarth** and John Ogden.

Manoury, Philippe (b.1952) – French composer, studied at the Paris Conservatoire and worked at IRCAM. Taught at the University of California, San Diego, between 2004 and 2012.

Marks, Dennis (1948-2015) – broadcaster, film maker and writer; he was Head of Music at BBC TV in the 1980s and General Director of English National Opera between 1993 and 1998.

Marsh, Roger (b.1949) – British composer, studied at University of York and in California. Lecturer in music at Keele Unversity (1978-88), then Professor at University of York.

Martinez, Odaline de la (b.1949) – Cuban-American composer and conductor; founder and artistic director of Lontano. The first woman to conduct at the BBC Proms (in 1984).

Martland, Steve (1954-2013) – British composer, born in Liverpool. Studied composition with Louis Andriessen in The Netherlands.

Master of the Queen's Music – a post in the Royal Household, awarded to a distinguished musician, usually a composer who would be asked to compose works for celebratory occasions. Since 2004, the post has been fixed-term, lasting ten years, with **Sir Peter Maxwell Davies** followed by **Judith Weir**.

Mathias, William (1934-1992) – Welsh composer. Studied at the RAM under **Lennox Berkeley**. Professor and Head of Department at University of Wales, Bangor (1970-1988).

Maxwell Davies, Sir Peter (1934-2016) – British composer and conductor. Studied at the University of Manchester and the Royal Manchester College of Music. Co-founder of the **Manchester School**. **Master of the Queen's Music** from 2004.

McCabe, John (1939-2015) – English composer and pianist. He studied at the Royal Manchester College of Music and in Munich. Apart from a period as Director of the London College of Music (1983-1990) he followed a freelance career recording the complete piano sonatas of **Haydn** and composing in virtually every genre.

McCartney, Sir Paul (b.1942) – Singer/songwriter/bass guitarist; founder member of The Beatles. Composer and lyricist of over 100 songs of which *Yesterday* is one of the most recorded.

McGonagall, William (1825-1902) – Scottish poet of Irish descent. Renowned (and lampooned) as 'the worst poet in the history of the English language'.

McPhee, George (b.1937) – Scottish organist and conductor. In 2013 he celebrated 50 years as Director of Music at Paisley Abbey.

Mellers, Wilfrid (1914-2008) – English music critic, musicologist and composer. Founding Professor of Music at University of York from 1964 to 1981. A specialist in the interaction of music with the English language.

Mence, Selga (b.1953) – Latvian composer. Head of the composition department of the Latvian Academy of Music since 2004.

Mercury, Freddie (1946-1991) – Singer, songwriter and lead vocalist of the rock group Queen. A charismatic stage performer, he is said to have had a four-octave vocal range.

Messiaen, Olivier (1902-1998) – French composer, organist, ornithologist and teacher. One of the major twentieth-century composers, his output was immense and incredibly influential. Though he wrote little for choir, his *O sacrum convivium* and *Cinq rechants* are regarded as masterpieces.

Messiah – Oratorio by George Frederic Handel (1685-1759) composed in 1742 and first performed in Dublin.

Miller, Glenn (1904-1944) – American trombonist, bandleader, arranger and composer. A major in the US Army Air Forces Band, he died when the plane he was flying in to France disappeared in the English Channel.

Milstein, Silvina (b.1956) – Argentinian composer. After emigrating to the UK in 1976, she studied at Glasgow University and held Fellowships at Cambridge University. She is a Professor of Music at King's College London.

Milton, John (1608-1674) – English poet. He served as a civil servant for the Commonwealth of England. Famed particularly for his epic poem *Paradise Lost* (1667).

Minimalism – A form of music using limited materials, repetitive patterns, drones and mainly consonant harmony. American composers such as **Steve Reich**, **Philip Glass** and **Terry Riley** are considered the pioneers in developing minimalist techniques while, in the UK, Michael Nyman is credited with coining the term as well as embracing many of minimalism's features in his compositions.

Minims – In music notation a half note consisting of two quarter notes (or crotchets).

Minnesota Composers Forum – Founded in 1973 by Libby Larsen and **Stephen Paulus**, the Forum was set up to create performing opportunities outside academic circles and to encourage performances of contemporary works in the Mid-West. The current name, American Composers Forum, was adopted in 1996 to recognise its nationwide scope.

Missa Brevis – A 'short mass' in Latin. The term is used either for a setting that is brief in duration or because it omits sections of the full mass.

Moniuszko, Stanisław (1819-72) – Polish composer, conductor and teacher. Regarded as the father of Polish national opera.

Monteverdi, Claudio (1567-1643) – The leading Italian composer of his generation and a critical figure in the evolution of opera and the transition from Renaissance to Baroque music. His *Vespers* (*Vespro della Beata Vergine*) of 1610 was composed for the dukes of Mantua and is famed for its rich variety of styles and choral and instrumental scoring.

Morecambe, Eric (1926-1984) – English comedian renowned for his partnership with Ernie Wise and their famous TV sketch with **André Previn** in which Morecombe 'performed' his own version of Grieg's Piano Concerto.

Morris, William (1834-1896) – English designer, novelist and poet. He contributed to the revival of British textile arts and production and to the development of the prose romance genre.

Mozart, Wolfgang Amadeus (1756- 1791) – Born in Salzburg he became one of the most astonishing musical talents of all time composing more than 600 works, of which the *Requiem* was left unfinished at his death but completed in 1792 by Franz Xaver Süssmayr.

Myers, Thalia (b.1945) – English pianist. A lifelong champion of new music, she has commissioned over 175 works including many for the Spectrum series published by the Associated Board [**ABRSM***] and intended to provide short, musically uncompromising but technically accessible piano pieces from some of the world's finest composers.

Nashe, Thomas (1567-c.1601) – English poet and playwright. His writings were controversial, noted for his biting satire and, in some cases, erotic content. 'Farewell, earth's bliss' was a verse from the masque, *Summer's Last Will and Testament* (1592).

Newman, Cardinal John Henry (1801-90) – British theologian and writer, who became an Anglican priest, later a Catholic priest and a Cardinal. He was canonised as a Saint in the Catholic Church in 2019. Amongst his writings is the poem *The Dream of Gerontius*, later set to music by **Edward Elgar**.

Newton, Sir Isaac (1642-1752) – English mathematician, theologian, astronomer, author and physicist. One of the most influential scientists in history.

Nielsen, Carl (1865-1931) – Danish composer, conductor and violinist. Composer of six symphonies and notable for the exploration of progressive tonality in his works.

Nono, Luigi (1924-1990) – Italian composer notable for his radical political views, his idiosyncratic development of serial technique and his interest in new sound sources and means of dissemination.

Nordheim, Arne (1931-2010) – Norwegian composer. His works focus around themes of solitude, death, love and landscape. He was an innovator in the integration of taped sound with live performance.

Nørgård, Per (b.1932) – Danish composer, regarded as a natural heir to **Sibelius** and **Nielsen**, but in the 1960s developing his own serial composition system based on the 'infinity series'.

Nucleus – British jazz-rock band, established by trumpeter Ian Carr, active between 1969 and 1989.

O'Donnell, James (b.1961) – Scottish organist and conductor. A graduate of Jesus College, Cambridge, he was Master of the Music at Westminster Cathedral before becoming Master of the Choristers at Westminster Abbey in 2000.

Oklahoma! – A musical, the first collaboration between lyricist Oscar Hammerstein II and composer **Richard Rodgers**. Premiered in 1943 it ran for 2,212 performances on Broadway and was made into a hugely successful film in 1955.

Oldham, Arthur (1926-2003) – English chorus master and composer. He founded the Edinburgh Festival Chorus and worked as choirmaster with orchestras in Paris and Amsterdam as well as the LSO Chorus and Scottish Opera.

O level – UK school examination, officially the General Certificate of Education: Ordinary Level, largely replaced by the **GCSE**.

Olson, Mel (1930-2001) – American choral conductor. Director of the Master Singers in Omaha, Nebraska, he was largely responsible for introducing the works of **John Rutter** to the USA.

Orbison, Roy (1936-1988) – American singer and songwriter who emerged as one of the most popular ballad singers of the 1960s.

Orton, Richard (1930-2013) – British composer and educator. He established the electronic music studio at the University of York in 1968 and pioneered performances of electro-acoustic music in the UK.

Osborne, Nigel (b.1948) – British composer, teacher and aid worker. Professor of Music at Edinburgh University between 1989 and 2012. Pioneered the use of music to help children in conflict zones such as Bosnia and Syria.

Owen, Wilfred (1893-1918) – English poet and soldier, killed one week before Armistice Day at the end of the First World War. His war poems had a huge influence on other poets and inspired settings by many composers, most notably **Britten** in his *War Requiem*.

Owens, Matthew (b.1971) – English organist and choirmaster. He has held positions at Manchester Cathedral, St Mary's Episcopal Cathedral, Edinburgh and Wells Cathedral.

Paciorkiewicz, Tadeusz (1916-1998) – Polish composer, organist and teacher. A traditionalist who eschewed the avant-garde, he nevertheless encouraged experimentation among younger composers in his role as composition professor and later Rector of the Warsaw Academy.

Palestrina, Giovanni Luigi da (c.1525-1594) – Italian composer who had a long-lasting influence on the composition of church music due to the technical perfection of his choral compositions.

Palmer, Samuel (1805-1881) – British landscape painter. Influenced initially by J.M.W. Turner, Palmer developed his own visionary style in pastoral watercolour paintings.

Panufnik, Sir Andrzej (1914-1991) – Polish composer and conductor who defected to Britain in 1954 and became a British citizen. He was Chief Conductor of the City of Birmingham Symphony Orchestra for two years but thereafter concentrated on composition, producing nine symphonies.

Park, Owain (b.1993) – English composer, conductor, organist and singer. Studied at Cambridge University. Founder and leader of the vocal consort Gesualdo Six.

Parry, Sir Charles Hubert Hastings (1848-1918) – English composer. A significant figure in the English musical renaissance as the teacher of, among others, **Vaughan Williams** and **Holst** at the **RCM**, and as a writer and theoretician.

Pärt, Arvo (b.1935) – Estonian composer. After struggles with the Soviet authorities in Estonia, he emigrated to Austria in 1980. During the 1970s he developed a distinctive style and technique called *tintinnabuli* (like the ringing of bells) and also converted from Lutheranism to Orthodox Christianity. He became the most-performed living composer in the world between 2011 and 2018.

Passio – A 70-minute passion setting in Latin of St John's gospel by **Arvo Pärt**. Completed in 1982, it is the first work in which Pärt fully embraced the *tintinnabuli* technique.

Patterson, Paul (b.1947) – British composer and teacher. Studied at the **RAM** where he later became Manson Professor of Composition and initiated several composer festivals.

Paulus, Stephen (1949-2014) – American composer, best known for his operas and choral music. Co-founder of the **Minnesota Composers Forum**.

Paz, Octavio (1914-1998) – Mexican poet and diplomat. After studying law and literature, he entered the Mexican diplomatic corps and served overseas while always writing poetry much of which was concerned with aspects of individual freedom and left-wing causes.

Pears, Sir Peter (1910-1986) – English tenor. As the professional and personal partner of **Benjamin Britten**, Pears enjoyed a successful career in opera and as a solo vocalist in oratorio and song recitals.

Penderecki, Krzysztof (1933-2020) – Polish composer and conductor. One of the most innovative composers of the post-Second World War period, notable for his use of tone clusters and extended instrumental techniques, his major choral works, the *Polish Requiem* (1984) and the *St Luke Passion* (1966), are remarkable for their devoutly religious sensibility.

Peter Grimes – Opera by **Benjamin Britten**, composed between 1942 and 1945 and premiered at Sadler's Wells Theatre in June 1945.

Peterson, Oscar (1925-2007) – Canadian jazz pianist and composer. In a career lasting over 60 years he enjoyed phenomenal acclaim, releasing over 200 recordings and winning eight Grammy Awards.

Petrassi, Goffredo (1904-2003) – Italian composer, conductor and teacher. He was an influential professor of composition at the Santa Cecilia Conservatory in Rome where his students included **Maxwell Davies**. His own music was characterised by neo-classical tendencies though later he embraced post-serial techniques.

Pheloung, Barrington (1954-2019) – Australian composer. After moving to London in 1972 he studied at the **RCM** with **John Lambert**. He wrote extensively for film but he is best known for his theme tune for the TV detective series *Inspector Morse*.

Piaf, Edith (1915-63) – French singer and actress. She specialised in songs about love, loss and sorrow with *La vie en rose* and *Non, je ne regrette rien* being the most famous.

Pianola – Also known as the player-piano, it was developed in the 1880s. It is fitted with a pneumatic mechanism which plays paper rolls. It attracted the interest of Stravinsky who wrote his *Étude pour Pianola* in 1917.

Pickard, John (b.1963) – British composer and teacher. After studies with **William Mathias** at the University of Wales, Pickard taught at Bristol University becoming Professor of Composition and Applied Musicology.

Poe, Edgar Alan (1809-1849) – American author, poet and critic, best known for his poetry and short stories that often feature mystery and the macabre.

Polanski, Roman (b.1933) – Polish-French film director whose output includes *Rosemary's Baby*, *Chinatown, Tess* and *The Pianist*.

Porter, Cole (1891-1964) – American composer and lyricist. Born into a wealthy family, Porter began composing when in his teens and wrote over 300 songs while at Yale University. He later achieved international acclaim for his Broadway musicals and film scores including *Kiss me Kate* (1948).

Poulenc, Francis (1899-1963) – French composer and pianist, renowned for his duo with the baritone Pierre Bernac. Largely self-taught, Poulenc developed his own distinctive compositional style that marks out his religious music such as the *Gloria* (1960), the demanding *Quatre motets pour un temps de pénitence* (1952) and for his cantata *Figure humaine*, written during the Occupation on poems by Paul Éluard.

Sadat, Anwar (1918-1981) – Politician. Anwar el-Sadat was the third President of Egypt from 1970 until his assassination by fundamentalist army officers.

Preston, Simon (b.1938) – English organist, conductor and composer. Having held posts at Westminster Abbey (as sub-organist), Christ Church, Oxford and then the Abbey again (as Organist and Master of the Choristers), Preston has pursued a career as a recitalist and freelance conductor.

Previn, André (1929-2019) – American conductor, pianist and composer. A versatile and prodigious talent, he enjoyed huge success in the fields of jazz, film music and classical conducting. He was Principal Conductor of the London Symphony Orchestra between 1968 and 1979 and was awarded an honorary KBE by the Queen in 1996.

Puccini, Giacomo (1858-1924) – Italian composer. Regarded by many as the greatest Italian opera composer after Verdi, his operas such as *La Bohème* (1896), *Tosca* (1900), *Madama Butterfly* (1904) and *Turandot* (1924) are the staple diet of companies all over the world.

Pulitzer Prize – Established in 1917, the Pulitzer Prize is awarded for excellence in journalism, literature and musical composition.

Quilter, Roger (1877-1953) – English composer known especially for his art songs and *A Children's Overture* (1914).

R&B – Rhythm and Blues, a term used for different kinds of African-American pop music developed since the Second World War.

Rachmaninov, Sergei (1873-1943) – Russian composer and pianist. After studies at the Moscow Conservatoire, he established a hugely successful career as a solo pianist while recognition of his compositional talent came slowly with his four piano concertos and the Second Symphony now recognised as masterpieces of the late Romantic style.

RAM (Royal Academy of Music) – The oldest conservatoire in the UK, it was founded in 1822 in Marylebone, London, and now provides training in instrumental and vocal performance, jazz, music theatre and opera.

Raksin, David (1912-2004) – American composer of over 100 film scores (perhaps the most famous being *Laura*) and more than 300 scores for TV programmes. He taught at the University of Southern California and the University of California, Los Angeles.

Rattle, Sir Simon (b.1955) – British conductor. An exceptional talent, Rattle came to widespread attention during his time with the City of Birmingham Symphony Orchestra from 1980 to 1998. In his subsequent appointments with the Berlin Philharmonic and the London Symphony Orchestra he has been notable for his advocacy for contemporary composers and music education.

Rautavaara, Einojuhani (1928-2016) – Finnish composer. One of the pioneers of serial music in Finland, he later adopted a more eclectic language embracing many influences including birdsong.

RCM (Royal College of Music) – Established in 1882 in South Kensington, London, the RCM offers professional training in all aspects of Western classical music plus research in performance practice and performance science.

Reich, Steve (b.1936) – American composer. With **Philip Glass** and **Terry Riley** responsible for the development of **minimalism** in the 1960s. Influenced by a trip to Ghana in 1970 and his studies of Balinese gamelan, his compositions explored percussive textures particularly in *Drumming*. But later he explored historical themes in works which reflect his Jewish heritage.

Repetiteur – A vocal coach and rehearsal pianist for opera companies.

Responses – In the Christian liturgy the Responses are said or sung in response to the Preces or Versicles said or sung by the priest or cantor. Sets of Responses have been composed by leading composers since the Book of Common Prayer was compiled in 1549.

Ridout, Alan (1934-1996) – English composer and teacher. After studies at the **RCM** and in the Netherlands he taught at the RCM, the universities of Birmingham, London and Cambridge and at The King's School, Canterbury. A prolific composer he wrote extensively for young people.

Riley, Terry (b.1935) – American composer regarded as the most significant figure in the development of **minimalism**. Influenced by composer La Monte Young, and by jazz and Indian music, Riley evolved a unique process of modular construction, exemplified in his 1964 work *In C*.

Rochberg, George (1918-2004) – American composer. Initially a proponent of serial music, he abandoned serialism after the death of his son in 1964. A distinguished and respected teacher, he served in the music department of the University of Pennsylvania until 1983.

Rodgers, Richard (1902-1979) – American composer known in particular for his music theatre works but also for over 900 songs and several film scores. His collaboration with Oscar Hammerstein II produced five hit musicals including ***Oklahoma!***.

Rolling Stones, The – English rock group founded in 1962 and one of the highest-earning and longest-active bands.

Roosevelt, Eleanor (1884-1962) – American diplomat and political activist. The wife of President Franklin D Roosevelt, she held positions as the US Delegate to the United Nations (1945-1952) and as Chair of the UN Commission on Human Rights.

Rorem, Ned (b.1923) – American composer. A prolific composer in all genres, Rorem is particularly well known for his opera *Miss Julie* (1965) and the many hundreds of solo songs.

Rossetti, Dante Gabriel (1828-1882) – English poet and painter. Along with William Holman Hunt and John Everett Millais, Rossetti was the founder of the Pre-Raphaelite Brotherhood. His poetry and art were inspired by Arthurian legends and medieval design.

RSCM – The Royal School of Church Music.

Rubato – From the Italian 'rubare', to rob, meaning the stretching or compacting of musical rhythm, phrases or beats.

Rumi (1207-1273) – 13th-century Persian poet and Sufi master who believed passionately in the use of music, poetry and dance as a path for reaching God.

Rushton, Edward (b.1972) – English composer and pianist. His composition professors included **Robin Holloway** and **James MacMillan**. He has lived and worked in Switzerland since 1998.

Russell, George (1867-1935) – Irish poet, painter, critic and editor. He was a fervent Irish nationalist but primarily used his writing rather than political activity to espouse the nationalist cause.

Rutter, John (b.1945) – see interview (page 215).

St Matthew Passion – The second of two Passion settings by **J. S. Bach** probably first performed on Good Friday in 1727 in St Thomas Church, Leipzig.

Saaremaa island – The largest island in the West Estonian Archipelago.

Saariaho, Kaija (b.1952) – Finnish composer based in Paris, France. After studies at the Sibelius Academy in Helsinki she moved first to Freiburg then to IRCAM in Paris where she developed her interest in computer-assisted composition and combining live performance with electronics.

Sacks, Oliver (1933-2015) – English-born neurologist and author. His studies of the impact of music on the brain led to his books, *Musicophilia - Tales of Music and the Brain* while *The Man Who Mistook His Wife for a Hat* became an opera by Michael Nyman (1986).

Sadat, Jehan (b.1933) – Wife of **President Sadat of Egypt** and human rights activist. She is the daughter of an Egyptian surgeon father and an English music teacher mother.

Salamunovich, Paul (1927-2014) – American conductor and educator. He was Music Director of the Los Angeles Master Chorale and an expert on Gregorian chant.

Sallinen, Aulis (b.1935) – Finnish composer. He studied at the Sibelius Academy of Music where he later taught composition. A prolific composer of operas and orchestral works, he was honoured by being awarded a lifelong 'Artistic Professorship' by the Finnish government which allowed him to concentrate solely on composition.

Salonen, Esa-Pekka (b.1958) – Finnish conductor and composer. He studied French horn, composition and conducting at the Sibelius Academy in Helsinki. After conducting posts with the radio orchestras in Finland and Sweden he was appointed Music Director of the Los Angeles Philharmonic in 1992.

Satie, Erik (1866-1925) – French composer and pianist. In his unique approach to composition and his idiosyncratic writing Satie was a major influence on the avant-garde of the early twentieth century. His most well-known pieces, the three *Gymnopédies*, have remained popular for over a century.

Saxton, Robert (b.1953) – British composer and teacher. He started composing at the age of six and received guidance from **Benjamin Britten** and Elisabeth Lutyens. He studied at both Cambridge and Oxford Universities and in Italy with **Luciano Berio**. Saxton has held teaching posts at the Guildhall School and Worcester College, Oxford.

Sayers, Dorothy L. (1893-1957) – English crime writer and poet. The creator of amateur detective Lord Peter Wimsey, she was also highly regarded for her translations of major classics including Dante's *Divine Comedy*.

Schnittke, Alfred (1934-98) – Russian-born composer of German heritage. After facing serious restrictions on the performance of his music in the Soviet Union, he emigrated to Germany in 1990 and enjoyed worldwide recognition.

Schubert, Franz (1797-1828) – Austrian composer of the late Classical and early Romantic period.

Schuller, Gunther (1925-2015) – American composer, conductor and educator. He became a professional horn player at the age of 15 and worked with Miles Davis in 1949. He was a pioneer in exploring the integration of classical and jazz techniques in compositions. He taught at the **Tanglewood** Music Center from 1965 to 1984.

Schumann, Robert (1810-1856) – German composer, pianist and critic. One of the great Romantic composers, particularly for the piano, Schumann also made a major contribution to the development of informed music criticism.

Schwarz, Rudolf (1905-1994) – Austrian-born conductor. He studied in Vienna and conducted there and in Germany. He was imprisoned by the Nazis from 1939 but survived internment in concentration camps and emigrated to England in 1947 to take up the post of principal conductor of the Bournemouth Municipal Orchestra. He later held similar positions with the CBSO and BBC Symphony Orchestra.

Sculthorpe, Peter (1929-2014) – Australian composer. Following studies in Melbourne and Oxford, Sculthorpe returned to Australia where he taught at the University of Sydney. His music is remarkable for its reflection of natural sounds and the music of indigenous peoples of Australia and neighbouring countries.

Second Vatican Council – Vatican II, as it was known, was convened by Pope John XXIII in 1962 to examine the relationship between the Catholic Church and the wider world. Its greatest impact on music was the advocacy of the use of vernacular languages in celebration of the Mass and the inclusion of folk and popular music idioms.

Seiber, Mátyás (1905-1960) – Hungarian-born composer who lived and worked in the UK from 1935. He studied with Zoltan Kodály and led the jazz department at the Hoch Conservatory in Frankfurt. In London he became professor of composition at Morley College at **Michael Tippett**'s invitation where he taught many significant British composers.

Serocki, Kazimierz (1922-1981) – Polish composer. Co-founder of the Warsaw Autumn International Contemporary Music Festival in 1956.

Shelley, Percy Bysshe (1792-1822) – English poet. He was one of the major English Romantic poets, regarded as a writer without parallel and a true radical in his political and social views.

Shelley, Howard (b.1950) – British pianist and conductor. An alumnus of the **RCM**, Shelley is particularly renowned for his performances and recordings of the whole of **Rachmaninov**'s output for piano and his direction of **Mozart** concertos from the keyboard.

Sherlaw Johnson, Robert (1932-2000) – British composer, pianist and scholar. He studied at the **RAM** and in Paris with **Messiaen** before teaching at various schools and universities. His recordings of Messiaen's piano and vocal music are regarded as milestones in the understanding and acceptance of the composer's music by a wider audience.

Shostakovich , Dimitri (1906-1975) – Russian composer and pianist. One of the great twentieth-century composers, producing 15 symphonies, three operas, six concerti and a large number of chamber works.

Shostakovich, Maxim (b.1938) – Russian conductor and pianist. The second child of Dimitri Shostakovich, Maxim studied at the Moscow and St Petersburg conservatories. In 1981 he defected to live in West Germany and then the USA though he returned to Russia after the fall of the Soviet Union.

Sibelius, Jean (1865-1957) – Finnish composer. Indisputably one of the most important symphonic composers of the early twentieth century.

Silvestri, Tony (Charles Anthony) (b.1965) – American lyricist and composer. While a poet and author in his own right, he has gained particular renown for creating tailor-made texts for composers, including choral works and operas.

Silvestrov, Valentyn (b.1937) – Ukrainian composer and pianist. Regarded initially as one of the most prominent avant-garde composers in the USSR, his early works were held in high esteem abroad but largely ignored in his homeland. His adoption of tonal and modal techniques and his embracing of the Orthodox religion led to a greater emphasis on melody in later works.

Singer, Malcolm (b.1953) – British composer, conductor and educator. He has held posts as Director of Music of The Yehudi Menuhin School and Professor of Composition at the Guildhall School.

Skempton, Howard (b.1947) – See interview (page 227).

Soft Machine – English rock band formed in 1966 and famed for its progressive jazz-rock idiom and its influence on the underground music scene.

Sol-fa/solfège – An educational method whereby skills in music such as aural perception, sight-reading and pitch recognition are taught. It evolved from a system invented in eleventh-century Italy by Guido of Arezzo.

Sondheim, Stephen (b.1930) – American composer and lyricist. He came to prominence as the lyric writer for **Bernstein's** *West Side Story* (1957) but then went on to produce the words and music for several musicals, with *Sunday in the Park with George* (1984) and *Sweeney Todd* (1979) probably being his most notable achievements.

Sorcerer's Apprentice, The – A symphonic poem by Paul Dukas (1865-1935) used by Walt Disney in his 1940 animated film *Fantasia*.

Sørensen, Bent (b.1958) – Danish composer. Regarded as one of the most original and distinctive composers of his generation, he won the Grawemeyer Award for Music Composition in 2018.

Sorley, Charles Hamilton (1895-1915) – Scottish poet and soldier. A captain in the British army, Sorley was killed in the Battle of Loos. Deeply conflicted in his attitude towards the First World War, his poetry has been ranked alongside other war poets, **Wilfred Owen** and Isaac Rosenberg.

Sousa, Conrad (1935-2013) – American composer. He studied at the Juilliard School and became composer-in-residence at the Old Theater, San Diego in 1959. He wrote five operas and extensively for choirs and the theatre.

Spem in alium – See **Tallis**

Staheli, Ronald (b.1947) – American conductor. He leads the choral and conducting division at Brigham Young University in Provo, Utah.

Stanford, Sir Charles Villiers (1852-1924) – Irish composer, conductor and educator. Studies in Cambridge, Leipzig and Berlin led to his appointment as professor of composition at the **RCM**, where he taught **Vaughan Williams** and **Holst**. Though a prolific opera and orchestral composer, he is chiefly remembered for his Anglican church music.

Star Wars – See **John Williams**.

Stevens, Halsey (1908-1989) – American composer, author and educator. He taught in four US universities before joining the faculty at the University of Southern California in 1946 and teaching there until 1976. His book on **Bartók**'s music is regarded as one of the finest composer studies ever written.

Stockhausen, Karlheinz (1928-2007) – German composer and theoretician. He is regarded as one of the most important, visionary and innovative composers of the twentieth century.

Stokes, Eric (1939-1999) – American composer, known for his humorous and eccentric compositions which combined traditional idioms with electronic music and other media.

Stones, The – See **The Rolling Stones**.

Stowe, Harriet Beecher (1811-1896) – American author and abolitionist. She is best known for her novel *Uncle Tom's Cabin* (1852) which strongly influenced anti-racism opinion in the USA and Europe.

Strauss, Richard (1864-1949) – German composer and conductor. Regarded as the natural successor to Wagner and Liszt, Strauss pursued a radical, dissonant harmonic style until the composition of *Elektra* (1909), after which he moderated this approach, demonstrating his immense skill in orchestral colour. His choral piece, *Der Abend* (Evening), is a rich 16-part setting of Schiller's poem.

Stravinsky, Igor (1882-1971) – Russian-born composer and conductor. One of the most important composers of the twentieth century, Stravinsky during his lifetime explored a wide variety of styles and techniques, influencing many other composers who followed him. His major choral works were *Canticum Sacrum* (1955), *Symphony of Psalms* (1930), and *Les Noces* (1923).

Street, Sean (b.1946) – British writer and broadcaster. A prolific poet, playwright and novelist, Street is particularly famed for his initiatives as a radio producer and he became Britain's first Professor of Radio, at Bournemouth University in 1999.

Swan Lake – A ballet with music by Pyotr Tchaikovsky (1840-1893).

Świder, Józef (1930-2014) – Polish composer and teacher. After studies in Katowice and Rome he taught theory and composition in the Katowice Music Academy.

Swift, Jonathan (1667-1745) – Anglo-Irish author. Swift studied for the priesthood at Trinity College, Dublin. In England he became one of the most prominent satirists of the era, advocating social reform particularly in Ireland. His best and most-renowned work is *Gulliver's Travels* (1726).

Symphony of Psalms – See **Stravinsky**

Szeligowski, Tadeusz (1896-1963) – Polish composer and educator. His stage works – two ballets and three operas – achieved huge popularity in his homeland. He founded the Poznań contemporary music festival and set up Poznań's symphony orchestra.

Szymanowski, Karol (1882-1937) – Polish composer and pianist. Though his early works were strongly influenced by German and Russian Romantic composers, he later developed a distinctive language which drew on folk music, Impressionism, atonality and oriental influences. His *Stabat Mater* (1926), a setting in Polish, uniquely incorporates Polish folk melodies and rhythms.

Tallis, Thomas (c.1505-1585) – English composer. One of the greatest composers of the first Elizabethan era, Tallis lived through the reigns of four monarchs, adapting his church music to the prevailing religious and musical doctrines. His 40-part motet, ***Spem in alium*** (c.1570), is one of the crowning glories of sixteenth-century music, a masterpiece of polyphonic writing.

Tanglewood – A summer music festival held on the estate of the same name in Western Massachusetts, USA. The resident orchestra is the Boston Symphony and each year a summer school attracts composers and performers from all over the world.

Tavener, Alan (b.1957) – Scottish conductor and organist. A graduate of Brasenose College, Oxford, he became a research graduate at the University of Strathclyde and founded the University's Chamber Choir. His Cappella Nova, formed in 1982, has more than 20 CDs to its credit and has dedicated itself to the performance of sixteenth-century Scottish choral music and contemporary works by the likes of **John Tavener** and **James MacMillan**.

Tavener, Sir John (1944-2013) – English composer. It was with the creation of *The Whale* in 1968 that he came to prominence, and works such as *In Alium* and *Ultimos Ritos* established him as one of the most popular contemporary music composers. His deep faith generated an extensive catalogue of religious works, most notable among these being *The Lamb* and *Song for Athene*.

Taverner, John (c.1490-1545) – English composer and organist. He was born and lived much of his life in Lincolnshire but was appointed Master of the Choristers at Christ Church, Oxford by Cardinal Thomas Wolsey. His mass settings, often based on *cantus firmus*, are some of the most complex and virtuosic works of that period.

Teasdale, Sara (1884-1933) – American poet. Her seven books of poetry attracted widespread admiration during her lifetime, charting developments in her own life and reflecting on love, beauty and death.

Telemann, Georg Philipp (1681-1767) – German composer. One of the most prolific composers of all time, Telemann's output is thought to have consisted of over 3,000 works. A close friend of **J.S. Bach**, he held prominent positions in Hamburg for 46 years.

Tennyson, Alfred, Lord (1809-1892) – English poet and Poet Laureate for most of Queen Victoria's reign. Poems such as 'Ring Wild Bells' and 'In Memoriam' have attracted the attention of numerous composers due to their craftsmanship and vivid imagery.

Thomas, Dylan (1914-1953) – Welsh poet. A popular poet during his lifetime, Thomas came to public attention through radio broadcasts and reading tours.

Thomas, Edward (1878-1917) – British poet of Welsh heritage. Thomas worked in London as a literary critic, writing poetry in his spare time, including the famous *Adelstrop*. He enlisted in the British army in 1915 and was killed at Arras.

Thomas, R.S. (Ronald Stuart) (1913-2000) – Welsh poet and Anglican priest, notable for his fierce Welsh nationalism and his poems about 'ordinary' people, particularly labourers and farmers.

Thompson, Randall (1899-1984) – American composer and educator. He was a prolific writer for choirs, especially male voice ensembles. At Harvard University **Leonard Bernstein** was one of his many distinguished students.

Tilson Thomas, Michael (b.1944) – American conductor and composer. In a career spanning over 50 years, he has held major conducting posts in the USA and was principal conductor of the London Symphony Orchestra from 1988 to 1995.

Tippett, Sir Michael (1905-1998) – British composer and conductor. A late developer, Tippett emerged as a composer after the Second World War following the premiere of the oratorio *A Child of Our Time* in 1944. His operas, including *The Knot Garden* (1970), reflected his engagement with psychoanalysis, modern mass media and American culture. Written for St John's College, Oxford, the Magnificat and Nunc Dimittis (1962) demonstrated his rigorous and affecting choral style.

Toge, Sankichi (1917-1953) – Japanese poet and activist. He survived the atomic bombing of Hiroshima where he had worked for a gas company. Some of his *Poems of the Atomic Bomb* (1951) are inscribed on his monument in the Hiroshima Peace Memorial Park.

Tolkien, J.R.R. (1892-1973) – English author, poet and academic. John Tolkien held professorial positions at Oxford University between 1925 and 1959. He is best known for his fantasy works, *The Hobbit* (1937) and *The Lord of the Rings* (1937-49).

Tomkins, Thomas (1572-1656) – Welsh-born composer and keyboardist. Born in St David's his first major appointment was as Organist at Worcester Cathedral in 1596. He was later a Gentleman of the Chapel Royal.

Tormis, Veljo (1930-2017) – Estonian composer. His gigantic output includes over 500 songs for choir, many of them based on ancient folk songs from Estonia and other Balto-Finnic cultures.

Tovey, Sir Donald (1875-1940) – British musicologist, composer, conductor and pianist. Tovey's teaching at the University of Edinburgh, his writings, especially the *Essays in Musical Analysis* (1939), and his editions of works by **Bach** and **Beethoven** were ground-breaking contributions to the understanding of the artistic and technical merits of classical music.

Trotter, Thomas (b.1957) – British organist. He was Organ Scholar at **King's College**, **Cambridge**, and won first prize in the St Albans International Organ Festival interpretation competition in 1979. He received the Queen's Medal for Music in 2020.

Turnage, Mark-Anthony (b.1960) – English composer. He studied with **Oliver Knussen**, **John Lambert** and **Gunther Schuller**, with whom he shares a deep interest in jazz, and has composed three operas and several large-scale orchestral works.

Twin Cities – A major metropolitan area in Minnesota, USA, so-called because of the close proximity of the cities of Minneapolis and St Paul across the Mississippi River.

Tyndale, William (c.1494-1536) – English scholar. His English translation of The Bible was the first to be drawn from Greek and Hebrew texts and the first to be printed (1526). His opposition to Henry VIII's annulment of his marriage to Catherine of Aragon led ultimately to Tyndale's execution in 1536.

Ustvolskaya, Galina (1919-2006) – Russian composer. A student of **Shostakovich** at the Leningrad Conservatory, she was highly regarded by her teacher and developed her own distinctive style which was not tolerated in the Soviet Union until very late in her life.

Van Gogh, Theo (1957-2004) – Dutch film director. His film, *Submission: Part 1*, criticised the treatment of women in Islam.

Vänskä, Osmo (b.1953) – Finnish conductor, composer and clarinettist. Studies at the Sibelius Academy led to his appointment as music director of the Lahti Symphony Orchestra. He later held posts with the BBC Scottish Symphony Orchestra and the Minnesota Orchestra.

Vasks, Pēteris (b.1946) – Latvian composer. Studies in Riga and Vilnius were followed by an orchestral career as a double bass player until composition took over with commissions for his works coming from all over the world.

Vaughan Williams, Ralph (1872-1958) – English composer. Considered to be the most significant figure in British music between **Elgar** and **Britten**, he made huge contributions to the understanding and appreciation of English folksong and church hymnody, while composing distinctive works in many genres, notably nine symphonies, vocal works like the *Five Mystical Songs* and ever-popular masterpieces such as the *Fantasia on a theme of Thomas Tallis* and *The Lark Ascending*.

Verdi, Giuseppe (1813-1901) – Italian composer. The dominant figure in Italian opera in the second half of the nineteenth century, notable particularly for his late operas, *Otello* and *Falstaff*.

Victoria, Tomás Luis de (c.1548-1611) – Spanish composer, one of the most significant exponents of Catholic church music, remarkable for its intricacy and multiple part writing.

Vishnevskaya, Galina (1926-2012) – Russian soprano. She enjoyed an international career between 1957 and 1982, singing major roles in Finland, the USA, the UK and Italy. With her husband Mstislav Rostropovich (1927-2007) she left the Soviet Union in 1974 to live in Paris.

Vingt Regards sur l'Enfant-Jésus – See **Olivier Messiaen**. A suite of 20 piano pieces, meditations on the infancy of Christ, composed in 1944.

Virtual Choirs – Groups of singers who do not meet physically but record their individual parts and submit the recordings to be collated into a performance. This phenomenon was initiated by Eric Whitacre in 2009 when he conducted 185 singers from 12 countries in his *Lux Aurumque*.

Vivaldi, Antonio (1678-1741) – Italian composer, violinist, teacher and priest. He was one of the greatest Baroque composers, known particularly for *The Four Seasons* and the *Gloria*.

Vogel, Edith (1912-1992) – Austro-Hungarian pianist and teacher. She made her debut in Vienna at the age of ten but had to emigrate to Britain in 1938 to escape Nazi persecution. She became a prominent teacher at Dartington Summer School and the Guildhall School and was regarded as an outstanding interpreter of **Beethoven** and **Schubert**.

Wagner, Richard (1813-1883) – German composer and conductor. Chiefly known for his operas including *The Flying Dutchman*, he established his own theatre in Bayreuth and had an immense influence on the musical language of his successors.

Wakeman, Rick (b.1949) – English rock musician. Studies at the **RCM** were interrupted by a developing career as a session musician before forming Yes, one of the most successful and influential progressive rock bands.

Wałęsa, Lech (b.1943) – Polish statesman. The first democratically-elected President of Poland (1990), he led the national federation of trades unions, Solidarność (Solidarity).

Wallace, John (b.1949) – Scottish trumpeter, conductor and educator. After a career as a soloist and orchestral principal, he became Principal of the Royal Conservatoire of Scotland from 2002 to 2014.

Wallen, Errollyn (b.1958) – See interview (page 249)

Walton, Sir William (1902-1983) – English composer. Over six decades he was one of the most significant symphonic composers in Britain while his oratorio *Belshazzar's Feast* (1931) became hugely-popular with professional and amateur choruses.

Warland, Dale (b.1932) – American conductor and composer. The formation of his own choir led to the establishment of the Dale Warland Choral Series published by G. Schirmer.

War Requiem – See **Benjamin Britten**

Washington, George (1732-1799) – American soldier and statesman. The first President of the United States.

Webb, Mary (1881-1927) – English poet and novelist. She was born in Shropshire and her poetry reflected her deep love of nature.

Webern, Anton (1883-1945) – Austrian composer and conductor. He studied with **Arnold Schoenberg** and developed his own radical musical language based on his teacher's twelve-tone technique. His *Six Orchestral Pieces* op.6 mark his move away from the **Mahler**-influenced early works to his own aphoristic, miniature language.

Weir, Judith (b.1954) – See interview (page 261)

Weiller, David (b.1957) – American conductor. He is Co-Director of Choral Studies and Associate Director of the University of Nevada, Las Vegas School of Music.

Wesley, Samuel Sebastian (1810-1876) – English composer and organist. He held positions at Leeds Parish Church and the cathedrals of Winchester and Gloucester. His anthems, such as *Thou wilt keep him in perfect peace*, and his hymns have been central to the Church of England tradition.

Whitman, Walt (1819-1892) – American poet. One of the most influential of nineteenth-century poets, his *Leaves of Grass* (1855) was considered controversial for its overt sensuality and its innovative free verse form.

Who, The – English rock band formed in 1964. Their rock opera *Tommy* (1969) was considered to be both a commercial and critical success.

Wicks, Allan (1923-2010) – English organist and composer. After studying at Christ Church, Oxford, he held organ posts at York Minster and Manchester Cathedral before becoming Master of the Choristers at Canterbury Cathedral (1961-1988).

Wilde, Oscar (1854-1900) – Irish playwright and poet. He was one of the most successful playwrights of the late Victorian era but courted controversy with his one-act play *Salome* (1891) on which **Richard Strauss** based his opera.

Willcocks, Sir David (1919-2015) – English conductor, organist, composer and educator. Following service in the army (1939-1945), Willcocks was Organist at Salisbury and Worcester cathedrals before being appointed Director of Music at **King's College**, **Cambridge** (1957-74). Director of the **RCM** from 1974, he also conducted The Bach Choir and served as editor of *Carols for Choirs*.

Willcocks, Jonathan (b.1953) – English composer and conductor. Alongside his composing, he has held posts at Portsmouth Grammar School and Bedales School, as well as being director of the Junior Department of the **RAM**.

Williams, John (b.1932) – American composer and conductor. The composer of over 100 film scores, many of which, like *Star Wars*, *Jaws* and the *Harry Potter* series, are considered to be among the most outstanding in cinematic history.

Wilner, Eleanor (b.1937) – American poet. She is notable for poetry that reflects culture and history rather than personal experiences. She was awarded the Robert Frost Medal in 2019.

Wood, Charles (1866-1926) – Irish composer and teacher. Primarily remembered as a composer of church music, Wood taught at the **RCM** and was Professor of Music at Cambridge University.

Woolf, Virginia (1881-1941) – English author. She is recognised as one of the most innovative writers of the first half of the twentieth century. In works such as *Orlando* and *To the Lighthouse* she explored modern themes and reflected a rapidly-changing society.

Wordsworth, William (1770-1850) – English poet. With **Samuel Taylor Coleridge** he is regarded as responsible for the English Romantic movement in literature.

Xenakis, Iannis (1922-2001) – Greek/French composer. He fled Greece in 1947 to avoid execution for his role in the Greek Communist Party. His training as an architect in Paris went hand in hand with music studies and he became a pioneer in the field of computer-assisted composition.

Yeats, W.B. (William Butler) (1865-1939) – Irish poet and playwright. He helped found the Abbey Theatre in Dublin and served as a Senator in the Irish parliament after independence. He received the Nobel Prize for Literature in 1923.

Zurbarán, Francisco de (1598-1664) – Spanish painter. He is known particularly for his religious subjects but also his chiaroscuro techniques in works like *Still Life, with Lemons, Oranges and a Rose* (1633).

Acknowledgements

The publisher would like to thank the following people without whose help this book would not have been published:

All our composers for giving freely of their time to be interviewed.

David Wordsworth for compiling the interviews and the appendices.

Sir Andrew Davis for contributing the Preface.

David Hill for contributing the Foreword.

Leslie East for his advice, his editing and for compiling the appendices.

Sidney Buckland for her assistance and proof reading.

To all our production team including Astrid Griffiths of Økvik Design and Halstan UK.

The publisher would like to acknowledge with thanks the following picture credits:

Cover © Belinda Lawley; **viii** © Todd Rosenberg Photography; **ix** © Nick Rutter; **xi** © Michael Tomlinson Photography; **p.2, 13** © Patrick Douglas-Hamilton; **p.14, 24** © John Bellars; **p.18, 66, 158, 187, 211** © Chris Christodoulou; **p.26, 31, 32, 37** © Marshall Light Studio; **p.38, 47** © Aivars Krastiņš; **p.48, 54, 59** © Brant Tilds Photography; **p.60** © Howard Goodall; **p.82, 89, 94** © Reinis Hofmanis; **p.96, 105** © Rhys Frampton; **p.106, 115** © Anne Marsden; **p.116** © Endre Balogh; **p.127** © Michael Stillwater; **p.128, 137, 139** © Mariusz Makowski; **p.132** © Bartek Barczak; **p.140** © Liz Isles; **p.144, 149** © Karina Lyburn; **p.150, 163** © Marc Marnie; **p.168** © Maarit Kytoharju; **p.177** © Jaakko Mäntyjärvi; **p.178** © Chris O'Donovan; **p.191** © Andy Stenz (Photography); **p.192, 201** © Peter Greig; **p.202, 207, 208, 213, 260, 271** © Benjamin Ealovega; **p.226, 235** © Jerry Butson; **p.236, 246** © Andy Holdsworth Photography; **p.242** © New Forest Chamber Choir; **p.248, 259** © Gillian Edelstein; **p.272, 282** © Marc Royce

Though every effort has been made to trace copyright holders, the publisher will be pleased to hear from anyone not acknowledged here.